HARD CALL

also by JOHN McCAIN *with* MARK SALTER

Faith of My Fathers

Worth the Fighting For

Why Courage Matters

Character Is Destiny

HARD CALL

GREAT DECISIONS AND

THE EXTRAORDINARY PEOPLE

WHO MADE THEM

JOHN McCAIN

WITH MARK SALTER

TWELVE

NEW YORK   BOSTON

Photo credits appear on page 457.

Twelve
Hachette Book Group USA
237 Park Avenue
New York, NY 10017

Visit our Web site at www.HachetteBookGroupUSA.com.

Twelve is an imprint of Grand Central Publishing.
The Twelve name and logo is a trademark of Hachette Book Group USA.

Library of Congress Cataloging-in-Publication Data

McCain, John
Hard call : great decisions and the extraordinary people who made
them / John McCain with Mark Salter.—1st ed.
p. cm.
Includes bibliographical references and index.
ISBN-13: 978-0-446-58040-3 (regular edition)
ISBN-10: 0-446-58040-6 (regular edition)
ISBN-13: 978-0-446-58142-4 (large print edition)
ISBN-10: 0-446-58142-9 (large print edition)
1. Biography—Miscellanea.   2. Decision making—
Case studies.   I. Salter, Mark.   II. Title.
CT105.M395 2007
920—dc22
2007006505

Book designed by Fearn Cutler de Vicq
Printed in the United States of America

FIRST EDITION: AUGUST 2007
10 9 8 7 6 5 4 3 2 1

For Roberta McCain and Lauralie Salter,
assured and intelligent decision makers, whose example
their sons have, with mixed success, tried to emulate

CONTENTS

HUMILITY

INSPIRATION

INTRODUCTION

I knew a man who slept through the night. He had nearly reached the end. Wounded, starved, delirious, and exhausted, he commanded himself to consider his situation carefully. The sights and sounds of salvation beckoned him and must have quickened the impulse to run toward it. In the last few days of his journey, he worried that he was losing his mind. He was slipping in and out of consciousness. He had caught himself arguing loudly with a Sunday-school teacher from his childhood. Thanking God for getting him this far, he briefly mistook his own voice for another American's. Now, he had to summon all that remained of his wits, and his formidable courage, to make the most fateful decision of his life: to make one last dash now or to wait for daylight. His choice might win a hero's welcome or indefinite pain and suffering; the blessings of a wife and children or the cruelty of an angered enemy; freedom or captivity; life or death.

He chose to wait.

Two weeks earlier, on August 26, 1967, Air Force Major George "Bud" Day had been shot down and captured north of Vietnam's DMZ. He had broken his right arm in three places, painfully sprained his knee, and battered his face when he ejected from his F-100 fighter jet. The North Vietnamese who captured him had roughly set his fractures, fashioned a crude cast for his broken arm, bound his ankles together, and put him in a hole in the ground until he could be transported north. Tough old bird that he was, Bud decided to go home instead. Late in his first night of captivity, he freed himself from the ropes, crawled out of his hole, and quietly began his trek to the other side of the DMZ and an American airfield, twenty miles or so to the south.

Over the next two weeks, he traveled at night and slept when he could during the day. He waded through rice paddies, dragged himself across jungle floors, climbed hills, crossed rivers, wandered in circles under dense jungle canopy, narrowly evaded recapture, and, once, risked exposing himself to enemy fire while floating down the Ben Hai River on two pieces of bamboo. He subsisted on dew and rainwater, a handful of berries now and then, and a couple of live frogs he swallowed out of desperation. He became ill, unable at one point to keep water down. He burned with fever. But he was tougher than most men, and braver. And he kept moving south.

Finally, near the end of the thirteenth day of his escape, he came to rest within a mile of a forward American air base. He watched helicopters and aircraft take off and land, signaled one or two unsuccessfully, and fought the impulse to run toward his countrymen as fast as a starving, half-dead man with a bum knee and a broken arm could. But he restrained himself. Given his condition and the powerful temptation posed by the prospect of imminent rescue from his miseries, his restraint strikes me as almost as superhuman as the astonishing feat of endurance and guts that had brought him so close to salvation. Of course, as I would soon come to know, Bud Day is no ordinary man.

He had the presence of mind and discipline in the most trying of circumstances to weigh the risks of hurried action. He assumed that the perimeter of the airfield was mined. And he worried that in the dark, a limping, crooked, sun-darkened scarecrow of a man hastily making his way toward the base might be mistaken for someone other than an American pilot by a wary sentry with a loaded M-1 and an aversion to taking chances. So, he concluded that he would wait for daylight to make his approach, and he lay down in the jungle for one last night.

It was a sound decision. It might have been the right one. The perimeter was likely mined, and he very well could have been mistaken for the enemy and fired upon. It was certainly a difficult decision, though. So much was at stake, and there were so many unknowns on which to base a truly existential decision. It was a very hard call.

He had made the decision not knowing if time would prove him right or wrong, not knowing anything for certain. Would he be captured in the night? Would he be alive in the morning? He knew only that he had exercised the discipline necessary to make the best decision he could. Cowardice had not restrained him, informed caution had—that and courage, the courage to endure another night of terror and suffering. He was aware of his situation, its risks and rewards. He had weighed his prospects as judiciously as time and circumstances allowed. And he chose well.

He had chosen well from the beginning of his odyssey to its end. When almost any other man in his condition would have rejected the idea of escape as impossible, he had risked it. Not rashly or mistakenly—he had assessed his circumstances correctly. He had not been tightly bound. He had not been kept in a cell but in a shallow, underground shelter. Perhaps, because his captors had not imagined that a man in his shape could manage an escape attempt, he hadn't been closely guarded. He was familiar with the terrain, and he had known the direction and distance to safety. He had had the cover of darkness.

He had believed in the mission. He had had confidence in his ability to accomplish it, not an irrational confidence born of conceit. He had known he had courage and stamina sufficient to overcome his injuries. He had known the time was right. His physical condition would decline with every day of captivity, and soon he would be taken north to prison. He did not act for himself alone, but for his family, to whom he wished to return. He was inspired by his duty to them and to the military code that exhorted captured Americans to escape if possible. He could see it was possible, when others would have seen the contrary.

His last decision, too, was a question of timing. Was it better to risk friendly fire and tripping a mine in the dark or to risk capture? He made a sound, informed, and hard decision that the risks of the former were greater than those of the latter. He would wait.

He had earned his freedom, fought for it, like no other man I have ever known. He should have had it.

As it turned out, he was to wait nearly six years for the freedom he had nearly grasped that night. He had risen with the dawn and made his way toward the base. In the open, several yards from the last jungle between him and safety, he was spotted by two North Vietnamese soldiers. They shouted at him to stop. He made a run for cover, and just before he reached it a bullet to his left leg brought him down. He hid in the bush as best he could. He lay still, trying not to breathe or groan from the pain, his heartbeat the only sound. He listened as his enemies tore madly through the jungle, shouting and firing indiscriminately. He lay still as one of them drew almost near enough to touch him but for a moment still could not see or hear him. And then he did.

They tortured Bud for his heroism on the long ride to Hanoi. They tortured him even more cruelly once he arrived at the dark, daunting, and dangerous prison they called Hoa Lo, the "fiery furnace." Torture could change a man forever. But it didn't change him. He was as tough, as brave, and as confident the day he left captivity as he had been the day he had almost escaped it.

He had made a sound decision, in a crucible few people ever encounter. It had probably been the right one. But it had not worked out as he had hoped. That was his misfortune, and he was man enough to accept it without crippling regret.

As unfortunate as his capture was for Bud, it was salvation for many others. Few leaders in Vietnam's prisoner-of-war camps were as honorable, brave, and inspiring as he was. The courage of his heroic escape attempt was recognized by a Medal of Honor, which was also given him for the trials he so bravely endured on behalf of all of us in the long years ahead. Included in the credit he can always claim is my life. But for Bud Day and his misfortune, I do not I think I would have ever left that prison. But that is another story.

I tell this part of Bud's story because it involved such a fateful and admirable decision. In the time I shared his circumstances, I would see him make other hard and, sometimes, life-risking decisions, and in my judgment they were usually the right ones. But I think this one, a decision with everything on the line, revealed all the attributes I most respect about good decision making and exemplary decision makers. It is one of the rare instances when the assessment of the quality of the decision doesn't depend most, or even much, on its outcome. The proof isn't always in the pudding, but it is often enough that we have come to accept that maxim as gospel. Not in this case. Part of the reason for that is that we can never know for certain whether, had he chosen the other course, he would be alive to tell the tale. But more,

it is because in the direst circumstances, suffering physically and mentally from extraordinary hardships, with no counsel, no assistance of
any kind, utterly on his own, with his emotions in tumult, he managed
to think clearly and carefully about his choice and make a sober, considered judgment. He committed himself to it, checked what was surely
a hypercharged survival instinct, and went to sleep.

He was as aware of his situation, the environment in which he must
make a decision, as was possible. He knew the terrain. He knew how to
navigate it. He understood the risks and the opportunities. He believed
he had the necessary resources—in this case, his own fortitude—to
achieve his objective. He had taken the measure of his enemies, understood as much as he could about their methods and resources. He
appreciated the potential for catastrophic mishap when an eighteen-
year-old sentry is startled in the dark.

He had known when the right moment was at hand to slip his
ropes, having sensed that it would soon pass. And when he made his
final decision, he sensed that the moment for his last effort had not
arrived.

He had foresight. He could see the possible where most others
would have seen disaster and hopelessness.

His foresight, as foresight often is, was rooted in his confidence.
Conceit is often mistaken for confidence. His was an instinct honed
from years of experience and preparation. He was sure of himself, but
it wasn't vanity that made him so. He trusted his strength and practical
sense. It had always served him well. Vietnam was his third war, and
this hadn't been his first existential decision. He compensated for his
weakness, his desperation. And he trusted he had the courage to stick
it out.

He acted with humility. He did not risk everything to avoid imprisonment and worse for his own sake but for that of the family he loved
well, and who needed him.

And, finally, he had been inspired, beckoned by duty and an officer's sense of honor.

I have long believed these—awareness, foresight, timing, confidence, humility, and inspiration—are the qualities typically represented in the best decisions and in the characters of those who make

them. What follows is a tribute to those qualities and to people who possessed them in character and action.

The stories in this book were chosen because they illuminate at least one of these qualities. Indeed, as in Bud Day's decision, many of them possess all the aforementioned attributes. But our purpose with each story is to focus on just one and to learn by example, if not how to make a difficult decision, then how to judge one after—and, possibly, before—it is made, to see if it can claim these qualities, which seem common to the best decisions.

We have not sought to provide a procedural formula for difficult decision making, such as Benjamin Franklin offered his friend, the British scientist Joseph Priestly. Write two columns on a piece of paper, he advised, listing the pros and the cons of a given course of action, and add items to each over time as they occur to you. Often the hardest decisions must be made without benefit of time to examine every possible consequence. Ideally, if we foresee that such a decision will eventually confront us, we can undertake an elaborate analysis before the moment for action arrives. But that is not always possible. Sometimes we must grasp the situation immediately or in a very short period of time, which allows only the most cursory review of our options and their potential outcomes.

We must prepare ourselves, of course, for such eventualities, by learning all we can about the situations in which we bear responsibility. We must understand, to the best of our ability, the people involved, with us and against us. We must know ourselves, our own strengths and weaknesses, and how best to employ the former and compensate for the latter. We must remember, almost instinctively, the lessons we have learned from earlier decisions, both those that succeeded and those that did not. And we must learn to act when necessary, no matter how challenging the obstacles, and to wait when caution is appropriate, no matter how urgently we feel the need to proceed.

But procedures for decision making will always vary, depending on the circumstances and our qualities. We all have our idiosyncrasies, the values, habits, instincts, cares, and superstitions—accumulated throughout our lives—that influence our judgment. When I assess a decision, I want to know all I can about the character of the decision maker before I examine the properties of the decision, its outcome, or how it was arrived at. When General Eisenhower alone gave the signal to launch the invasion of Europe, he wrote a statement claiming all blame should it fail and giving all credit for success to the courage and resourcefulness of his soldiers. That tells us a lot about Eisenhower's character and offers evidence of the quality of his decision that is as important as the factors or procedures he used to make it. That he accepted his enormous responsibility so honorably, and with such gravity, suggests that it was made with great care and with humility. It seems obvious that who decides is as important as what is decided.

In the end, it is always character that most moves history, for good or ill.

I cannot offer a several-step, how-to-make-a-great-decision plan for beginners. I would be hard pressed to provide a cogent description of how I make decisions. The ways I have arrived at important decisions, both right and wrong ones, have varied over the years. I hope this has resulted in a progressively better approach. But I have blundered often enough in recent years to forswear such a boast.

My life has been blessed with the good company of many people of exemplary character and sound reason, who made hard calls with courage and humility. I have learned from their examples. If I fail to heed those lessons when making an important decision, the fault doesn't lie with the stars, but with my own deficiencies. When I have done well it is because I have had the best teachers, whose examples made a hard call clearer to me and, in some instances, easier to make.

I knew a man who slept through the night, when everything hung in the balance. He would accept whatever the day brought, whether it be joy or sorrow. He had done his best and had taken his rest. And that, my friends, is all that is required of any of us.

AWARENESS

Naval aviators claim to have invented the term "situational awareness" to describe an aviator's comprehension of the tactical situation he encounters when flying a mission—how well he keeps track of everything that is happening or likely to happen around him. Where is he in formation? Where is the ground? How close is he to the target? What's his fuel level? How is his aircraft performing? Are his avionics functioning correctly? Are weather conditions hampering the operation and increasing its risks? Where is the enemy, or where is he likely to be? What are the scope, location, and range of the enemy's air defenses? Is he evaluating new information he perceives or that is communicated to him and altering his expectations accordingly? These are but a few of the scores of variables he must keep track of to increase the likelihood of his mission's success.

There are more subjective judgments involved in the decisions he must make during his mission. How good a pilot is he? How good are the other pilots in his squadron? How experienced are they? How fatigued? How good is the enemy? How experienced? How stressed? What personality attributes of his or his squadron mates might affect his judgment? Is he steady under pressure? Are they? Is he brave enough? Does flying seem natural to him, or is it a complex and exacting chore that makes him anxious and distracts him from the achievement of his mission? Is he the overconfident type? Do the other fliers' reactions to the situation, the weaknesses and strengths of their personalities, cause him to take risks he shouldn't or to elude his responsibilities? Is he so gung ho or so flushed with adrenaline that he is heedless of increasing danger? Is he the type who, when he hears the tone that warns him the enemy's weapon system has locked onto him, keeps barreling in on his target, or does he take immediate evasive maneuvers? He must understand and try to compensate for all these variables as he makes decisions that will affect the outcome of the mission and, perhaps, determine whether he lives or dies.

That's what they taught me in aviation school anyway. And personal experiences reinforced the lesson. On my last combat mission in Vietnam, having survived several mishaps that could have but did not cost me my life, I wasn't as acutely aware of the danger to my own well-being that the mission entailed. Instead of interpreting my previous experiences as evidence that things can and often will go wrong when flying, particularly in dangerous and stressful conditions—an awareness that should have made me more heedful of the danger—I had developed a false sense of my own invulnerability. And that characteristic of my ego, which I felt no need to check, discounted the danger I personally faced. I placed too much faith on what was beyond my knowledge or control: luck. And my luck ran out that day. When I heard the warning tone that an enemy SAM battery had locked onto me, I was moments away from dropping my bombs on target. I thought I had enough time to do my job and still evade the missile I knew would probably be coming my way. I also allowed my desire to get the hell away from Hanoi, which, thanks to Soviet assistance, had become the most heavily air-defended city in history, to encourage me to strike first and evade second. I didn't want to come back for a second run. I had five and a half very long years to regret my decision and the lapse in self-awareness that prevented me from recognizing the cockiness that had blinded me to one of the immutable principles of war and life: luck is unreliable.

Obviously, not every important decision involves stakes that are so consequential. But gaining the most acute awareness of both the objective and subjective circumstances in which you make a decision, in the time allotted for making it, increases the quality of every decision. The first question you need to answer is: What are the stakes involved? What is at risk and how much is it at risk by your decision? If the stakes are grave—life or death, the success or failure of an important enterprise, the well-being or peril of a loved one—you will proceed cautiously and expend every effort and every last second to gather relevant information before you decide. If your object would be irretrievably lost by the wrong decision, you will feel that burden even more. If the stakes are not so grave, or if you know you will have time to compensate for a bad decision, then you might have the space to consider bolder action—one that might carry a greater risk of failure but will achieve more significant success if it proves to be right. Of course, sometimes circumstances are so dire that only a bold decision can rescue you from them. If that's the case, good luck. You're going to need a lot of it, and a lot of courage. Perhaps you are not required to make any decision at all but have glimpsed an opportunity to advance a particular interest. Do you know what it could cost you? Is it worth the risk? Are you confident you understand the environment, so that your gamble is more than an expression of your desires, that it has a decent chance to succeed?

Time is the second consideration. When does the problem become unsolvable? When will the opportunity pass? Will you have another opportunity to recover from the wrong decision? What is the last moment you have to decide, and do the chances of success diminish or increase by waiting? Is patience a virtue or a risk? How much time do you have to think and to discuss it with others? Is more information attainable in any realistic time frame? Are you required to make a decision on the spot? If so, then you answer the third critical question.

Are you prepared for the decision? Do you know your business? Have you already gained the knowledge to make the call? Do you know what you don't know? Have you trained to follow an urgent-decision protocol that can be executed in the time available? Are you experienced in making right decisions on the spot or at length in an environment like the one you now confront, with the same players involved and similar risks and rewards at stake? If the situation involves human opponents, do you know how prepared or experienced they are? Do they know what they don't know? Are you reasonably sure you have the means to execute the decision? Does it matter? Are there other people with more experience and better preparation to whom you can turn for advice?

If you have more time to make a decision, then you must make yourself more aware. You can gather more information, consult a wider circle of advisers, study your situation and review similar decisions, seek answers to questions you know are pertinent, and identify questions that aren't immediately apparent.

Fourth, do you have confidence, an informed confidence, that the information you are using to make the decision is reliable? Are your assumptions no more than groupthink, conventional interpretations of situations that may differ in important, perhaps unknown ways from the one you are currently in or that have not been reassessed in light of incoming information? Or are they based on observations of the specific situation? Have you weighed conflicting evidence and come to a sound conclusion as to which is more accurate? The answer to these questions may well rely on personal knowledge you possess about the sources of that information. Has the source been reliable in the past? Is it experienced with providing such information? If it is human intelligence on which you rely, what are your sources' qualifications for locating and evaluating relevant information? What are their motives? Could they have hidden motives? Have they given you reason in the past to doubt their judgment? Do they have the ability to separate the important from the extraneous? Do they understand your needs? Do they see the situation in the same way or differently than you do? Do you know why? Remember, garbage in, garbage out, as computer programmers say. False information is often perpetuated and will lead you to not only one bad decision but possibly several if it forms the premise of your strategic thinking and is not exposed as false in good time.

A large part of the reason the United States invaded Iraq was our confidence that Saddam Hussein possessed chemical and biological weapons and was making significant progress in developing nuclear weapons. That confidence was in part based on information from previously unreliable or questionable sources. Part of it was based on the comfort we took from the fact that the intelligence services of many other countries shared that assumption. Leave aside the question of whether we would have invaded had we known the true state of his weapons programs: some have argued we shouldn't have; others, myself included, argued that Saddam still posed a threat that was best to address sooner rather than later. I mention this issue only to illustrate how false information perpetuated other mistakes. Soon after the invasion, we devoted time and manpower and the priority concentration of our civilian leadership to efforts to scour Iraq for weapons that weren't there, when it would have been far better to concentrate our efforts and our soldiers on more critically important tasks, such as securing conventional arms depots and dealing with the pockets of resistance we left behind in the race to Baghdad. The political and military mistakes we have made in Iraq offer a variety of examples of insufficient awareness. Books, rather large ones, have been written to cover them all. An important part of awareness is anticipating the decisions you will have to make if your initial decision proves successful. For instance, we were well aware of the quality of the Iraqi army, the conditions we would fight in, the stability of the regime we sought to destroy, even the character of the tyrant we deposed. We designed a force and an operational plan to dispense with them quickly. But we did not plan for or have the force ready to deal with our success. We didn't know what would happen in Iraq if we achieved our initial objective by the means we employed, and we were very slow in realizing what was needed when it did happen. That proved to be a very serious and tragic mistake.

The last and indispensable component of awareness is the most subjective: personal knowledge of the people involved in and affected by your decision. And the most important part of that equation is self-awareness. Are you better at seeing the big picture and less adept at gathering and evaluating details? Are there people around you to compensate for that? Are you patient? Impulsive? Are you intimidated by a lack of consensus among your advisors? Are you dismissive of dissent? Do you have a tendency to focus on finding support for a judgment you have already made and to discount contradictory evidence? Once you've made up your mind, are you intent on moving on? Or will you change your mind even late in the game, if other facts come to light? Are you too prone to doubts? Or are you the kind of person whose treasured hopes have in the past trumped lessons learned from hard experience? What are your most common mistakes? Do you work well under pressure, or are you much better when you have time to wait on more information, on additional help, or for events to become clearer? Have your instincts served you well in the past? If so, do you trust them more than contradictory facts or the advice of experienced counselors? Most important, do you know these things about yourself? What have you done to compensate for them? Have you a team designed, at least in part, to compensate for your shortcomings? These are but a few of the many personal questions that have to be answered before making an informed decision. And they should be asked and answered before you are confronted with the need to make a decision.

What do you do when a routine checkup leads to an unfortunate diagnosis and you are confronted with choosing between two or more forms of treatment? Do you simply ask the doctor for his or her advice and give your assent to the decision? Do you know your doctor well enough? Is your trust based on anything more than familiarity and amiability? If your doctor is not qualified to make that recommendation, he or she will likely send you to someone who is. Have you sought additional opinions? Have you searched for information about the nature of your disease? What are the rates of success for each proposed treatment? Do you know how much time you have before your situation becomes so acute that it limits your options? Do you understand the nature of the proposed treatments? Do you know enough about yourself to know if you can withstand mentally and physically some treatments better than others? If surgery is required, have you taken care to find the best surgeon available? Have you chosen a hospital that is well regarded for the kind of surgery or treatment you need?

In short, the better aware you are, the more sound your decision. What is the most common observation made by someone who made the wrong call? "I really didn't know."

THE MAHATMA
AND THE INTRUDER

B ranch Rickey changed things. The "smartest man in baseball," according to *Time* magazine, he was the author of many of the game's most important innovations. As general manager for the St. Louis Cardinals, he had started the farm system by purchasing controlling interests in minor-league teams so that they would develop young talent for his club. He used sophisticated statistical analyses to evaluate players' performance. Knothole gangs, sliding pits, batting tees, and helmets were all his ideas. He believed the ability to hit, throw, and field were God given, but everything else about baseball could be taught, and he pioneered blackboard coaching to teach both fundamentals and newly designed plays. He was the shrewdest judge of talent in the business. He developed an extensive scouting network to find the most promising young athletes in the country, develop their potential in his farm teams, and turn them into pennant-winning ball-players. A master trader, he had an uncanny ability to recognize just when a star player's talent had peaked and trade him before his decline was noticeable, reaping better players and handsome payments in the bargain.

When he started with the Cardinals, they were $175,000 in debt and the worst team in baseball. When he left, they were one of the most profitable teams, the home of the "Gashouse Gang," one of the best teams in the National League in the 1930s, and the owners of six league pennants and four World Series victories.

He was a square block of a man in a shapeless suit, bow tie, and fedora, with a shock of dark hair draping his brow. He had a meaty face, a cigar wedged in the corner of his mouth, and bushy eyebrows; he looked owlish behind his big spectacles. He vibrated with the energy and gushing sanctimony of his theatrical nature. The child of a strict Methodist upbringing on an Ohio farm, he neither swore nor drank and turned every sportswriter's question into an occasion for a long sermon on baseball and morals and anticommunism and the American way. Reporters referred to his office, where he preached to them, as "the Cave of the Winds." He treated rotary clubs, his family, and the occasional knothole kid to the same windy sermonizing that wearied the usually indefatigable New York press. He was "a mixture of Phineas T. Barnum and Billy Sunday," *Time* magazine said, "who is prone to talk piously of the larger and higher implications of what he is doing."[1]

He was both pious and cunning and a bottom-line man. He never attended Sunday games, out of deference to his devout mother and the strictures of his faith. But he listened to them on the radio, and, as his critics never tired of pointing out, he didn't object to the fact that the Sabbath was the most profitable day of the week at ballparks. He was an outspoken advocate of prohibition who kept company with some of baseball's hardest drinkers. He was devoted to his wife, an exemplary father to his six children, strict in his decorum, and averse to gambling; but when he was with the Brooklyn Dodgers he retained as manager and protected the tempestuous, hard-drinking Leo Durocher, Leo the Lip, whose two favorite activities were cussing at umpires and shooting dice with some of the New York nightlife's more unsavory characters. He preached the virtue of honesty but had few qualms about using deception in the service of a higher cause, especially winning ball games. He was a prominent Republican and quite conservative—when he was with the Cardinals, he had considered running for governor of Missouri. It was said "his enemies were (in no particular order) Roosevelt, communism, and welfare."[2] Yet the great plan he was conceiving even in his years in St. Louis would put him in league with the most radical forces in the country, including the American Communist Party.

He was the highest-paid executive in baseball, and the most tight-fisted. He was infamous for the low salaries he paid his players. The owner of a team in the Negro Leagues remarked, "I've heard Mr. Rickey is very religious. If such is true, his religion runs towards the almighty dollar."[3] He once rebuked his best hitter, who was demanding a salary commensurate with his contributions to the team, "We lost with you and we can lose without you." Jimmy Powers of the New York *Daily News,* less impressed with Rickey's shrewdness than he was disdainful of his miserliness, tagged him with the uncomplimentary moniker "El Cheapo."

He was tireless, working from dawn to late in the evening, except on Sundays. He had two professional obligations, which he pursued relentlessly: to win and to make as much money doing it as possible. "Luck," he said, "is the residue of design." When he arrived in Brooklyn in 1942, the Dodgers had just won a pennant, but it was an aging team with a weak minor-league system, and it took Rickey a couple years to turn things around. He built a better farm system, quadrupled the size of his scouting staff, and, in those World War II years, signed a crop of players too young to be drafted, to much ridicule from the exuberantly hyperbolic New York press, that by war's end was to yield some of the best players in the game. He traded away some of the club's most popular players. The Dodgers finished seventh in the league in Rickey's third year with them. The fans and the sportswriters were merciless. But he inspired his players' loyalty and a nearly religious reverence for his motivational powers and genius. He called them by their first names. They called him Mr. Rickey. He insisted on it.

The Professor, the Brain, El Cheapo, and the Deacon were four of the many nicknames reporters assigned him, but the one that fit the best, and stuck, was "the Mahatma," invented by sportswriter Tom Meany to describe the man who was "a combination of God, your father and a Tammany Hall leader."[4]

He was, for all his theatricality, imperiousness, guile, and hard-nosed business practices, a man with deep convictions. He believed in change, not just in the game he loved but in the country. He often remarked in public that he wanted to use his talents for causes "that mattered outside the park."[5] Early in his life, he had played professional ball for a few years. But cold-eyed judge of talent that he was, he knew he would never be much of a success at it. He could hit all right, but he wasn't much of a fielder. In a single game in 1907 he had thirteen stolen bases charged against him. He went to Ohio Wesleyan University to make something of himself, and then to the University of Michigan, where he obtained a law degree. One afternoon, when he was still with the Cardinals, he unexpectedly lamented to his son his frustration that he had never employed his talents for a more meaningful social purpose than winning baseball games.

> I completed my college course in three years. I was in the top ten percent of my class in law school. I'm a Doctor of Jurisprudence. I am an honorary Doctor of Laws. . . . You have to admit, boy, that I am an educated man. . . . And I like to believe that I am an intelligent man. . . . Then will you please tell me, why in the name of common sense, I spent four mortal hours today conversing with a person named Dizzy Dean.[6]

He had coached the baseball team at Ohio Wesleyan. A young black man, Charlie Thomas, was the team's catcher and best hitter. According to Thomas, Rickey had always taken "a special interest in my welfare."[7] In South Bend for a game against Notre Dame, Thomas was denied a room when the team checked into its hotel the night before the game. "Why don't you have a room for him?" Rickey asked the hotel manager, who replied, "Because our policy is whites only." Rickey prevailed on the innkeeper to allow Thomas to sleep on a cot in his room. As Rickey subsequently told the story, after making the rounds to check that his players were settled into their rooms for the night, he returned

to his own room to find Thomas sitting on a chair, sobbing and rub-
bing his hands as if he were trying to remove their color. "Black skin,
black skin," he cried. "If only I could make them white, Mr. Rickey."
Although Thomas remembered the incident as less dramatic than his
coach's account, Rickey claimed he had forever after been haunted by
the memory of it. "I vowed that I would always do whatever I could
to see that other Americans did not have to face the bitter humiliation
that was heaped upon Charlie Thomas."[8]

However much Rickey might have embellished the story, there is
little doubt that his religious faith had instilled in him a sincere aversion to injustice. He revered Abraham Lincoln and was an avid reader
of books on slavery and Jim Crow laws. He corresponded with noted
academics who had written about segregation and theorized about
methods to weaken its hold over the American conscience. His daughter Jane recalled another example of Rickey's moral commitment to
justice from his years in St. Louis. Rickey had accompanied her to court
to challenge a traffic ticket she had received. While there, his attention
was drawn to an African American, a suspect in a murder case, whom
the police were abusively interrogating. Rickey intervened, upbraided
the police, reminded them that the man had rights, and gave the suspect his card with an offer to represent him. The man was subsequently
released, and Rickey hired him as his chauffeur.[9]

It is clear that the decision for which Branch Rickey will always be
remembered, while certainly consistent with his bottom-line sensibility, had a moral component as well. In the beginning, he was careful
to reveal his higher purpose to only a few people who would appreciate it and to insist to everyone else that he had done it only to help the
Dodgers win the pennant. He used his guile to ensure a successful outcome, to make it acceptable to baseball and the public. But to make it
work, he would need more than cunning and an adroit public-relations
campaign. Branch Rickey was going to change things in baseball and
America, and he needed a man with guts to help him do it, the guts to
endure the unendurable for the sake of a good cause. He dispatched
his scouts to scour the country for the man who could do it. They
found him playing shortstop in the Negro Leagues for the Kansas City
Monarchs.

His wife, Rachel, said that what first attracted her to Jackie Robinson when she was a nursing student at UCLA and he was a four-letter
star athlete there was his dignity, the way he "walked straight" and
"held his head up . . . proud of not just his color, but his people."[10] He
was not a meek man whom racism had accustomed to servility. He had
always stood up for himself, seldom accepted abuse without challenge,
and had gotten himself into plenty of scrapes to prove he was a better
man than those who treated him cruelly. When just a small boy, he was
taunted on the streets of Pasadena, California, with cries of "nigger,
nigger, nigger." His family counseled him to ignore such insults, but
he couldn't. "Cracker, cracker, cracker," he retorted, "and when the
rocks came flying, small as he was, he picked them up and flung them
back."[11]

At the urging of her brother, Burton, who had immigrated to
California several years before, Mallie Robinson had moved her five
children from Cairo, Georgia, to Pasadena when Jackie was barely
more than a year old. Her philandering husband had abandoned the
family's sharecropper cabin not long after Jackie was born, consign-
ing them to even deeper poverty. Their abusive white landlord, who
remembered Mallie "as the sassiest nigger woman ever on this place,"
added to her burdens.[12] She used the family's meager savings to purchase the train tickets, and with several members of their extended
family moved to Pasadena, where she found work as a maid for several
wealthy families.

She was a religious woman and a strict but kindhearted and attentive mother. She left their home in the dark early-morning hours,
walked miles to her place of employment, and returned home well
into the evening, every week of the year. She assigned each child the
responsibility to look after the next youngest one. Willie Mae, the
second youngest, looked after Jackie. Jackie, the youngest, looked
after himself. Pasadena offered more opportunities to the Robinson
family than Georgia had, but they remained in poverty, struggling to
afford two meals a day, some days only one, and some days no more than
a piece of bread, sugared and dipped in milk. And if they had hoped
to escape the oppression of the Jim Crow south, Pasadena imposed
its own injustices, segregated as it was by custom rather than law. The

Robinsons, along with Mallie's sister's family, managed to buy a modest white frame house in a working-class neighborhood. They were the only black family on Pepper Street, and they were not welcome. They hadn't been in the house long before one of their neighbors burned a cross on their front lawn. Jackie's oldest brother, Edgar, put out the flames. Stones were hurled at their windows, and various other attempts were made to drive them from the neighborhood. They stuck it out, in the house they called "the castle," for the refuge it provided them, and in time their steadfastness won the grudging respect of their neighbors.

There were no black schools in Pasadena, and at the predominately white schools the Robinson children attended they were expected to keep to themselves and to submit quietly to their inferior status. On their way to and from school, they were subjected to verbal and physical abuse from white kids, and even by adults who rolled down their car windows to shout insults or warnings to them. Once, when Jackie and a few friends had jumped into the local reservoir to escape the misery of hot summer day, they were arrested by a sheriff's deputy who remarked, "Look there, niggers are swimming in my drinking water." At the county jail, one of the boys complained he was thirsty. The sheriff told one of his deputies, "The coon's hungry. Go buy a watermelon."[13] Jackie remembered people in Pasadena as "less understanding, in some ways, than southerners . . . they were more openly hostile." He had always been made to feel, he remembered, "like an intruder," and he resented it for the rest of his life.[14]

But Robinson would have had to agree that California also offered more opportunities to prove himself equal to or better than any white kid there than the south would have. For him, those opportunities were found mostly on the playgrounds of the city's parks and the playing fields of his schools, on teams that were integrated many years before southern teams were. Long after Jackie Robinson had left California, those who knew him on those playgrounds recalled that they had never seen an athlete like him.

His mother had taught him to be proud and not to let the ignorance of others weaken his self-esteem. She taught him to be assertive in defense of his rights. She taught him to hold himself upright when his dignity was challenged but to respond without letting his passion get the better of him. She tried to instill in her children the faith in which she abided, the belief that to be a person of quality in the eyes of God is all that really matters. But Jackie had trouble keeping his rage in check. Insults were not something he found easy to bear quietly. He had his share of fights and got into a fair amount of trouble with the police. For a brief time, he ran with a gang of self-styled tough kids, though their crimes never rose above the level of petty vandalism. But a young minister who took an interest in Jackie persuaded him to stay out of gangs and channel his frustration and energy into athletic competition. And to his and America's good fortune, Jackie took the lesson to heart. He soon understood that sports offered the better place to vent his anger and assert his dignity. "Jackie wasn't a very likable person," a friend from childhood remembered, "because his whole thing was just win, win, win, and beat everybody."[5] Jackie played as if he were intent on showing every doubting white person who had ever treated him unfairly that he was a man to be reckoned with.

There was hardly a sport in which he didn't excel when he put his mind to it, from football to Ping-Pong. At Pasadena Junior College and then at UCLA he was a standout in track and field, football, basketball, and baseball. One observer called the UCLA point guard "the best basketball player in the United States"; another considered him the best halfback in the country. (He averaged twelve yards per carry.) He won trophies for golf and tennis. He was a champion swimmer. He set records for the broad jump and surely would have competed and medaled in the Tokyo Olympics in 1940 had they not been canceled following the outbreak of World War II. His brother Mack had won a silver medal in the 1936 Munich Olympics, finishing behind Jesse Owens in the two-hundred-meter dash, and had returned to Pasadena only to struggle to find work as a janitor.

Powerfully built, naturally agile, with an explosive first step, a fraction under six feet, and fearless, Jackie was an intimidating presence on the court and field. He was pigeon-toed, which gave him a staggered, awkward gait when he walked. But he ran like a race car. It was often remarked that Jackie could hit full speed by his third stride, and when he barreled down the sidelines carrying the football for

UCLA, woe to the brave defensive tackle who tried to get in his way. He brought the fast break to the patient offensive sets of UCLA basketball and burned his opponents off the dribble. In baseball, which was not his favorite sport, "he was the bandit on the bases who sometime stole second, third and home in succession."[16] But more than any other quality, Jackie was remembered for a competitiveness so fierce that it left a lasting impression even on people who saw him play only once. He was unyielding, and he was tougher on himself than any other player. If he felt he hadn't played well, he became sick to his stomach. In every game, no matter how unimportant, he wanted to beat the other side just as badly as it was possible to beat them. He simply burned to win.

Whatever resentment he may have encountered from white team-mates and students, most of it disappeared as he proved his athletic prowess, and his legend as the best athlete at UCLA (and perhaps in California) spread throughout the state. Despite his celebrity, he was a reserved young man and wary of people who treated him like a star, assuming some of them would have once shut their homes and neighborhoods to his family. He had suffered a cruel blow not long after he had arrived at UCLA when his older brother Frank, whom he was closest to, was mortally injured in motorcycle accident and had died in the hospital in great pain, which Jackie had witnessed. At times, his reserve could slip into solemnity, which could be misperceived as surliness. He neither smoke nor drank, and until he met the elegant, proud, and strong-willed Rachel Isum, he dated infrequently. He played cards skillfully on team road trips, but not out of a weakness for gambling. It was just another form of competition to him, and he played to win. He still had his share of trouble, as he always found it hard to suffer a slight quietly, and with his hard-hitting approach to sports he found himself getting a reputation in some quarters for being something of a thug. The anger that motivated him on the field wasn't extinguished by his successes and popularity. He knew that sports might have won him a privileged place in college, but after that there would be few opportunities to profit from his talents, as any white kid would if he had half of Jackie's heart and talents.

He left UCLA in 1941, in the spring of his final semester, because he felt he could no longer afford to remain there. He had obligations to his family that he felt required him to begin making a living. His mother tried to persuade him to graduate, as did Rachel, with whom he had by then become seriously involved. When she challenged him, noting his good grades and how important a degree would be in the future they might have both suspected they would share, he told her he had thought about it a lot and had "come to the conclusion that somebody has to help my mother. She has worked herself almost to the point of collapse. . . . I just can't feel right inside, knowing that she needs help and not giving it when I know I can."[17] UCLA offered to pay his expenses for the last months of the school year, but he would not be dissuaded. When Jackie Robinson made up his mind to do something, he did it.

He had little clear idea what he would do for work, but he hoped it would involve sports. He worked and played baseball at a camp for kids for a couple of months, before playing football for a semipro team and working construction jobs in Honolulu. He came back to Los Angeles in December, on board a ship that had left Honolulu two days before the attack on Pearl Harbor. He played semipro basketball for the Los Angeles Red Devils until he received his induction order from the army in March 1942, and reported to Fort Riley, Kansas for basic training.

When he asked to play on Fort Riley's baseball team, the coach, a young captain, told him it was for whites only and said to another white officer, "I'll break up the team before I'll have a nigger on it."[18] The football coach offered him a place on his squad, but Jackie turned him down in retaliation for the earlier snub. When a full colonel, who had a son on the team, advised him that he could order him to play, Jackie acknowledged his authority to do so but reminded him that he couldn't order him to play well.

Despite these unfortunate encounters, Jackie acquitted himself well at basic training, earning good marks for discipline, character, and marksmanship. Yet he was turned down when he applied for Officer Candidate School. As luck would have it, heavyweight boxing champion Joe Louis was also stationed at Fort Riley at the time and had become friends with Robinson. When Louis learned Robinson's application had been denied, he intervened with a friend at the War Department, who investigated reports that qualified black candidates were routinely turned down for the school. Not long after, the decision to reject his application was reversed, and in January 1943 he was commissioned a second lieutenant. He marked the occasion by buying an engagement ring for Rachel. Three years and one temporary breakup would pass before they finally made it to the altar. By then, Jackie and Rachel's lives were about to change, and the country along with them, more than either could have anticipated when they first became engaged.

Robinson never saw combat during the war, having remained stateside for the duration. Two other incidents of his brief military career are worth noting, the first while he was still stationed at Fort Riley as the morale officer for an all-black company. He had listened to his soldiers complain about the many indignities they were forced to endure on the base because of their skin color, particularly the fact that only a few tables were available to black soldiers at the PX, while white soldiers were generously accommodated. Jackie promised the men he would take the matter up with the white major who served as provost marshal. The next day, he phoned Major Hafner and asked if the segregation of the PX was official policy or just custom. Hafner told him it was both. After Robinson protested, Hafner, who did not know he was speaking to an African-American officer, asked Jackie, "How would you like to have your wife sitting next to a nigger?"[19] With that, Jackie exploded and dressed the major down in terms that are supposed to be the privilege of officers addressing a subordinate, not someone of superior rank.

Not much later, Jackie was transferred to an all-black tank battalion, although he had no training in tank warfare, at Fort Hood, which was located in a part of Texas not known then for its hospitality to newly arrived African Americans, even a freshly commissioned second lieutenant. Robinson proved a good officer, and the platoon he commanded received the best evaluation of any on the base. He made a very favorable impression on the battalion commander, who was a fair and competent officer. One evening Jackie took a bus from the officers' club to the base hospital, where he was to have his ankle, which he had injured playing football, X-rayed to see if he was fit for overseas duty. He took a seat near the front of the bus. The white bus driver ordered him to move to the back. Lieutenant Robinson forthrightly refused, citing a recent directive from the Department of the Army that officially desegregated buses on army bases. The driver, now angry, persisted in demanding that he relinquish his seat. Jackie told him to mind his own business. When some of the white passengers took noisy offense at what they perceived as his arrogance, Jackie told them where they could go, too. After several further futile exchanges, the driver got off the bus to fetch the dispatcher and a couple of MPs. In short order, the MPs took Jackie to the assistant provost marshal, Captain Gerald Bear, who began dressing him down for trying to "start a race riot." Jackie held his ground, and when the captain's civilian secretary, who believed Texas's segregation laws should apply on as well as off the base, insulted him, he returned the favor.

The next morning, Jackie's battalion commander, Colonel Bates, was asked to sign papers charging him with insubordination, disturbing the peace, conduct unbecoming an officer, insulting a civilian, and refusing a lawful order from a superior officer. Bates refused to sign. So Fort Hood's commanding general immediately transferred Robinson to another battalion, whose commanding officer was happy to see him court-martialed. The injustice of Robinson's predicament provoked other African-American officers at the base to contact the NAACP, and soon leading African-American newspapers took up his cause.

He was assigned a skilled attorney, who easily demolished the testimonies of Captain Bear, the two MPs, and a few other eyewitnesses. The senior officers who heard the case, including one African-American officer, were all fair-minded men. The trial ended in an acquittal four hours after it had begun. Four months later, Jackie was honorably discharged from the army.

He accepted a job coaching basketball at Samuel Huston College, a small black college in Texas. It ended after one season, when he received an invitation to try out for the most celebrated team in the Negro Leagues, the Kansas City Monarchs, the team where Buck O'Neil played and managed, and where Satchel Paige, over forty and still the best pitcher in the game, hurled his fastballs. The Monarchs dominated their league. They had always had the best pitchers, hitters, fielders, and base runners. They were a colorful cast of characters, with names like Cool Papa Bell and Double Duty Radcliffe, and in the off-hours of their raucous itinerant life, they caroused with the best of them. Their coaching was poor, the training nonexistent. The teams were chronically short of equipment, even baseballs. The rules were lax. Pitchers used all manner of doctored balls, greased with Vaseline, scuffed with emery boards, nicked with penknives. The playing style was freewheeling. But the Monarchs prepared for every game and took the field intent on winning.

When Jackie arrived to play shortstop, his teammates didn't consider him to be an exceptional ballplayer physically. He didn't have the arm to play shortstop and wasn't as quick defensively as he was running the bases. But they were impressed with his intelligence. "Jackie didn't have the ability at first," remarked a teammate, "but he had the brains."[20] He learned some of his skill at base running, his ability to keep the entire infield in jitters trying to guess when he was going to steal another base, from Cool Papa Bell, one of the best base thieves ever. Most impressive was his competitiveness, which was as keen as it had been at UCLA. He wanted to win as much as or more than any man on the team, and he hit .387 that season.

But he didn't enjoy life in the Negro Leagues: the low pay, the rough life on the road, the broken-down buses, the long rides through the Jim Crow south and the assaults on his dignity they often entailed, the crummy hotels, the sloppy officiating, the erratic play, the hard drinking, and other excesses. He wanted more, and the fact that his race still got in the way of the success he knew he could attain made him seethe. He'd flame up over practical jokes, insults, and disrespect, no matter where they occurred. On more than one occasion, things got violent. A teammate recounted the many occasions when the team bus would pull into service stations in Mississippi, "where drinking fountains said black and white and we had to leave without our change, he'd get so mad."[21] On one memorable occasion, the Monarchs' manager had to run back to the bus to summon the other players for help when a store owner called Jackie "boy." "Jackie's gonna get us killed," he warned.[22] Jackie tried to quit the team once and was persuaded by the offer of a raise to stick it out. But by the end of the season, he was finished with the Monarchs. He was going to Montreal to play baseball for the Royals, the Brooklyn Dodgers' AAA farm team. Branch Rickey had asked him to be the first African American to play baseball in the major leagues. And Jackie Robinson had said yes.

As a national institution, baseball both reflected American society and had helped at critical moments to weave its disparate elements into a more coherent whole. It had served to restore national unity after the Civil War. Although St. Louis, Washington, and Cincinnati were the only major-league cities located near the south, the game was followed as avidly in southern newspapers as it was in the north and midwest. Early in the twentieth century, baseball was firmly established as the national pastime, beloved by rich and poor alike, white and black, every ethnic group, in every city and state. Kids played the game on city parks and streets and in farm pastures.

The great waves of immigrants from eastern and southern Europe yielded some of the best players in the game. Joe DiMaggio's father was a Sicilian fisherman. Hank Greenberg was the son of Orthodox Jews who had emigrated from Romania. The presence in the game of so many players of diverse (if white) ethnic heritage, often first-generation Americans themselves, inspired the loyalty of new immigrants who had never seen or heard of the game before they arrived at Ellis Island, and it hastened their assimilation into the mainstream culture of their new country. But baseball, as powerful a unifying force as the military or any other national institution in America, also reflected in the 1940s the falseness and injustice of the "separate but equal" myth employed to justify the Jim Crow laws of the south and the de facto segregation of the north. African-American players, no matter how outstanding they were, had their own leagues. The major leagues were for white players and for the occasional mixed-race, Latino, Native American, or Asian player, but no one of obviously African heritage. There was no statute enforcing the segregation of organized baseball. Nor was there ever an official policy in the major leagues to exclude African Americans. The autocratic Judge Kenesaw Mountain Landis, baseball's long-serving commissioner, frequently professed baseball had neither â written or unwritten policy barring black players. But everyone knew the score. There was an unwritten rule. And Landis was an implacable foe of integrating baseball.

World War II wrought many social changes in the United States, among them the migration of southern blacks to the north, where jobs were more plentiful and segregation less brutal. Major-league owners couldn't have helped but notice that Negro League teams were starting to draw record attendances at games played in northern ballparks. Moreover, the recognition that African Americans had served, sacrificed, and fought with distinction in the war influenced white attitudes about race relations, providing greater power to moral arguments advanced on behalf of integration, and helped motivate the civil-rights advances of the forties and fifties. A national Fair Employment Practices Committee had been established in 1941 to investigate allegations of discrimination in government hiring. The New York State Assembly sanctioned a similar committee. Black newspapers, civil-rights leaders, and a number of white sportswriters in the north, including Jimmy Powell at the New York *Daily News,* became more vocal advocates during the war for the integration of baseball. New York mayor Fiorello La Guardia formed a Committee on Unity, made up of prominent civil-rights leaders in the city, to ensure that the city enforced fair employment and housing practices.

In Boston, a civil-rights activist on the city council had threatened to impose blue laws that would effectively close the city's two major-league ballparks on Sundays. To avert the threatened financial catastrophe, the Red Sox agreed to allow three players from the Negro Leagues to try out for the team in April 1945. The tryout was simply a public-relations ploy, and none of the players was signed. They hit a few balls, shagged some flies, and were dismissed with nothing more than thanks, although Red Sox manager Joe Cronin conceded they had ability. Two of the players weren't surprised that the Red Sox hadn't really been interested in signing them and took the disappointment in stride. But the third player was genuinely angered by the charade. Wendell Smith, the sports columnist for a leading African-American newspaper who had arranged for the tryouts and brought the three men to Boston, remembered Jackie Robinson telling him after, "Listen, Smith, it really burns me up to come fifteen hundred miles to have them give me the runaround."[23]

The war had also drained the major leagues of some its best talent. Many of the players who had returned to the game after the war had sacrificed their prime playing years to answer their country's call to arms, and the leagues were in need of new talent. Mountain Landis had died unexpectedly in 1944, but the new commissioner, a former U.S. senator and governor of Kentucky, A.B. "Happy" Chandler, was hardly known for his enlightened views on race relations. The mounting pressure on New York's three major-league teams, the Yankees, Giants, and Dodgers, to integrate caused the Yankees' president to write the new commissioner, describing the situation as "increasingly serious and acute" and warning that if something wasn't done immediately to prevent it, "we will have colored players in the minor leagues by 1945, and in the major leagues shortly thereafter."[24] But Chandler surprised journalists who inquired about his views on the subject by remarking, "If a black boy can make it on Okinawa and Guadalcanal, hell, he can make it in baseball. . . . Once I tell you something, brother, I never change. You can count on me."[25]

Branch Rickey observed these developments and understood their import with the alertness of a man who had been waiting patiently for years for the right time and opportunity to seize his place in history. He knew that opportunity would not present itself while he was in St. Louis, a deeply segregated border-state city. But he had been set on integrating the Dodgers since he came to Brooklyn in 1942. He approached the problem carefully and employed deception to mask his true intention. He knew that signing a black player to play for the Dodgers could not appear to be a concession to the pressure being exerted on the leagues by civil-rights activists, newspapers, and left-wing politicians, and he cautioned advocates, sometimes angrily, that they were setting the cause back by appearing to force the issue. Astute observer of social progress that he was, however, he knew their efforts were shaping the environment and accelerating the time when he would dare his great experiment. Still, he intended to argue to Brooklyn's fans, players, and owners that his decision to sign a black player was in the best interests of the team, to help them win ball games and to fill the seats at Ebbets Field, and not because he had been moved to embrace the cause of social justice. In his heart, however, he held a nobler purpose. "I couldn't face my God much longer," he later explained, "knowing that His black creatures are held separate and distinct from His white creatures in the game that has given me all I won."[26] Were he to succeed in this most important assignment, he would have to find just the right man, a strong man with courage and character, who could take the abuse that was sure to come his way and answer not with his fists or mouth but by proving himself an exceptional ballplayer and gentleman.

Rickey devised a plan to integrate the Dodgers that was to proceed in six stages.

1. The backing and sympathy of the Dodgers' directors and stockholders, whose investment and civic standing had to be considered and protected.
2. Picking a Negro who would be the right man on the field.
3. Picking a Negro who would be the right man off the field.
4. A good reaction from the press and public.
5. Backing and thorough understanding from the Negro race, to avoid misinterpretation and abuse of the project.
6. Acceptance of player by his teammates.[27]

Rickey first approached George McLaughlin, bank president, part owner of the team, and member of the Dodgers' board of directors, to discuss his plans. McLaughlin gave his blessing to the project but counseled Rickey about the opposition he would encounter from fans and players: "If you find the man who is better than the others, you will beat it; if you don't you're sunk."[28] A few weeks later, Rickey met with the team's directors and won their acquiescence to his plan and their promise to keep his intentions a secret, even from their families. Rickey kept his own family and closest associates as much in the dark as was possible. He then dispatched his scouting team to find his man.

To obscure his intentions, he told his scouts, some of whom might have resigned had they known they were recruiting a black man, that he planned to establish a new Negro league, the United States League, and he needed players to fill its rosters. He announced the plan in May 1945, promising to clean up the dubious practices and improve the freewheeling play of the Negro Leagues.* He took a member of Mayor La Guardia's antidiscrimination committee into his confidence and suggested the formation of the subcommittee to examine the feasibility of integrating baseball, admitting that it would serve as a ruse to convince integration advocates that something was being done, relieve pressure on New York baseball, and allow Rickey to work secretly and on his own timetable to search for the right player. He met with the man who called the Dodgers' games on the radio, Walter Lanier "Red" Barber, and told the Mississippi-raised sportscaster in confidence, "There is a Negro player coming to the Dodgers. I don't know who he is and I don't know where he is and I don't know when he is coming. But he is coming. And he is coming soon."[29] Rickey knew that the immensely popular Barber had it within his power to influence Brooklyn's fans either decisively for or against an African American on their team's roster. He believed Barber could be persuaded to support him, because Rickey knew him to be a fair man, even if influenced by his southern heritage. Barber reacted to the news silently but was deeply disturbed at the prospect. He kept the news to himself but considered quitting the Dodgers. Eventually, as Rickey had known he would, Barber decided to stay with the team and just "broadcast the ball."[30] When Jackie Robinson arrived and proved himself on the field, Red Barber was to be one his most vocal and ardent supporters.

Rickey queried black sportswriters about who they thought were among the best prospects in the Negro Leagues. Wendell Smith, who had brought Robinson to the Red Sox tryouts, spoke highly of Jackie, confirming reports Rickey had already received from his scouts. Thinking that he might have found his man, he traveled to California in person to investigate Robinson's background.

Robinson's biographer, Jules Tygiel, described what kind of man Rickey was looking for:

---

*The United States League folded after one season.

The candidate did not have to be the best black ballplayer, though he naturally needed superior skills. Rather, he had to be the most likely to maintain his talents at a competitive peak while withstanding pressure and abuse. He needed the self-control to avoid reacting to his tormentors without sacrificing his dignity. "How can a man of worth and human dignity and unsullied personality bend enough?" Rickey later explained his thinking. . . . In addition to his composure on the field, the candidate had to be an exemplary individual off the field as well. "We could know about his playing ability in uniform," reasoned Rickey, "but what about out of uniform? . . . his associates, his character, his education, his intelligence." When Rickey had completed the portrait of the ideal path breaker, he concluded, "There were just not many such humans."[31]

Yet Branch Rickey found one.

Jackie Robinson met almost all of Rickey's requirements exceptionally well. He was a good ballplayer, quick and competitive, and an extraordinarily gifted athlete, who had the proven ability and the intelligence to improve his play in whatever role assigned him. Rickey admired the way he used his quickness and brains to unsettle an opposing team's infield. He laid down bunts with great skill and was a clutch hitter, best with two strikes on him. He had the drive. No one could doubt that. He was college educated, a relative rarity in professional baseball at that time. He was well spoken and carried himself with dignity. He had played on integrated teams at UCLA and had been popular among the school's predominantly white students and fans. He had been raised well, overcome adversity, and showed admirable discipline in pursuing his achievements. He had served as an officer in the army. He did not smoke, drink, or possess any other unacceptable vices, as far as was known. He was engaged to a fine young lady, whom he would soon marry. He had heart, courage, and toughness. What Rickey didn't know for certain, and would need to ascertain, was whether Jackie's explosive need to prove himself, and the pride and anger that drove it, could be channeled productively and exclusively on a baseball diamond. He admired the fact that he stood up for himself, and he wasn't overly worried by the many instances when Jackie's temper had erupted in righteous indignation. But he couldn't let that happen on or off the field when he came to the Dodgers.

Rickey had read a report of the events that led to Robinson's court-martial and acquittal, and he admired his refusal to submit to injustice. "A man of ideals," Rickey noted, "a battler." But he didn't know if Jackie could fight his battles with the patience and shrewdness Rickey would expect of him. Before he had that last and most critical assurance, Rickey would have to put his man to the test. He sent one of his best scouts, Clyde Sukeforth, to Chicago, where the Monarchs were playing, to bring Jackie to Brooklyn.

The three-hour encounter between Branch Rickey and Jackie Robinson at the Dodgers' front office at 215 Montague Street on August 28, 1945, is one of the most cherished legends in baseball. Three eyewitness accounts—Rickey's, Robinson's, and Sukeforth's—vary in minor respects but agree on most of the important ones. All the participants remembered the encounter as dramatic, exhausting, and poignant. Rickey informed Robinson that contrary to what he might have been told, he was not being considered for a job in the new Negro league but for a contract with the Brooklyn Dodgers, with a year playing for the Montreal Royals before they brought him up, and he wanted to know if he had the stuff to endure the inevitable torrent of abuse that would greet the first black man in the big leagues. Rickey imagined every possible scenario Robinson would encounter and playacted them. Sweating, cursing, panting, contorting himself, bringing his scowling, beefy face to within an inch of Jackie's, Rickey mimicked surly waiters, bigoted train conductors, obnoxious hotel-desk clerks, insulting fans, biased umpires, enraged opponents who assailed his dignity with spikes, fists, beanballs, and bats, and anyone else whose abuse Jackie would have to endure without retaliation. Robinson recalled that Rickey's "acting was so convincing I found myself chain-gripping my fingers behind my back."[32]

"You're playing shortstop and I come down from first, stealing with my spikes high, and I cut you in the leg. As the blood trickles down your shin, I grin at you and say: 'Now, how do you like that, nigger boy?' Then in the World Series: So we play for keeps there, Jackie, we play it to win there, and almost everything under the sun goes. I want to win in the most desperate way, so I'm coming into second with my spikes flying. But you don't give ground. You're tricky. You feint, and as I hurl myself, you ease out of the way and jam that ball hard into my ribs. As I lie there in the swirling dust, my rib aching, I hear that umpire cry, 'You're out,' and I jump up, and all I can see is that black face of yours shining in front of my eyes. So I yell, 'Don't hit me with a ball like that, you tar baby son of a bitch.' So I haul off and sock you right in the cheek."[33]

With that, Rickey swung his fist at Jackie's head, and he reacted with a plaintive "Mr. Rickey, do you want a ballplayer who's afraid to fight back?" giving Rickey the opening to state exactly who it was he wanted: "I want a ballplayer with the guts not to fight back."

"We can't fight our way through this, Robinson. We've got no army, there's virtually no one on our side. And I'm afraid that many fans will be hostile. We'll be in a tough position. We can win only if I convince the world that I'm doing this because you're a great ballplayer and a fine gentleman. If you're a good enough man, we can make this a start in the right direction. But let me tell you, it's going to take an awful lot of courage."[34]

Then an exhausted Rickey read from Giovanni Papini's *Life of Christ,* "Ye have heard that it hath been said, An eye for an eye, and a tooth for a tooth: But I say unto you, That ye resist not evil: But whosoever shall smite thee on thy right cheek, turn to him the other also."

Robinson understood. "What you want me to say is that I've got another cheek," he responded.[35] Yes, that was what Rickey wanted to hear. "For three years, Jackie, three years," there could be no incidents on or off the field. Sukeforth remembered several minutes passing before Robinson finally gave his assent. "Mr. Rickey, I think I can play ball in Montreal. I think I can play ball in Brooklyn. . . . If you want to take this gamble, I promise you there will be no incident." And with that, it was done. Under a framed portrait of Abraham Lincoln that adorned Rickey's office wall, Robinson signed an agreement to play for Montreal for a $3,500 signing bonus and $600 per month. The following year he would play for the Dodgers for a $5,000 salary, the lowest salary a rookie could receive under league rules. Mr. Rickey never parted with a buck too easily.

The Dodgers made the announcement two months later. "We made this step for two reasons," the press release stated. "First, we are signing this boy because we think of him primarily as a ballplayer. Secondly, we think it a point of fairness." To everyone but his family and closest confidants, Rickey said he had hired Robinson because he would help win ball games and put more people in the seats, abjuring any larger goal than that. To African-American audiences, he quietly warned that they must restrain their enthusiasm and avoid giving any impression that one race had triumphed over another, or they would endanger the great experiment. For the most part, they heeded Rickey's counsel, launching a "don't spoil Jackie's chances" campaign to curb boisterous ballpark demonstrations.

Jackie Robinson experienced all the abuse Branch Rickey warned him would come his way and then some. The Royals' manager, Mississippi-born Clay Hopper, had beseeched Rickey not to make him accept an African American. "Do you really think a nigger is a human being," he asked a perturbed Rickey, whose reaction was not recorded for posterity.[36] He played spectacularly for the Royals. In his first game, he hit safely four times, including a three-run homer, scored twice, and stole two bases. Soon enough, he had the fans and his teammates on his side, but not without enduring constant taunts of "nigger, go home," beanballs, spikes and hard outs, black cats tossed onto the field, and every other conceivable insult and injury. He kept his promise to Rickey. There were no incidents. He kept his rage bottled up, or channeled it into his game.* He nearly had a nervous breakdown in the process. By the end of the season, he led the league in batting and led the Royals to victory in the Little World Series. When he was called up the following year, a chastened and changed Clay Hopper told him,

---

* One of the incidents with a cat, which occurred during a game in Syracuse as Jackie walked to the plate, resulted in a Robinson triple that drove in three runs.

"You're a great ballplayer and a fine gentleman. It's been wonderful having you on the team."[37]

He arrived in Brooklyn to much acclaim and a cold welcome from his teammates. During spring training, outfielder Dixie Walker, beloved by Dodgers fans as the "People's Cherce," circulated a petition among the team's southern players asking to be traded rather than play with Jackie. Several signed. Shortstop Pee Wee Reese, a Kentucky gentleman, declined. Rickey had Leo Durocher put a stop to it and told the players that any Dodger who couldn't accept Jackie as a teammate would be traded soon enough. Only one took player took him up on the offer.

His debut at Ebbets Field, on April 15, 1947, with twenty-six thousand fans in the stands, more than half of them African American, was a disappointment to Jackie. He went 0–3 against the Boston Braves. In his first month as a Dodger, he found himself mired in a hitting slump, and his defense was off. He had trouble adjusting to first base, a position better suited for left-handers. He would be moved to second base, the position best suited to his talents, the following year, but throughout his rookie season Eddie Stanky, who had signed Walker's petition, started at second base for the Dodgers.* Jackie was even a little hesitant on the bases at first.

There was also, of course, plenty of vile mistreatment directed at him, which he endured stoically. The abuse from opposing teams and fans, as well as the adulation of adoring African-American fans, bothered him. The latter he found terribly embarrassing on days when he hadn't performed up to his or Rickey's expectations. He was heckled constantly with the worst racial epithets. He received death threats. He was hit by more pitched balls in his first season than some players were in their entire careers. In St. Louis, Cardinals right fielder Enos Slaughter, out by a mile, jumped in the air when he reached first base and intentionally spiked Jackie in the leg. In an early-season three-game home stand against the Phillies, infamous for the insults hurled from their dugout at opposing batters, he caught the worst abuse of his rookie season. Led by their redneck manager, Ben

---

*Stanky was traded at the end of the season to clear the position for Jackie, who endured the brunt of the fans' displeasure over the loss of the popular Dodger.

Chapman, they shouted, "Go back to the cotton fields, nigger," and, "Hey, snowflake, which one of the white boys' wives are you dating tonight?" Even Stanky couldn't take it and yelled his own epithets at the dugout bullies. A Phillies pitcher later confessed that Chapman had threatened to fine any pitcher fifty dollars if they refused to throw at Jackie.

With minor exceptions, Jackie was treated civilly by the other Dodgers, but initially they kept their distance from him, and he from them. Observing their interactions in the Dodgers locker room, *New York Post* reporter Jimmy Cannon described Jackie as the "loneliest man I have ever seen in sports."[38] Rickey had given Wendell Smith a job with the team, basically to keep Jackie company on the road. But what appeals to the better angels of their natures couldn't do, the taunts and injuries inflicted on him by the Dodgers' opponents did. The team rallied to Jackie, a welcome development symbolized by an act of kindness in a particularly brutal game in Cincinnati. When the taunts became almost unendurable, the great Pee Wee Reese walked over to Jackie and draped his arm around his shoulder. The gesture silenced the Reds' bench and showed whoever saw it that Jackie Robinson was a Brooklyn Dodger, and the Dodgers were happy to have him.

By May, he had come out of his slump, gone on a fourteen-game hitting streak, and started playing the kind of baseball he and Branch Rickey expected him to play. True to his word, he never responded in kind to the cruelty he experienced during his first years with the Dodgers. When he and the many African Americans who soon followed him to the big leagues were accepted and appreciated throughout the country, and Jackie was released from his promise, he was to give back whatever abuse he received. The picture of Jackie arguing a call with the umpire or giving an opponent a piece of his mind became a common sight. But in his first few years, he just played the game all the harder. Opposing teams learned that if you made Jackie Robinson mad, it made him only all the more determined to beat you. Call him a "nigger," and he'd steal another base on you. Question his parentage, and he might smash a line drive that would nearly shave your head on its way to left field. He was extraordinary on the bases. He stole twenty-nine in his rookie season. He broke every opposing pitcher's concentration, made every infielder jumpy. He brought a scrambling, exciting kind of play back to the majors that hadn't been seen since Ty Cobb ran the bases. And he did it all with class and dignity. By the end of the season, *The Sporting News,* which just the year before had editorialized against baseball's integration, named him their first ever rookie of the year. He had hit .297 for the season, including twelve home runs and forty-two successful bunts, and helped the Dodgers win another pennant. Two years later, he was voted league MVP.

He played ten seasons for the Dodgers before retiring. He was twenty-eight when he started with them, old for a rookie. In his years with the team, the Dodgers won six pennants and their only World Series championship. He went into business, made a decent living, fought in the civil-rights struggles of the fifties and sixties, and always stuck by his principles, no matter what other people thought. He had chosen to live his life the hard way, for the sake of his own self-esteem and the dignity of his race. The stress had taken its toll. Afflicted by diabetes, blind, suffering from heart disease, and looking twenty years older than his fifty-three years, he died in 1972.

Branch Rickey had left the team years before Jackie, in 1950, after a falling-out with the owners. He took his wizardry to the Pittsburgh Pirates, where he recruited the great Roberto Clemente, and then spent his last two years in baseball with his original team, the Cardinals. He died in 1965 at eighty-three, in the middle of a speech. Reporters who had once endured his sermons from the "cave of the winds" thought it a most appropriate end. One assumes Mr. Rickey did, too.

Rickey was the man who built two of baseball's greatest dynasties, but he will always be remembered for the decision he made so skillfully to bring America's game to all Americans, to do something as big outside the ballpark as it was inside. He had seen something in Jackie Robinson that was greater than his athletic prowess. He had looked for a great baseball player with principles, courage, and dignity. The man he found had those qualities, as well as a temper he really didn't mind showing when provoked. He was a brave and driven man, but an often angry one. And Rickey saw something else in Jackie Robinson that maybe even Jackie wasn't sure he possessed. He saw a man with the courage and strength to maintain his composure under the most trying circumstances, a man whose pride could become a self-effacing dignity. He saw the man who could represent on the field and off the ideal American, and who could make integration, and long-delayed justice for his race, heroic to white America. They shook hands on the deal and made their country a better place.

SATISFACTION GUARANTEED

The fire began around nine o'clock on a breezy Sunday night in October on the west side of Chicago in a barn in the alley behind the O'Leary house. Within an hour, it had reduced much of the west side to ashes. By midnight, strong winds from the southwest had driven the flames north, across the south branch of the Chicago River, and toward the heart of the city's business district. It consumed everything in its path: homes, saloons, churches, theaters, businesses small and large, city hall, the courthouse and city jail, Potter Palmer's stunning new hotel, and the State Street bridge across the north branch of the river, which carried the fire to the north side and the opulent mansions of Chicago's rich. By the early hours of Tuesday morning, the winds had finally died down, and a light rain had fallen to subdue the firestorm. In the smoke and ash-choked air, the city lay in ruins. The fire had burned a path four miles long and nearly a mile wide. Many thousands of buildings had been destroyed, more than two hundred million dollars' worth of damage inflicted. Hundreds had perished, thousands were injured. One third of the city was homeless. Few had escaped the great Chicago fire of 1871. Other cities, rivals for its opportunities, expected, not unhappily, that Chicago had breathed its last.

But the greatest boomtown in America—situated so advantageously on the shore of Lake Michigan, at the nexus of the country's growing network of railroads, with access, by river and rail, to the rich farmlands of the Mississippi River valley and the grain stores and livestock of the Great Plains, the city where fortunes were won and lost at such a prodigious pace that even New York, the great citadel of American capital, looked on with envy—was imperishable.

Among the charred ruins of the city's newest shopping district was its preeminent wholesale and retail dry-goods establishment. The firm of Field, Leiter and Company had opened the doors of its new six-story store on State Street only three years earlier. The event had been a spectacle. Uniformed, well-groomed, and impeccably polite staff welcomed a throng of the city's wealthiest patrons to the most elegant department store in the city. Dominating the newly widened State Street, the emporium's Corinthian columns rose from the meticulously swept avenue and sidewalk to support the immense marble and limestone commercial palace. The wholesale department, the firm's largest and most profitable division, occupied the upper floors. But the first floor boasted the main attraction: the retail division. Gentlemen and ladies swept into the gas-lit, lavishly furnished, ornately painted hall and beheld with excitement the elegantly arranged shelves and tables, heaped with the finest luxury goods from New York, Europe, and the Far East. These leading citizens and proud patrons of the young, rising commercial capital had seen nothing like it in their city, and they were thrilled. The owners, Messrs. Field and Leiter, observed the reaction and—if not thrilled, as they were not given to exuberant display—were quietly pleased, as had become their custom when their innovative practices and the diligent application of their business principles met with success. "Satisfaction guaranteed" was the firm's motto. And that day, everyone was satisfied. As the visionary Marshall Field had known they would be.

HE WAS BORN IN 1834 on his father's two-hundred-acre farm near Conway, Massachusetts, one year after the frontier town of Chicago, with a population of three hundred and fifty hardy souls, was incorporated. At sixteen, he quit his formal education and his father's plow and accepted a position as a clerk in a small dry-goods store in nearby Pittsfield owned by a Congregationalist church deacon, Henry Davis. The young clerk, so shy and taciturn he had earned the schoolboy sobriquet "Silent Marsh," struck his employer as ill suited for the sociable life of a country merchant, bargaining and gossiping with customers. If a boy wasn't convivial enough to make friends, he probably wouldn't prove sharp enough to make a profit. But what Deacon Davis and his customers might have initially mistaken for insecurity and diffidence proved to be a composed and serious nature and an observant, absorbing mind. Neither charm nor glibness explained his eventual popularity with customers, especially women, but his informed interest in their needs and preferences did. He gained his customers' confidence by his evident interest in understanding them, and when he spoke to them he talked of things that interested them, information he had learned from listening intently to them and making a thorough study of the merchandise favored in popular women's journals.

Five years later, in 1855, when he set off to follow his older brother, Joseph, to the Illinois boomtown on Lake Michigan, where quick-witted, hardworking merchants were hustling to seize opportunities from the promise of the opening west, he carried in his pocket a reference from his bereft employer testifying to his budding talent for commerce:

> I can without qualification commend him as a young man of unusual business talent. . . . His character and principles as well as business qualifications are such I cannot doubt he will meet that success in life which usually accompanies industry, perseverance, and integrity when combined with strict energy of character.[1]

Not long after he reached the city, Field found a job as a clerk for Chicago's largest wholesale dry-goods establishment, Cooley, Wadsworth and Company, where his "strict energy of character" quickly caught the eye of a rising junior partner there, John Farwell. Years later, Farwell observed that his former associate and later rival had a "wonderful comprehension of feminine nature. He had the merchant's instinct. He lived for it, and it only."[2] Scrupulous in the exercise of his assigned duties; eager in the assumption of additional responsibilities; enterprising in learning all he could about his trade, Field rose rapidly in the esteem of his employers. Though still quiet and reserved, he questioned the company's traveling salesmen about business conditions in their territories and about the popularity of goods in other towns and cities. He kept a careful record of which goods sold well and which didn't, and of the surplus and shortages in the company's inventory. He spent a lot of time in the store's retail section, observing the purchasing behavior of women, who were its main customers, noting what goods attracted them and how they responded to the manner and methods of the salesmen who waited on them. He became a sharp judge of quality in both goods and services and disdained both cheap merchandise and heavy-handed salesmanship. Farwell, recognizing that Field's talents were squandered as a stock clerk, successfully proposed to the company's senior partners that they send the young man out on the road as a traveling salesman, where his obvious knack for the trade and the opportunity to further his practical education in the dry-goods business would profit the company and Field alike.

He didn't care for the rough life of a traveling salesman, but he was quite good at the job. He was not like other salesmen. He wasn't slick or garrulous or entertaining but formal and reticent. Yet he again won over his customers, small-town merchants and wholesalers, with his dependability, his business acumen, and his unusually acute discernment of their situation, knowledge he had gained by careful research. He knew what they needed and didn't press them to order more merchandise than they needed or things they couldn't sell. His solicitousness earned the loyalty of old and new customers, added scores of new orders to the balance sheet of Cooley, Wadsworth and Company, and gratified the firm's senior partners, who agreed to make him a junior partner in 1860.

In the five years it took Field to rise from stock boy to partner, the company had survived the financial panic of 1857 and the ensuing depression in 1858. Reorganized in 1857—Wadsworth was out, replaced by Field's benefactor, John Farwell—the company opened a new store and warehouse even as it struggled to avoid the fate of many Chicago wholesalers, who went under as banks failed and credit grew scarce in the turbulent times, and to keep pace with the astonishing, apparently depression-proof success of their chief competitor, Potter Palmer.

Potter Palmer came to Chicago from rural New York a few years before Marshall Field arrived. With borrowed money and his own savings, Palmer had opened a small store in 1852 on Lake Street, the center of the city's growing dry-goods business district. He immediately set about capturing the carriage trade by using the lessons he had learned operating a store in Lockport, New York, and the innovations he had observed in the famous Broadway emporium of New York City's "merchant prince," Alexander Turney Stewart.

Unable to secure much credit, he couldn't supply his new store with copious quantities of stock, but what goods he did acquire would be esteemed for their high quality. He took care to display them attractively on the store's shelves and tables and, in a seldom-utilized space, his storefront windows. He was the first merchant to cater primarily to women, attracting their attention with items of special interest to them, which he took care to know of and acquire. He welcomed them unescorted to his store, novel behavior in those days, and they were treated with elaborate courtesy and solicitousness. He was a sound judge of people as well as of goods, and he employed staff who possessed a measure of his own qualities and adhered faithfully to the principles of his tradecraft. Salesmen were instructed to memorize the names and preferences of their clientele and were forbidden to pressure customers into purchases, but they were to be quick in responding to questions and attentive to all their needs. "The customer is always right" was the central creed of the Palmer system, no matter how difficult or demanding that customer might be, in an era when customers were usually treated, if not rudely, seldom deferentially. Although he was intent on catering to an upper-crust market, people of any class and means were welcome at Potter Palmer and Company, whether they came to purchase or just admire his wares.

He ran a cash-based business, extending credit rarely and only after extensive investigation. But in a break with the practice of the day, when the price of goods was never declared but arrived at by haggling, Palmer had a one-price-and-one-price-only policy, posted clearly every day. And, more often than not, that price was substantially lower than what his competitors offered for goods of similar quality. In time, when he had sufficient resources, he advertised heavily and imaginatively, promising the most sought-after goods at the lowest prices. He advertised regular bargain sales, though such practices were then only employed in bad economic times, when sales had dangerously declined. His greatest innovation was his return policy. Special customers were allowed to purchase goods on approval. "If your husband doesn't like it," Palmer told them, "bring it back, and I'll refund your money."[3] His competitors ridiculed the policy, confident its rube author would soon learn an overdue lesson about human nature when his customers returned goods after they had been used for whatever occasion they had borrowed them.

When the panic hit in 1857, his competitors began slashing prices, which in many instances presaged going-out-of-business sales. Palmer's retail and wholesale business still managed to undersell them. He surveyed the mounting chaos calmly. His aversion to indebtedness, his credit policies, and the growing profits he earned from his innovations, not the least of which was his goods-offered-on-approval policy, helped him build up considerable cash reserves to ride out the storm. While others were liquidating inventory, he was planning bigger purchases from manufacturers in Europe and Asia. When merchants were leasing space in their stores and warehouses to bring in desperately needed revenue, Palmer was expanding into larger quarters. When most of his rivals were desperately seeking credit from failing banks, Palmer's ledger showed increasing profits. He closed his wholesale business, but only to place himself in a more advantageous position to outpace his retail rivals. When Marshall Field tried to pick up some of Palmer's former merchant customers, he found it hard going when he couldn't promise them, as Palmer had, an unrestricted return policy. By the end of the panic, with his profits rising along with his reputation, Potter Palmer was the man to watch in Chicago's battered dry-goods trade.

And no one watched closer than Marshall Field, a smart and serious student of human nature and commerce, intent on making his own fortune by showing the same initiative and attention to business.

As a junior partner at Cooley and Farwell, Field was given responsibility to manage the sales and credit department, which, with exacting attention to detail, he streamlined and systemized. Within a year, he was made a full partner. But as he watched with growing admiration their biggest rival's continued expansion and innovations, Field chafed over his leading partner's innate caution and lack of imagination. By 1863, an ailing Cooley departed Chicago. The company reorganized as Farwell, Field and Company, and made its bookkeeper, Levi Leiter, whose motto was "cash the rule, credit the exception," a junior partner.[4] Field began instituting his own innovations, drawn from his own experience and observations and his appreciation for the Palmer system.

Chicago boomed amid the wild inflation of the Civil War years. Many merchants prospered, but Palmer prospered most. He undersold competitors, whose prices rose as inflationary pressures grew, by 10 to 20 percent. He spent months in New York personally overseeing and expanding purchases for his emporium. He relocated to a stunning five-story marble edifice. He got back into the wholesale business. He famously announced that henceforth his money-back guarantee to select unsatisfied customers would be extended to all. His decisions elicited yet more disapproval and scorn from his competitors—except for his young and now biggest competitor, who noted it all with approval. Field had also kept his company's prices well below what his other competitors offered. He instituted a one-price-only policy and improved the quality of customer service. He expanded both the firm's wholesale and retail businesses. He relocated to larger quarters to accommodate his increased inventory. He followed Palmer to New York to observe current fashions and retail practices and to take charge of his company's wholesale purchases. Soon the firm's business equaled and threatened to surpass Palmer's. And Marshall Field was becoming the wealthy man he had set out to be when he first left his father's farm. Shrewd judge of character that he was, Palmer returned his rival's respect and, unbeknownst to Field, devised a plan that would combine the geniuses of the two men, who between them invented retail shopping.

In 1864, two years after he became a named partner, Field left Farwell, Field and Company and took Levi Leiter with him. That year, Palmer's doctor warned the energetic businessman that the pace of his frenetic activities was seriously damaging his health. Palmer, a bachelor who had had little time for anything but business, decided it was time to enjoy life. He would find a suitable partner to take over the business while he went off to Europe to enjoy a few years of leisure, recharge his imagination, and consider new business opportunities. He knew only one man who could fit the bill. He approached Marshall Field and offered to sell both his retail and wholesale businesses to Field and Leiter for 20 percent below the estimated value of his inventory. With Civil War prices at their inflated peak, it was an expensive proposition. But Field knew his business as well as he knew his adopted city, and he was confident that each would grow to mutual advantage. He accepted. Palmer kept several hundred thousand dollars of his own in the new firm and left for Europe. In January 1865, Field, Palmer, and Leiter opened for business under new management in Potter Palmer's store.

Disaster struck almost immediately. When General Lee laid down his arms at Appomattox Courthouse, five years of spiraling prices came to an abrupt end, igniting a new financial panic and price wars that threatened economic chaos in cities all over the country, nowhere more so than in Chicago. Palmer had built his business on the principle of always offering quality goods for less, and Field had been his eager disciple. Now as merchants slashed prices over and over again, Field struggled to maintain the practice as revenue dwindled, not only threatening the capital he needed to carry out his ambitious plans but endangering the new company's solvency. He and Levi offered to sell back part of the business to Palmer, but their partner counseled patience and fortitude. He had ridden out financial panic before. Take advantage of low prices to increase buying, he advised; profits will return soon enough.

They bought as much new inventory as they could without burdening the firm with debt. To encourage other struggling merchants to increase their wholesale purchases, Field persuaded Leiter to soften a little the strict credit policy that was his pride. Field knew that whatever few bad loans they incurred would be more than offset by the strengthened loyalty of most of their customers when good times returned. Field also employed his peerless sense of quality in people and goods to improve his sales force, hiring enterprising, honest people, giving them specific responsibilities and wide latitude, at wages below the current average but with the promise that with hard work and exercised intelligence they could someday join the rolls of the firm's partners. But the most important contributors to Field and Leiter's astonishing success during the postwar panic were the improvements they made to the singular experience of shopping at their establishment.

By the end of their first year, Field, Palmer, and Leiter had sold eight million dollars' worth of goods and recorded three hundred thousand dollars in profit. In his constant pursuit of opportunities to get the best goods at the lowest cost, Field sent his buyers to Europe. After traveling there himself, he decided to open an office in Manchester, England, to directly manage the store's European buying. He dispatched his brother, Joseph, to run it, and Joseph did so ably, with a reputation for driving a hard bargain. Field helped make Chicago a federal port of entry so the goods he purchased abroad wouldn't be held up at length in New York's customshouse. Business flourished. Most of the firm's business was in wholesale and was to remain so for many years. But the retail end was to grow in the coming years to unexpected heights, as the enterprising Field devoted more and more of his attention and talents to making his retail division, and its dazzling innovations, one of Chicago's leading attractions.

By 1867, Field and Leiter had enough capital to buy out Potter Palmer, who was content to turn his attention full-time to his real-estate investments. Palmer had begun buying up property on a narrow, unattractive street that held rows of small, dingy wooden taverns, groceries, and boardinghouses but which offered a more advantageous location than Lake Street, where most of the dry-goods business resided. Once Potter Palmer acquired nearly a mile of State Street, he persuaded the city to widen the avenue, and he began to build the most elegant commercial building in Chicago. When it was complete in 1868, Field, Leiter and Company leased it for a considerable sum.

And then, in 1871, Field watched it burn down.

He arrived quickly at the site to oversee the desperate efforts to save the store. He knew immediately it was futile. The store would be lost. So he ordered the employees to save as much of the inventory as they could before the flames consumed the building. He dispatched men to secure as many horse-drawn wagons as they could, as a chain gang of staff handed merchandise out of the store and onto the wagons, which Fields directed to the lakefront, where they might be spared from the fire. They worked feverishly into the night and managed to salvage more than two hundred thousand dollars' worth of goods.

When the fire finally burned out, all that remained of the store "was a crude sign reading: 'Cash Boys and Work Girls will be paid what is due them Monday 9 A.M. Oct. 16th at 60 Calumet Ave. Field, Leiter & Co.'"⁵ Three weeks later, Field, Leiter and Company opened for business in an old railroad carbarn, its salvaged merchandise cleaned and displayed as attractively as possible.

The next year, Field and Leiter moved the wholesale division to a new building on Madison Street. And two years later, on the anniversary of the fire, they moved their retail operations to a new building leased from the Singer Company on State Street. Potter Palmer had responded to the great fire with his usual confidence and eye for opportunity. He had lost thirty-two buildings in the fire but immediately set about rebuilding State Street, grander than ever. From the ashes he raised the city's most elegant hotel, the fireproof Palmer House. He built it as a gift to the woman to whom he had, at long last, surrendered his comfortable bachelorhood, the formidable Bertha Honoré Palmer, who would become Chicago society's preeminent hostess. His new State Street showcases included the building his former partners now occupied. When the store reopened, the country was gripped by yet another financial panic, worse and longer lasting than the panic of 1857. But Field, like his mentor, kept his cool under duress. His company had little debt and plenty of cash. Levi Leiter's zeal for tight credit, and Field's preference to pay cash for his properties and goods, put them in good stead to weather this latest storm.

They informed their wholesale customers that they would continue to offer credit on the usual terms, providing somewhat better terms to smaller merchants, and signaling their confidence that they could keep on doing business during the downturn. They continued to undersell their competitors, though not without a struggle. When the depression lifted in 1876, with the west and its capital, Chicago, flourishing well ahead of the rest of the country, eastern manufacturers and merchants began to relocate there. The new competition and resulting price war strained Field, Leiter and Company, but the partners remained confident that they would continue to grow and prosper. They struggled, especially when A. T. Stewart's firm opened up a wholesale house in Chicago. The two companies matched price cut for price cut, advertisement for advertisement, innovation for innovation. But eventually A. T. Stewart surrendered and closed its Chicago operations. Field, Leiter and Company resumed its preeminent position in the city's dry-goods trade. And then calamity struck again.

On November 14, 1877, their new retail store burned to the ground. Two weeks later, they opened for business in an exhibition hall Field had leased on the lakefront. Less than two years later, they welcomed their customers to a new store on State Street purchased from the Singer Company for a considerable sum, an immense six-story structure, built on the site of their former State Street location, where it has remained ever since.

Of all the fateful decisions Marshall Field made over the course of his hugely successful career, none showed his mettle more than the course of action he followed during the traumatic events of the 1870s. Few businessmen could have managed these transformations following adversity with the skill and speed he did, with the attention to all the details of his business as meticulous as ever, despite the addition of such heavy burdens. And he did it all while steadily building market share and devising endless innovations to increase it further. Once he was reestablished in his latest, very expensive store on State Street, he began to help his competitors to relocate theirs. He knew whatever increased trade they enjoyed would profit him as well, as ever bigger crowds thronged the broad avenue that he and Potter Palmer had built.

Many of his ideas, of course, emulated those of Potter Palmer. Yet they were also the product of his extraordinary self-confidence, based on an almost uncanny awareness of himself, his city, his business, and human nature. He showed unusual talents as a merchant from a very early age, as John Farwell had noted years before. But nature didn't provide him with an unerring instinct for business, for seizing his opportunities and taking chances, for making just the right decisions at just the right time. Nature might provide higher intelligence to some than to others. But more than nature, hard work on his father's farm, at Deacon Davis's store, and at Cooley, Wadsworth and Company shaped the man and his rectitude. His quiet, composed personality reinforced the calm and purposefulness he maintained when confronting calamity, but it also masked his observant eye; just as his reticence, wrongly perceived as shyness or insecurity, made him a better listener. He watched how people reacted to goods and services. He knew his market before he built it. He learned his business before he reinvented it.

His competitors scoffed at some of his decisions as sure to prove ruinous: the expense of the goods he purchased; his consistent underselling; the offices and factories he established all over the world; the trust he invested in his customer with his liberal return policies; the authority he gave his employees; the immense financial investments in his stores; and the many expensive amenities he offered his customers. But he was never the incautious businessman they took him for. Unlike many of theirs, his enterprise never failed. It always prospered.

While he occasionally argued with Leiter over the excessive and often gratuitous lengths his partner went to preserve his strict credit policies, he appreciated their general soundness. Whenever possible, he built his stores and acquired his merchandise with cash. He was always prepared for setbacks and disasters and could respond to them more readily than could his rivals. His vast store of knowledge acquired through his years of study and practice gave him insights others lacked. Where others saw only the risks of particular enterprises or ideas, he knew them to be reasonable and timely. He never believed he took a risk. "I have tried," he explained, "to make all my acts and commercial moves the result of definite consideration and sound judgment. There were never any great ventures or risks. I practiced honest, slow-growing business methods, and tried to back them with energy and a good system."

In 1881, Marshall Field and Levi Leiter dissolved their partnership. Leiter had grown tired of the retail trade, disparaging it as unreliable, vulnerable to economic downturns, and far less profitable than their wholesale business, despite the enormous expenses required to implement Field's endless ideas and improvements. Field bought him out for far less than the business was worth. He knew the company's most valuable assets were the men they had recruited as partners—the energetic, able young men who had pledged themselves to Field's system. Before he approached Leiter, Field secured commitments from most of the men to remain with him. Leiter was wise enough to understand—when Field confronted him with the offer and the information that their best subordinates intended to follow their mentor—that the company would be worth less to him than to Field. So he left.

Many of the company's junior partners had risen from clerks and salesmen, where they were paid less than the prevailing wage. They preferred the prestige of working for the finest establishment in Chicago, where the tradecraft they learned would give them an advantage in any future enterprise, and for the promise that should they prove themselves to the discerning eye of their employer to be industrious, enterprising, imaginative, loyal, and of good character, they would eventually share in the company's ever-growing profits. Field was stingy with praise and ever aloof. But he knew his people, monitored their progress, and rewarded them, often without comment, when he reasoned they had earned it.

Some employees might attain such opportunities eventually, but while they labored in the company's lower echelons, they made do with long hours and meager pay. Field despised unions and went to considerable lengths to keep them out of his business and restrict their growth elsewhere. But he had no desire to profit exclusively from the labor of his employees. He was not a miser enthralled with the bottom line of his company's ledger and insensitive to the aspirations of human capital. He held fast to his principles and expected his employees to do likewise. He wished them to rise as he had risen, with hard work and initiative, and if they did he would see that they were appropriately rewarded.

Marshall Field knew something else his erstwhile partner didn't: that retail had a more promising future and was well worth the expense and labor he invested in it. He understood his city would weather whatever misfortune and catastrophe befell it. Chicago would grow as prodigiously as the west. It was the financial capital of the west, the center of a sprawling network of railroads that brought the bounties of the settled frontier to Chicago, where they were collected, processed, dressed, and resold to markets throughout the country. Chicago might prosper in fits and starts, but its population would always grow and its profits rise, and all classes—the wealthy, the middle class, and the working poor—would prosper with it. And Marshall Field and Company would offer the best goods at the lowest price, accompanied by the latest amenities available to an ever-growing number of appreciative customers.

Marshall Field and Company was the first retail establishment to invest in electric lights. It was the first to provide public restrooms, coatrooms, waiting lounges, a citywide delivery system, information desks, a bridal registry, and theater-ticket booths. It was the first to install telephones and eventually operate its own central switchboard. It opened a post office in the store. It was the first to dress up its store-front windows with elaborate Christmas displays. It was the first to open tearooms and dining rooms for its customers. Legend has it that Field discovered that an employee had shared her lunch with a hungry customer and realized it would profit the store to keep customers on the premises instead of watching them suspend their shopping to fill their stomachs. The company always remained in the vanguard, years ahead of any of its competitors, in the quality of its service and the comforts and opulence of its surroundings.

The story goes that one afternoon as Field made his rounds in the State Street store, he witnessed a heated exchange between a clerk and a female customer. "What are you doing?" Field demanded of his employee.

"I'm settling a complaint," the clerk replied.

"No, you're not," he was told. "Give the lady what she wants."[6]

Many of the innovations in both Field's retail and wholesale trade were devised by the men to whom he had given large responsibilities and authority. And none proved his judgment sounder than John Shedd and Harry Gordon Selfridge. A farm boy from New Hampshire, Shedd started as a salesman in the wholesale division and rose quickly to become its general manager. Quiet, hardworking, intelligent, tasteful, and as careful a student of his business as was his employer, Shedd expanded the wholesale business's traveling sales force and assigned new salesmen specific goods, which they would become expert in promoting. He devised a general system for purchasing. He eased credit rules somewhat. Wholesale business boomed under his management, and while Marshall Field was not one to shower even the most successful subordinate with praise, he saw to it that the valuable John Shedd became a wealthy man in his employ.

Harry Selfridge, a short, dapper, energetic schoolteacher's son from Jackson, Michigan, "mile-a-minute Harry," started as a stock boy, turned down a better job to work in retail, the trade he was uniquely suited to, and eventually became the store's manager. He had all the skills of a natural showman, an innovative promoter, and an advertiser, with a keen eye for new opportunities. He shared Field's devotion to customer service. He stressed the importance of courtesy to staff and customers and exhorted the staff to embrace wholeheartedly the principles that their visionary founder had conceived and employed to enormously profitable effect. Customers were always to be addressed as "Sir" or "Madam," and employees would never address one another by first or last name. "Mr.," "Miss," or "Mrs." must always precede a surname. He convinced Field to hire buyers exclusively for the retail business. He hired others for the specific task of dressing the store's windows. He opened a bargain basement and proved the merit of the idea to a skeptical Field when it posted twenty-five million dollars in annual sales. He started the practice of annual sales to clear out old inventory and make room for the new. He kept his employees happy, despite their low wages, with lunchrooms, their own restrooms, and school for the youngsters who carried money to and from the clerks, until Harry automated their work with new pneumatic tubes.[7]

In 1893, the much-heralded World's Columbian Exposition was to open, and an immense faux-marble metropolis, "the White City," was to be erected on the Chicago lakeshore. Selfridge recognized the singular opportunity this offered Marshall Field's to spread its reputation around the world. He encouraged Field to make the store as big an attraction to the thousands of out-of-town and foreign visitors as anything on offer in the White City.

After buying additional properties over the years, Marshall Field's had expanded considerably, built and furnished under the management of Harry Selfridge and the approving eye of Field to dazzle dignitary and working woman alike. It was the first modern department store, and it was, as Field and his bright lieutenant had known it would be, among the most popular Chicago attractions in the year the Columbian Exposition had spread the city's fame to the four corners of the world.

In 1902, with Selfridge's encouragement, Marshall Field ordered neighboring buildings demolished so he could erect his grandest emporium to date, a massive twelve-story neoclassical palace with Corinthian columns occupying the entire block, resplendent in design, furnishings, and goods, with steam-powered elevators and revolving doors. One hundred and fifty thousand people swarmed into the store during its first three days. All were greeted courteously by salesclerks and partners and handed gifts to commemorate the occasion. Marshall Field's was once again the talk of the town.[8]

Harry Selfridge departed two years later. He eventually moved to London, where, in short order, he opened Britain's first and most famous department store, Selfridges. John Shedd remained as Field's second in command. Both men, for the rest of their working lives, sat at desks beneath portraits of the man who had taught them their trade.

Marshall Field died in 1906. He caught a cold while playing golf on a snowy New Year's Day. In about two weeks, he was dead from pneumonia. The store closed, and the Chicago Board of Trade suspended trading to honor his passing. He had given generously to many civic projects: the University of Chicago, the natural history museum, the art museum. But his greatest monument was the business he had built, with his industry, intelligence, and the pioneering decisions he had made in a pioneering city.

Three years after Field's death, John Shedd, who succeeded his mentor as president, constructed yet another massive addition to the flagship store on State Street, topped by an extraordinary Tiffany ceiling, with 1,600,000 separate pieces of colored glass. People flocked to see it and to spend a few pleasant hours among the lavish amenities and impeccable service offered free of charge by Marshall Field and Company, the largest department store in the world.

ROCKET MEN

At 11:38 a.m., January 28, 1986, on an unusually cold morning at Cape Canaveral, Florida, the space shuttle *Challenger*'s two solid rocket boosters ignited, the bolts holding the *Challenger* to the launchpad were blown off by explosives, and the shuttle began liftoff. Designated Shuttle Mission 51-L, the launch marked the twenty-fifth flight of the shuttle program. In five years of operational history, it had successfully employed all four shuttle orbiters in its fleet: *Columbia, Discovery, Atlantis,* and *Challenger. Challenger*'s seven-person crew included mission commander Dick Scobee; shuttle pilot and decorated Vietnam War naval aviator Mike Smith; three mission specialists, Judith Resnick, Ellison Onizuka, and Ron McNair; payload specialist Air Force captain Greg Jarvis; and a junior-high-school history and social-studies teacher from Concord, New Hampshire, Christa McAuliffe.

A half second before launch, T–0, and unnoticed at the time, puffs of dark-gray smoke blew from the lower field joint on the right-side solid rocket booster, near the strut that secured it to the external fuel tank, which contained liquid hydrogen and oxygen. Solid rocket boosters are much more powerful than liquid-fuel rockets, but once they are

ignited they cannot be shut off. Every precaution must be taken in their design, construction, and service to make certain that they are sound and will operate safely.

At T+28 seconds, the shuttle's three main engines began to throttle down from full thrust to prevent the pressure of the dense lower-atmosphere air from pulling the shuttle apart. At T+37, the first of three strong wind shears were sensed and compensated for by the *Challenger*'s guidance, navigation, and control system. At T+40, the shuttle was supersonic, having passed Mach 1 at nineteen thousand feet altitude. At T+52, the shuttle engines throttled back up to full thrust as the shuttle approached Max Q, the point at which the aerodynamic drag on the vehicle is greatest.

Seven seconds later, T+59, a plume of smoke began to grow from the right solid rocket booster as burning gas leaked through a growing hole in the booster's lower field joint. At the same time, the booster's internal pressure began to drop. At T+64, flames from the burning gas penetrated the external tank and ignited its liquid-hydrogen tank. A tenth of a second later, a bright glow was visible between the booster and the external tank. At T+66, pressure within the fuel tank began to drop dramatically.

At T+72, the rear strut holding the booster to the external tank gave way, and the booster begins to move erratically, rotating around an upper strut. In the crew's last recorded statement, *Challenger* pilot Mike Smith uttered "Uh-oh."

In the next second, the bottom of the liquid-hydrogen tank failed and released its contents, resulting in a sudden forward thrust that propelled the hydrogen tank into the liquid-oxygen tank, while simultaneously the booster swung on its upper strut and struck the external tank. A bright flash occurred between the external tank and the *Challenger* orbiter as leaking fuel and gases mixed and ignited. At T+73.162, in a plume of white vapor and flames, at an altitude of 48,000 feet, the vehicle began to break up. *Challenger* abruptly veered from its course and was instantly torn apart, while the two solid rocket boosters broke away and continued flying. Despite the appearance of a huge fireball, the shuttle was not blown apart by an explosion caused by the burning gas. It disintegrated under extreme aerodynamic pressure. The crew cabin separated and continued ascending until it reached sixty-five thousand feet, escaping the massive vapor cloud before arcing downward toward the Atlantic Ocean. Although at least some of the crew were thought to have remained briefly conscious following the vehicle breakup, they would have quickly passed out when their cabin lost pressure. Descending at more than two hundred miles an hour, they were killed by the force of the impact with the ocean surface.

"The decision to launch the *Challenger* was flawed."

Given the enormity of the catastrophe, the summary sentence that opens chapter 5 of the report that explained how and why the disaster had occurred is a model of understatement. Of course, the twelve-thousand-page report of the Presidential Commission on the Space Shuttle Challenger Accident provides copious detail about how the decision was flawed, as well as the physical cause of the shuttle's demise. But sometimes nothing gets a message across more directly than an understated recognition of the obvious, even if the language seems too banal to describe what was both a terrible human tragedy and a huge blow to American confidence in the future of our space program.

President Ronald Reagan announced the formation of the commission on February 3, 1986, and selected former Secretary of State William P. Rogers to chair it. The thirteen other members of the Rogers Commission were all well-qualified choices, most of whom had considerable experience with the space program. They included Neil Armstrong, the first man to walk on the moon; Sally Ride, the first female astronaut; Chuck Yeager, the famous Air Force test pilot who first broke the sound barrier; and Richard P. Feynman, winner of the 1965 Nobel Prize for physics.

Four months later, on June 6, 1986, the Rogers Commission issued its report. It confirmed what countless press stories had already reported, that the *Challenger*'s destruction was caused by the failure of two of the O-rings used to seal the field joints of the four segments of the right solid rocket booster and prevent hot gases and flame from the booster's motor from burning through the joints and potentially reaching the external fuel tank. The report attributed the failure to the O-rings' defective design, which allowed the hot combustion gases to erode them when, among other things, cold temperatures caused the O-rings to harden and not remain securely fitted in the joints.

That is what happened on the morning of January 28, when overnight temperatures had fallen to the low twenties, and the temperature at launch was thirty-six degrees. Until then, the lowest temperature recorded for a shuttle launch was fifty-three degrees, at the January 24, 1985, launch of the shuttle *Discovery*. Engineers at Morton Thiokol, which designed the solid rocket boosters, had never tested them at temperatures that low and did not possess any data for how temperatures much below fifty-three degrees would affect them. But they had an idea, and cause to worry.

The commission saved its most distressing disclosure for chapter 5 of its report, entitled, "The Contributing Cause of the Accident." Thiokol executives and engineers had discussed the potential O-ring problems with NASA managers at the Kennedy Space Center and Marshall Space Flight Center in Huntsville, Alabama, the night before the launch and had initially recommended that it be canceled. What occurred next was a case study in how group dynamics and external considerations that should not be central to a decision can cause decision makers to discount or neglect critically important information, which rendered them, in this case, fatally unappreciative of the magnitude of their decision.

The launch should have been canceled. Information was discussed that provided sufficient reason to do so, but its full weight did not receive due consideration.

Morton Thiokol engineers were aware of the problem as early as 1977 and had ordered design changes then. In 1981, after the second space-shuttle launch, NASA analysts noticed that gases had charred the O-ring seals. In 1985, the *Discovery* launch also bore evidence of O-ring erosion from escaping gases. Thiokol engineers began to study the effect of lower temperatures on the seals and had ordered improvements that had not yet been implemented by the time of the *Challenger* launch.

In August of 1985, Thiokol engineer Roger Boisjoly and NASA analyst Richard Cook separately wrote memoranda to their superiors expressing their concerns that the O-ring flaws could result in a catastrophe. "It is my honest and very real fear," Boisjoly wrote,

> that if we do not take immediate action to dedicate a team to solve the problem with the field joint having the number one priority, then we stand in jeopardy of losing a flight along with all the launch pad facilities.

That same month, a Thiokol supervisor, A. R. ("Arnie") Thompson, noted in an in-house memo that "the O-ring seal problem has lately become acute."

As it turned out, at least half of the shuttle flights prior to the *Challenger*'s final flight had experienced problems with the field-joint seals, and all had returned safely to earth. In 1985, NASA had classified the problem as a "launch constraint"—in other words, anticipation of O-ring erosion was sufficient reason to cancel a launch. But on six previous occasions, the constraint had been overridden. NASA managers became accustomed to the defect, as they had become accustomed to other problems with the shuttle. The risks to the shuttle from O-ring erosion became acceptable. While the managers possessed information for a fuller appreciation of the danger, practice had made them less wary and less aware of the magnitude of the potential disaster their negligence invited.

Compounding this overconfidence were the political and economic worries that hastened NASA's urgency to launch *Challenger*. The
space program no longer enjoyed quite the exalted place it had once
held in the public's affection and in government appropriations. To
the public, space flight had become routine and less of a thrill than
it had been during the Mercury and Apollo missions. Reductions in
federal funding for the space program began with the last Apollo
flight to the moon, and congressional skepticism about the shuttle's
practical applications, combined with competition from the European
Space Agency, worried NASA managers. An ambitious flight schedule
was intended to establish the shuttle as a dependable, reusable space-
transportation system with a range of applications—military, scientific,
and commercial—that would eventually make the program financially
self-sufficient. It was also intended to make each launch more cost-
effective. These imperatives impaired NASA's judgment and over-
sight. The priority of mission-safety concerns slipped as political and
economic considerations became more influential in engineering and
management decisions, and information that should have raised alarm
was compartmentalized or qualified or disregarded.

The *Challenger* launch had been delayed a record number of times
for various mechanical and weather-related problems. The next shuttle
mission was scheduled in a month's time, leaving little time to rebuild
the launchpad, so NASA managers were anxious to get *Challenger* into
orbit. Engineers at Rockwell International, the primary contractor for
the shuttle, informed NASA's manager of the shuttle program, Arnold
Aldrich, that ice on the launchpad elevated the risk that *Challenger* could
be damaged during takeoff. Aldrich agreed to push back the launch
by an hour to give inspectors additional time to assess the situation,
but the engineers did not firmly recommend cancellation. Neither did
Aldrich appear to have given cancellation appropriate consideration.

More serious were the concerns raised by Alan McDonald, Morton
Thiokol's project director, and Thiokol engineers Boisjoly and Thomp-
son, in a telephone conference with NASA managers at Kennedy and
Marshall that began at 8:45 the night before the launch. Boisjoly and
Thompson had been given an hour to prepare a presentation docu-
menting the problems with the boosters' joint seals and the worrisome

effects of cold temperatures on the O-rings' performance. After presenting their concerns, they recommended that the launch be delayed until temperatures at Canaveral reached fifty-three degrees, the lowest temperature at which they had reliable data about the O-rings' effectiveness.

NASA managers expressed surprise and annoyance at the recommendation and challenged the conclusion. A senior NASA executive at Marshall was reported to have said he was "appalled" by Thiokol's recommendation, and the company's vice president for the Space Booster Program, Joe Kilminster, asked for five minutes to discuss the problem with his engineers off-line, during which the engineers continued to voice objections to the launch.

In a final review, with only senior Thiokol executives involved, Vice President for Engineering Robert Lund was asked by Senior Vice President Jerald Mason to put on his "management hat."[1] The result of their discussion was an agreement that while cold temperatures threatened the integrity of the primary O-rings in the booster field joints, the data were inclusive, and secondary O-rings in each of the joints ought to seal effectively. In simultaneous discussions at Kennedy, engineer Arnie Thompson continued to press for postponement. The second teleconference between all parties began at 11:00 p.m. Joe Kilminster explained Thiokol's conclusions and provided the company's "engineering assessment"—or reassessment in this case—that the launch could remain on schedule. NASA's senior manager at Marshall, George Hardy, asked Kilminster to put Thiokol's recommendation in writing.

Thus was the space shuttle *Challenger* launched on its fatal flight of January 28, 1986. No one individual involved in the decision deserves exclusive or even primary blame for its consequences. The systematic downgrading of technical problems and aggregating of mistaken assumptions that were reinforced with every successful shuttle mission led the seven astronauts to their doom. Waiving launch constraints had become routine at NASA, and every dodged bullet reinforced NASA's false confidence. Practice had made imperfect the situational alertness of the decision's many authors. Important but not critical considerations were accorded a higher priority than the primary imperative, that the *Challenger* return safely to earth. The shuttle had to keep flying. The mission would succeed because it had to succeed.

In a dissenting and harsher view included in the Rogers Commission report, Richard Feynman made the following observation:

> It appears that there are enormous differences of opinion as to the probability of a failure with loss of vehicle and of human life. The estimates range from roughly 1 in 100 to 1 in 100,000. The higher figures come from the working engineers, and the very low figures from management. . . . Let us make recommendations to ensure that NASA officials deal in a world of reality in understanding technological weaknesses and imperfections well enough to be actively trying to eliminate them. They must live in reality in comparing the costs and utility of the Shuttle to other methods of entering space. And they must be realistic in making contracts, in estimating costs and the difficulty of the projects. Only realistic flight schedules should be proposed, schedules that have a reasonable chance of being met. If in this way the government would not support them, then so be it. NASA owes it to the citizens from whom it asks support to be frank, honest, and informative, so that these citizens can make the wisest decisions for the use of their limited resources. For a successful technology, reality must take precedence over public relations, for nature cannot be fooled.[2]

An illuminating observation on the problems inherent in the kind of group dynamics that fatefully underlay the decision to launch the *Challenger* was authored by a professor of philosophy, Marcia Baron.

> It is a sad fact about loyalty that it invites . . . single-mindedness. Single-minded pursuit of a goal is sometimes delightfully romantic, even a real inspiration. But it is hardly something to advocate to engineers, whose impact on the safety of the public is so very significant. Irresponsibility, whether caused by selfishness or by magnificently unselfish loyalty, can have most unfortunate consequences.[3]

As apt as the above observation is as an explanation for some of the flaws in NASA's decision making, it excludes from consideration examples when single-mindedness, even in engineers, can drive progress toward a goal by encouraging attentiveness to all relevant information and by necessitating escape from bureaucratic mind-sets that ignore, minimize, or misinterpret that information. The trick is to remain fixed on the right goal, to recognize what it is you are deciding. The right goal at stake in the *Challenger* decision should have been a safe and successful flight, which, more than any other consideration, would affect NASA's future, which was the preoccupation of NASA management. Here they made a common mistake. They gave priority to an ultimate goal, and to the institution organized to achieve it, over the decision at hand. They worried that a postponed launch would jeopardize support for the program, without adequately weighing the risks to the program, not to mention human life, posed by the decision to launch in cold temperatures. To get there, they had to discount information that should have alerted them to those risks. They had to become willfully uninformed. The result: a horrible tragedy for seven families and an end to confidence that the shuttle would eventually become a commercially viable "space truck" that would pay for itself.

The decision maker who is successfully single-minded in achieving a larger goal knows that progress toward that end is made or lost by various decisions along the way. Each decision must be made with priority given to understanding whether it is the best decision in the situation at hand, recognizing that the right decision, whether it initiates or withholds action, will better serve the future goal. A *Challenger* launch was not especially important to the future of the space program; a safe launch was.

––––

WHEN THE FATHER OF modern rocketry was sixteen years old, he climbed a cherry tree to prune its branches. He looked skyward and began to dream. "I was a different boy," he later wrote, "when I climbed down from the tree." He had a purpose, which he would keep through the years, through disappointment, sickness, ridicule, rejection, and success. "How wonderful it would be," he thought, "to make some device which had even the possibility of ascending to Mars, and how it would look on a small scale, if sent up from the meadow at my feet."

It has been more than one hundred years since Robert Goddard beheld the future from the limbs of a cherry tree. In the course of his life, he invented the liquid-fueled rocket, built a gyroscope to help stabilize its flight, designed the first multistaged rocket, launched rockets that broke the sound barrier and set records for attaining the highest altitude, developed solid-fuel rockets that were fired from handheld launching tubes—bazookas—and conceived the basic theories that would one day carry man to the moon. He held more than two hundred patents for his inventions. Every liquid-fueled rocket that flies today is based on his invention.

He had been a frail boy in Worcester, Massachusetts, often in poor health but a voracious reader with an aptitude for mathematics, physics, and chemistry. From childhood, he was enthralled by the idea of reaching the heavens by human device and fascinated by fireworks, kites, and balloons. He had read H. G. Wells's classic, *The War of the Worlds,* and believed that human spaceflight would not always be strictly an invention of science-fiction writers. He wrote a paper in 1907, while still an undergraduate at Worcester Polytechnic Institute, which proposed the means for stabilizing airplanes. Studying the propulsion of firework rockets, he realized that gunpowder as a means of propulsion was limited. In 1909, he had worked out the mathematical formulas for rocket propulsion using liquid hydrogen and liquid oxygen. While convalescing from tuberculosis in 1914, he registered his first two patents, one for a rocket propelled by gasoline and nitrous oxide, and the second for a three-stage rocket.

In 1916, the Smithsonian Institution gave him a small grant to continue his rocket experiments in his laboratory at Clark University, where he taught physics. There he proved by experiments in airtight chambers that rockets could fly in a vacuum, and he built his first liquid-fueled rocket motor. In 1919, the Smithsonian published his paper "A Method of Reaching Extreme Altitudes," which explained the arithmetic behind his theories of rocket flight and his experiments with liquid-fuel propulsion. Near the end of the monograph, he suggested that using his methods of propulsion, a rocket with enough fuel and size could even reach the moon. The claim, unconventional but perfectly accurate, elicited a great deal of ridicule, which would plague Goddard for many years.

Nature, *The New York Times* sneered, did not agree with Professor Goddard's theories of rocket ships and flights. The paper published a front-page story about Goddard's theories and in an editorial the next day mocked them, dismissing Goddard's work as lacking "the knowledge ladled out daily in high schools."

That experience instilled in Goddard a lifelong distrust of the press and cautiousness about revealing his discoveries to people who lacked his rare combined talents as a physics theorist and a practical engineer. But rather than let elitist derision and popular ignorance discourage him, he pursued his work as diligently as ever but as quietly as he could. It was hard to keep quiet, however, a ten-foot rocket named Nell, propelled by gasoline and nitrous oxide, fired from his aunt Effie's farm in 1926, which ascended forty-one feet before terminating its two-and-a-half-second flight in a cabbage patch. As brief and limited an ascent as Nell had achieved, it was the first successful launch of a liquid-fueled rocket.

The accomplishment put Goddard ahead of two other pioneers of rocket science and spaceflight exponents, the provincial Russian schoolteacher Konstantin Tsiolkovsky, who in 1903 had published *Investigations of Space by Means of Rockets,* and German physicist Hermann Oberth, who had privately published *The Rocket into Planetary Space* four years after Goddard had published his groundbreaking article. Like Goddard, both men suffered the disdain of established science and opinion leaders, and both men, like Goddard, refused to be constrained by the limits and derision offered by the hidebound conventions of their contemporaries.

Not long after a local reporter in 1929 had written an account of Goddard's latest rocket launch under the headline, "Moon Rocket Misses Target by 238,799½ Miles," Goddard decided he would be better off continuing his work outside the skeptical gaze of the press. With funds provided from the Guggenheim Foundation and additional support raised by an early enthusiast of his work, Charles Lindbergh, Goddard decamped for the deserts of New Mexico. There he remained for the rest of his life, where he developed rockets of ever greater size, range, speed, and sophistication. And while public acclaim still eluded him, and the government took little interest in his rockets, physicists elsewhere took notice, especially the members of the Verein für Raumschiffahrt, the German Society for Space Travel.

Throughout much of the thirties, innocently and in the interests of science, Goddard shared his research with his German counterparts, who took his work far more seriously than did the U.S. government. Though some of his German admirers eventually worked for the Nazi war effort and utilized Goddard's research in the development of weaponry, most of what Goddard provided them was publicly available in his many patent applications. One physicist in particular, a disciple of Hermann Oberth, had been inspired by "A Method of Reaching Extreme Altitudes" and was to use Goddard's rocket designs as the model for the most fearsome weapon in the Nazi arsenal, the Vergeltungswaffe 2, "Revenge Weapon 2," the V-2 rocket.

Goddard tried unsuccessfully to interest the U.S. Army in the military applications of his rockets, remarking to one uninterested general who had watched one of Goddard's rockets ascend into the heavens, "We could slant it a little and do some damage."[4] Meanwhile, in the country where Goddard was acclaimed as a visionary, his admirer was working toward that end. In a remote research facility on the Baltic coast, in the little German village of Peenemünde, Wernher von Braun led a rocket team under the authority of the Luftwaffe, which built the liquid-fueled rockets that were to terrorize London in the last months of the war.

Von Braun was an officer in the SS, though he later claimed to have been compelled to accept the commission, and his missiles were built by slave labor, assigned from the concentration camp at Buchenwald, whose suffering he had personally observed. He later argued that he had never been a real Nazi, just a scientist doing what scientists do, employed in the service of the Nazi war machine out of civic duty and dire necessity. It is perhaps plausible that von Braun was never sincere in his Nazi affiliation, disdained the party's ideology and practices, and, as he also claimed, was appalled by the conditions imposed on his slave labor force. In fact, late in the war he was arrested and briefly held by the SS, but this appears to be more the consequence of a power grab by Heinrich Himmler than any evident disloyalty on von Braun's part.

It is much clearer, however, and damnable that he was never moved to protest Nazi crimes against humanity or sabotage his work in the hope that it would hasten the regime's destruction.

Stained though his reputation is, Wernher von Braun was also a brilliant and visionary scientist. He shared with Robert Goddard a childhood obsession with rockets and space travel. He read the same books and treatises, took the same inspiration from H. G. Wells, challenged the same conventions, and grasped the same future that Goddard did. When von Braun was confirmed in the Lutheran church, his aristocratic Prussian parents commemorated the occasion by giving him a telescope, igniting his lifelong passion for space exploration. After reading Oberth's seminal work in the 1920s, he brought a singular concentration to his math and science studies, which he had shown little enthusiasm for previously. By the time the Third Reich required his services, he was preeminent in the field of rocket science, second only to his mentor, Oberth, in the esteem of Germany's scientific community.

In the last days of the war in Europe, with the Red Army approaching from the east, von Braun led five hundred members of his team toward the American lines and surrendered to the first GI they encountered. The scientists had hidden their V-2 records in an abandoned mine shaft to safeguard them. Von Braun disclosed the location to American intelligence officers, as well as the location of the remaining V-2 components. The U.S. government approved the transfer of von Braun and his team to the United States in what came to be known as Operation Paperclip, so designated because the army indicated which of the Germans were selected for work in the United States by attaching a paper clip to their files. Within months, they were relocated to Fort Bliss outside El Paso, Texas, and directed to assist a score of government scientists at the Army Ordnance Corps test site at White Sands, New Mexico, in reassembling and testing V-2s that the army had shipped from Germany.

Among the Americans who had the opportunity to inspect von Braun's handiwork was Robert Goddard, who recognized it, for the most part, as his own invention. One of the captured German rocket men, rumored to have been von Braun himself, remarked when queried about the V-2's design, "Why don't you ask your own Dr. Goddard? He knows better than any of us." If it struck Goddard as odd that enemy scientists showed a better understanding and respect for his work than did his American contemporaries, he never said so. He was surely accustomed by then to the ironies attending his long and often lonely campaign to prove the theories—and their practical applications—that he had conceived as a young man. He never built another rocket, though. The preeminent American scientist and engineer of rocket technology died of cancer not long after inspecting the V-2.

The "paper clip" scientists remained at Fort Bliss until 1950. While there, von Braun had a lot of free time on his hands. America was war-weary and wasn't much interested in missiles. Von Braun continued developing a concept he had long held for a space program, which he published two years later in a series of articles in *Collier's Weekly Magazine*, "Man Will Conquer Space Soon!" which included visions of lunar landings and a manned expedition to Mars. To get there, von Braun conceived a wheel-like space station, two hundred and fifty feet in diameter, to serve as a space platform, which would be serviced by reusable space vehicles ferrying astronauts and equipment to it. Thus, history records that von Braun himself conceived the idea for the space shuttle, although the reusable vehicle NASA eventually built has been used in missions considerably less grand than the one he envisioned.

In the meantime, the army had other work for von Braun. He and his team were transferred in 1950 to Huntsville, Alabama, where von Braun directed the army's ballistic-missile development team at Redstone Arsenal. He remained in Huntsville for the next twenty years, becoming a naturalized citizen in 1955.

He once told a friend, "When I landed on the American continent in 1945, I had one burning hope: that this step may enable me to contribute to the launching of the first satellite."[5] It was a dream he had nursed for years. When he was fifteen, von Braun had calculated the speed necessary for a rocket to put a satellite into orbit. But the military wanted von Braun to do for the United States what he had done for Germany: build a ballistic missile as a weapon of war. The United States was again at war, in Korea, and might have need of a weapon that could eventually be used to deliver nuclear warheads in an attack

against a new enemy, the Soviet Union. Von Braun designed the missile, the Redstone rocket, a seventy-foot direct descendant of the V-2,
with a detachable warhead, first launched in 1953 and used for the first
nuclear-missile tests.

As he worked on the Redstone, he and his team also developed on
their own initiative early plans to use the rocket to carry a satellite into
orbit. They were discouraged in their endeavors by the government's
lack of urgency to get into space. In 1948, Defense Secretary James
Forrestal had ordered that any satellite work be limited to basic design
research, and no actual development should proceed. At the beginning
of the Redstone project, von Braun turned to a colleague, Ernst Stuhlinger, and remarked, "With the Redstone, we could do it!"

"Do what?" Stuhlinger asked.

"Launch a satellite, of course!"[6] Von Braun urged his superiors
to authorize development of a satellite project and continued working with his team to prepare for the eventuality by planning necessary
modifications to the Redstone.

In 1954, the government finally showed signs of interest in satellites.
Von Braun and other enthusiasts from the military and industry were
ordered to Washington to discuss a joint effort to launch a satellite.
Von Braun proposed launching a five-pound satellite into orbit atop a
modified Redstone. The navy agreed to develop the satellite technology, and a green light was given for Project Orbiter.

Von Braun and his associates had prepared a paper for the meeting,
and he argued that "since it is a project which we could realize . . . it is
only logical to assume that other countries could do the same. It would
be a blow to U.S. prestige if we did not do it first."[7] He and his fellows at Redstone were well aware, even if Washington wasn't, that the
Soviets were working on launching a satellite into orbit. Von Braun's
single-minded pursuit of his interests did not blinker his vision to
events outside his immediate environs. On the contrary, it made him
acutely alert to information from any source about any development
that had relevance to his work, information that was not difficult to
obtain. Soviet scientists were quite candid about their plans to reach
space first, and von Braun strained to convince his superiors that he
should be allowed to make it a contest.

For a variety of reasons, he was not allowed. Interservice rivalries in the armed forces hampered efforts to develop a joint satellite project. In 1955, the White House announced that the United States intended to launch a satellite in time for the International Geophysical Year, an international scientific effort beginning in July 1957, which would showcase advances in all the earth sciences. Von Braun intended his Redstone Orbiter to be the vehicle that would achieve the American triumph. But a committee of scientists appointed by the Pentagon chose a project under development at the Naval Research Laboratory, an elegantly designed but untested Vanguard satellite-launch system. "This is not a design contest," von Braun protested. "It is a contest to get a satellite into orbit." And in that endeavor, von Braun was miles ahead of anyone else.[8] But the committee was unmoved. The Vanguard, they insisted, had more "dignity." "Dignity," von Braun huffed, "this is a Cold War tool. How dignified would our position be if a man-made star of unknown origin suddenly appeared in our skies?" But Project Orbiter was finished.

The crestfallen scientists at Huntsville were ordered to return to making military missiles and terminate all satellite research and development. But von Braun had other ideas. He told his team that they would continue work on a new modified two-stage Redstone missile, the Jupiter, as well as develop a third stage for some future purpose. Eventually, he told them, confident that the navy's Vanguard project could not do what he knew he could, "we will be called upon to launch a satellite . . . [and] we will quickly add that third solid rocket stage . . . put the satellite on top, and we are in business, and even without transgressing the limitations they have clamped on us." He eventually persuaded Washington to allow him to build an even more powerful, four-stage rocket, the Jupiter-C, which was ready to launch in September 1956—strictly for military purposes, of course.

Throughout 1956 and into 1957, indications that the Soviets would soon launch a satellite were frequent and convincing. No one felt more distressed by the news than the man who knew he could have done it first. On October 4, 1957, a public-relations official at Huntsville burst into a meeting of army brass and von Braun's senior team and announced, "Soviet Russia has launched a satellite."

"We could have done it . . . two years ago," von Braun observed. The generals stared at him, as if waiting for guidance about what could now be done. He was ready. "Give me the word," he told them, "and we will have an American satellite in orbit in sixty days."⁹ A month later, the Soviets launched another spacecraft, carrying a mutt named Laika.

President Eisenhower took the news with his usual equanimity. He knew that the United States was far ahead of the Soviets in missile research, and he didn't particularly care if they had won a minor race. We would stay ahead of them in the long run. But the American people, and their representatives in Congress, were considerably more disturbed. They wanted answers about how we could have let the Soviets embarrass us. Most of all, they wanted an American satellite in space, now.

Two weeks after *Sputnik*'s launch, von Braun had presented a paper at a conference offering what he called "The Lessons of Sputnik." It was a terrible blow to national prestige, he had admitted, and we "have made grave errors of judgment."¹⁰ But, he reassured his audience, "we have lost a battle . . . we have not lost the war. If we only remember that it is more important to get United States satellites up there, rather than Army, Navy, or Air Force satellites."¹¹ A few days after Laika embarked on his final journey, the White House ordered von Braun's team to resume Project Orbiter.

One last action had to be attempted before von Braun would have his chance. On December 6, 1957, a little before noon, the Vanguard, carrying a small satellite in its nose cone, fired its engines, rose four feet into the air, and crashed to the ground in a ball of fire and a cloud of black smoke. The satellite, however, separated cleanly from the missile and escaped the destruction. Its antennae popped and began transmitting signals. The satellite, at least, had worked perfectly.

Von Braun's team at the Army Ballistic Missile Agency was ordered to get a satellite launch system ready as quickly as possible. At 10:48 p.m. on January 31, 1958, a four-stage Jupiter-C rocket, carrying in its nose cone a satellite four feet long and six inches in diameter, launched from Cape Canaveral. The rocket sped into the night sky and quickly disappeared from view. Within five minutes, unobserved and untracked by anxious scientists and government officials, all four stages had launched successfully. Ninety minutes later, Goldstone tracking station in the Mojave Desert reported, "Goldstone has the bird." *Explorer 1,* the first American satellite in space, had deployed safely in orbit and begun transmissions to earth. "We have firmly established our foothold in space," declared the man who had done more than any other to get us there. "We will never give it up again."

In 1960, von Braun's employment with the army ended. He became the first director of the Marshall Space Flight Center for the newly created civilian space agency, NASA. There he remained happily, the most popular and persuasive booster of America's space program, for ten years. His Redstone rockets carried America's Mercury astronauts into space, and a Redstone descendant he designed, the Saturn V, carried Americans to the moon. Von Braun died in 1977 at the age of sixty-five.

Throughout his career, he was in full command of all knowledge and opportunities that could further his dream of human exploration of space. He encouraged action within the bureaucracies that managed America's space program and avoided the inhibitions that vast institutions can often impose on creative minds. He was a loyal champion of NASA. But his highest loyalty was to his dream, and every decision he made, employing all the knowledge and experience he could gain, was to further the adventure he had always been convinced was within the grasp of humanity.

"Don't tell me that man doesn't belong out there," he told *Time* magazine. "Man belongs wherever he wants to go."[12]

FORESIGHT

I skate where the puck is going to be, not where it has been." That's how Wayne Gretzky concisely explained the skill that made him one of the greatest hockey players of all time, perhaps the greatest. How did he know where the puck would be? Instinct? Perhaps. What is instinct, though? Is it acquired, or is it a natural gift? I don't rule out the possibility that some have a nose for opportunity, a sixth sense, but the people I have known or studied who have possessed that instinct have acquired it through experience, a lifetime of careful preparation. In Gretzky's case, playing and practicing with his teammates would have prepared him to know when and where they would pass the puck. And like all the most successful professional athletes, he took care to know his opponents. He would know where they were likely to pass the puck, and he would get there before they did.

Many believe foresight is like a sixth sense, but it is more explicable than that—more often than not, it is acquired by industry and study. However, it does seem more prevalent in people who are by nature more imaginative. "The best decision makers," the steel magnate Charles Schwab said, "are capable of seeing the present as if it were already the past." Yet they first had to understand how the present came to be, to imagine what could make it a thing of the past. Great statesmen who have been praised for their ability to see around the corner of history knew their history before they looked beyond it, and they understood the forces that drove it in one direction or another. They grasped the whole of the situation they were in before they conceived of the force that could change it. Napoleon, one of his generals commented, "had only to glance through his telescope to sum up the position and forces of an entire army" and know where and when to strike at it.

As wondrous as it might seem, genuine foresight is not really the mark of some special genius that is inexplicably bestowed upon the few and withheld from the many. It is rather more human than that. Most often, as was the case with Winston Churchill, a man of intelligence and imagination, foresight is the achievement of painstaking inquiry and the disciplined application of reason to acquired knowledge, in order to perceive a previously unseen pattern, reason, need, opportunity, or predictive behavior. Some may have more of a gift than others for divining an insight from accumulated information, mentally processing all they have learned to reach conclusions swiftly and surely. But the possession of foresight is not, at least in the secular concerns of human beings, a divinely granted quality. Industry and diligence are within the capacities of anyone, and as they are the necessary qualities of deductive reasoning, so, too, are they often the means to a singular insight. Awareness, then, is indispensable to foresight.

Those who truly understand their environment know that it isn't static. The status quo may be more or less resistant to change, but it will change. Whether it changes for the better or worse, as far as you're concerned, may very well depend on your action. If you have profited by the existing situation, you might be reluctant to risk changing it. You might oppose efforts by others to change it. But eventually someone or some event will force the change you resisted. Better to seize the opportunity, if you can see it, to change it in ways that serve the purposes for which you are responsible.

It is fair to say that people who have shown extraordinary foresight are often rather unconventional. They are less influenced by traditions that evidence no greater quality than longevity. They are less encumbered by groupthink or peer pressure. They look for opportunities to take calculated risks. They aren't afraid to be bold, though for some, boldness is more an expression of vanity than it is the confidence to venture a considered if daring gambit. People whom history has proclaimed as visionaries have often appeared more reckless than their contemporaries and have failed more often than they have succeeded. Churchill's admirer Lord Birkenhead once observed about his friend: "When Winston's right, he's right. When he's wrong, well, my God."

If the foresight you thought you possessed led you astray, do you labor to find its flaws, and apply the lesson to the next time an insight stirs you to action? Or do you write it off to misfortune or the failings of others and venture forth in the same way the next time? Do you sharpen your foresight by understanding why it failed and how to correct it? Or does failure make you timid? Foresight might be gained by the timid, but without the guts to act upon it, it is as useful as a wonderful singing voice to a monk who has taken a vow of silence.

The most impenetrable quality of foresight is the imagination to conceive as a whole the future you think you possess the means to shape. Schwab likened it to "a vision, a dream of the whole thing." Yet more likely one has simply observed in a limited environment the effect of an idea, an invention, or a tactic and begun to wonder about its potential to work a larger change. Finding no reason to suggest that a small invention is by nature unsuited to a bigger challenge, you might imagine how profoundly it could alter an industry or science or a nation or the world. Curiosity and discernment are the attributes of the visionary.

Our founding fathers read the history of ancient republics not to imitate their glories but to avoid their flaws. The first priority of human beings and the political institutions they form is self-interest, which pursues power to seek advantage over others. Governments that do not account for that basic instinct, even republics, will be corrupted into extinction. So they devised a system of divided government, each institution circumscribed by the authority of the others, to account for man's vices rather than rely on his virtues.

Foresight penetrates confusion and turmoil caused by change and identifies signs that suggest a new direction. In 1985, Andy Grove and Gordon Moore, the president and CEO of Intel respectively, met to discuss ways to address the competition from Japanese manufacturers that was threatening their profits in the market they had created, the memory-chip business. Others were complacent in thinking that Intel's main product would continue to prosper in a changing marketplace— the growing demand for and increasing supply of personal computers would expand the market enough that greater competition wouldn't dilute their profits. But Grove and Moore feared otherwise. The unexpectedly rapid growth of competition suggested to them that the trend would accelerate even more, and a downward spiral of Intel's market share and profits would ensue. So they imagined themselves not as the victims of change but as its agents. Grove asked Moore to imagine they had been fired by the company's board of directors, and a new CEO with fresh eyes had been brought in to address the problem. "What would he do?" Grove asked.

"He would get us out of memories," Moore replied.

"I stared at him, numb," Grove recalled. Then he suggested to Moore, "Why shouldn't you and I walk out the door, come back, and do it ourselves?"[1] In that moment of clarity, the idea that would produce the microprocessor was conceived, and Intel's dominance of a new market, which would earn the company exponentially greater profits, was set in motion.

It is not hard to perceive in our times the need for foresight. Change is happening all around us, some good and some of it disconcerting. The growth of the global marketplace, which no country has promoted more effectively than ours, offers a host of opportunities for the society that recognizes them. But it causes dislocations as well. Even skilled American jobs are increasingly migrating overseas. When you ask business executives to explain the root cause of the development, they almost universally point to the problem of American education. We spend more per student on our children's education than almost any other country. But too many students are not learning the skills that will make them attractive to employers, who can hire employees with the same or better skills than Americans at much lower cost. Unless we systemically reform our education system so that our children acquire more proficient or unique skills, we are going to find it increasingly difficult to compete for jobs with the Chinese and Indians. Some suggest that as standards of living rise in countries competing with us for jobs, the American worker will become cost attractive to global businesses. But other less developed countries will become our new competitors.

If any endeavor in our country is in need of innovation and leaders with foresight, it is education. The institutional obstacles to systemic change are immense. The resource-consuming administration of education bureaucracies, politically influential unions that serve the interests of teachers and not students, and timid school boards all resist real change and its most effective agent, competition.

People outside the system might find it easier to grasp the problem and perceive the remedies. But the impediments within the system are so averse to change that the most effective agent of change, the person who understands the reality and forces progress toward a new ideal, will have to come from within: The teachers who decide to organize to force changes in more than their compensation packages—or even to leave their schools to form a new one, unencumbered by conventions that retard progress. The government agency that allows it. The school board that requires administrators to teach. The union official who doesn't resent competition from private schools but learns from it to improve the quality of public education, even if one of those improvements makes quality the condition for tenure rather than longevity.

Profound change doesn't always require consensus. Sometimes it is achieved when just a few people see the way ahead and decide to set in motion events that will overtake resistance, change the unsatisfactory status quo, and leave something better in its place.

"I HEAR THE STEADY DRUMMER"[1]

On July 1, 1911, the German gunboat *Panther* entered the Moroccan port of Agadir and dropped anchor. The government of Kaiser Wilhelm II had dispatched the warship to emphasize Germany's insistence that it be compensated with territory in the French Congo for accepting France's effective control of Morocco. To our modern eyes, the appearance of one small and lightly armed warship (carrying a brass band among its company, for heaven's sake), which by itself could not possibly hope to contest France's influence in the North African kingdom, seems a rather innocuous gesture. But to the great powers of Europe in 1911, it was shockingly provocative. The action exacerbated distrust of Germany's larger intentions and hastened the day when Europe was to commence the four years of unprecedented slaughter remembered as the Great War.

Anxiety over Germany's militarism was already mounting in European capitals. Its large and well-disciplined standing army was always a worry, as were the Germans' inexhaustible supply of grievances over what they generally perceived as a lack of respect from most of the great powers. Most worrisome in recent years had been the Kaiser's relentless determination to build a powerful navy. Germany had never been much of a seafaring nation. Its longest coastline and most of its naval bases were along the icy waters of the Baltic Sea, separated by the Danish peninsula from a smaller coastline and ports on the North Sea. The Kiel Canal in Schleswig-Holstein linked the two seas but was too narrow to permit the passage of the great fleet of massive battleships Germany was now intent on building. Unlike Britain and France, Germany did not have extensive overseas possessions that required the maintenance of a large navy.

After unification in 1871, German military power resided in its Prussian-dominated Imperial Army. Although the Kaiser, cousin to many of the other crowned heads of Europe, had long admired the Royal Navy of his British uncle, Edward VII, many British leaders worried that the Kaiser's plans represented more than battleship envy. Unlike Germany, Britain had never relied on a standing army to defend itself from invasion. The island nation, and the vast empire it had built, claimed the most powerful navy in the world as its first line of defense. Since Admiral Nelson's time, the essence of British national pride and security resided in the confidence that Britannia ruled the waves. No other sea power was her equal. As Britain entered the twentieth century, it was determined to defend that supremacy from all challengers.

Britain's chancellor of the exchequer, David Lloyd George, who just two years before had opposed the Royal Navy's plan to build six new battleships, was as stunned as anyone by Germany's precipitous action at Agadir. With the encouragement of his friend and colleague the home secretary, he gave a speech on July 21 in which he assured his audience of bankers that Britain always preferred to maintain peaceful relations with other powers.

> But if a situation were to be forced upon us in which peace could only be preserved . . . by allowing Britain to be treated as if she were of no account in the Cabinet of nations, then I say emphatically that peace at that price would be a humiliation intolerable for a great country like ours to endure.

Lloyd George spoke for the whole of His Majesty's government when he made the speech. Foreign Minister Edward Grey had conveyed that very sentiment in cables to European capitals in the days after the Agadir incident. The crisis was eventually resolved through negotiation, and Germany backed down, nursing yet another wound to its much injured pride. But at the time of Lloyd George's speech, anxiety was still acute, and Germany expressed its outrage over the chancellor's remarks in a cable that scarcely couched its belligerent tone in the typical language of diplomacy. Grey summoned Lloyd George and the home secretary to the Foreign Ministry, where he showed them the German response. Outraged in turn, they prepared a cable informing Berlin, diplomatically, that Great Britain would not be dictated to or intimidated by the Kaiser's government. The home secretary had joined Lloyd George in arguing against the six new battleships. Agadir had also forced him to reconsider his previous views. "Germany's action at Agadir," he wrote, "has put her in the wrong & forced us to consider her claims in the light of her policy and methods."[2] Years later, he recalled his thoughts about this harbinger of the war to come, and the flurry of diplomatic exchanges that had concentrated the minds of European statesmen in the summer of 1911.

They sound so very cautious and correct, these deadly words. Soft, quiet voices purring, courteous, grave, exactly-measured phrases in large peaceful rooms. But with less warning cannons had opened fire and nations had been struck down by this same Germany. So now the Admiralty wireless whispers through the ether to the tall masts of ships, and captains pace their decks absorbed in thought. It is nothing. It is less than nothing. It is too foolish, too fantastic to be thought of in the twentieth century. Or is it fire and murder leaping out of the darkness at our throats, torpedoes ripping the bellies of half-awakened ships, a sunrise on a vanished naval supremacy, and an island well-guarded hitherto, at last defenceless? No, it is nothing. No one would do such things. Civilization has climbed above such perils. The interdependence of nations in trade and traffic, the sense of public law, the Hague Convention, Liberal principles, the Labour Party, high finance, Christian charity, common sense have rendered such nightmares impossible. Are you quite sure? It would be a pity to be wrong. Such a mistake could only be made once—once for all.[3]

In a little more than three months' time, the home secretary would be responsible for guarding against such a catastrophic mistake. By then he had assumed a new office and a new title, First Lord of the Admiralty Winston Spencer Churchill.

Germany's naval buildup had begun in the last decade of the nineteenth century, with the Kaiser's appointment of Admiral Alfred von Tirpitz as secretary of state for the Imperial Navy. Tirpitz shared the Kaiser's conviction that Germany needed a great fleet to become a world power, and under his leadership Germany began to develop both a high-seas fleet and a submarine fleet. Tirpitz believed, and the Kaiser concurred, that were the German navy to become, if not equal to, then powerful enough to threaten serious damage to the British fleet, Britain would be persuaded to stay out of any future war between Germany and other European powers. Their purpose gained greater urgency after Britain and France concluded the Entente Cordiale in 1904, ending a centuries-long history of hostility between the two greatest European powers, and after the Anglo-Russian Entente in 1907. Together with a French entente with Russia, the agreements formed the Triple Entente, which, though not a formal military alliance, clearly augured that should Germany and the Austro-Hungarian empire go to war with France and Russia, Great Britain would enter the war on the side of Germany's enemies. Add to this the fact that, should it come to war, Germany's strategic plan for the western front (called the Schlieffen Plan for its author, Field Marshal Alfred Graf von Schlieffen) envisioned an initial attack from its right flank on France that required the German army to first invade Belgium. Great Britain had signed a treaty with Belgium in 1839, pledging to defend Belgian neutrality.

Still, Kaiser Wilhelm and his formidable naval minister believed that a prodigious buildup of the Imperial Navy could convince his British cousins to remain neutral, irrespective of their 1839 treaty obligations—the "little scrap of paper," as the German chancellor called it. Rather than risk its naval supremacy and, thus, the security of its empire, Britain would avoid conflict with Germany, Tirpitz reasoned, and accede to German ambitions to become a world power. Toward that end, the German Reichstag authorized a buildup that would eventually give Germany the second largest navy in the world.

The naval arms race between Germany and Great Britain accelerated in 1906 when the first of Britain's modern battleships, the fearsome HMS *Dreadnought,* was completed and Germany responded by announcing it intended to build dreadnoughts of its own. The man who had overseen the *Dreadnought*'s design and construction was a towering figure in British naval history—second only, perhaps, to the great Lord Nelson—Admiral of the Fleet John Arbuthnot Fisher. Jackie Fisher, as he was popularly called, though never to his face, had been made first sea lord (the equivalent of a U.S. chief of naval operations) in 1905. He had begun his naval career as a young midshipman in the days when Her Majesty's ships still spread canvas for power. In a career that was to span sixty years, he became the most modernizing force in the British navy.

He was an imperious, impatient, argumentative, short-tempered, and visionary reformer, who seemed to make nearly as many enemies as admirers. As first sea lord, he ran roughshod over hidebound officers who esteemed the navy's quaint traditions over efficiency. He thoroughly revamped naval training. He sold off scores of obsolete ships, dry-docked others he considered unfit for service in a modern navy, and commissioned 161 new warships, including twenty-two new battleships. He pushed for the construction of a submarine fleet. He valued speed above all other qualities in a ship. Accordingly, he was reluctant at first to support the construction of dreadnought-class battleships, as he feared their heavy armor would make them too slow for modern naval warfare and vulnerable to mines and torpedoes. He preferred to build faster and lighter armored battle cruisers. Armor was a lesser concern to Fisher. Speed was everything. As he would later tell his protégé, Winston Churchill, speed was the "first of all necessities . . . so as to be able to fight

When you like
Where you like
and *How you like.*[4]

Nevertheless, when the British government, mindful of German naval ambitions, ordered the construction of the *Dreadnought,* Fisher oversaw every aspect of its construction and insisted on improvements to its weaponry that exceeded any previous ship's firepower. It was Fisher who convinced the government to replace the biggest gun in the fleet arsenal and in the world—the twelve-inch gun, which fired an 850-pound shell—with the 13.5-inch gun, firing a 1,250-pound shell. He also argued for the conversion of the fleet from coal to oil fuel, a very controversial position, considering Britain at that time had no oil reserves of its own but plenty of good Welsh coal. He succeeded in building some fifty destroyers and a greater number of submarines that burned oil. But the pride of the navy, the great British battleships of the line, *Dreadnought* and pre-*Dreadnought,* were still stoking coal in their boilers.

He oversaw the creation of a new Home Fleet in 1906, with seven battleships drawn from the Atlantic, Mediterranean, and Channel fleets. "Our only probable enemy is Germany," Fisher observed, which "keeps her whole fleet always concentrated within a few hours of England. We must therefore keep a Fleet twice as powerful concentrated within a few hours of Germany." Fisher explained why the Home Fleet's cruising grounds would be in the North Sea, citing Nelson's dictum "your battleground will be your drill ground."[5]

Fisher received a peerage in 1909, adopting the motto "Fear God and Dread Nought" for his coat of arms, and retired to Lake Lucerne in Switzerland the following year. He departed the navy convinced that war between Britain and Germany, and a tremendous clash between their navies, was inevitable and imminent, and he came astonishingly close to predicting the date of the start of "the battle of Armageddon": October 1914.

So, too, did the man who relied on Fisher as his principal advisor foresee the coming conflict with an uncanny accuracy. In the midst of the Agadir crisis, Prime Minister Herbert Asquith convened a meeting of the Committee of Imperial Defence on August 23. Churchill, his blood up, prepared a memorandum and circulated it to committee members in advance of the meeting. Churchill's son and biographer, Randolph Churchill, called it "one of the most prescient strategic documents that Churchill ever wrote." He not only anticipated that

Germany would launch its initial offensive in the west but predicted "the military timetable of the German invasion of Belgium and France in 1914 . . . almost to the day."[6]

"By the twentieth day," Churchill warned, "the French armies will have been driven from the line of the Meuse and will be falling back on Paris. All plans based on the opposite assumption ask too much of fortune." But contrary to the Schlieffen Plan's assumptions, which held that Germany could quickly defeat France before Russia had fully mobilized its armies on the eastern front, Churchill envisioned the torturous stalemate on the western front that was to become an awful reality. Russia, Churchill believed, would be in position to apply "growing pressure from the thirtieth day." Germany's extended lines, the huge numbers of soldiers she would need to accomplish her objectives, and Great Britain's deployment of an expeditionary force to France would stall Germany's advance. By the fortieth day of the war, Germany would "be extended at full strain both internally and on her war fronts," a strain that would become increasingly "more severe and ultimately overwhelming." At that point, Churchill forecast, "opportunities for the decisive trial of strength" would arrive. But that trial would demand

> heavy and hard sacrifices from France, who must, with great constancy, expose herself to invasion, to having her provinces occupied by the enemy, and to the investment of Paris, and whose armies may be committed to retrograde or defensive operations. Whether her rulers could contemplate or her soldiers endure this trial may depend upon the military support which Great Britain can give; and this must be known beforehand, so that we may know, before we decide, what they must be prepared to do.[7]

Churchill proposed that a British force of 107,000 soldiers be deployed to France at the commencement of hostilities, with another 100,000 added from the British army in India by the fortieth day. In almost all its particulars, Churchill's memorandum envisioned the early course of the war and the bloody stalemate that would soon obtain in the miserable trenches of the western front. When the war did come in 1914, former Prime Minister Arthur Balfour would praise the memorandum as "a triumph of prophecy."

Asquith, impressed by Churchill's vigorous resolve to prepare the country for war, began to consider him for the admiralty. He shared Churchill's concern that the fleet and the curious lack of urgency in the navy's planning for the war were inadequate to the challenges they would face. Churchill had written the prime minister of his doubts. "Are you sure that the ships we have at Cromarty are strong enough to defeat the whole of the [German] High Seas Fleet?" he questioned. "If not, they should be reinforced without delay."[8] On September 27, Asquith offered the admiralty to Churchill. When Asquith's daughter, Violet, encountered Churchill moments later and offered him tea, he looked at her "with grave but shining eyes. 'No, I don't want tea. I don't want anything in the world. Your father has just offered me the Admiralty.'"*[9]

Churchill is such a well-known and revered figure in this country that his biography does not require detailed elaboration. Americans are most familiar with his heroic leadership in World War II and his steadfast courage before then, when he was a lonely voice warning of the rising threat of Nazi Germany during his "wilderness years." Less well remembered is the first part of his political career, his meteoric rise to power at a very young age, his sudden fall, and his subsequent recovery. His was a life without equal in modern times. At times, his story seems too dramatic for fiction, much less biography. (Indeed, many accounts of incidents in his remarkable life have been, if not entirely invented, much embellished, though surely not to the extent that they diminish his singularity.) Many who recall his first turn as first lord of the admiralty remember only the incident that led to his downfall, the disastrous Dardanelles campaign and the wholesale slaughter of Australian, New Zealander, and British soldiers on the beach at Gallipoli. I think Churchill was made a scapegoat for the mistakes and irresolution of others. But that is not a universal opinion and is perhaps best left for another book. For the purposes of this chapter, it is sufficient

---

*Churchill's appointment was announced on October 24, just five days shy of his thirty-seventh birthday.

to examine the critical decisions this young man of destiny made when he prepared the Royal Navy for the Battle of Armageddon both he and Jackie Fisher believed was inevitable.

From the moment he arrived at the admiralty, Churchill exuberantly immersed himself in the work of comprehensively understanding the tradition-bound world of the Royal Navy, its strengths and flaws, and the challenges it would face from its likely foe. Robert Massie, in his superb study of the British and German naval-arms race, *Dreadnought,* described the routine Churchill instituted on his first day in office. He had a large chart of the North Sea hung on the wall behind his desk. Then, "every day the duty officer marked with small flags the position of the principal ships of the German Navy. Each morning, on entering the room, Churchill stood before the chart and studied the whereabouts of the High Seas Fleet. His purpose 'was to inculcate in myself and those working with me a sense of ever-present danger.'"[10]

Like Fisher, his intention was to modernize, and to do that he would have to know the state of affairs. He was a man with many opinions, and the swiftness with which he conceived them and the belligerence with which he often defended them sometimes gave the impression he was impulsive. But rarely did he lack the facts to explain and argue his views. He was quite diligent in that regard. Among the perquisites of the portfolio was the admiralty's yacht, the *Enchantress,* which became Churchill's office and home for most of the next four years, and which conveyed the new first lord to most of His Majesty's naval bases and shipyards, where he undertook to master every detail of navy tactics and capabilities. He appeared to be everywhere at once, inquiring, badgering, and learning. Everything arguably within his purview quickly became the object of his keen interest, from gunnery to the morale of his sailors. "I got to know what everything looked like," he wrote, and "where everything was and how one thing fitted into another. In the end, I could put my hand on whatever was wanted."[11] He was fascinated with airplanes and immediately understood their utility in warfare. He spent hundreds of hours in the air learning how to fly, until he very reluctantly acceded to the demands of his anxious wife, Clementine, to suspend the training. He crawled into the cramped quarters of gun turrets and learned how they worked. "From dawn to midnight one's whole mind was absorbed," he remembered.[12] And he used the whole of his formidable mind to push on a reluctant admiralty the reforms he believed were necessary to prepare the fleet for war. "In matters of technical advance, the First Lord was always in the van, always supporting the pioneers, always sweeping aside the obstruction of the unimaginative."[13]

It became Churchill's practice to solicit information and opinions from junior officers and ordinary seamen, while oftentimes ignoring or arguing with their infuriated seniors. The respect he showed them, and the increase in pay and other material comforts he won for them, made him a favorite with the ranks. He was seldom as well received by senior officers, who resented his abrupt manner with them and the changes he was forcing to time-honored naval traditions in which they located their self-esteem. An apocryphal anecdote that attained the status of legend had Churchill dismiss the notion that naval traditions merited respect. "And what are they?" he asked. "Rum, sodomy, and the lash. Good morning, gentlemen." In later years, Churchill denied having made the caustic remark but expressed a wish that he had. Even the king, who had spent fifteen years in the navy and risen to the rank of captain, earned Churchill's contempt when he failed to appreciate the soundness of his first lord's judgment. In a letter to Clementine, Churchill lamented his sovereign's obtuseness. "The King talked more stupidly about the Navy than I have ever heard him before. Really it is disheartening to hear this cheap and silly drivel with which he lets himself be filled up."[14]

Churchill had been alarmed by the admiralty's lack of coordination with the War Office and what he feared was the navy's desultory planning for war. He was dismayed to discover that the navy had yet to formulate a plan to transport an expeditionary force to France in the event of war. As home minister, he had been surprised to learn he was responsible for protecting the navy's stores of gunpowder. During the Agadir crisis, his request that the admiralty provide a force of Marines to protect the storage depots was refused. One of his first acts as first lord was to establish the Naval War Staff, modeled on the Army General Staff and charged with coordinating war plans with the War Office. This he achieved over the objections of the sea lords he had inherited, who preferred to keep their war plans to themselves and away from the prying curiosity of the War Office and politicians in general. In his first year at the admiralty, Churchill replaced three of the four sea lords.

For advice in selecting their replacements, he turned to the man who was to become his most valued counselor and ardent champion, the mercurial and brilliant Jackie Fisher. Fisher and Churchill had known and admired each other since they had spent a two-week holiday together in France in 1907. They had recognized each other instantly as kindred spirits in intellect, personality, and opinions concerning the Royal Navy. The day before he assumed the office of first lord, Churchill cabled Fisher in Switzerland that he would like to see him as soon as practical. Fisher arrived three days later. Churchill informed him of his plans to prepare the navy for war, and asked his advice. He later described Fisher as "a veritable volcano of knowledge and inspiration; and as soon as he learned what my main purpose was he passed into a state of vehement eruption. . . . Once he began, he could hardly stop. I plied him with questions and he poured out ideas."[15]

Though appointments to senior commands, war planning, and the disposition of His Majesty's ships were important to Fisher and Churchill, their main focus was on making the improvements in ship design and accelerating the construction of new ships that would maintain their advantage over the High Seas Fleet. They first concentrated on plans to increase the caliber of ships' guns. Fisher had prevailed on the government to increase the caliber of the new dreadnoughts from twelve inches to 13.5 inches. Now, Churchill proposed a new fleet of five superdreadnoughts that would boast a battery of eight fifteen-inch guns, each firing a 1,920-pound shell. His plan was enthusiastically supported by Fisher, who, with typical resort to hyperbole, declared that "to achieve the supply of this gun was the equivalent of a great victory at sea; to shrink from this endeavor was treason to the Empire."[16]

"Enlarging the gun," Churchill wrote, "meant enlarging the ships, and enlarging the ships meant enlarging the cost." He had no time to develop a trial gun to test. The keels would soon be laid for the new battleships, the *Queen Elizabeth* class. Germany was widening the Kiel

Canal so that its ships based in the Baltic could quickly reach the North Sea without steaming north around Denmark. By the Kaiser's permission, Churchill had been extended the privilege of examining the new German naval law that authorized the canal's widening as well as another increase in ship construction. He concluded from the document that the law "put four fifths of the German navy permanently on war footing." The canal would be completed by 1914, and this alarming development meant that the warning time for a German attack would be reduced to a few hours. The superdreadnoughts must have the new guns. A clash between the German and British fleets would emphasize the "importance of hitting first, hitting hardest and keeping on hitting."[17] After consulting a second time with Fisher, who urged him on, Churchill ordered the full-scale development of the new guns, without knowing with any certainty that they would work. No gun of their size had ever been constructed or even contemplated by another navy. "From this moment on," he wrote, "we were irrevocably committed to the whole armament, and every detail in these new vessels, extending to thousands of parts, was redesigned to fit them."[18]

He had instructed that one of the big guns be ready and tested four months in advance of the others. Should it fail, it would still be too late to recover the costs of production, but it would at least settle the question of whether Churchill had achieved an enormous advance in the superiority of British battleships or had authored a complete disaster. The naval estimates (annual budgets) he had submitted to the government were vastly larger than past ones. His estimate for 1914 would constitute the largest navy budget in British history and the largest in the world. A shocked Lloyd George, who as chancellor of the exchequer was responsible for finding the money to pay for Churchill's plans, complained that "Winston is getting more and more absorbed in boilers."[19]

As the day of the gun's trial neared, Churchill was fraught with anxiety. "Fancy if they failed," he worried. "What a disaster. What an exposure. No excuse would be accepted. It would all be brought home to me—'rash, inexperienced,' 'before he had been there a month,' 'altering all the plans of his predecessors' and producing this 'ghastly fiasco.'" But, he wrote to his first sea lord, "risks have to be run in peace as well as in war, and courage in design now may win the battle later on."[20]

When the new fifteen-inch gun proved a "brilliant success," Churchill next turned to the problem of speed.[21] The new guns and their heavier shells added more weight, so Churchill ordered that the *Queen Elizabeth* dreadnoughts would carry four instead of the five turrets of the existing dreadnoughts, and more boilers were added. But the new battleships would be protected with thirteen and a half inches of steel armor, making them even heavier. Fisher would have preferred that they sacrifice armor for speed, but Churchill balked at the suggestion. The hugely expensive new ships of the line, he maintained, must be able to take a punch. And, as both Fisher and Churchill knew, they would be vulnerable to that new and troubling weapon of naval warfare, the torpedo. But Fisher reminded Churchill that the most important purpose was to bring the enemy to battle, with the British fleet in position to "cross the enemy's T," the tactic that involved steaming perpendicular to the enemy's line of battle, subjecting it to an all-ships' broadside, and then enveloping it. For this to occur, speed was more critical than armor. "Do you remember the recipe for jugged hare in Mrs. Glasse's Cookery?" he wrote Churchill. "First, catch your hare."[22] To achieve this level of superiority, the new dreadnoughts would have to possess the speed of the lighter armed battle cruisers, twenty-five knots or more. But their size, armor, and guns would restrict them to no more than twenty-one knots.

One remedy was evident to both men: oil. Oil was more combustible and burned hotter than coal, and it produced steam faster, which in turn enabled a ship to accelerate more rapidly and to rely on fewer boilers. Oil-burning ships created less smoke, making them less visible at a distance to the enemy. Oil obviated the need for huge numbers of sailors to be assigned to stoke coal, and it could be stored in more distant places on board, allowing for greater efficiencies in the ships' design. Moreover, ships would no longer need to endure the manpower-intensive process of taking on coal, which, Churchill observed, "exhausted the whole ship's company."[23] At any given time, a quarter of the fleet might be in port coaling. Ships that burned oil could be replenished from tanks onshore with a turn of a valve. Even more important, they could be refueled at sea. "The advantages conferred by liquid fuel were inestimable," Churchill wrote, as it enabled a ship to steam faster, carry more armament, use less manpower and remain at sea longer.[24]

But the decision to convert the fleet from coal to oil would be the most controversial of all Churchill's reforms. Britain produced no oil. It produced coal. "The oil supplies of the world were in the hands of vast oil trusts under foreign control," Churchill recognized. "To commit the navy irrevocably to oil was indeed to take arms against a sea of troubles."[25] First among the troubles, as always, was the navy's resistance to change and the concern of its commanders that a conversion from oil to coal would sacrifice too great a strategic advantage. One of Churchill's predecessors as first lord, William Palmer, had rejected the idea in 1904, saying, "The substitution of oil for coal is impossible, because oil does not exist in this world in sufficient quantities." Changing to oil, even if a reliable supply could be secured, raised other problems as well. Chief among them was oil's highly flammable nature. Coal was inert. An enemy shell striking a coal-storage bin would not instantly ignite the solid fuel. A direct hit on an oil tank would set off an immediate inferno and greatly increase the destructive capability of the enemy's guns. Storage tanks ashore would be vulnerable to enemy attack, and the lost fuel would be more difficult to replace than coal.

Yet Churchill was convinced that "if we overcame the difficulties and surmounted the risks, we should be able to raise the whole power and efficiency of the navy to a definitely higher level; better ships, better crews, higher economies, more intense forms of war power—in a word, mastery itself was the prize of the venture."[26]

Churchill wanted new destroyers and battle cruisers designed to burn oil as well. As mentioned, Fisher had managed to have oil burners authorized for a number of new destroyers. But after their construction, the admiralty, worried about the scarcity and expense of oil, reversed itself and ordered future destroyers to return to using coal. The oil-burning destroyers sustained speeds of thirty-three knots. Their coal-burning successors could manage only twenty-seven. Churchill was determined to put an end to the folly. "Building slow destroyers!"

he lamented. "One might as well breed slow race horses." He recognized that if he could persuade the government to accept oil for the new superdreadnoughts, he wouldn't encounter much resistance to his insistence that other new ships have the same advantage. "The camel once swallowed, the gnats went down easily."[27]

But it was a hugely expensive and risky venture. To overcome the daunting opposition to the conversion he would need not only to persuade the government that the advantages outweighed the risks but also to find some means of securing a reliable oil supply at a cost that would not distress beyond endurance the guardians of the royal treasury, who were already showing signs of fatigue with their tireless young colleague's hugely expensive reforms. He could not do it alone. And so, in 1913, he again enlisted the service of his comrade Jackie Fisher. He asked Fisher to chair a Royal Commission on Oil Supply, and the old man readily agreed. Within six months, the commission issued its report making a powerful and persuasive case for the conversion to oil and the acquisition of a four-year supply. Churchill had faced enormous resistance. The navy's increasingly prodigious budgets were driving Lloyd George and other fiscally prudent ministers wild. "On more than one occasion, I feared I should succumb," he wrote. But in the end, with Fisher's help, Parliament and the wary admirals relented, and the sum of ten million pounds was authorized for the construction of tanker ships and storage tanks. Churchill had also dispatched agents to the Middle East to find and control a steady supply of oil. In 1914, one month before the "guns of August" would commence their four-year cannonade, Churchill secured for the British crown a 51 percent controlling interest in the Anglo-Persian Oil Company for 2.2 million pounds.

Churchill and Fisher also feared that Germany was working on converting its fleet to oil, and this only reaffirmed their conviction that the advantages in speed and flexibility that oil afforded the fleet outweighed the strategic risks. Their concern was misplaced. Germany was beginning to use oil to supplement coal by spraying it on coal to increase its combustibility. But German warships would not convert to exclusive use of oil until after World War I. By the time Armageddon arrived, the Royal Navy would have the advantage.

The conversion to oil was a bold and risky decision, yet in the end it didn't provide an indefinite strategic advantage to Britain. The United States had already begun to build oil-fueled battleships, and after the war all the major sea powers concentrated on building oil-fueled fleets. But with respect to the crisis in which the world was about to convulse, Churchill's decisions assured that the British navy, on which Britain's security depended to an extent greater than did any other power, was to remain second to none. The decision to build an oil-fueled Fast Division was only one of those critical decisions, but it was one of the most important ones. The remarkable confidence Churchill showed in plunging ahead with such monumentally consequential changes is now a historically well-respected feature of his character. But it is important to remember that at the time he prepared his navy for war by using his intellect, industry, and the often irresistible force of his arguments, he was only in his thirties. Yet in challenging the weight of generations of experience and knowledge possessed by his opponents, he saw what they could not see. He believed possible what they dismissed as impossible. And he was able to do it because he had compensated for his lack of comparable experience by teaching himself everything he needed to know to make his decisions.

His naval budgets were premised on his firm intention to build two ships for every one Germany commissioned. He offered to suspend or limit ship construction should Germany do the same. When Germany rejected the offer, he proceeded with his plans confident that with the will and resources he could maintain Britain's superiority in quality and number of warships.

As he would be in advance of the next war, he was Britain's most discerning and outspoken messenger of Germany's bellicose intentions, and he saw the urgent need to take actions today that would secure his island nation. The German High Seas Fleet could serve only one purpose, he argued: to threaten war. Otherwise it was only an expensive luxury for a nation with few colonial possessions. But for Britons, he reminded his countrymen, a powerful navy was something else entirely. In a speech to Parliament in 1913 defending the budget he had proposed, Churchill observed that other powers did not need a navy to defend themselves. "They build them so as to play a part in the world's affairs. It is sport to them. It is life and death to us."[28]

Churchill had worried that the Home Fleet had no protected wartime anchorage near the waters where it would confront the High Seas Fleet. He located one in Scapa Flow in Scotland's Orkney Islands, where the fleet could keep a watchful eye on the Heligoland Bight, through which the Kaiser's dreadnoughts would have to pass in the event of war. And when war did come, Churchill and the fleet were ready.

On June 28, 1914, Serb nationalist Gavrilo Princip shot and killed Austrian Archduke Ferdinand and his wife as their carriage passed through a narrow Sarajevo street. A month later, on July 23, after receiving assurances from the Kaiser that Germany would come to Austria's aid in a war with Russia, Austria sent Serbia an ultimatum, which British Foreign Minister Edward Grey described as "the most formidable document that was ever addressed from one state to another." No nation that valued its sovereignty could have accepted its terms.

The British cabinet had been absorbed with the questions of Irish Home Rule when the event that triggered it all occurred. When, following an exhaustive debate on the question, Grey read to his fellow cabinet ministers the menacing tone and demands of the Austrian ultimatum, Churchill remembered:

> We were all very tired, but gradually as the phrases and sentences followed one another, impressions of a wholly different character began to form in my mind. As the reading proceeded it seemed absolutely impossible that any State in the world could accept it, or that any acceptance, however abject, would satisfy the aggressor. The parishes of Fermanagh and Tyrone faded into the mists and squalls of Ireland, and a strange light began immediately . . . to fall and grow on the map of Europe.[29]

Serbia attempted a placating response, but Austria insisted on the full acceptance of its demands. Serbia refused. The two nations went to war. Russia, as expected, mobilized to defend its Serb allies. Germany did the same on behalf of Austria. France was bound to Russia. Germany launched its western offensive, violating Belgian neutrality and drawing Great Britain into the war. And thus commenced four years of atrocious carnage, as nineteenth-century military tactics encountered twentieth-century weaponry.

Churchill and the British government still harbored hope that a Europe-wide war could be avoided, but that hope diminished with every passing day. And Churchill would not invest the security of his country on the wager. With the king, he had just overseen the greatest naval review in British history, with 223 ships of the Home Fleet, which would be renamed the Grand Fleet, passing in salute. Normal procedure after the review would be to disperse the ships and extend two weeks of liberty to her crews. Churchill called the admiralty the night he learned of the Austrian ultimatum and ordered the fleet not to disperse and to await further orders. He sent armed guards to protect the nation's arms depots and oil-storage tanks. He dispatched anti-aircraft batteries to positions along the North Sea coast. He cabled the commander of the Mediterranean Fleet to prepare for an outbreak of hostilities. And then, quite extraordinarily, on his own initiative he ordered the fleet to its war station at Scapa Flow. "I feared to bring this matter before the Cabinet," he later wrote, "lest it should be mistakenly be considered a provocative action likely to damage the chance of peace."[30]

In *The World Crisis,* Churchill provides this memorable description of the Grand Fleet's passage.

We may now picture this great Fleet, with its flotillas and cruisers, steaming slowly out of Portland Harbour, squadron by squadron, scores of gigantic castles of steel wending their way across the misty, shining sea, like giants bowed in anxious thought. We may picture them again as darkness fell, eighteen miles of warships running at high speed and in absolute blackness through the narrow Straits, bearing with them into the broad waters of the North the safeguard of considerable affairs. . . . If war should come no one would know where to look for the British Fleet. Somewhere in that enormous waste of waters to the north of our islands, cruising now this way, now that, shrouded in storms and mists, dwelt this mighty organization. Yet from the Admiralty building we could speak to them at any moment if need arose. The king's ships were at sea.

Six days after he gave the order, Germany invaded Belgium, and Great Britain was at war. Churchill summoned his mentor, Jackie Fisher, then seventy-four years old, to return to his last command as first sea lord.

Germany recognized that its High Seas Fleet was no match for the superior force that Churchill had assembled. For the first two years of the war, it sought to avoid a clash involving the entire fleets of both nations. It attempted to draw only parts of the British fleet into battle, hoping to diminish it piecemeal until such point as rough parity was achieved and Germany could challenge for control of the North Sea. It never succeeded. In 1916, the German fleet finally entered the North Sea in force, but the action was taken in the expectation that it would take some of the lightly armored battle-cruiser squadrons (commanded by Churchill's former naval secretary, Vice Admiral David Beatty) unawares, overwhelm them, and escape back into the Baltic before the rest of the British fleet could arrive. The plan met with initial success. Beatty's squadron was subjected to a tremendous barrage from the German fleet. Three of his best ships were destroyed, along with almost all the lives of the ships' companies.

The tide turned when suddenly the German fleet discovered that it was being fired upon by the big guns of four *Queen Elizabeth*–class oil-fueled superdreadnoughts, which it never expected to arrive on the scene so quickly. It was a ferocious battle. Casualties were heavy on both sides, although Britain suffered the most losses. Nevertheless, the German fleet was eventually forced to run for its ports in the Baltic. The Kaiser's High Seas Fleet never again challenged Britain for control of the North Sea. Although the battle was fought to a draw, Britain had attained its strategic objective, and thus the Battle of Jutland is considered a victory for the Grand Fleet, Winston Churchill's creation.

By that time, both Churchill and Fisher had left the scene. They had clashed bitterly during the failed Dardanelles campaign. When Fisher resigned in protest, his action forced Churchill to leave as well. Years later, Churchill was to hail the results of Jutland to defend his farsighted decisions as first lord of the admiralty, citing no less an authority than Admiral Tirpitz himself, who acknowledged that the speed of the superdreadnoughts had turned the tide. Churchill was to command a battalion in the trenches of France before returning to rebuild his shattered political career. He was to return to the loftiest heights of power before falling again, as he took on his familiar role of watchful defender of his country, alert to dangers of a rearmed Germany.

When, at length, his foresight was proved again with Nazi Germany's invasion of Poland, Neville Chamberlain sent for him and offered him his old command, first lord of the admiralty. And all the British ships at sea flashed the signal, one to another, "Winston is back."

PATENT NUMBER 174,465

In 1832, Samuel Finley Breese Morse sailed home from Europe on the packet *Sully*. He was a gifted artist with a growing reputation for portrait painting. While a far from wealthy man, he was politically active and well connected socially. As a student at Yale, he had shown little enthusiasm for subjects other than art, except for a particular interest in the embryonic science of electricity, an interest he had avidly maintained. Naturally, he was pleased to discover that Dr. Charles T. Jackson, a noted American physician and scientist, had also booked passage on the *Sully*. Jackson shared with Morse his excitement over the latest European experiments in electricity.

In 1820, French physicist André-Marie Ampère had established the theoretical relationship between electricity and magnetism. In 1825, British scientist William Sturgeon had invented the electromagnet. Sturgeon fashioned a seven-ounce piece of iron into a horseshoe shape and ran a current of electricity through a coil wrapped loosely around it. The current magnetized the coil, which Sturgeon demonstrated by

using the seven ounces of iron to lift a nine-pound iron bar. When Sturgeon cut the current, the magnetic field disappeared. A few years later, an American inventor, Joseph Henry, demonstrated the potential application of powerful electromagnets to communicate over long distances by transmitting an electric current through a mile's length of wire to an electromagnet, causing a bell clapper to strike.

In conversation with Morse, Jackson said these experiments confirmed Benjamin Franklin's discovery that "electricity passes instantaneously over any known length of wire."

Morse is reported to have responded by asserting, "If the presence of electricity can be made visible in any part of the circuit, I see no reason why intelligence may not be transmitted instantaneously by electricity."[1]

The idea of an electric telegraph had been proposed before, but Morse, his extraordinary imagination fired by his conversation with Jackson, conceived of its limitless potential. "If it will go ten miles without stopping," he thought, "I can snake it to go around the globe."[2] While still on board the *Sully,* he began to sketch drawings that led to his first prototype telegraph in 1937 and the alphabet he coded as numbers of electric impulses.

Alfred Vail, the son of a wealthy industrialist, happened to observe

Morse's slow and impractical invention and was enthralled by the machine's potential. He quickly formed a partnership with Morse, arranged for his father to finance their enterprise, and, as he was a more accomplished mechanic than Morse, began improving Morse's crude prototype at the family's Speedwell Ironworks in Morristown, New Jersey. On January 6, 1838, Morse and Vail successfully tested their latest model, transmitting an electric current through two miles of wire to an electromagnet that pulsed the coded message "A patient waiter is no loser." Morse, who had initially used numeric codes to represent words in a telegraphic dictionary, soon devised a simpler approach: an alphabet that used codes for each letter. Controversy over who really invented the Morse code, Morse or Vail, has endured for years. But Vail never challenged Morse's authorship claim and, in fact, testified to Morse's work on the coded alphabet in a letter to his father in 1838.

They spent the next few years refining their invention and demonstrating it to influential audiences in Boston, New York, Philadelphia, and Washington. Morse took on other partners, including an influential congressman, and by the time he filed the first patent for his telegraph in 1840, Vail's share of the partnership had been reduced to 8 percent. Morse managed to secure a congressional appropriation in 1843 to construct the first experimental telegraph line between Washington and Baltimore. On May 24, 1844, Morse sent a message, "What hath God wrought," from the chamber of the Supreme Court to the B&O Railroad depot in Baltimore, where Vail received and transcribed it.

Vail supervised the building of additional telegraph lines and was responsible for some of the telegraph's most important early innovations. Morse concentrated a good deal of his efforts on promoting his invention to receptive audiences in the United States and Europe and on securing additional backers and government support for an extensive telegraph network. By 1846, telegraph lines ran from Washington to Baltimore, Philadelphia, New York, Boston, and Buffalo.

In 1848, Vail received a modest salary as superintendent of the Washington and New Orleans Telegraph Company. Late that year, he wrote Morse from his office in Washington that he intended to return to New Jersey: "I have made up my mind to leave the Telegraph to take care of itself, since it cannot take care of me . . . and bid adieu to the subject of the Telegraph for some more profitable business." Morse devoted much of his time to suing upstart telegraph companies for patent infringement. He held all patent rights to his telegraph, even those for inventions that were credited to Vail. In 1854, the U.S. Supreme Court upheld his patent claims, and all American companies using his system were obliged to pay Morse royalties. He became an immensely wealthy man, who gave generously to many charities, helped found Vasser College, and remained rich and famous until his death in 1872.

In 1850, fifty separate telegraph companies were in operation and were soon to be paying Samuel F. B. Morse royalties. A relative latecomer to the industry that seemed to boom overnight, the New York and Mississippi Valley Printing Telegraph Company was founded in 1851 by a group of Rochester, New York, investors, led by Hiram Sibley, to operate a telegraph line from upstate New York to St. Louis. Initially, the New York and Mississippi Valley did not rely on Morse's patents but used instead a device built by a Vermont inventor, Royal E. House, that electrically imprinted letters, rather than Morse's dots and dashes, on tape. Almost immediately, Sibley's company began buying up competitors in the chaotic and proliferating industry, and it reincorporated five years later as the Western Union Telegraph Company, with licenses to use both the Morse and House patents.

Western Union intended to establish a monopoly west of the Hudson River. With the completion of the first transcontinental telegraph line in 1861, it was well on its way. During the Civil War, both Union and Confederate armies relied on the telegraph to communicate orders and information between commanders in the field and their respective governments. They considered telegraph lines nearly as invaluable to the war effort as railroads and took care to protect and extend them. In 1866, Western Union introduced the first stock ticker. That same year, the first successful transatlantic telegraph cable was laid by the iron-hull SS *Great Eastern* carrying 2,300 nautical miles of heavy copper and steel cable, and the ever-accelerating information revolution that continues to this day began to shrink the world.

The company had grown from a half-million-dollar business at its inception to a forty-one-million-dollar corporation ten years later. In 1870, it started a service to standardize time in the United States, and the next year introduced transfer of money by wire, which eventually became its primary business. By the late 1870s, Western Union was the largest corporation in the country, boasting 212,400 miles of telegraph lines carrying thirty million messages per year to 8,500 telegraph offices. It carried on its books fifty-five million dollars in assets, and it owned a one-third stake in its principal manufacturer, the Western Electric Company. William Vanderbilt, son of the railroad titan Cornelius, was its largest shareholder, and William Orton, a former teacher and bookstore owner, was its powerful president.

In 1876, a Boston patent lawyer, Gardiner Greene Hubbard, offered to sell to William Orton for the sum of one hundred thousand dollars the patents to a device his son-in-law had invented. Orton is reported to have declined the offer with the tart observation, "What use could this company make of an electrical toy?" leaving Hubbard little choice but to promote the device, the telephone, on his own. Two years later, Orton ruefully observed to associates that he would gladly pay twenty-five million for the patent, were he offered it again.

The telegraph had changed the world. But it is in the nature of human beings, whether motivated by native curiosity, compassion, or commercial opportunity, to search ceaselessly for innovations in even the most revolutionary technology. Such endeavors lead, inevitably, to the invention of technologies that render obsolete the marvelous invention that had first attracted their interest and labor. The man or woman who comprehends distant possibilities propels science, commerce, and human experience toward the unclaimed future. Gardiner Hubbard was such a man, as was his son-in-law, Alexander Graham Bell.

Bell was born in Edinburgh, Scotland, in 1847 to a family of renowned elocutionists. His grandfather, Alexander Bell, had limited success on the British stage before earning distinction as an orator and "celebrated Professor of Elocution," who specialized in correcting speech defects. His two sons, Alexander Melville and David, shared his profession, and Melville's eminence as a speech teacher eventually exceeded his father's. Melville fell in love with and married Eliza Grace Symonds, a talented pianist ten years his senior, whose deafness inspired her husband's greatest accomplishment. In 1864, he devised a physiological alphabet, "Visible Speech," using symbols to represent the position and movement of the throat, tongue, and lips as they produced sounds. Bell employed his system as a means to instruct the deaf how to speak and how to read the speech of others. He is rumored to have been the model for Professor Higgins in George Bernard Shaw's *Pygmalion.*

Melville Bell supervised his three sons' training as elocutionists. His second son, Alexander Graham, who had inherited his mother's musical bent, used his father's conception of visible speech to excel in his own right as a teacher of the deaf. Young Aleck had also shown early promise as an amateur inventor but was more adept at conceptualizing inventions than actually producing them. He lacked the dexterity and mechanical proficiency to manufacture elaborate practical applications of his theories.

Bell's fascination with the mechanics of speech led to his exploration, at nineteen, of the relationship between vowel sounds and musical notes. Holding tuning forks in front of his open mouth, Bell vocalized vowels and learned that each one consisted of two pitches, and that in a given sequence one will rise while the other falls. His delight in the discovery led him to the research of a German physicist, Hermann von Helmholtz, who had already noted the phenomenon. As Bell told the story, his unfamiliarity with the German language resulted in a "very valuable blunder." Helmholtz had devised the means of reproducing vowel sounds by running an intermittent electric current to an electromagnet situated near tuning forks, which it caused to vibrate. Struggling to read Helmholtz's German, Bell concentrated on the illustrations the physicist included in his book *On the Sensations of Tone.* He concluded mistakenly that Helmholtz had transmitted vowels by telegraph. Helmholtz had made no such claim, but Bell later claimed that had he understood that, "I might never have commenced my experiments."[3] Bell's inaccurate conclusion excited him. He assured friends that the day was fast approaching when speech and music would be transmitted by telegraph, and he began his own experiments with telegraph equipment, electromagnets, and tuning forks. His ear for music and skill as a pianist, inherited from his musical mother, aided his experimentation and planted the idea that telegraphy could be greatly improved if a means could be devised to transmit more than one message at a time through a single wire, using differently pitched electric currents.

The death from tuberculosis of his two brothers and Alexander's own poor health convinced Melville Bell to move his family to North America. They settled in Brantford, Ontario, in 1870. The following year, Alexander moved to Boston, where he accepted teaching positions in quick succession at the Boston School for Deaf Mutes, the Clarke School for the Deaf, and the American Asylum for the Deaf in Hartford, Connecticut, before opening in late 1872 his own School of Vocal Physiology in Boston.

A leading center of learning, Boston welcomed into its elite circle of scientists and inventors the young teacher, whose use of his father's system of visible speech was producing astonishing results among his deaf pupils. He was offered and accepted a position as a professor of speech at Boston University in 1873. His exposure to the latest advances in science and technology excited his renewed interest in developing a mechanism to telegraph multiple sounds simultaneously, as did another Boston inventor's success in building a duplex telegraph.

Bell resumed work on his "harmonic telegraph" in a borrowed laboratory at Massachusetts Institute of Technology, using instead of tuning forks flexible metal strips like organ reeds, which an electromagnet caused to vibrate and produce multiple and differently pitched signals. He also began experimenting with an undulatory current rather than an intermittent one. The former could convey amplitude as well as pitch as it varied in intensity, just as sound disturbs the density of the air. Bell conceived of the notion that an electric current could conduct the vibrations of a multitude of reeds activated by a human voice to a receiver at the other end of the circuit, which, through the vibrations of its own reeds, would reproduce the voice.

The apparatus required to pick up and reproduce all the frequencies of the human voice, which Bell called a harp transmitter, was seeming too large and complex to work reliably. But a fortuitous occurrence offered a potential remedy. Bell was shown a new invention at MIT, the phonautograph, a device similar to an ear trumpet with a membrane stretched over its mouth, which was connected to a stylus. When a person spoke into the trumpet, it vibrated the membrane, which caused the stylus to etch the sound wave onto a piece of glass. It was essentially a rudimentary facsimile of the human ear, with the membrane acting as the membrane of the eardrum, which moves by vibration the bones in the inner ear.

The invention inspired Bell to interrupt his work on the harmonic telegraph and experiment with a more accurate and smaller-scale facsimile of the inner ear, which could form the basis of a less cumbersome mechanism to conduct and receive speech. A diaphragm with one magnetized reed in its center vibrating sympathetically to the sound of a human voice could, he reasoned, replace all the reeds in his harp transmitter and transmit audible sounds by vibrating a membrane in the receiver. "At once the conception of a membrane speaking telephone became complete in my mind," Bell explained, "for I saw that a similar instrument to that used as a transmitter could also be employed as a receiver."[4] Bell continued his experiments during a summer holiday at his parents' home in Ontario. He returned to Boston with the first sketches of the invention that was to make him famous.

Charles Williams's machine shop in Boston was a popular attraction for inventors of the day. Renowned for their skills, Williams's mechanics were adept at working with budding and established inventors. Thomas Edison was a frequent customer, as were many other well-known inventors. In the summer of 1874, Alexander Graham Bell hurried into Williams's shop, eager to find an assistant who possessed the dexterity Bell woefully lacked. He grabbed the first man he encountered, the rough, uneducated, profane, but unusually bright Thomas Watson and, after enthusiastically explaining his conception, convinced the young mechanic to help him construct his harmonic telegraph. It can be fairly said of Bell that he was favored by fortuitous happenstance. In no other instance was this truer than in his chance meeting with Thomas Watson. Watson, for all his coarse ways, was not only a gifted mechanic but as enthusiastic and nearly as bold a conceptual thinker as Bell.

Through his work with the deaf, Bell met Gardiner Hubbard, whose daughter, Mabel, was one of Bell's students and his future wife, and Thomas Sanders, a wealthy leather merchant in Salem, Massachusetts, and father of another of his students. Both men admired Bell and were impressed with his experiments. They agreed to provide him financial support in exchange for a share of the patent rights to the harmonic telegraph. Hubbard, a patent attorney, particularly understood the need for the device, as Western Union, stringing wire across the country, had become overwhelmed by the volume of telegraphs waiting to be transmitted over its lines one at a time.

Bell shared the results of his acoustic experiments with Watson, who was equally captivated by the idea of transmitting human speech by wire. They had labored in the attic of Charles Williams's shop on several different harmonic telegraphs, none of which had worked as well as they had hoped. Both men wanted to set the device aside to begin work in earnest on Bell's new idea. Watson later recalled, "Had his harmonic telegraph been a well-behaved apparatus that always did what its parent wanted it to do, the speaking telephone might never have emerged from a certain marvelous conception that had even then been surging back of Bell's high forehead for two or three years."[5]

Hubbard, however, insisted that a market existed for the harmonic telegraph, while it was uncertain what profitable use could be made of a telephone. Both Bell and Hubbard knew that another inventor who worked for Western Union, Elisha Gray, was working on a multiple transmitter, and Hubbard urged Bell to finish and patent his harmonic telegraph as quickly as possible. Bell rushed to Washington in February 1875 to file patent applications for his invention, only to find that Gray had already filed applications for his transmitter. However, the technology Bell had used differed in important respects from Gray's invention, and on that basis Bell was granted two patents. While in Washington, Bell took the opportunity to meet with Joseph Henry, the physicist whose powerful electromagnet had once inspired Samuel Morse and who now served as president of the Smithsonian Institution. Bell discussed with Henry not only the harmonic telegraph but also the idea that he could not let go of, the telephone. Contrary to the sentiments of Bell's financial backers, Henry grasped the genius of the young inventor's conception and offered him two words of advice: "get it."

Four months later, on June 2, 1875, as Bell and Watson still struggled to perfect their harmonic telegraph, fortune intervened again. While Bell worked at the tedious chore of tightening the receiver's tuning screws, Watson, in another room, pulled at a metal reed that had stuck to the transmitter's electromagnet. Suddenly Bell, holding the receiver to his ear, heard a sound quite different from any other he had heard over wire. The reed Watson had plucked, tightened in its contact screw, vibrating near the pole of the magnet, had acted as a diaphragm and induced an undulating current that varied in intensity and reproduced an audible twang at Bell's end. They tested their accidental discovery repeatedly through the course of the day, always achieving the same result. Bell left Watson with instructions to fashion the speaking telephone he had sketched the previous summer, using lambskin membrane as a diaphragm. They tested the invention the next evening, after Williams's mechanics had left for the day. When Bell sat at the receiver, he failed to hear Watson two floors below speaking into the transmitter. When they changed places, Watson claimed he could faintly hear the sound of Bell's voice but not well enough to distinguish the words he spoke. Watson theorized that Bell's voice was easier to hear because of its deeper resonance and that his own hearing was more acute than Bell's. They worked to resolve the problem of unintelligible, one-way communication until Bell went to Ontario later that summer. They resumed perfecting the device when he returned in September. In the course of their experiments, they determined that partially submerging a wire in a conducting liquid improved its ability, when vibrated by the sound waves of the human voice, to vary in intensity and produce an undulating current.

Bell had alerted Hubbard to their discovery before he left for Canada, and Hubbard finally grasped the invention's importance, even if he remained uncertain about its commercial application. Neither Hubbard nor Saunders had received any return on their investment in the harmonic telegraph. Funds had run low, and Bell had to return to teaching to cover his personal expenses, which would soon multiply after he married Mabel Hubbard, to whom he proposed in November. The strain of work caused his chronically fragile health to decline. Still, working with his accommodating assistant late into the evenings after a full day of teaching, Bell labored through the fall and winter of 1875 to complete his marvelous conception.

Sensing that success was imminent—and also, no doubt, the close approach of Elisha Gray, who was again working on a similar invention—Bell traveled to Washington the next February to file a patent application for "the method of, and apparatus for, transmitting vocal or other sounds telegraphically, as herein described, by causing electrical undulations, similar in form to the vibrations of the air accompanying the said vocal or other sounds, substantially as set forth." He arrived just hours before Gray. Both men were well aware of each other's work. The society of American inventors in the nineteenth century was a small and largely transparent one. Bell knew that Thomas Edison was also working on a telephone, as was an Italian immigrant, Antonio Meucci, who was, in fact, the first person to invent a telephone but not the first to file a patent application. Though Gray obviously felt motivated by Bell's obsession to conduct similar experiments, both he and Edison lacked Bell's appreciation for the importance of his discoveries. In 1875, Gray wrote to his attorney, "Bell seems to be spending all his energies on [the] talking telegraph. While this is very interesting scientifically, it has no commercial value."[6]

On March 7, 1876, Bell received U.S. patent number 174,465 for his "improvements in telegraphy," considered to be the most commercially valuable patent ever granted. It was to expire in seventeen years. Three days later, Bell and Watson were back at work on the patented invention, with Bell at the transmitter and Watson at the receiver when Bell uttered, or so legend has it, his famous cry, "Watson, come here, I want you." Reportedly, Bell had spilled on himself some of the battery acid he was using as a conducting liquid, and his appeal for help was inadvertently transmitted over the wire and received by Watson in another room. Historians understandably find the account dubious. Neither man recorded the incident in the meticulous daily logs they kept. Further, it seems a rather sedate reaction from someone who had just been burned by battery acid. Even a gentleman would be forgiven for using stronger language to describe such an accident. Yet, whatever transpired between them on that fateful day, Alexander Graham Bell and Thomas Watson had succeeded in making their telephone work, and the events the discovery then set in train would, as Bell had envisioned, change the world utterly.

On June 25, Bell took his invention to the Centennial Exhibition in Philadelphia, where a stunned emperor of Brazil, Dom Pedro II, held a receiver to his ear and remarked excitedly, "I hear. I hear," as Bell, on the other end, exclaimed a Shakespearean soliloquy. Word of the astonishing discovery began to spread. Bell and Watson staged many other public exhibitions in Canada and the United States, the most successful of which was a call placed from Salem to Boston over twenty miles of borrowed telegraph wire. They installed their first telephone for free in Charles Williams's shop and ran the first dedicated telephone line over the first telephone pole to Williams's home. Within a year, two hundred other customers leased Bell's telephones. Over the next two months, the number tripled. Most of Bell's early customers were businessmen who could afford the expensive leases and who appreciated an alternative means of communication, which didn't require them to employ the services of a skilled telegraph-key operator. By 1878, five thousand phones had been leased.

Still, the telephone's commercial application was uncertain. Initially, all telephones operated over private lines, limited to connecting just two phones over relatively short distances. The public exhibitions Bell and Watson gave emphasized the telephone's use as a broadcasting system. Bell would read from Shakespeare, or Watson from the newspaper. Occasionally, a singer was employed to demonstrate the invention's facility in conducting complex arrangements of musical notes and tones over wire. All that changed with the establishment of the first central switchboard in New Haven, Connecticut, in 1878, with twenty-one subscribers. Other cities quickly opened their own switchboards. In Hartford, Connecticut, a famous early subscriber thought the invention both marvelous and vexing. He eventually wrote a satire of a telephone conversation, as well as a letter to the "father-in-law" of the telephone, Gardiner Hubbard, to complain that Hartford's switchboard closed at night and that his service was frequently interrupted when he used it to practice cursing. He signed the letter with his pen name, Mark Twain.

Gardiner Hubbard deserves the lion's share of the credit for developing the business plan that was to make him and his partners very wealthy men. Initially, he had organized the Bell Patent Association with Bell, Sanders, and Watson, promising to share any profits that might result from a successful patent application. Watson, for his invaluable part in the telephone's invention, received a 10 percent share. In July 1877, Hubbard drafted the contract that established the Bell Telephone Company, which issued five thousand stock shares to Bell, Mabel, Hubbard, his wife and brother, Sanders, and Watson. With little operating capital with which to expand their business, Hubbard devised a system to license their patent to local agents, who agreed to construct transmission lines and switchboards and install the telephones to subscribers they served on a geographically exclusive basis. Most important, all telephones installed by local licensees were to be leased, not purchased, from the parent company.

For the first years of the company's existence, all its telephones were manufactured exclusively in Charles Williams's shop, perhaps out of gratitude for his early involvement and his willingness to accept frequently late payments from the chronically strapped company. This arrangement maintained the company's control of the industry and fueled its rapid expansion without requiring the company to invest immense capital. It provided the company with a reliable revenue stream, if not, initially, huge sums of capital. The whole enterprise, of course, depended on Bell's firm hold on his patents. If the patents were infringed, wealthier challengers would quickly overrun Bell's business and drive it into bankruptcy. This proposition was to be sorely tested in the years ahead.

None of this would have occurred had William Orton not turned down Hubbard's offer in 1876. Before the establishment of the first switchboard, Hubbard worried that the partners might never be able to market the telephone as anything more than a novelty or to find the backing to develop the industry's infrastructure. The one hundred thousand dollars he hoped to obtain from Orton would repay the investment of Thomas Sanders, who had yet to recoup a single dollar. And he made the proposal confident that should Western Union purchase the patent, the telegraph company would offer well-compensated positions to the telephone's inventors and their partners.

Understandably, Orton's rejection of the offer is considered one of the greatest business blunders in history. But Orton was not a stupid man. On the contrary, he was a man of proven executive ability who had risen from modest beginnings to run the largest corporation in the country. He had overseen the company's immense expansion, bought or destroyed virtually all its competition, and had authorized the purchase of a controlling stake in its own manufacturer, Western Electric, which had been founded by Elisha Gray.

He was an impressive man, and he had good reason to believe that he saw the future of his industry clearly. After all, the company he led was as great and entrenched in his day as Microsoft is today, maybe more so. But he could not foresee the value of any invention that did not improve the business that had made him wealthy. A harmonic telegraph would have interested him, and he had employed Elisha Gray to invent one. But he could not make the leap to grasp that there could exist an entirely new system of communication, which would compete with and eventually supplant the telegraph. The telegraph had been operating profitably for forty years, but in Orton's mind it was still in its infancy, and the astonishing growth it had experienced would be exceeded in the years ahead. Yes, the telephone offered the immediacy of the telegraph. So what? Why invest enormous capital in developing a new communications industry that would do only what the telegraph had already succeeded in doing, obliterating time and space with instantaneous communication? Hubbard failed to see that the telephone offered potential customers things the telegraph didn't: intimacy, ease of operations, and instant two-way communication.

Alexander Graham Bell, of course, was not a businessman. He was a teacher of the deaf with an ear for sound, a talent for conceptual thinking, and the amateur inventor's enthusiasm for the limitless wonders of science. When chance discoveries seized his imagination, he acted. He was not concerned with improving a corporation's bottom line but only with refining his conception and finding the means to make it real.

He married Mabel Hubbard in 1877, and the couple left on an extended European honeymoon. While in London, Bell tried to find British investors who would purchase the rights to his patent. Toward that end, he drafted a prospectus that contained a memorable paragraph expressing a vision of the telephone's utility that had eluded William Orton.

It is conceivable that cables of telephone wires could be laid underground, or overhead, communicating by branch wires with private dwellings, country houses, shops, manufactories, etc., etc., uniting them through a main cable with a central office where the wires could be connected as desired, establishing direct communications between any two places in the city. . . . Not only so, but I believe in the future wires will unite the head office of the Telephone Company in different cities, and a man in one part of the country may communicate by word of mouth with another in a different place.[7]

That vast difference in conception affected the relationship between Bell and Western Union years after Orton had passed on Hubbard's offer. It didn't take Hubbard long to realize he had made a mistake by offering the patent to Orton. Orton authorized purchase of the rights to both Elisha Gray's and Edison's telephones and, with his company's own patents pending, formed subsidiary telephone companies to compete with Bell. Edison soon invented a new transmitter that was greatly superior to Bell's, using a carbon diaphragm and battery-induced current rather than a voice-activated one, sparing its users the necessity of speaking so loudly to make themselves heard on the other line that they, or so the joke went, frightened the horses in the streets outside their homes.

Bell and Hubbard's patents were to expire in 1893, and both men knew they must challenge any infringement immediately or watch their business be destroyed by the capital and infrastructure advantages of their huge competitor. By 1879, Western Union claimed the greater share of the telephone-exchanges market in New York and Chicago. But Bell's place in the struggle would be limited to using his knowledge and speaking ability to serve effectively as the company's witness in the coming trials to defend his patent. Watson served as the company's first head of research and development in what could be fairly described as the precursor to the legendary Bell Telephone Laboratories, devoting considerable time to inventing a call bell to obviate the necessity for a user to thump the transmitter to alert the person on the other end of the line to the call. Hubbard and Sanders would organize the company's full response to the daunting challenge posed by Western Union.

Sanders approached a group of wealthy New England investors and convinced them to join Bell's directors in forming the New England Telephone Company, which would soon merge with Bell and provide the parent company with much-needed capital to expand into a nation-wide licensing company. Hubbard persuaded a talented railway-mail superintendent, Thomas Vail, to become Bell's first general manager, ignoring his superior's warning that he was abandoning a promising career with the post office for the uncertain rewards of a struggling telephone company. (Vail was a distant relative of Samuel Morse's disappointed associate, Arthur Vail.) Vail's first act as general manager was to send a copy of Bell's patent to every Bell agent and exhort them to fight against encroachments from any competitor. "We have the original patents," he assured them. "We have organized and introduced the business and do not propose to have it taken from us by any corporation." Vail also recognized that were the company to expand to generate the capital it desperately needed, it would have to contract the services of additional manufacturers. Williams's shop could not possibly keep pace with the demands for phones the company now envisioned.

Another improved transmitter, equal to or even superior to Edison's device, was offered to Bell by its inventors. Watson recognized its effectiveness and recommended its purchase. Reorganized as the National Bell Telephone Company after the merger with the New England Telephone Company, Hubbard, Sanders, and Vail were now prepared to join the battle in earnest. They were game, if seriously overmatched. Bell could claim a net worth of less than half a million dollars at the time, while Western Union, backed by the Vanderbilts, boasted nearly one hundred times its capital. But they had sufficient sums to hire competent legal representation to complement the confident assurances of their star witness that his invention deserved to hold exclusive right to his patent.

Western Union began offering telephone service in Massachusetts, Bell's first and most important market. National Bell Telephone filed suit on September 12, 1878, charging Western Union's American Speaking Telephone Company and Elisha Gray with patent infringement. Bell, as expected, proved a compelling witness. Moreover, Gray could not provide any documentation to prove he had been developing his own telephone prior to his application for a patent. Bell produced logs and other documents testifying that he had conceived of the idea for a working telephone as early as 1874. Before a judgment was rendered, Western Union agreed to a settlement with National Bell.

The reasons for the giant company's surprising decision were several. Bell's testimony and much of his case convinced Western Union that its competing claim was weak. Still, the company had the means and strength to protract the litigation for years, if it so chose. But the company also had to worry about the threat posed by the notorious and dogged financier Jay Gould, a perennial Vanderbilt rival, who controlled a competing telegraph company and had proposed an alliance with Bell. Most important, the settlement they negotiated with Bell seemed to serve the telegraph company's immediate interests, protecting its primary business. Western Union could argue, if it so chose, a stronger claim for its Edison transmitter and challenge Bell on this and other grounds, but it decided to forbear. Under the terms of the settlement, Western Union abandoned the telephone business and assigned all its telephone patents to National Bell. In return, Bell would provide Western Union with a 20 percent royalty on all telephones it leased. Moreover, Bell agreed not to use its local telephone exchanges, which were generally restricted to a fifteen-mile radius from the central switching office, "for the transmission of general business messages, market quotations, or news for sale or publication in competition with the business of Western Union."[8] Thus, the settlement appeared to divide the telecommunications market between Bell, which would gain control of local markets, and Western Union, which improved its dominance in the lucrative market for long-distance service.

Western Union had made what appeared to all concerned to be a sound business decision. Western Union's president, Norvin Green (William Orton had died the year before), expressed his satisfaction that the company had escaped "a bitter and wasteful competition."[9] But, in fact, Western Union had again failed to grasp the real challenge Bell posed to its business. No concession could be won from Bell that would prevent its becoming not just a successful competitor but the master of an entirely new market, from which Western Union had now withdrawn.

Immediately after the settlement was announced, Bell's stock doubled and continued its rapid growth and corresponding accumulation of wealth, under the able leadership of Thomas Vail. In 1881, National Bell bought a controlling interest in Western Electric, which became the principal manufacturer of telephone equipment. By 1887, 167,000 Bell telephones were serving markets in every city in America, and each user paid Bell handsomely for the privilege. For the next eighteen years, Bell would fight and defend lawsuits from six hundred competing claimants. It won every single one, thanks in large part to the testimony of Alexander Graham Bell, who never failed to win over the sympathies of juries.

When Bell's patents expired, scores of competing telephone companies sprang up, many of which soon claimed important markets from Bell. J. P. Morgan, as a principal investor in the company, stepped in to rescue Bell's monopoly by employing his usual business tactics, confronting competitors with a choice between selling to Bell or being destroyed. After another round of mergers in 1885, the company organized a subsidiary company, the American Telephone and Telegraph Company, AT&T, which eventually became the holding company for the entire Bell enterprise. In 1909, Vail convinced AT&T's directors to purchase its old rival, Western Union, from Jay Gould's son and heir, George.

Both Bell and Watson had tired of the business many years before. The pressure of endless litigation and their disinterest in the complexities of operating a huge business encouraged them to pursue other interests. Bell continued inventing new technologies, which, had the telephone not overshadowed his every future accomplishment, themselves would have earned him considerable fame. He resided in Washington, where he continued his work with the deaf, founded the leading scientific journal, *Science,* and succeeded his father-in-law as president of the National Geographic Society. Occasionally, the company they had founded asked Bell and Watson to reprise on special occasions their old roles as the instrument's inventors. Vail concentrated his efforts on developing Bell's long-distance business, a risky but ultimately profitable venture.

In 1915, Bell agreed to inaugurate the company's introduction of coast-to-coast service by placing a call from New York to his old friend Watson, in San Francisco. Bell had long ago abandoned the hope that the greeting he and Watson had used—"hoy," not "hello"—would become the standard exchange between two telephone users. Yet he persisted in using the greeting himself. "Hoy, hoy, Watson," Bell called.

"Hoy, Bell," Watson replied. Then the two old friends dispensed with the script the company had written for them and conversed for twenty-three minutes as if they were any other two friends catching up after a long separation.

These two men had together invented one of the most disruptive technologies of all time. What they had unleashed all those years before from the attic of Charles Williams's machine shop changed human communication forever. Bell had glimpsed the future, but even he could not foresee all of his discovery's implications. The telephone was to create scores of new industries and destroy scores of others that failed to comprehend Bell's vision.

Western Union, the first of those disadvantaged companies, had to rely on wire transfers and other businesses it developed to sustain its profitability. The telephone had killed the telegraph, though it continued in ever-diminishing use for decades. In a press release in 2006, the company announced with regret that "Western Union will discontinue all Telegram and Commercial Messaging services," finally surrendering to the fate that Alexander Graham Bell, teacher of the deaf and amateur inventor, had known was inevitable when a leading man of commerce had dismissed his invention as a toy.

TURNING POINT

The turning point came too late for Chris Gueffroy. In the dark early morning of February 6, 1989, near the Britz Canal in East Berlin, the twenty-year-old waiter and a friend attempted to cross the Berlin Wall. They mistakenly believed that the standing order for East German border police to use deadly force to prevent escapes had been relaxed. As they climbed a metal fence, guards opened fire. Gueffroy was hit ten times, sustaining a mortal wound to the heart. Though seriously wounded, his friend survived and was sentenced to three years in prison for attempting to cross the border illegally. The guards received government commendations. To encourage their strict attention to duty, border guards were rewarded for shooting escapees. Guards who failed to stop an escape attempt were often imprisoned. The families of victims were instructed not to publicize the deaths of their loved ones. The official report noting the cause of death was changed from "shot in the heart" to "heart injury." Nevertheless,

Gueffroy's family saw to it that a notice of his death was published in the newspaper.

The Berlin Wall was first constructed in 1961 to halt the huge migration of Germans from the oppression and deprivations of the Soviet-controlled sector of Germany to the political freedom and economic opportunity of the west. In its twenty-eight-year history the Wall had been reconstructed on several occasions, evolving from a simple wire fence in 1961 to an imposing complex, completed in 1980, of thirteen-foot-high reinforced cement barriers, metal fences, barbed wire, a well-lit no-man's-land between fence and wall called the "death strip," antivehicle trenches, 302 watchtowers, and twenty bunkers that stretched ninety-six miles from the center of the city to the Berlin suburbs. One thousand East Germans are believed to have been killed while attempting to cross it. Chris Gueffroy was the last victim. Nine months after an AK-47 round had pierced his heart, tens of thousands of East and West Germans swarmed to the Wall and jubilantly knocked down, piece by piece, the entire gross impediment to liberty. Two men very different from each other, whose decisions had led to the stunning event, watched it on television. Both of them had seen it coming, one considerably earlier than the other.

In June of 1982, Leonid Brezhnev was secretary-general of the Soviet Communist Party. Soviets troops were in Afghanistan. Cuban soldiers were in Angola. Six months before, the communist regime in Poland had declared martial law and imprisoned the leaders of Solidarity. The buildup of Warsaw Pact conventional forces in Europe begun in the seventies had given the east a three-to-one quantitative advantage over NATO. More alarming, the Soviets had deployed a new intermediate-range ballistic missile, the SS-20, which had greater range, accuracy, and power than their existing SS-4s and SS-5s. NATO relied on theater nuclear weapons to counter the Soviet's advantage in conventional forces. The deployment of SS-20s undermined the strategic balance. To restore it, NATO planned to deploy in Europe nuclear-armed cruise missiles and the Pershing II intermediate-range ballistic missile. The decision sparked widespread public protests in the west and the beginning of the nuclear-freeze movement, which believed that improvements to NATO's deterrent capability needlessly increased east-west tensions and made a nuclear-weapons exchange in Europe more likely.

NATO and the Soviet Union had entered into negotiations in 1981 to limit nuclear arsenals in Europe, but the new American president, Ronald Reagan, had insisted on what his administration referred to as the "zero-zero" option, which proposed the complete elimination of NATO's Pershing IIs and nuclear-armed cruise missiles in exchange for the complete elimination of Soviet SS-20s, SS-4s, and SS-5s. The proposal was dismissed by the advocates of a nuclear freeze and many eminent foreign-policy "wise men" in the west as unserious and unattainable. American-Soviet arms-control negotiations had never produced an actual reduction of nuclear arms but had sought to place ceilings on future increases. President Reagan's stubborn insistence on the proposal was viewed by his many critics as further proof that the old man lived in a black-and-white Hollywood dreamworld, where an honest man could always do the right thing and good always triumphed over evil, rather than in the dark-gray realities of the Cold War, where American presidents were expected to reside. More unnerving, he didn't seem terribly affected by their disapproval. They mistook him for a fool.

His approach to arms control was of a piece with his conviction that another, better world was achievable in our lifetimes, a world in which American interests were better secured and American ideals, which represented the natural aspirations of mankind, were ascendant in the darkest corners of tyranny. A romantic idyll, his critics scoffed. The consensus shared by many western statesmen and foreign-policy analysts held that the Soviet Union and its empire, whatever the deficiencies of its economic and political system, was a powerful and stable adversary, and the balance between the superpowers an enduring one. American policy concentrated on maintaining that balance, not risking its disruption with schemes conceived in a fantasist's dreams of a brighter tomorrow.

Yet it was an unrepentant Ronald Reagan who took the podium in the Royal Gallery of Westminster Palace in June of 1982 to share with the British Parliament and the world his confidence that the time had arrived to move beyond containing the Soviet threat. He spoke of the terrible danger, unknown in centuries past, of global annihilation posed by the nuclear arsenals of the two superpowers and of the doctrine of mutually assured destruction upon which the strategic balance between east and west rested.

What, then, is our course? Must civilization perish in a hail of fiery atoms?
Must freedom wither in a quiet, deadening accommodation with totalitarian evil?

No, he assured the world, "It may not be easy to see; but I believe we live now at a turning point."

In an ironic sense Karl Marx was right. We are witnessing today a great revolutionary crisis, a crisis where the demands of the economic order are conflicting directly with those of the political order. But the crisis is happening not in the free, non-Marxist West, but in the home of Marxist-Leninism, the Soviet Union. It is the Soviet Union that runs against the tide of history by denying human freedom and human dignity to its citizens. It also is in deep economic difficulty.... The constant shrinkage of economic growth combined with the growth of military production is putting a heavy strain on the Soviet people. What we see here is a political structure that no longer corresponds to its economic base, a society where productive forces are hampered by political ones.

He was convinced that the great Soviet empire had begun its inevitable decline and that a resolute west led by a determined United States should act to accelerate it. He did not wish to sound "overly optimistic," he said, and then proceeded to make the claim that was to cause sober-minded solons in the capitals of the western world to wonder whether his was just empty rhetoric or if he was simply intellectually incapable of understanding the realities of the world.

The Soviet Union is not immune from the reality of what is going on in the world. It has happened in the past—a small ruling elite either mistakenly attempts to ease domestic unrest through greater repression and foreign adventure, or it chooses a wiser course. It begins to allow its people a voice in their own destiny. Even if this latter process is not realized soon, I believe the renewed strength of the democratic movement, complemented by a global campaign for freedom, will strengthen the prospects for arms control and a world at peace. . . .

The march of freedom and democracy will leave Marxism-Leninism on the ash-heap of history as it has left other tyrannies which stifle the freedom and muzzle the self-expression of the people.

And so, he argued, "let us be shy no longer. Let us go to our strength. Let us offer hope. Let us tell the world that a new age is not only possible but probable." In an overdue nod to reality, his critics argued, he recognized that efforts to achieve such an improbable vision "will long outlive our generation." But he was intent on starting the project now, on his watch.

The only part of his prediction that proved inaccurate was the last qualification. Few others would have dared believe that the Soviet regime would collapse several generations hence. *Time* magazine's report of the speech included the observation, "To some listeners, Reagan sounded as if he were predicting imminent Soviet economic collapse—a view with which many of the most pro-American NATO leaders emphatically disagree."[1] Reagan's assessment of the Soviet Union's structural weaknesses was mocked by eminent western Sovietologists, many of whom, when less than a decade later he was proved correct, did not have the grace to credit the old man for his wisdom. They attributed the empire's collapse to the very weaknesses he had described and they had underestimated, and they declared these forces would have produced the same result whether or not Ronald Reagan had ever been elected president.

"The Soviet Union is not now nor will it be during the next decade," wrote professors Seweryn Bialer and Joan Afferica, "in the throes of a true systemic crisis, for it boasts enormous unused reserves of political and social stability."[2]

What did Reagan see that his critics did not? What was the basis for his convictions? His beliefs were not uninformed, as his detractors assumed. He saw the economic, political, and ideological hollowness of the Soviet system better than they did. He knew they were nearly bankrupt and tremendously overstretched. They had the largest military in the world. While the United States had reduced its forces after the Vietnam War, the Soviet Union had added four hundred thousand men to its armies. But the Soviets were falling far behind in the development and application of high technology to their weapons systems. Reagan's first order of business upon becoming president was to initiate a huge buildup of American defenses, increasing military spending by 25 percent in each of the first two years of his presidency. With the almost nonexistent growth produced by its inherently flawed economic system, the Soviets would be hard pressed to keep up. The drain of men and resources into Afghanistan and the incessant demands for economic support by its vassal and client states were taxing Moscow's ability to maintain the status quo, much less rise to the challenge of a reinvigorated and rearming adversary. Reagan sensed their exhaustion and, in it, the west's opportunity to upset the strategic balance, which had been the patient and disciplined work of nearly forty years of statecraft, and win the Cold War.

It was that knowledge that informed his vision, but it was something else that gave it its power. Ronald Reagan had risen from modest beginnings to prosper and enjoy a comfortable and purposeful life and to eventually, at a late age, become the president of his country. And throughout his life he credited America, the country where anyone with initiative and a little luck could succeed as he had, for the opportunities he had enjoyed and the meaningful life he had lived. To him it was beyond dispute that liberty, equal justice, and free markets—the American creed—were indispensable to successful societies, and thus a system conceived in their antithesis, where the individual and all his works was subordinate to the state, would inevitably fail. And if that antithetical system posed a threat to our own, then it must be made to fail. And so he set about to do it.

Even before his Westminster speech, President Reagan had made clear that he saw the future differently than most and would seize what opportunities he could to hasten its arrival. In 1981, he assured the students and faculty of Notre Dame, "The West won't contain communism. It will transcend communism. It will dismiss it as some bizarre chapter in human history whose last pages are even now being written." And less than a year after the Westminster speech he delivered his famous (or infamous, depending on your perspective in those days) "evil empire" speech to the National Association of Evangelicals in Orlando, Florida, in which he accused the Soviet regime of being "the focus of evil in the modern world." And he closed his remarks by quoting Tom Paine: "We have it within our power to begin the world over again."

That stunned the cognoscenti and was denounced as empty name-calling at best, and at worst a dangerous provocation sure to worsen superpower relations. That his message was welcomed by the millions of oppressed people suffering under Soviet domination seemed to matter less. Reagan was not without allies, two of the more important of whom were the redoubtable Margaret Thatcher and the Polish pope, who was intent on using his pontificate to help liberate his fellow Poles. But to many critics, Reagan's assault on the rhetorical conventions of Cold War statecraft and what they assailed as his blustering Manichean worldview were cause for great alarm in a world where two rival superpowers had the power to destroy the earth many times over. What alarmed them more was his refusal to limit his advocacy to the stagecraft of his presidency, at which even his harshest critics conceded he was unusually gifted. He was intent on speaking his mind, and he was just as intent on backing his words with action. And this, in their view, augured nothing but ill for reducing tensions between east and west and for any hope of progress in the preferred theater for détente, arms-control negotiations.

The Reagan strategy to destabilize the Soviet empire was laid out in the National Security Decision Directives he signed over the course of eight months in 1982 and 1983. The first was NSDD-32, signed by the president on May 20, 1982, which authorized the United States "to neutralize the efforts of the U.S.S.R. to increase its influence" by, among other efforts, providing covert assistance to anti-Soviet groups in eastern Europe, particularly the Solidarity labor union in Poland. Since Lech Walesa had led striking shipyard workers in Gdansk in August

1980, Solidarity's popularity had grown to threaten the very legitimacy of the Communist Party's supremacy in Poland. The Kremlin, worried that the challenge would spread to other eastern European satellites, had urged the Polish government of General Wojciech Jaruzelski to put an end to it. Martial law was declared on December 31, 1981. President Reagan was outraged and insisted on an American response that would both punish the Soviets and help Solidarity in its moment of greatest need. NSDD-32 provided the basis for several years of covert support to a movement, in the center of the Soviet empire, dedicated to its destruction. Three weeks after he signed it, Reagan met in the Vatican with Pope John Paul II to discuss their mutual plans to support the forces of freedom in His Holiness's homeland.

Reagan signed NSDD-66 on November 29, 1982, which established "the security-minded principles that will govern east-west economic relations for the remainder of this decade and beyond." It made the disruption of the Soviet economy—by denying it financial support, access to high technology, and international assistance to complete a natural-gas pipeline—the stated goal of U.S. policy. The National Security Council aide who drafted it, Roger Robinson, described it as "tantamount to a secret declaration of economic war against the Soviet Union."[3]

NSDD-75 was signed on January 17, 1983, two months after Leonid Brezhnev's death and the succession of the ailing Yuri Andropov to the leadership of the Soviet Communist Party. NSDD-75 committed the United States to not simply containing but reversing Soviet expansionism by, among other things, promoting "the process of change in the Soviet Union toward a more pluralistic political and economic system."

The economic sanctions imposed on Moscow were important, and none more so than the U.S. attempt to prevent completion of the huge natural-gas pipeline the Soviets were building. Although opposition from western Europe allies to Reagan's efforts to prevent the transfer of western technology to the project eventually prevailed, the Reagan administration managed to delay its completion for two years. More devastating to the Soviet economy, however, was the president's successful effort to lower the price of oil by working with the Saudis to hugely increase supply. Oil generated 80 percent of the Soviet Union's hard-currency earnings. When the price of oil dropped from thirty dollars per barrel in 1985 to twelve dollars per barrel, the effect on the Soviet economy, which was already approaching zero annual growth, was devastating.

The Reagan Doctrine, a term coined by columnist Charles Krauthammer, was used to describe the administration's material support for indigenous guerrilla movements in Third World Soviet client states, such as Afghanistan, Nicaragua, and Angola. That support was important, particularly in Afghanistan, where the war was a huge burden for the Soviets. But it was just a part of Reagan's strategy. And while western skeptics of the strategy were dismissive, in Moscow they understood its potency. Yevgeny Novikov, a senior staff member of the Soviet Communist Party Central Committee, recalled, "There was widespread concern and actual fear of Reagan on the Central Committee. He was the last thing they wanted to see in Washington."[4]

Consequently, the Soviets resorted to ever harsher denunciations of the United States and the reckless cowboy who led it, in an attempt to exacerbate western anxiety that Reagan was provoking by his brinkmanship a dangerous confrontation between east and west. In 1983, the Soviet news service, Tass, declared Reagan was gripped by a "bellicose, lunatic anti-communism." Two weeks before his death, Brezhnev told an audience of Soviet generals that Reagan was conducting a policy of "adventurism, rudeness, and undisguised egoism" that would, if unchecked, "push the world into the flames of nuclear war."

After a Soviet MiG shot down a commercial Korean airliner that had strayed into Soviet airspace on September 1, 1983, relations between the superpowers appeared to have reached their nadir. Reagan rightly denounced the shootdown, which caused the deaths of sixty-one Americans, among others, as a "crime against humanity." Andropov accused the U.S. government of trying to provoke war and violating "elementary norms of decency." *Time* magazine, which made Reagan and Andropov its men of the year for 1984, cited Soviet comparisons of Reagan to Adolf Hitler and Andropov's declaration that Reagan had dispelled "all illusions" that the policy of détente could be sustained while his administration remained in office. The Soviets walked out of negotiations in Geneva to limit nuclear forces in Europe and refused to resume negotiations on strategic nuclear limitations and conventional-force reductions.

The escalating hostility in Soviet rhetoric and diplomacy succeeded in further distressing much of the western public but had less of an effect on the president it was intended to dissuade. Despite widespread public protests, the first cruise missiles arrived in England in November 1983, and the following month the first Pershing IIs were deployed in West Germany. Even more distressing to the Soviets and his critics in the west was Reagan's televised address earlier in the year, on March 23, 1983, announcing a new defense policy, the Strategic Defense Initiative (SDI). The United States, he declared, intended to develop an antiballistic missile system that would render "nuclear weapons impotent and obsolete." For obvious reasons, SDI became the chief focus of Soviet concern and diplomacy. Although a strategic missile defense was never completed or deployed, the initiative became the most successful element of Reagan's strategy to win the Cold War. In time, it convinced a new and considerably more enlightened Soviet leader that the Soviet Union could not prevail in an arms race with the United States and that its initial attempts to do so had accelerated its demise and rendered its empire unsustainable.

A feature of much criticism in the west of Ronald Reagan's statecraft was his failure to engage Soviet leaders personally beyond the occasional exchange of letters. Summits between American and Soviet leaders, which typically concluded with the signing of agreements worked out weeks in advance, were believed to offer the best opportunity to overcome impediments to greater cooperation. Détente thrived on summitry, yet in the first term of the Reagan presidency, no summits had been planned. Responding to criticism that he was intentionally rejecting a valuable tool of Cold War diplomacy, Reagan shrugged off the suggestion by noting that Soviet leaders "keep dying on me." Yuri Andropov died of kidney failure in November 1984 and was succeeded by the also ailing Konstantin Chernenko, who died a little more than a year later.

In Chernenko's successor, Ronald Reagan believed he had a Soviet leader with whom, in the words of Margaret Thatcher, he "could do business." Only fifty-four years old, energetic, with a quick wit and an engaging personality, Mikhail Gorbachev offered a stunning contrast to the dour, stodgy bureaucrats who had long typified the Soviet Politburo. Born in 1931 to a peasant family and raised near the city of Stavropol in the famine-stricken North Caucasus, he had had a tough childhood. Both his grandfathers had been victims of Soviet repression. Stavropol was occupied by the German army in World War II, and his father had been gravely wounded in the war. Mikhail was a bright and industrious student, and he worked alongside his father on a collective farm. In 1949, for his work in bringing in a record crop, he received the Order of the Red Banner of Labor and was admitted to Moscow State University to study law the following year. He joined the Communist Party in 1952 and after graduating in 1955 married fellow student Raisa Maximovna Titorenko, with whom he had one child, a daughter, Irina.

He rose quickly through a succession of party posts. In his student days and his first years as young party apparatchik, he showed the appropriate respect for the cult of personality created by the ruthless and paranoid Joseph Stalin. He was a genuinely committed and earnest communist. But he had enough realism about the inadequacies and inequities of Soviet life, developed in his own experiences as a child of the collective, not to embrace official propaganda as an invariably accurate portrait of society. Like other members of his generation, Gorbachev was surely impressed by Nikita Khrushchev's denunciation of Stalin at the party's twentieth congress in 1956 and welcomed the limited and short-lived openness in Soviet life that followed. One assumes, also, that he was disappointed when repression returned in force after Khrushchev's fall from power.

In 1970, he was appointed the first secretary for the Stavropol region, and the following year he became a member of the party's Central Committee. He moved to Moscow in 1978 and became a member of the Politburo two years later, the youngest member in Soviet history. He was a protégé of Yuri Andropov, the former head of the KGB, who appreciated Gorbachev's intelligence and political and administrative skills. Although Andropov himself remained a member in good standing of the old order, he was an intelligent man who despised the endemic corruption of the Brezhnev years. He recognized the need for an energetic reformer with a reputation for honesty to modernize the exhausted Soviet economy and the decrepit institutions of Soviet power, and he groomed Gorbachev to succeed him. After Andropov's death, the party could not yet bring itself to trust the supreme office in the land to a young man whose instinct for reform might threaten their privileges; it turned instead to the trusted apparatchik, Chernenko. But the next year, the decay of the Soviet state and the challenge of the Reagan administration convinced even the more obdurate Politburo members that something must be done to revitalize the economy and government and that someone must be found who could compete on the world stage with the determined former movie actor who was driving them to despair. So they turned to Mikhail Gorbachev. They could have had no idea what that was going to bring about.

Gorbachev surely never set out to destroy communism and the Soviet empire. On the contrary, he intended to make necessary changes, even radical ones, to modernize the economy and government because he believed they were essential to preserve the party's leadership of the Soviet Union and its satellites in an enlightened and more effective form. He began immediately, purging from the Central Committee, Politburo, and ministries officials he judged incompetent and corrupt or who would pose an obstacle to his reforms. His economic and political reforms were limited at first, but they were real, and just the beginning. Even he could have had no idea what would come from his "new thinking."

When Gorbachev assumed office, he shared the general Soviet view of Reagan as an implacable foe and warmonger. But he knew also that Reagan's strategy was effective. So he brought his flair for public relations to diplomacy and relations with the United States. He sought an accommodation in which he would offer real arms reductions in exchange for the United States' agreement to abandon its plans for a strategic-defense system. Toward that end, he announced in April 1985 that the Soviet Union would suspend its deployment of SS-20s in Europe, and in September he proposed a 50 percent reduction to the nuclear arsenals of both superpowers. Two months later, he met Reagan in Geneva.

No agreements had been worked out in advance. And the Geneva summit did not produce any. Gorbachev's offer of serious arms reduction, as attractive as it was to Reagan, could not dissuade him from pursuing his dream of rendering nuclear weapons obsolete. Reagan insisted that no hostile intentions were behind SDI. Gorbachev dismissed the assurance: "It's not convincing. It's emotional. It's a dream. Who can control it? Who can monitor it? It opens up an arms race in space."⁵ He countered with an assurance that the Soviets would never launch a first strike against the United States, which Reagan declined to accept on trust.

Yet despite the fruitlessness of their negotiations, the two leaders got on remarkably well. Reagan had greeted his guest outside, standing coatless and smiling in a sharp wind, looking vigorous, elegant, and in command. Gorbachev had emerged from his limousine, quickly doffed his hat, and bounded up the stairs to greet his host. Their first meeting occurred beside a roaring fire in a lakeside mansion borrowed by the American side for the occasion. It was expected to be a brief welcoming encounter, lasting no longer than fifteen minutes before the respective delegations joined them to begin the hard and detailed negotiations. Reagan had told his aides that he wanted more time for personal diplomacy and not to interrupt them until he told them to. The meeting, billed as the fireside summit, lasted more than an hour, and despite their unresolved differences both men emerged with considerably warmer feelings for each other. They later strolled alone along the lake and talked informally. Reagan did not shrink from raising every disagreement between their two governments, including those over Afghanistan, Poland, and human rights, particularly the refusal to allow Jews to emigrate. He did it in his usual genial but determined manner, and Gorbachev did not respond with the indignant lecture on the subject Americans expected from Soviet leaders. And despite the failure to come to terms on arms-control issues, the two men agreed to work toward a 50 percent reduction of strategic arms and agreed to another summit in Washington the following year. Reagan was confident that the summit would ultimately prove to have been an important success. "The real report card," he promised, "will not come in for months or even years."

Although he and Gorbachev had had sharp exchanges in private and in the presence of their aides, Reagan later remarked how impressed he had been with Gorbachev's willingness to listen and to consider seriously the U.S. point of view. "There was warmth in his face and his style," he later remembered, "not the coldness bordering on hatred I'd seen in most senior Soviet officials I'd met until then."[6] Gorbachev allowed to associates that Reagan had struck him as a more congenial and open-minded person than he had been led to expect.

In the months following the summit, the press lamented that the "spirit of Geneva" was in danger of being lost. The Soviets announced a moratorium on nuclear tests, and Gorbachev urged the United States to do likewise. The proposal was welcomed by many, including senior Democrats in Congress. Reagan, who knew that testing was necessary to ensure our existing weapons were reliable, refused. The Reagan administration also announced in 1986 that because of Soviet cheating, the United States no longer felt obliged to abide by the terms of the unratified SALT II. Gorbachev dispatched former Soviet ambassador to the United States Anatoly Dobrynin to inform the president that the U.S. moves had jeopardized the promised Washington summit. Reagan paid little heed to the threat, recognizing it correctly as "game-playing," and wrote in his diary that "my feeling is the summit will take place, if not in June in July, sometime after the [U.S. congressional] election."[7]

The summit was more seriously threatened by several unexpected events. Soon after Reagan had returned from Geneva, the Iran-Contra scandal was discovered, and the administration became the target of congressional and special-prosecutor investigations. Two weeks after the Dobrynin meeting, U.S. Air Force and Navy bombers struck Tripoli and Benghazi in retaliation for Libya's involvement in a terrorist bombing of a West Berlin nightclub in which an American serviceman had been killed. Ten days later, the Chernobyl nuclear reactor outside Kiev exploded. The Soviet government's handling of the crisis bore little trace of glasnost, and Gorbachev was soon consumed with his own scandal.

Despite these multiple distractions, Reagan sent a "sweeping new arms reduction proposal to Gorbachev," which called for the complete elimination of all ballistic missiles, while both sides would continue research on defensive systems and commit to jointly deploy any system that proved effective.[8] Not unexpectedly, Gorbachev dismissed the idea, as did the American foreign-policy establishment, as "an attempt at upholding the pretense of a continuing dialogue."[9] Few believed an American president would seriously offer such a proposal.

The last breach in superpower relations occurred on August 30, when the Soviets arrested an American reporter, Nick Daniloff, in retaliation for the FBI's arrest of a Soviet spy working at the United Nations, and announced that they were going to try him for espionage. In Reagan's own words, the arrest made him "mad as hell."[10] For the next several weeks, the Daniloff affair preoccupied U.S.-Soviet relations. The Soviets offered to release him if the United States would release their spy. Reagan refused. On September 12, Reagan offered to release the Soviet agent, who did not have diplomatic immunity, to the custody of the Soviet embassy, where he could await a trial, if Moscow immediately released the American reporter. The Kremlin had no immediate reaction to the offer. On September 17, the Soviet ambassador was notified that the United States intended to expel twenty-five suspected KGB agents stationed at the UN unless it received immediate notification that Moscow intended to release Daniloff.

Two days later, Soviet Foreign Minister Eduard Shevardnadze arrived in Washington and met with the president. Shevardnadze brought with him a letter from Gorbachev in which the Soviet leader did not mention Daniloff or offer a response to Reagan's earlier letter but proposed an impromptu twenty-four-hour meeting in either London or Reykjavik, to see if further arms-control progress was possible. The meeting would be a presummit to prepare for the Washington summit if both sides agreed that was still worthwhile. There would be no formal agenda and no intention to reach any final agreements. Reagan refused to accept the offer until Nick Daniloff was freed. According to his diary, he took the opportunity to complain about the arrest and "give [Shevardnadze] a little run down on the difference between our two systems." He recalled, "I enjoyed being angry."[11]

After another two weeks of back-and-forth negotiations, Moscow and Washington finally reached an accommodation. Daniloff was to be released, along with an imprisoned Soviet dissident. In exchange, the Soviet spy was to be tried quickly and deported to Moscow. The matter resolved, the administration accepted Gorbachev's offer of an informal summit and recommended Reykjavik as the venue, since it is closer to equidistant from Washington and Moscow than London is. The meeting was scheduled for October 11, 1986. When it was over, Reagan summed up the experience and his feelings thusly: "My hopes for a nuclear free world soared briefly, then fell during one of the longest, most disappointing—and ultimately angriest—days of my presidency."

In his last CIA briefing prior to the meeting, the president was informed, "Gorbachev's strategy requires keeping a lid on current defense spending in order to modernize the economy and allow it to compete more successfully with the U.S. over the long haul." The great utility of SDI was its influence in convincing Gorbachev that the Soviet Union could simply no longer afford the Cold War, and to bring it to an end it would have to become a changed power in every respect. Scholars argue over how important SDI was to the conclusion of the Cold War and the collapse of the Soviet empire, but it strikes me as beyond doubt that this welcome outcome of east-west rivalry would not have arrived as expeditiously as it did had not Reagan remained so committed to finding some better means to protect the world than the deterrent effect of mutually assured destruction.

"Reagan's SDI was a very successful blackmail," remembered Gennady Gerasimov, the Soviet Foreign Ministry spokesman at the time. "The Soviet economy couldn't endure such competition."[12]

SDI was more than blackmail to the man who most sincerely advocated it. Reagan knew that it served his strategy to exploit Soviet weaknesses, and he believed that "the Soviet economic tailspin would force Mikhail Gorbachev to come around on an arms reduction agreement we both could live with."[13] But his support for SDI was rooted more in his genuine revulsion at the fact that the Cold War balance of power rested on so terrible a threat. Ronald Reagan was more genuinely dedicated to the idea of a world without nuclear weapons than the most ardent nuclear-freeze proponent. While his critics on the left and in Moscow saw him as captive to the military-industrial complex, he saw the world as a brotherhood of man, in which people were either well or poorly served by their governments, but all of whom shared in their hearts the same values, the same aspirations for peace, freedom, and prosperity.

In an irony lost on the antinuclear movement, the wisest critics of Reagan's vision of a world free of the terror of nuclear weapons were on the right. Nuclear weapons were necessary to compensate for the Warsaw Pact's huge advantage in conventional forces, they argued. Peace had been maintained for decades by their deterrent effect. Without such weapons, what threat could so surely restrain the Soviets from initiating a war? But the man whom the left saw as a B-movie gunslinger had a dream of peace—an unrealistic one, perhaps, but a sincere one. And he believed that anyone who shared the same terrible responsibility he possessed must in his heart feel a kinship for that dream.

Gorbachev came to Reykjavik to tempt Reagan with his own dream. And for moment, as Reagan himself recorded, his hopes soared.

The American side arrived in Reykjavik expecting only to prepare the ground for a successful Washington summit. Gorbachev's purpose, according to an aide, was "to sweep Reagan off his feet with our bold, even risky approach to the central problem of world politics."[14] Their first meeting began at 10:40 in the morning, in a modest guesthouse provided by Iceland's government. Only interpreters and note takers were present for that first exchange. After an hour, they were joined by their foreign ministers, George Shultz and Eduard Shevardnadze. Gorbachev handed Reagan a written draft of his "bold" proposal, offering to reduce each side's strategic arsenal by 50 percent and to eliminate entirely intermediate-range missiles in Europe, leaving aside France and Great Britain's own arsenals: the zero-zero option Reagan had initially proposed. In exchange, the United States would agree to adhere strictly to the Anti-Ballistic Missile Treaty for ten years and to refrain from testing all "space-based elements of anti-ballistic missile defenses in space."[15]

It was, indeed, a bold proposal, and it stunned the American side. Even the most stalwart hawks in the American delegation were impressed, none more so than the president, but he balked at the last condition. He had not come to Reykjavik to use SDI as a bargaining chip. Gorbachev repeated his offer. Reagan insisted that SDI was intended for pacific purposes, and a ten-year moratorium on developing it was unacceptable. He believed, incorrectly, that a strategic-defense system could be developed and deployed far sooner than that. He again assured Gorbachev that strategic defense would never be used to win a nuclear exchange with the Soviet Union and repeated his offer to share the technology with the Soviets.

"We're not in a press conference," Gorbachev responded. "There's no reason to speak in banalities." He acknowledged that the Soviet Union lacked the resources to develop a system of its own, so their response would "not be symmetrical but asymmetrical." As for Reagan's offer to share the technology with them, he was contemptuous. "I cannot take your idea . . . seriously. You are not willing to share with us oil well equipment, digitally guided machine tools, or even milking machines. Sharing SDI would provoke a second American revolution! Let's be realistic."[16] Reagan held firm. But both men authorized their delegations to work through the night to see if the agreement for sweeping reductions could be negotiated.

Many people would be surprised to learn that Reagan insisted on being personally involved in negotiations that were so comprehensive and detailed. The conventional view of Reagan was of a genial, big-picture leader (less charitably, a naïve and lazy one) who was disengaged from complex and difficult discussions. He might not have possessed a technocrat's grasp of all the arcana of arms-control negotiations, but he had self-confidence in his skills as a negotiator and a reverence for his historical responsibilities. And unlike most statesmen, he did not fear entering into important negotiations without agreements in hand that had been worked out in advance. His periods of silence, which others often mistook for disengagement, might have been strategic. In a perceptive column, *Washington Post* columnist Meg Greenfield described Reagan's decision-making process as reflecting the skills he learned in labor negotiations as president of the Screen Actors Guild. He arrives with a set of core convictions, patiently waits out his adversary's attempts to shake him free from them, and then, in the final hour, yields something attractive to the other side "but that can be interpreted as furthering the original Reagan objective."[17]

In the morning, American negotiators reported to the president that they were close to achieving genuinely breathtaking agreements: the complete elimination of intermediate-range missiles in Europe and a 50 percent reduction in strategic weapons. Thrilled, Reagan believed that "literally, a miracle is happening."[18] Reagan and Gorbachev rejoined the negotiations after breakfast and agreed to delay their departures in the hope that a final agreement could be achieved that would stun the world as much as it had stunned the delegations.

In fast, almost chaotic discussions, the two leaders drove the delegations to the brink of Reagan's dream of nuclear abolition. They first reached agreement on the elimination of the missiles in Europe. The Soviets would be allowed to keep one hundred intermediate-range missiles east of the Ural Mountains, targeted at Asia, and the United States an equal number for Asia, based in Alaska. All others would be eliminated. When Reagan explained that NATO would have to retain some tactical nuclear weapons to counter the Warsaw Pact's larger armies in Europe, Gorbachev offered to negotiate deep reductions in their conventional forces as well. An agreement for a 50 percent reduction in strategic arsenals appeared within reach. But when Gorbachev again insisted on a U.S. commitment not to test a ballistic-missile defense, Reagan again attempted to persuade him of the security such a system would provide both sides. Neither man budged but agreed that talks should continue. The principals left the negotiations while their aides searched for some way to square the circle.

With Reagan's approval, the American side proposed to restrict research, development, and testing of SDI to the terms of the ABM Treaty for five years, during which time strategic arsenals would be cut in half. During the following years, both sides would continue reducing all ballistic missiles until they were completely eliminated. At that point, both sides would be free to introduce defensive systems. When the two leaders resumed negotiations, the Soviets countered with an offer to substitute "strategic offensive arms" for "offensive ballistic missiles," which would include all nuclear weapons. Finally, they offered to allow testing of a defensive system, but only in the laboratory. The prohibition of space-based testing would remain. Both leaders engaged in yet another round of futile attempts to persuade the other, while suggesting arms-reductions agreements that envisioned the impossible. Reagan told Gorbachev he could commit to the abolition of all nuclear weapons.

"We can do that," the Russian responded.

"Let's do it," Secretary of State Shultz interjected.[19] But neither man would relinquish his position on SDI.

The American side offered to accept the Soviet proposal only if the word "laboratory" was omitted. Gorbachev refused. "One word, one lousy word," Reagan lamented. Unexpectedly, an agreement to rid the world of the terror of nuclear annihilation was literally within his grasp. Such an agreement would have provoked enormous controversy in the west, as it would have ceded conventional-force superiority to the Soviets. Reagan was sincere in his desire to achieve it, but not at the cost of SDI. Gorbachev referred to Reagan's refusal to trade SDI for an agreement as "some invisible force [that] suddenly stayed the President's hand."[20] It was hardly invisible. He had insisted from the beginning that SDI was not a bargaining chip. Gorbachev had simply failed to believe it. Even in a world of drastically reduced nuclear arms, future threats could arise from other nations. To Reagan, SDI was a hedge against the possibility that someday leaders who did not share his and Gorbachev's commitment to peace might threaten the world with these terrible weapons, and he had a commitment to his country to ensure that it was adequately defended.

"I am asking you to change your mind . . . so hopefully we can both go out and bring peace to the world," Reagan pleaded.

"I can't do it," Gorbachev responded. "But if we could agree to ban research in space, I'd sign in two minutes." With that, both men and their associates ended the discussion and prepared to leave. No one outside the room, even other staffers, had any idea what had happened. As Reagan and Gorbachev emerged, Reagan told his staff there would be no joint statement. In full view of the press, Gorbachev told him he was "sorry it didn't work out. I don't know what else I could have done."

"You could have said yes," a bitterly disappointed Reagan retorted.

It would be a while before the press and the world knew the details of just how close the two superpowers had come to monumental agreement, but the stern look on Reagan's face and a press briefing by a dispirited Secretary Shultz clued them in that something remarkable had been attempted and failed. On Air Force One, Reagan was disconsolate. He had nearly had it in his power to "begin the world over again," and it had slipped out of his grasp. He did not doubt that he was right. But he grieved over the chance that had been lost.

The chief of staff of the Soviet armed forces, Marshal Akhromeyev, who had come to Reykjavik to ensure that Gorbachev, eager for an agreement that would reduce Soviet defense spending so he could get on with economic restructuring, did not sacrifice the interests of the military. He had a more optimistic view of what had been achieved. "This was a great moral breakthrough in our relations," he observed, "when both sides looked far into the future." Gorbachev, too, in the press conference he held in Reykjavik after Reagan had departed, remarked, "Reykjavik was not a failure. It is a breakthrough, which allowed us for the first time to look over the horizon." Soon Reagan, who had left Reykjavik dejected, would recover his optimism, seize the opening glimpsed at Reykjavik, and confidently return to using his presidency as a force to remake the world.

Gorbachev, although he had not accepted Reagan's assurances regarding SDI, returned to Moscow confident that Reagan was genuine in his commitment to peace between the superpowers. And he argued to his Politburo that SDI should not prevent the Soviets from coming to an agreement that would reduce the necessity of spending money they could not afford in a race they could not win. Within one year of Reykjavik, both sides signed an agreement in Washington to eliminate intermediate-range missiles in Europe, the first actual reduction of nuclear weapons in history.

Gorbachev's visit to Washington was an enormous public-relations success as well. Americans were impressed by the engaging modern politician, so unlike his predecessors, who amiably walked the streets of their capital shaking hands and kissing babies. No less impressed was the American president, the old movie actor. He had a professional respect for Gorbachev's adroit political skills. More important, like his fellow citizens he believed in Gorbachev's sincerity as a man of peace.

He had believed that when he went to Berlin six months before the Washington summit, determined to encourage Gorbachev to be the historical figure Reagan believed he wanted to be. Standing before the Berlin Wall, within view of the Brandenburg Gate, Reagan delivered the speech that had divided his advisors, some of whom worried it might risk progress toward superpower accommodation for the sake of an emotional but unrealistic rhetorical flourish. Reagan believed otherwise. He felt sure the moment was at hand to to end the Cold War and the division of Europe. He had organized his government's policies toward that end, and whatever his personal regard for Mikhail Gorbachev, he never wavered from pushing the Soviets into a position where they would, in effect, have to surrender and accept the free world's terms for peace. Now he was intent on reminding his friend that they both had responsibilities to history. "General Secretary Gorbachev," he said, "if you seek peace, if you seek prosperity for the Soviet Union and Eastern Europe, if you seek liberalization: Come here to this gate! Mr. Gorbachev, open this gate! Mr. Gorbachev, tear down this wall!"

What was in it Ronald Reagan that let him see the future, a future few others believed was imminent or possible at all? What gave him the strength to make such hard decisions, to accept disappointment so manfully, to bear criticism so lightly, to confront opposition so confidently? I think it was one thing, one conviction more than any other, a conviction born of his own success. He believed in his country and its values, and he never doubted that America was on the right side of history. That was the task he felt was his historic responsibility, the focus of his leadership of the free world: to impart to Mikhail Gorbachev his faith in the power of liberty. It was the faith that gave him eloquence, allowed him to command the world stage, and made him the man who, in the words of his friend Margaret Thatcher, "won the Cold War without firing a shot." And it gave his friend Gorbachev cause to reflect, "Who knows what would have happened if he wasn't there?"

Reagan was right, both in his faith in freedom and his faith in Mikhail Gorbachev. And he was right in his conviction that the time was at hand to "begin the world over again."

———

MIKHAIL GORBACHEV soon pressed his colleagues to accept deep, unilateral reductions in Soviet conventional forces. He pressed them to withdraw all Soviet forces from Afghanistan, and then from other client states. He pressed them to reduce the commitments to their empire that were bankrupting them. He suggested that it was time to reconsider the

Brezhnev Doctrine, first declared when Soviet tanks crushed the Prague Spring in 1968, that no nation, once forced into the Soviet empire, could ever leave it. He argued that these difficult decisions were economically necessary, that without them there could be no reform, no salvation. He did not intend that the Soviet Union itself would dissolve and the Communist Party would relinquish its leadership of the Soviet state. But the party, the government, the terms of its empire would all have to change if they were to continue to exist at all. When the inevitable came, and he faced a decision whether or not to prevent by force the liberation of eastern Europe, he acted wisely and let it happen.

In Yugoslavia in March 1988, Gorbachev spoke of a new order in Europe: "We are interested in eliminating the divisions of Europe. What we need is an honest and effective policy of good-neighborliness. . . . Economic alliances and cooperation and the gradual advancement towards a common European market are the vital prerequisites for the peaceful future of Europe." And the long-oppressed people of eastern Europe took him at his word. The empire came apart. In Hungary, General Secretary János Kádár, who had partially embraced Gorbachev's call for perestroika and glasnost, had nevertheless failed to satisfy his country's desire for immediate and comprehensive change. He was replaced by Károly Grósz, who legalized opposition parties and began to prepare for open, multiparty elections. Martial law in Poland ended in 1988. The following year, Solidarity was recognized as a legitimate party, and in June elections were held for the national legislature. Solidarity won all but one of the seats in the upper house and every open seat in the lower house. The Jaruzelski government had reserved a majority of the lower house seats for the Communist Party but bowed to the inevitable. Solidarity was the choice of the Polish people, and Jaruzelski agreed to step down and join in a coalition government as a junior partner with Solidarity. A solidarity leader, Tadeusz Mazowiecki, became the Polish premier, marking the Warsaw Pact's first peaceful transfer of power from the Communist Party to a freely elected government.

In May, Hungary announced that it would open its border with Austria and immediately proceeded to do so. On its other border with East Germany, people traveled freely between the two socialist countries. No wall had been necessary to prevent the permanent migration of East Germans, because Hungary had not offered an escape route to the west. Now it did, and the first hundreds of East Germans crossed into Hungary as "tourists," with no intention of ever returning. Some of them were forcibly returned to East Germany, but by August the flow of westbound refugees had grown so numerous that the Hungarian government announced that any East Germans entering Hungary were now free to continue traveling to the country of their choice.

Other eastern Europe regimes in Bulgaria, Czechoslovakia, Romania, and East Germany were appalled and recognized that the course of these events, if unchecked, would soon threaten their regimes. East Germans who had traveled to Czechoslovakia had taken sanctuary in the West German embassy. Three thousand demonstrators in Prague, shouting antigovernment and anti-Soviet slogans, had marked the anniversary of the Soviet invasion in 1968 before club-wielding police had broken them up. Events in Hungary and Poland were sure to exacerbate the situation. Communist leaders looked anxiously to Moscow to make it clear that any further challenges to the Brezhnev Doctrine would not be tolerated. China had briefly tolerated a popular uprising in Tiananmen Square before ruthlessly repressing it in June. The remaining orthodox communist rulers of eastern Europe hoped they could convince Gorbachev that the same sort of response would be appropriate now. But Gorbachev's government made it clear it had no intention of intervening. The Brezhnev Doctrine was dead. In response to the situations in both Poland and Hungary, Moscow had expressed surprise but declared that it was no longer the business of the Soviet Union to dictate how the people of Poland and Hungary governed themselves or what policies they followed.

The man who had supervised the construction of the Berlin Wall in 1961, Erich Honecker, had ruled East Germany since assuming the post of party general secretary in 1971. He intended to remain in charge a good while longer, and he expected the Wall, which the west viewed as a symbol of tyranny, would remain the symbol of the inviolability of the socialist state. He scorned Gorbachev's reforms. A year and a half after Reagan had called for the Wall's destruction, Honecker declared that it would "still stand in fifty or hundred years."

In October 1988, as East Germany prepared to celebrate the fortieth anniversary of its founding, the Honecker regime was experiencing signs of growing popular unrest. Protests by prodemocracy activists were occurring almost weekly in several East German cities. As Honecker awaited the arrival of Mikhail and Raisa Gorbachev, who had agreed to be the honored guests for the anniversary celebration, he supervised plans to keep them removed from any public demonstration. Yet when Gorbachev arrived in East Berlin, he was greeted by enthusiastic crowds chanting, "Gorby, Gorby, help us." Gorbachev knew what Honecker refused to recognize: East Germany could not avoid the changes that were sweeping the empire. The Cold War was ending. In June, he had traveled to Bonn, and in a joint statement with West German Chancellor Helmut Kohl agreed that "the priority task . . . [of] overcoming the disunity of Europe" would be achieved only if the "right of all peoples and states to freely determine their fate" was respected. In an address before the East German Politburo, Gorbachev offered an observation intended for the recalcitrant Honecker: "One cannot overlook the signals of reality. Life itself punishes those who react too late." Before he returned to Moscow, he commented on the country's unrest and the future of the country. "The people themselves decide."[21] And according to the man who was soon to replace Honecker, Egon Krenz, Gorbachev had turned to Krenz and a few other "trusted German comrades" as he prepared to board his flight for Moscow and advised them to "take action."[22]

The end came swiftly. On October 9, two days after Gorbachev had warned him to embrace reform, Honecker prepared for a mass demonstration planned for that evening in the central square of Leipzig. He had met that morning with Chinese Vice Premier Yao Yilin, who presumably had offered his own thoughts about how the regime should deal with popular unrest. Honecker emerged from the meeting to warn that the government would not tolerate any further "attempts . . . to destabilize socialist construction or slander its achievements."[23] He then ordered the East German military to crack down on the Leipzig demonstrators. All that happened next is not known for certain. What is known is that the demonstration proceeded, and fifty thousand East German marched peacefully. East German troops remained in their barracks.

Egon Krenz claims he traveled to Leipzig to countermand personally Honecker's order. He may have, but he is hardly the most reliable source. A Honecker favorite and one of his closest aides, Krenz and his commitment to democratic reform must be viewed as more a matter of opportunism than a genuine change of heart. Many accounts suggest the decisive intervention came from Moscow through the Soviet commander attached to the East German army, who counseled the soldiers not to disrupt the demonstration. Gorbachev is reported to have been in daily contact with the Soviet command in East Germany. Some reports even suggest that Soviet tanks blocked the gates at the East German military compound near Leipzig.

Whatever occurred, Moscow did not intervene to prevent the resulting collapse of the Honecker regime. The next day, the East German Politburo met in emergency session. On October 13, the government released prisoners who had been arrested at earlier demonstrations. On the sixteenth, Honecker's retirement and the elevation of Krenz was announced. Larger and larger prodemocracy demonstrations became an almost everyday occurrence. On November 4, five hundred thousand demonstrators marched in downtown East Berlin demanding freedom. On November 9, the government announced that henceforth East Germans would be free to travel to the west. And with that, it was over. East German authorities might not have anticipated how the new travel decree would be interpreted. But the people of East Berlin had little doubt. They rushed to the Berlin Wall, as their fellow Germans on the other side did the same, and in that carnival of free expression tore it down. Within days, the other communist regimes in eastern Europe collapsed.

On December 3, Mikhail Gorbachev and President George H. W. Bush met on the island of Malta to formally declare the Cold War over. By October 1990, Germany was one country again and remained in NATO. The next year, four months after a coup in which Gorbachev was briefly held under arrest failed, the Soviet Union itself dissolved. Mikhail Gorbachev became a private citizen, which he remains to this day.

He did not anticipate the progression of events that was launched by his commitment to change. But he didn't intervene to prevent it either, and history will richly reward his forbearance. The man who became his partner, Ronald Reagan, who had decided to initiate the bold and controversial policies that hastened the destruction of an evil empire, had seen it all coming, although even he was surprised at the speed with which it happened.

The world he envisioned and which Gorbachev came to accept is not permanently fixed in history yet. Russia today, under a corrupt leadership that shows little regard for the democratic values Reagan assured us were invincible, appears intent on restoring some semblance of an empire—by subtler means if possible, by threats and intimidation if necessary. But a world of free, independent nations at peace with one another remains within our reach, as Reagan, the clear-eyed idealist, believed. We need only have the faith and courage to make it so. Those who doubt it should appreciate how richly ironic history can be and remember the man, mocked as an idle dreamer who didn't believe in walls, who proved to be wise.

TIMING

How many initiatives, causes, products, and proposals have been inaugurated with the sponsor's assurance that it represented "an idea whose time has come"? So many and so frequent are such boasts that were one to take them seriously, it would appear there comes a time for every half-baked notion, worthless consumer item, groundless conceit, and empty gesture. Infinity couldn't accommodate them all. Poor Victor Hugo, who coined the adage "An invasion of armies can be resisted, but not an idea whose time has come." He could never have imagined the invasion of ideas launched in the vain hope they would prove irresistible—and of which it could be unkindly said that the army of Vanuatu, if it has one, would prove harder to ignore.

Timing isn't everything. Quality matters more. But good ideas have often failed because the time was not yet propitious for their introduction, and moments have passed when a sound decision might have seized an important opportunity or averted a disaster. Important decisions, be they personal, professional, or historical, often have proved effective because their authors sensed a moment arriving or passing in which they could do some good: The statesman who sees in contemporary political, social, or military developments forces aligning to create a hinge of history that a decisive action might move in a new and better direction. The entrepreneur who finds evidence that a new market is taking shape and strikes first to meet a demand that even the consumer may not have yet realized exists. The athlete who interprets the slightly delayed reaction, or the ache in his shoulder imperceptible to anyone but him, as signs that his best playing days are over and decides to retire at the peak of his achievements rather than in their shadow.

Like foresight and other attributes of good decisions, correct timing derives from the first quality, awareness. The awareness of a situation that reveals to the potential decision maker a need or opportunity has arisen that others are either unwilling or not yet in a position to address. A crisis occurs that demands an urgent decision, but the decision maker is aware it is not yet so acute that he or she cannot wait for further developments that might ameliorate it or until the information needed to make a sound decision is complete. Or, conversely, the awareness that the crisis will not wait on future events or additional information, and the decision must be made immediately with the information at hand. A sense that the other players involved in making a decision or the people affected, whose acquiescence is essential for the decision's success, are ready or not quite ready to do so.

Supreme Court Justice Felix Frankfurter agonized over the right decision in *Brown v. Board of Education.* A decision that seems to later generations so obviously right was a hard call to him. He abhorred segregation. He was a Jew and a naturalized citizen of the United States who deeply believed in assimilation and "the transforming powers of American culture, especially public education."[1] He was the first justice to hire an African-American law clerk. But then he personally abhorred the death penalty as well and had voted to affirm its constitutionality. He was a "leading apostle of judicial restraint" and vigilant critic of judicial activism. "The Supreme Court to Felix Frankfurter," historian Richard Kluger wrote:

> was hallowed ground, its resources to be spent frugally, never dissipated in hollow proclamations beyond its power to enforce. If the Court was to retain its majesty, it dared not venture where it has no business—onto the battlefields of the legislature and into the backrooms where current policy was carpentered. . . . The Court was to remain above the battle, reaching down to tip the balance only when one or the other side was in open violation of the great organic law of the land.[2]

Stare decisis, respect for the Court's precedents, was important to him but not as important as the right of each American citizen. And so he decided, after painstaking review and reflection, to vote to overturn the Court's *Plessy v. Ferguson* decision and the specious "separate but equal" doctrine it had established, which had been used to justify the segregation of public education.

He was the fifth justice to decide in favor of striking down *Plessy*, with four other justices opposed. The decision then would have been made by the narrowest of majorities. Frankfurter wisely reasoned that were a deeply divided Court to render such a monumentally important decision, it would diminish the authority of the decision in the public's eye. And in the parts of American society where resentment of the decision would be strongest, a closely divided decision would make resistance to its enforcement all the more bitter and sustained. Chief Justice Fred Vinson supported upholding *Plessy*, and his views had influenced three other justices to uphold the precedent. So Frankfurter conceived a "Fabian strategy" of delay and skillfully managed to put off the Court's decision to its next term, after changes in membership might occur and the prospect for a less divided or even unanimous decision would be brighter.

As the Court had yet to take even an informal vote, although all nine justices knew where the majority lay, Frankfurter suggested several questions to be put to counsel for both sides in a reargument of the case. Vinson wasn't in any hurry and was amenable to the suggestion. By the time the Court's next term arrived, Vinson had died, and Earl Warren had been confirmed to replace him. Together, Frankfurter and Warren worked masterfully to produce a unanimous decision to overturn *Plessy*. Frankfurter's keen attention to timing had made the right decision more effective.

Warren wrote the Court's opinion in the case, which ordered the desegregation of public schools "with all deliberate speed." It is hardly surprising that Frankfurter, careful steward of the Constitution, guardian of the values of justice contained therein, and a man with an impeccable sense of timing, had suggested to Warren that he stress the timeliness with which the Court expected its decision to be enforced.

The importance of timing decisions is really just a question of whether they will prove more effective at a certain time than at others. If the decision, as in *Brown v. Board of Education,* will right a terrible injustice whose victims have suffered long enough or settle some other urgent moral question, is the moral imperative greater than the benefits from waiting for circumstances more favorable to the proposed remedy? It takes a wise person to make that call. And wise men like Frankfurter and Abraham Lincoln have chosen the latter course.

In matters less grave, the decision is obviously easier. Does it matter that much if a college student defers a decision on choosing a major or allows herself to be tracked as a premed student only to later discover she would find greater professional fulfillment as an engineer? Probably not, assuming she has not waited until it is too late to make the change, even if it requires an additional investment of time and expense. Wrong decisions that involve only personal considerations are usually correctable before they have done too much damage, and even then the consequences are rarely so grave they cause regret that is insufferable—not in every instance, but in most. Human beings are resilient, and never more so than in unfortunate predicaments we have caused for ourselves and ourselves alone. But for those who make decisions for others, considerations of timing are weighted with much greater import, for a decision delayed or rushed may do harm to others. Regret that bears guilt for failing others is a harder burden to carry. Timing then becomes a much harder thing to decide. Yet history offers innumerable examples of where timing proved to be the critical factor in a decision's success, even when it entailed delays in redressing a grievous wrong. We should weigh carefully the arguments involved in such dilemmas. But in the end, I think one of the most laudatory distinctions awarded to decision makers can be fairly claimed by those who have chosen to wait for the right moment to act: they did the right thing, and their timing was perfect.

THE MASTER STROKE

My staff members had completed their review of the defense appropriations bill for 2002 and had handed me a list of questionable projects that the Appropriations Committee had marked for funding, many of which had not been requested by the Defense Department. This is standard practice in my Senate office for every appropriations bill. Before debate begins, we search for projects of dubious merit, post them on my office website, and select several of them for amendments I offer to strike them from the bill. I routinely lose these amendments by wide margins. Members of Congress from both parties defend the practice of earmarking funds for projects in their districts and states as one of the most prized advantages of incumbency and as important to their re-elections. Seldom is much consideration given to whether a particular pork-barrel expenditure has value to anyone other than the recipient and the member who succeeded in getting it funded. Aware of this, appropriators often go to considerable lengths to hide the item in prosaic language that offers little information about its intended recipient, its sponsors, its real purpose, or which commercial concern would benefit from it.

On this occasion, however, one very large appropriation caught my attention immediately. It provided thirty billion dollars to the Air Force to begin replacing its aging refueling tankers with a new fleet of planes. In the first place, it was not clear to me that the current fleet of tankers needed to be replaced. Many of them had been in service for forty years or more, but I wasn't aware of any studies indicating they were no longer capable of performing their mission. On the contrary, these aircraft, initially built to refuel the country's first jet bombers, the B-47 and B-52, were considered some of the most durable and dependable planes in the Air Force. The B-52 itself, old warhorse that it is, is still in service after fifty years and performing amazingly well. Why did we need to replace the tankers that refueled them? Eventually, the Air Force and the new tankers' advocates on Capitol Hill argued that the current fleet was suffering from corrosion problems. Subsequent investigation proved this to be a deliberately exaggerated concern.

If the corrosion problem was real and urgent, why then didn't the Air Force request the money to replace the fleet in its own budget submission to Congress? That question was the most nettlesome one to me. The Air Force had not budgeted for the new tankers or included them in its "unfunded priorities" list of items that the service would like to have if Congress were to make additional funds available. In this instance, because the Air Force didn't have enough money to buy new tankers, it had proposed, and the Appropriations Committee had agreed, to acquire a new tanker fleet by leasing for ten years up to one hundred planes, converted from commercial use. At the end of the lease, the Air Force would return the tankers to the manufacturer or, presumably, purchase them for some additional figure. The cost of the lease seemed exorbitant to me, and the scheme itself seemed dubious and shrouded in secrecy. If estimates were accurate, the ten-year lease for planes that had a life span of thirty to forty years would cost more than it would to buy them.

I chaired the Senate Commerce Committee at the time and used my authority to subpoena documents related to the proposal from both the Air Force and the defense contractor involved. Also at my request, the Senate Armed Services Committee held hearings to investigate the necessity of acquiring new tankers and the proposed lease, its practicality, its terms, and its genesis. The facts we uncovered led to an investigation by the Defense Department's inspector general and eventually by Department of Justice attorneys. The proposal had originated with Boeing, which worried that the market for its 767s was shrinking, and the Air Force had readily agreed. Hundreds of e-mails between Air Force personnel and Boeing executives exposed a sad tale of government and corporate corruption that eventually led to criminal convictions of the Air Force's chief procurement officer and Boeing's chief financial officer. The investigations also brought about the resignations of the secretary of the Air Force, several of his subordinates, and the president of Boeing.

Obviously, the corruption discovered in the investigation reflected poorly on the Air Force and helped expose the negligence that had become prevalent in Pentagon procurement practices. But it also cast a shadow over a once proud and principled industry leader and marked a precipitous decline, if not in its profitability, in its character. During the same period, Boeing employees were caught and the company fined for stealing documents from its largest competitor, Lockheed Martin. Boeing had long had a sterling reputation for integrity, quality, and bold innovations that kept it in the vanguard of the extraordinary post–World War II expansion of the aircraft industry. For many years, Boeing seemed to anticipate before its competitors the needs of its commercial and government markets and had taken chances to meet those needs without ever compromising its strict standards of quality or corporate ethics. The very aircraft the leased tankers were intended to replace was itself one of Boeing's greatest achievements, the KC-135, better known by its commercial designation, the 707. Its development was one of the proudest moments in Boeing history, and it was the product of one of the two most brilliant decisions made by the company's legendary president and chief executive, William McPherson Allen.

He hadn't wanted the job. He wasn't an engineer like his predecessors, Phil Johnson and Claire Egtvedt. He surely hadn't been an early aviation enthusiast and pioneer like Boeing's legendary founder, Bill Boeing. He was the son of a mining engineer, raised in rural Montana. He wasn't a businessman, although he understood the business. He was a lawyer whose wife had died two years earlier, leaving him with two young daughters to raise on his own.

He was educated at Harvard Law School, where he discovered, he said, that he wasn't as smart as the other students, "so I made up my mind to work all the harder to make up for it."[1] After graduating in 1925, he brought that ethic to the Seattle law firm of Donworth, Todd and Higgins, which served as counsel to the nine-year-old Boeing Company. He eventually became Boeing's chief outside counsel. He was involved in many of the decisions that accelerated the young company's development, eventually oversaw all of its contracts and financing, and had been given a seat on its board of directors in 1931. His friend Phil Johnson died of a cerebral hemorrhage near the end of World War II, and Boeing's directors searched for months for a successor before deciding the company's lawyer was the best man for the job. Stunned and surely flattered, he turned them down anyway. After they urged him to reconsider, he wrote in his diary the reasons for and against the move.

> AGAINST—1) I do not feel I have the qualifications, that's the all-compelling reason. 2) trouble lies ahead. 3) Lack of seniority: if I don't make a success of it. I would resign, then where would I be? 4) Worry. Could I physically stand it? 5) less time with the children. Heaven knows it is little enough now.
> FOR—1) a little greater material return. 2) It would be a new challenge.[2]

The positive side of that ledger hardly seems as compelling as the sound reasons not to take the job. But, in the first of many great decisions, Allen accepted the board's offer and became Boeing's fourth president.

His reference to "little greater material return" wasn't an understatement. His salary was barely larger than it had been at his law firm, fifty thousand dollars. In today's dollars, it would be ten times that, but even so, with chief-executive compensations now reaching stratospheric levels of tens and hundreds of millions of dollars in annual salary, stock options, and other benefits, it seems a rather paltry sum.

Allen's approach to his job might also seem a little antiquated, and sadly so, in today's corporate climate of scandals and ethical corner-cutting, when businesses reinvent themselves as exclusively financial ventures and when management's focus on stock prices crowds out their concern for providing better products to their customers. For too many businesses today, diversification, risk aversion, and mergers are the easiest route to keeping Wall Street happy and increasing the value of shares in the company that are so generously provided to their executives. Though the company has since shown welcome signs of reform, Boeing had at times abandoned the practices that had once made it an admirable as well as an exceptionally successful company. While still profitable, Boeing had set a course that would have shocked Bill Allen, who once proclaimed that he would build the 707 "even if it takes the resources of the entire company."

On the night he decided to become Boeing's president, Allen made a list of the qualities he would have to possess to do the job well enough to at least keep his self-respect.

Must keep temper—always—never get mad.
Be considerate of my associate's [*sic*] views.
Don't talk too much—let others talk.
Don't be afraid to admit that you don't know.
Don't get immersed in detail—concentrate on the big objectives.
Make contacts with other people in industry—and keep them!
Make a sincere effort to understand labor's viewpoint.
Be definite; don't vacillate.
Act—get things done—move forward.
Develop a postwar future for Boeing.
Try hard, but don't let obstacles get you down. Take things in stride.
Above all else be human—keep your sense of humor—learn to relax.
Be just; straightforward; invite criticism and learn to take it.
Be confident. Having once made the move, make the most of it.
Bring to the task great enthusiasm, unlimited energy.
Make Boeing even greater than it is.[3]

When Bill Allen took the helm of Boeing, it was in the heavy-bomber business. In its earliest years, it had manufactured seaplanes. Later, it had entered the mail-delivery business, until Congress passed a law denying a government mail-service contract to the same company that manufactured the planes that would deliver it. After World War I, Boeing began to produce planes for the growing commercial-aviation market. In 1935, it built the four-engine "299," and in 1939 the fabled "Stratoliner," the first passenger plane with a pressurized cabin. Boeing's "Clipper" ships were the first to provide transatlantic passenger service. But with America's entry into World War II, all that changed. For the army, Boeing built the biggest and most capable bombers ever conceived: the B-17 "Flying Fortress" and the larger and longer-ranged B-29 "Superfortress," in quantities that staggered the imagination as well as our enemies. In the last full year of the war, the Boeing assembly line was producing 350 "forts" every month and had become an immensely large company.

Boeing was prepared at the war's end for substantial reductions in government orders for heavy bombers and had begun an orderly workforce reduction. But moments after the chairman of Boeing's board of directors announced Allen's appointment as president, the company received notice from the Army Air Corps that the cuts in bomber production would be immediate and far more drastic than anyone at Boeing had anticipated. Orders for B-29s were reduced to fifty for the current month, and to ten for each of the next five months. After that, who knew? The company had already completed nearly that number. On his first day as president, September 1, 1945, Boeing lost over a billion and a half dollars in contracts, and both its Seattle and Wichita plants ceased operations. Forty thousand employees were laid off. When he had included in his sparse list of reasons for accepting the position "It would be a new challenge," he couldn't have possibly imagined just how big a challenge it would prove and just how quickly it would arrive.

Nevertheless, the next day Allen convened a meeting of Boeing's senior executives and announced that the company would begin converting the B-50, a follow-on to the B-29, to a commercial airliner, the "Stratocruiser." To keep the price low enough, they would have to manufacture at least fifty of them. So Allen ordered fifty. He knew the planes would be big enough, fast enough, and with a long enough range to attract airline purchases. But he made the decision without having in hand an order for a single one. That was not how things were done in the aircraft industry of the time. You got the order, and then you built the plane. Allen didn't think he had a choice. Thousands of his employees were out of work, and their families were threatened with destitution. And Boeing might not survive an extended shutdown. So he gambled.

One year later, Boeing had managed to sell fifty-five of the new airliners but had lost, as Allen expected it would, more than thirteen million dollars on the deal. No matter. His gamble had paid off in more important ways. He had kept his assembly line running, his engineers working, and his company together. Boeing had become a much smaller company, but not for long.

Boeing would build jet-engine bombers. In March 1946, the Air Force created the Strategic Air Command (SAC) and was intent on accelerating plans conceived during the war to acquire a fleet of jet-engine bombers and reconnaissance planes. Boeing hurried to win the business and did so with a high-altitude, medium-range, six-engine B-47, capable of midair refueling, the first complete jet-engine strategic bomber. The first prototype took its successful test flight in December 1947. In the fourteen years the B-47s were in service, the Air Force purchased more than two thousand of them. Its revolutionary design remains the basic model for every large aircraft in existence.

The Air Force, however, was not completely satisfied with the aircraft's capabilities. It was fast enough, but SAC wanted a longer-range bomber, preferring a fleet that wouldn't have to be based outside the United States to be effective overseas. Boeing worked to meet that requirement as well. In 1954, the Air Force took possession of a Boeing-manufactured long-range bomber, the mighty B-52 "Stratofortress," the biggest bomber in the world, still in service more than fifty years later and performing, as it always has, magnificently. Among the many achievements credited to the B-52 is the part it played in the decision that would make Bill Allen the greatest aviation-industry leader of all time.

He did not appear to have a gambler's personality. He was reserved, thoughtful, patient, plainspoken, and straightforward in style. Friendly but not gregarious, conservative and careful but not timid, the tall, thin, bald pipe smoker couldn't have looked more unlike the dashing and audacious types who dominated the aviation industry at the time. But he had nerve, however obscured behind his placid demeanor.

He instituted long-overdue changes in Boeing's management that had allowed seniority to dictate personnel decisions rather than merit.

His personal ethics were unassailable, and he imposed a strict code of conduct on his employees. His executives were instructed to refuse offers of free plane rides and meals from the airlines, and his salesmen were forbidden to dispense anything more than token gifts to their customers. During his years as Boeing's president, the company headquarters were located in a nondescript low industrial-park-type office building adjacent to its main plant and Boeing Field, which the company used to test and deliver its planes.

In 1949, Allen rode in the navigator's seat in a B-47 while visiting the company's Wichita plant. He flew back to Seattle on a prop-drive plane that seemed to crawl in comparison. According to legend, his decision to manufacture high-speed jet-transport planes was first formed in that experience, when he glimpsed the future of commercial aviation—fast, convenient long-distance transportation for the multitudes. The following year, Allen went to visit the British aircraft manufacturer de Havilland, where the "Comet," a jet-transport plane, was in production. While Allen might have been impressed by the Comet's design, the real surprise of his visit was that the plane was built almost entirely by hand. With its advances in engineering and its tooled-up assembly lines and state-of-the-art wind-tunnel tests, Boeing, if it had the financing, could quickly outpace its British competitor and at less cost. But Boeing was a small player in commercial aviation.

Still, Allen saw the necessity for the jets. He knew the Air Force would need them, whether they knew it then or not. And the airliners, who still carried long-distance passengers on big prop planes, would want them, too. Airline leaders, like Juan Trippe at Pan American World Airways, were entrepreneurs who had entered the business with confidence in its limitless potential. They had a knack for sensing the next big thing that would make commercial air travel an increasingly common experience. Allen knew the world was shrinking, overseas markets were opening, corporations had global concerns, and the American economy was expanding rapidly. He knew there would be passengers for his jets. When the airline executives recognized their need, Allen wanted Boeing to be the first company capable of meeting it. Now, he sensed, was the right time to move ahead. And he had the gambler's nerve to act on his intuition.

By the time Allen returned to Seattle from England, the Korean War had begun. The B-52's first test flight was to occur just days later. Allen knew that Air Force orders for the big bomber, should the test prove successful, would increase to meet wartime demands. At the end of 1951, Boeing's profits for the year were estimated at seven million dollars. Boeing's comptroller felt confident they would double earnings the following year. Allen knew he would have the capital, barely, necessary to start production on a jet transport. And he felt certain that once the Air Force took possession of the B-52s and put them into operation, it would recognize the necessity of acquiring refueling tankers that could fly as fast as the planes they serviced.

A preliminary radical design for a jet transport had already been drafted by Boeing engineers. But the question of going ahead hadn't been formally put before Boeing's board of directors. First, Allen instructed his secretary to type a questionnaire that would ask Boeing's senior executives about the feasibility of building the plane, its estimated cost, its capabilities, the markets it could serve, and what changes in management and operations its production would require. When his executives answered the questions to his satisfaction and unanimously affirmed his intuition to build the thing, he scheduled a board meeting to pitch the proposal for April 22, 1952.

The directors were shown the proposed design, with its long wings swept back at a thirty-five-degree angle, carrying pods for four powerful Pratt & Whitney engines beneath them, and a long fuselage that could carry fuel, troops, or commercial passengers. They were as impressed by the design as they were shocked by its price tag. Allen told them that the first prototype would probably cost fifteen million dollars ($110,000,000 in today's dollars), and if and when Boeing went into full production of the plane the retooling and other assembly-line changes required would cost tens of millions more. "The sum," they realized, "was larger than the value of the company."[4] Allen alleviated their concern somewhat by suggesting that he was confident he could persuade the IRS to allow the investment as a deduction. Still, were they to give the go-ahead for the hugely expensive prototype, they would do so with only Bill Allen's nose for timing and opportunity. But there wasn't a market yet. Like his decision to build the B-50, the decision to build a jet transport would be made without a single order from the Air Force or the airliners or even an assurance of their interest in the plane. And should there prove to be a commercial market, de Havilland had a three-year head start on Boeing. If Bill Allen's gamble failed, it would bankrupt the company.

The decision to build the Dash 80, as the prototype was called, was announced on August 30, 1952. Boeing intended to build a much bigger, faster, and longer-range jet than the Comet. Production teams worked around the clock, and in the strictest secrecy, in a complex nicknamed the Walled Village. Less than two years later, Dash 80 was ready to fly.

On May 21, 1954, Boeing's chief test pilot, Tex Johnston, shook Bill Allen's hand, climbed into his seat, and taxied the plane onto the runway at Boeing Field. The prototype was painted yellow and brown, as if it were a commercial airliner and not an Air Force tanker. At two o'clock, the four big engines revved up, and Dash 80 sped down the runaway for two thousand feet, lifted up, and roared skyward in a steep ascent. The news cameras, reporters, Boeing employees, representatives from the Air Force and the airlines, Bill Boeing, and a relieved Bill Allen watched the plane execute all of its performance tests with graceful ease and land safely ninety minutes later.

During a later test in front of an international audience, Johnston, who liked to help his company sell airplanes by employing a little showmanship, executed an unplanned roll, to the delight of his entire audience, save one. When he landed, a Boeing official informed him that Allen would like to see him in his office immediately. When Johnston strolled in, Allen greeted him cordially and inquired about his family. Then he mentioned that he had heard Johnston had rolled the plane, and asked him, "What do you think you were doing?"

"I thought I was selling airplanes," the pilot replied.

"Don't do it again," Allen shot back, "and say hello to your wife for me."[5]

Not long before the plane's first test flight, the Air Force had finally indicated possible interest in acquiring it. But to meet the discussed delivery date of October 1956, Allen had to order full-scale production to begin before the government had made a final decision, and he had to use Boeing's own capital to cover the costs. The Air Force preferred a design by Lockheed, but Lockheed had only a paper drawing. Boeing had a plane. A year later, the tanker order from the Air Force came through, and over the course of its production run Boeing was to build 564 KC-135s. Half of Allen's strategic gamble had paid off.

Now Allen directed his team to concentrate on the airline industry, knowing that the Air Force's embrace of jet transports would encourage the airliners to make the same move. Boeing was able to use the same tooling used to manufacture the KC-135, which would give them a time advantage over any domestic competitor, but converting the KC-135s into 707s did require a number of design modifications, with every part of the plane standardized to make it relatively easy to customize the plane to meet the airlines' specific requirements. Douglas Aircraft Company, the most experienced and successful commercial-airliner builder, had begun work on a jet airliner, the DC-8, with a design almost identical to the 707, and de Havilland's Comet would soon be on the market. Boeing had to race to stay ahead. Initial cost estimates for the 707 were one million dollars more per plane than the airlines were willing to spend. Allen ordered his production team to make whatever changes necessary in design and production to lower the cost to the airliners' number.

The race with Douglas was a struggle. Douglas's sales team was much more experienced in selling planes for commercial aviation, and it had the advantage of being able to say yes to any airliner's specifications. All they had was a plane on paper, which they could lengthen or widen to satisfy their customers' wishes. Boeing already had a prototype, so making changes of that kind would be a more difficult and expensive proposition.

Bill Allen and Juan Trippe liked and respected each other. Trippe wanted Pan Am to be the first airliner to offer passenger jet service. So he was the first to order twenty 707s from his friend, but he also announced that he had placed an order for twenty-five DC-8s for later delivery. Douglas was offering Pan Am a plane better suited to their needs—several inches wider so that it could accommodate more passengers. United Air Lines followed with an order for thirty DC-8s. The airlines were more accustomed to doing business with Douglas, which had built most of their current fleets while Boeing had concentrated, profitably, on winning government contracts. Bill Allen knew that a bigger move into the commercial market was necessary for Boeing to thrive, and he was determined to be an industry leader. Boeing had a plane, and could deliver it faster. All it had to do was prove as accommodating to customers as was its chief competitor. But that would be expensive and require yet another daring decision by Bill Allen.

American Airlines wanted a longer and wider plane for its overseas routes. Douglas promised to give it to them. Allen had to decide whether to stick with the plane already in production or design and build a bigger one, with room for rows of six seats across, as the airline had demanded. It would be another huge expense for the company, already stretched thin by the production costs it had borne on its own. He decided to do it. While American executives might still have preferred the DC design, Allen had the plane, which he promised to deliver before Douglas had a prototype. Boeing got the contract.

Juan Trippe was the first to put the 707 into operation, in 1958. The jet age began. The 707 was fastest jet airliner in the world, at six hundred miles per hour, with the longest range, the highest possible altitude, and the ability to carry two hundred passengers, twice the capacity of the Comet. Douglas never would catch up. When it was acquired by McDonnell Aircraft Corporation in 1967, it still hadn't sold enough DC-8s to cover the costs of their production. In one master stroke, brilliantly timed by a modest, capable lawyer, Boeing was on its way to becoming the biggest producer of commercial airliners in the country.

His latter-day successors, in competition with Europe's Airbus, reversed the direction Bill Allen had set for the company and began to rely on military contracts at the expense of their commercial-aviation business. And that overreliance led to some pretty bad decisions and ethical lapses that would have deeply shamed Allen. The company has improved, and it should recover that sense of itself and the future of its business that made Bill Allen the best gambler in the business and Boeing the greatest aircraft manufacturer in the world.

On a fishing trip in Alaska in 1965, Allen discussed with his friend and fellow gambler Juan Trippe the explosion in overseas travel that had followed the introduction of the popular 707. Trippe estimated that thirty-five million passengers traveled overseas by air that year, and he expected a 200 percent increase in fifteen years. But mass international air travel would reach the heights he envisioned for it and be profitable only if he had bigger planes. He told Allen he needed a jet two and a half times larger than the 707, though the plane had been flying commercially for only seven years.

"If you build it," Trippe told his friend, "I'll buy it."

"If you buy it," Allen responded, "I'll build it." And thus, another bold and well-timed decision began the story of the Boeing 747, the jumbo jet, and the age of mass travel overseas, and the smaller world Bill Allen had seen coming.[6]

SELL THE SHAVE, NOT THE RAZOR

King Camp Gillette was a man particularly given to blinding insights. They never crept up stealthily or formed slowly in his imagination. As he told it, his visions struck him all at once, completely formed and publicly presentable. Each one electrified him, a jagged bolt of lightning to the brow as he hurried along the Damascus road. And each one occasioned in him a grandiose exclamation: *destined to change man's conception of industry; our fortune is made*. His passion for his ideas may lend a bit of comical charm to his historical character. More interesting, his enthusiasms so completely overtook him that he became a man of extraordinary contradictions, capable of pursuing with equal intensity two opposing identities: socialist utopian dreamer and a hustling, happy capitalist. He was an American original: practical and starry-eyed; worried and optimistic. He had visions both fanciful and keen. His utopian schemes belong to the former category.

But his famous invention, which was both a physical product and a business strategy, and his decision to commit himself diligently over many years to its realization, changed American commerce forever. And perhaps that is what unites the two pronounced sides of his personality and kindled his exuberant resilience to skeptics. King Gillette liked to change things. And he had an instinct for it, a salesman's sense of timing and possibility, which, in turn-of-the-century American commerce, made him the brilliant innovator he believed he was as a social reformer. And it gave legitimacy to his boasts. He did, indeed, change our conception of industry, and he made a fortune doing it.

His family moved to Chicago, that city of restless enterprise and reinvention, in 1859, when King Gillette was four years old. His father, George, a sometime patent agent and amateur inventor, ran a wholesale hardware business. His mother, Fanny, a formidable and enterprising woman, spent more than thirty years collecting and experimenting with recipes before coauthoring *The White House Cookbook,* still in print and selling to this day. It was from Fanny, Gillette's biographer Russell Adams suggests, that King Gillette inherited "his lifelong belief in efficiency, and his hatred for wasting time."[1]

Gillette and his two brothers, George and Mott, attended high school in Chicago before the Great Fire of 1871 convinced their father to seek his fortune elsewhere and move his family to New York, where he opened another hardware business with his two older sons. At seventeen, King went his own way, working first as clerk for a rival hardware wholesaler. At twenty-one, he began his career as a traveling salesman, which remained his livelihood for more than thirty years. Hardworking, clever, and engaging, Gillette excelled at his profession, working for a succession of employers who recognized and rewarded his talent for selling everything from hardware to household cleaners to bottle caps.

Having inherited his parents' ingenuity, he spent his free time inventing and patenting improvements of the hardware products he sold, "which made money for others," he later remarked, "but seldom for myself."[2] His more notable patents were for improvements to the durability of beer kegs and the tap-and-valve system used to draw the beer. The itinerant life of traveling salesman afforded him little time, and his income, while respectable, hardly gave him the additional resources necessary to develop and market his inventions. But Gillette had all the attributes of a ceaseless striver: persistence, self-confidence, inquisitiveness, and imagination. He was occasionally frustrated but undaunted in his efforts to make a fortune from his innovations. And he was as quick to appreciate promotional strategies, particularly the importance of paid advertising, as he was to perceive a need for a product, should he ever find the means to bring it successfully to market.

In 1890, he married Atlanta Ella Gaines, and the following year he accepted a position as the New York and New England regional sales representative for the Baltimore Seal Company. The company's founder and president, William Painter, took an instant liking to his new star salesman, and Gillette found in Painter a kindred spirit. Like Gillette, Painter was a man of exceptional ingenuity and drive. Unlike Gillette, he had already made a fortune from his inventions. Gillette admired him and respected his advice, which Painter dispensed freely to his young protégé.

For the rest of his life, Gillette credited Painter for focusing his fertile imagination on the search for a paradox, a disposable indispensable, until he seized upon the idea that was to revolutionize business. Not long after Gillette went to work for him, Painter renamed his company the Crown Cork and Seal Company, in tribute to the product he had just brought to market. Until Painter patented his invention, bottles of carbonated beverages had been sealed with reusable rubber stoppers held in place by a wire brace. Painter had devised a cheaper, and most important a disposable, substitute: a cork-lined tin bottle cap, which when crimped over the bottle top resembled an upside-down crown. Once opened, the bottle could not be resealed by the consumer, and the cap was discarded. But the crown bottle cap was so much cheaper than its predecessor that soft-drink bottlers scrambled to order and reorder the new invention, and the rubber stopper became obsolete. Crown Cork and Seal flourished. The bottle cap became the industry standard until the invention of the twist-off cap late in the twentieth century, and the company entered the ranks of the Fortune 500, where it remains to this day.

Most Americans in the nineteenth century were still thrifty people who spurned luxuries. They bought goods as infrequently as possible and declined any service they could, with a little time and trouble, do for themselves. They valued durable products that could be kept in good working order by the owner's strict attention to their care. But America was changing. It was becoming more populated and prosperous, its cities more crowded, and its frontiers more firmly settled. Social mobility, the great attraction of American life, was ever more achievable and unbounded. The American middle class was growing, and the average American's standard of living was improving. Americans then and now remain one of the world's most industrious peoples. And while expanding wealth affords its beneficiaries more leisure, American life has always been distinguished by its hurried and hectic qualities, even in the pursuit of relaxation. As incomes rise, so does a growing appreciation for convenience.

William Painter had an instinct for his times. So did his talented and ambitious employee, King Gillette. Employer and employee enjoyed each other's company, and Gillette was often invited to Painter's summer home. On one such occasion, as Gillette was describing his frustration with the failure of one or another of his patented inventions to bring him much in the way of material reward, Painter counseled him to follow his model.

"Why don't you try to think of something like the Crown Cork, which when once used is thrown away, and the customer keeps coming back for more?" Painter advised him.

"It's easy to give that kind of advice," Gillette responded. "But how many things are like corks, pins, and needles?"[3]

Irrespective of his initial reaction, Gillette took the advice to heart and applied the restless imagination that was his most distinguishing feature to the task of finding a practical application for its inspiration. As he bounced along the railroad tracks of the American northeast, traveling from one destination to another hustling the wares of the employer whose success he sought to emulate, the search for his own Crown bottle cap became an obsession. "I applied the thought to every material need, but nothing came of it," he later wrote.[4] And however diligently he hunted for his disposable product, his concentration was shared with his other grand obsession, social reform.

By the standards of the day he was well paid for his talents as a salesman. But in the estimation of his enterprising family and his own, an appreciable skill at selling someone else's goods was hardly a measure of success. Gillette was thirty-six years old when he took the job with Painter's company, and his son and only child, King Gaines Gillette, was born that same year. Incessant traveling became less attractive to the new husband and father, who desired a more settled life. But the necessity of providing for his family kept him on the road, and the frustration he felt surely provided much of the impetus for his conception of a better organized society. In that pursuit, however, the savvy understanding of human nature Gillette showed as a salesman succumbed to his overheated imagination of the perils of free-market competition.

As usual, Gillette claimed a sudden revelation had struck him when he described the genesis for his idea to perfect society and, if truth be told, his intended assumption of God's responsibility for human nature's design. Peering out a hotel window in Scranton, Pennsylvania, on a rainy morning, he observed the daily traffic jam of wagons and people come to a halt as a broken-down grocery wagon blocked their progress. According to Russell Adams, he "immediately imagined all the ultimate destinations of the foodstuffs borne by the broken wagon, then backtracked to the sources of the goods." In that instant, his previous perception of a world divided into separate political and industrial entities was dispelled and replaced with "the thought that is destined to change man's conception of industry. . . . Industry as a whole is one vast operative mechanism. Included in it are the governments of every country, and our combined system of social, political and industrial economy."⁵

Never content to keep his visions to himself, Gillette soon began work on a book that decried the competition inherent in free-market capitalism as socially and economically ruinous. Influenced by his own observations as well as the work of other utopian dreamers of his day, with which he was familiar, he proposed that all of humanity be organized in one publicly owned corporation that would manage all industry. The entire population of the United States, some sixty million people at the time, would hospitably reside in blocks of skyscrapers near Niagara Falls, which would supply the newly consolidated nation with an adequate source of hydroelectric power. He helpfully included in his book an illustration of his towering megalopolis. In his worldwide corporate community, "selfishness would be unknown," he declared, "and war would be a barbarism of the past."

As visions go, Gillette's was certainly a comprehensive one. That it was as ludicrous as it was ambitious was not apparent to his many fellow reformers and budding socialists, who heralded *The Human Drift* after its publication in 1894. Gillette quickly rose to minor prominence in the social-reform movement of the late nineteenth century. His ideas were frequently published in a leading radical magazine, *Twentieth Century,* and reformers encouraged him to assume political leadership of the movement to repair the wrongs of capitalism. That he was unable to devote his full attention to their cause was a decidedly fortunate decision, for Gillette and for the rest of the country. His genius was better suited to more practical endeavors. And had he not returned to his other obsession, he would have eventually been choked to death with frustration.

His zeal to rescue humanity from the depredations of capitalism was to prove futile, of course. And yet, in an amusing quirk of fate, his dogged determination to find his own bottle cap, a product that was both necessary and inexpensive enough to continuously repurchase, would alleviate a small misery of mankind and earn him the grateful recognition of millions of satisfied customers.

In his satiric poem *Don Juan,* Lord Byron compared shaving, that tiresome daily chore, to the pain a woman suffers in childbirth.

Condemn'd to child-bed, as men for their sins
Have shaving too entail'd upon their chins,
A daily plague, which in the aggregate
May average on the whole with parturition.

This view was shared by many of Gillette's fellow sufferers in the early nineteenth century, especially those who assumed personal responsibility for keeping their chins beardless rather than relying on the skill of a local barber. Great skill was required when gingerly scraping across one's face and neck a finely ground blade of Sheffield steel, a task best left to professionals, lest the hasty or clumsy user prove the aptness of its informal label—the cutthroat razor.

Fashions come and go, no less so with men's facial hair. But necessity, more often than whimsy, dictated changing styles of how men groomed their whiskers. Cavemen, it is believed, used clamshells as rudimentary tweezers to pluck their beards one whisker at a time to prevent them from becoming the habitation of lice and other vermin. Pieces of flint or obsidian (volcanic glass) were commonly used in the earliest attempts at cutting rather than plucking whiskers. Advances in metalworking in ancient India and Egypt produced the first permanent razors, made of copper, and the beardless fashion prevalent among the ruling classes. Again, the practice was evidently intended to deter lice infestation and to help one keep cool in those warm climates, but it became in time the mark of a civilized person, who daily shaved both face and head and wore wigs to distinguish himself from barbarians.

Shaving became more widespread as much of the known world capitulated to the armies of Alexander the Great, who had himself shaved twice a day, and always before battle. Alexander may have been fastidious about his appearance, but more than vanity inspired the habit. In combat, a beard offered the enemy a welcome handhold to grasp in his attempt to lop off one's head. Likewise, Julius Caesar kept clean shaven at all times, employing a specially trained slave to pluck the whiskers from his face. Beardless Alexander and Caesar immortalized a Greco-Roman ideal of male appearance that dominated their cultures until the Emperor Hadrian grew a beard, reportedly to cover his poor complexion. The style then further declined when long-haired and bearded barbarians stormed the gates of Rome.

William the Conqueror helped revive the style when he ordered his Norman soldiers to disguise themselves as shaved and tonsured monks in advance of their invasion of England. And knights returned from the Crusades beardless, having adopted the look preferred in the sumptuous palaces of Arab princes.

Then, too, when beards came back into fashion, a practical purpose usually influenced the change. The popularity of men's beards during the American Civil War is partly attributable to the fact that advances in warfare reduced the frequency of hand-to-hand combat. Stonewall Jackson was shot from his horse, not dragged off it by his impressive whiskers. But more often than not, simple convenience encouraged men to sprout beards. Shaving in the field was time-consuming and, depending on the steadiness of the hand that wielded the straight razor, posed another hazard for men who faced enough danger as it was.

No matter how exotically men fashioned their beards—curled, brushed, or trimmed like the topiary in their gardens—one fact more than any other encouraged their growth: shaving was a difficult and inconvenient procedure. Most men paid a barber to shave them. Obviously, a daily trip to the barber wasn't in the cards for men of modest means. Hence, they either let their beards grow or limited themselves to one or two shaves per week. Those men who developed the skill to shave themselves had to prepare their beards for the experience. Softening and lathering one's beard required water, which in the nineteenth century wasn't as easily available as it is today. Warm water was an even greater inconvenience. Add to that the time involved in stropping the blade before every shave to keep it sharp; routine trips to a cutler to have it honed; the ever-present risk of cutting oneself or worse; and the infection that often developed in the wounds, and it is easy to see why shaving was considered such a cursed nuisance.

In the late nineteenth century, a hollow, ground Sheffield steel straight razor cost the modern equivalent of seventy dollars or more. They were expected to last a lifetime or longer and were often treated as family heirlooms, passed on, like a watch, from father to son. For men who traveled frequently for a living, like King Gillette, the straight razor was of little utility. No matter how steady your hand, shaving over a small sink in a swaying railroad car was a complicated and dangerous business.

To address the needs of the modern nineteenth-century traveler, the Kampfe Brothers of Brooklyn, New York, filed the first patent for a safety razor. They based their Star razor on an earlier design by an English manufacturer who invented the first hoe-shaped razor, with a short blade set perpendicular to the handle. Their owners surely welcomed the decreased danger involved in shaving. But the new safety razors still required considerable care to use. The blade was a short wedge of forged steel, sharpened to a cutting edge on one side. Just like a straight razor, it dulled after use and had to be routinely stropped and honed. Trying to strop the small, extracted blade was a more awkward task than holding a straight razor by its handle and briskly swiping the long blade along a leather strap. Nevertheless, the Star razor quickly gained popularity, especially among the growing ranks of salesmen. Gillette owned one. And it was while he was preparing himself for his morning shave with his new Star razor that he at last conceived of his disposable bottle cap.

In the spring of 1895, Gillette found that the blade of his razor had become dull and required stropping. In his own account, the idea for an inexpensive disposable struck him like a thunderbolt, and he immediately began working on inventing one. Russell Adams convincingly argues that the process of invention was a more deliberate and evolving one. The idea did begin to take shape in Gillette's mind while he shaved, and as he studied his expensive Star razor and its wedge of forged steel, he posed himself the critical question: was it necessary to use so much steel to produce a cutting edge? As he explained years later in testimony during one of many suits to protect his patent,

> The thought occurred to me that no radical improvements had been made in razors, especially in razor blades, for several centuries, and it flashed through my mind that if by any possibility razor blades could be constructed and made cheap enough to do away with honing and stropping and permit the user to replace dull blades by new ones, such improvements would be highly important to the art.[6]

Gillette, the man who habitually dreamed up ideas to improve human existence, had focused the practical side of his active imagination on a chore faced routinely by half the human race and grasped that it was ripe to be commercialized to an extent that had exceeded anyone else's imagination. The growing population of American cities and the rising class of office workers, like salesmen, were an unexploited market for an affordable daily shave. And that was what Gillette proposed to sell them: a convenient and comfortable shave. The razor would be ingenious but hardly the elegant heirloom its users treated with reverence. To encourage sales, he intended to sell the razor for less than it cost to manufacture and accustom its users to the idea of regularly replacing the blades, where he would make his profits. His insight fortunately coincided with industrial-age advances such as mass production and the rolling mill, which would make this idea, unlike his world corporation, an achievable ambition. But Gillette did more than invent a useful product. His razors-and-blade business model, more than any other invention, engendered the dynamic consumer product market that fuels the American economy to this day.

Soon after he conceived the idea, without having produced so much as a drawing of his radically new razor, he wrote to his wife to announce, "I've got it; our fortune is made." He set about the task of inventing the first disposable razor blade with his customary indefatigability. It was to take eight years of toil and frustration before Gillette brought a product to market. Despite setbacks in manufacturing and a chronic shortage of financing, he never once doubted his conviction that he could produce and sell an invention unequaled in its improvement over the standard then in use. "There has never issued from the patent offices of the world," he later boasted, "any article of invention to meet an individual need, which has equaled or approached the Gillette razor in its saving of time over the system it has displaced."

Once the idea took hold of him, Gillette could talk of little else, importuning friends and mere acquaintances with his thoughts on various designs and the certainty of the device's commercial success. He whittled a model razor from a piece of wood and showed it to friends in only occasionally successful efforts to impart to them a little of his enthusiasm. He made scores of drawings before settling on a modified version of the hoe-type razor already in use. He had recently moved his family to Boston, where he now spent his free time frequenting machine shops and soliciting help in fabricating the critical component: a wafer-thin piece of steel sharpened to a fine cutting edge on both sides, which could be inexpensively manufactured. But the machinists he approached were unanimous in their opinion that so thin a piece of sheet steel could not withstand forging to take or hold a cutting edge. Gillette, who knew next to nothing about metallurgy or cutlery, attempted to forge several thin blades himself, but not one worked well enough to cut a single whisker. He met with no better success when he put the question to metallurgists at MIT. Financial backers were proving just as hard to come by. For four frustrating years, he found little encouragement for his idea. The farsighted William Painter was one of the few people who grasped the genius of it and encouraged Gillette not to abandon it. "The razor was looked upon as a joke by all my friends," said Gillette. "A common greeting was 'Well, Gillette, how's the razor?' If I had been technically trained, I would have quit."[7]

In the summer of 1899, Gillette found a Boston machinist who was willing to fabricate, under Gillette's supervision, a few prototype blades. They worked well enough for Gillette to file the first of many patent applications for his razor. But the method of the blade's manufacture was costly and time-consuming and unlikely to produce inexpensive blades in sufficient quantities so they could be sold cheaply to the consumer. Gillette did now possess, however, a working model he could use to attract investors and, hopefully, someone who could devise a manufacturing process that produced a cheaper and better blade at a cost affordable to the average workingman.

In 1900, a friend of Gillette who had invested a small sum of capital in the project showed the model to an MIT-trained chemist and experienced inventor, William Emery Nickerson. Although Nickerson grasped the commercial viability of a disposable razor blade, he was initially skeptical that it could be produced. He thought the blade in Gillette's model was "rather too stiff for the handle" and was uncertain he could improve it.[8] Eventually, he was persuaded to take up the challenge for a salary of forty dollars per week, and within weeks he assured Gillette and his small group of investors that it could be done. A delighted Gillette founded the American Safety Razor Company in 1901. The next year, as William Nickerson was hard at work developing a method to harden sheet steel and a machine that could automatically sharpen the thin blades, Gillette proposed to rename the company the Gillette & Nickerson Safety Razor Company. "Nickerson" was dropped for its obvious suggestion of the perils of shaving that the safety razor was intended to avoid. Gillette insisted that his name remain in the company's title.

It took William Nickerson three years to develop the machinery and technique to produce the disposable blade. After much experimentation and many delays, he discovered that a wide enough blade, in an improved design of Gillette's prototype handle, could hold its shape well enough to cut a man's beard cleanly. And he perfected a means to harden a thin ribbon of steel, as well as a machine that held it rigid enough to give the blades their cutting edge.

Since he first conceived of the idea of a disposable razor blade, Gillette had continued in the employ of Crown Cork and Seal. He had no other means to support his family during the eight years it took to develop the product and bring it to market. Now, just as Nickerson's work had progressed to the point where he could declare that with a little more work and sufficient financing Gillette's vision could be realized and "no man can set a limit to it," the fledgling company teetered on the brink of bankruptcy. Nickerson's work had exhausted all the company's capital and then some. By the summer of 1902, the Gillette Safety Razor Company was as much as twelve thousand dollars in the red, and its small board of directors despaired of finding additional capital. Nickerson took up that challenge as well and soon convinced a group of New York investors to put up a $150,000 in exchange for a 51 percent share of the company's stock. But Gillette and his investors refused to relinquish control of the company and rejected the offer.

Gillette turned reluctantly to a Boston businessman, John Joyce, who had lost a substantial sum in one of Gillette's earlier inventions. Joyce and Gillette had remained on good terms, and as the astute businessman listened to Gillette describe his invention and its financial woes, he saw instantly the razor's commercial potential. He agreed to invest enough money in the company to enable it to bring the razor to market but insisted on terms that were highly favorable to him. He would purchase as much as one hundred thousand dollars in company bonds at a 40 percent discount and would receive an equivalent amount of company stock. His investment would earn him a seat on the company's board, and, if the venture failed to progress satisfactorily, Joyce would be allowed out of the agreement after an investment of thirty thousand dollars. Gillette and the company's other directors had little choice but to agree to the terms and admit Joyce to the board, where he quickly made his presence felt.

In 1902, with Joyce's money and urging, the hardworking Nickerson rushed to complete the manufacturing process. When, at last, the production line of Gillette razors and blades began to run, the directors met to set a price for their product. Gillette's original idea to sell the razors as a loss leader and make a profit on the blades clashed with John Joyce's bottom line. The blades were proving more expensive to manufacture than anticipated. To sell them at an affordable price, which was essential for Gillette's scheme, would provide too small a profit margin, if any. The blades themselves might have to be sold at a loss, and the company would have to make up the lost return on the sale of the razor handles until their market grew substantially and improvements in the manufacturing process produced blades at a lower cost. At Joyce's insistence and over Gillette's objection, the board of directors set the price for the handle at five dollars, twice as much as the cheapest straight razor and one third of the average worker's weekly wage. A package of twenty blades would sell for a dollar. In time, the company returned to Gillette's original business model to give away the razor and sell the blades. As Gillette had envisioned, it reaped vast profits from the decision. But for now, Gillette had to hope that the convenience and novelty of the Gillette safety razor and its low-priced disposable blades would attract enough customers to make his fortune.

The company signed a contract with the Chicago firm Townsend and Hunt, which, in exchange for exclusive retail rights, agreed to purchase fifty thousand razor sets over the next year and assure sales of one hundred thousand per year for the next four years. In October of 1903, the first ads for the new razor appeared, announcing: "We Offer a New Razor." Sales were hardly brisk in the first months of their availability. Fifty-one razors and 168 packages of replacement blades had been purchased by the end of the year. Nevertheless, Gillette and his fellow shareholders were encouraged that a market existed for a five-dollar razor and expected higher sales in the immediate future. To increase their returns, the directors soon reduced the number of blades in a replacement package from twenty to a dozen.

Until sales met the company's expectation, King Gillette had to continue earning a living as a salesman for Crown Cork and Seal, in which capacity he was transferred to London in November 1903.

He was, of course, very reluctant to leave just as his invention was finally entering the marketplace. But he had little choice. His company was not yet in a position to pay him a salary. So he resigned as company president, and he and his wife and son set sail for England on the same day the U.S. Patent Office issued two patents for Gillette's "new and useful improvements in razors," and assigned to the company the exclusive rights to its manufacture and sale for a period of seventeen years.[9]

Nickerson's sharpening machines weren't working efficiently enough to keep up with projected demand. Entire batches of razors were ruined in the first months of 1904 due to malfunctioning machinery. In an effort to raise capital other than his own to refine the manufacturing process, Joyce proposed the company sell overseas sales rights for one hundred thousand dollars. Gillette hurried back to Boston in time to attend the directors' meeting when the sale was put to a vote and successfully argued against it. Moreover, the board elected a new slate of officers. John Joyce was chosen as the company's new president and King C. Gillette assumed the office of vice president, for an annual salary of eighteen thousand dollars. He quit Crown Cork and Seal, moved his family back to Boston, and started purchasing additional shares of Gillette stock.

His clashes with Joyce over various decisions grew more frequent and harsh. And the stakes were substantially larger than when they had squabbled over the price of the first razor handle. In 1904, sales of the Gillette safety razor totaled ninety thousand, and their satisfied owners had purchased ten thousand replacement-blade packages. Gillette became convinced that he must seize control of the company from Joyce, who was then its largest shareholder. With his usual energy, he kept adding shares to his holdings and persuaded the board of directors to expand from five to seven members. Gillette saw to it that the two new directors were picked by him and could be relied upon to support his successful effort in 1907 to wrest the company's presidency from John Joyce.

The company continued to wrestle with production problems, rapidly rising demand, frequent disagreements between the company's two largest and hardheaded shareholders, and complex litigation to protect its patents from infringement by an ever-increasing number of copycat razors. But through it all, the company prospered beyond anyone's initial expectation except for King Gillette's.

Gillette had always believed that advertising to entice American men to accept the profound change in their shaving habits would be critical to the company's success.[10] From the moment the first razors went on sale, the company invested twenty-five cents in advertising for every razor sold. The advertising budget would grow substantially, and Gillette applied his energy and genius for marketing innovations to promoting his invention. Early advertising focused on the new razor's convenience, celebrating the blade's limited life span as a welcome end to the tiresome necessity of stropping and honing a razor, and promoting the quality and comfort of its shave. "You cannot cut yourself," one early ad assured men, promising "Security from infection . . . and the satisfaction of being free from the barbershop habit."[11]

King Gillette's most inspired promotion would be the trademark head-and-shoulders photograph of himself on every package of blades. He looked the model of the successful, well-groomed, Gay Nineties American male: his head turned slightly to the left, wearing a wing collar, his hair parted neatly in the middle, and, but for his bushy mustache, sporting a smoothly shaven face. The photograph in time became almost iconic. Foreign men looking to buy razor blades would oftentimes ask their local retailer for the "kind with the man's face."[12] King Gillette became one of the most famous men in the world.

Immensely wealthy and tired of his ongoing battles with John Joyce, King Gillette retired from actively managing the company in 1913, although he retained the title of company president until his death. He moved to California, began investing in real estate, and traveled the world as the company's goodwill ambassador, urging on every male old enough to shave his indispensable razor with the disposable blade. With his unerring sense of timing and opportunity in the world of commerce, he could often be relied upon to offer the company profitable advice. In no instance was this truer than when he advised the company's directors to see to it that every American soldier leaving for Europe in World War I had packed a company-designed metal shaving kit with a Gillette safety razor and an adequate supply of replacement blades. When the war ended, American doughboys had used 3.5 million

Gillette razors and 32 million blades and took their new shaving habits home with them, as well as their preference in razors.

Once he retired from daily management of the company, Gillette returned to his utopian schemes with renewed vigor and, thinking bigger than ever, enlarged them beyond his earlier fanciful conception of a megalopolis on the banks of the Niagara. He incorporated his "World Corporation" in Arizona, promising "horizonless farms, and trafficless streets bordered with grass and flowers."[13] He offered the presidency of the corporation to former president Theodore Roosevelt for an annual salary of one million dollars. T.R. wisely declined the offer, and the thousands of subscribers Gillette had hoped to find for the corporation never materialized either.

This man of startling contradictions and limitless zeal never found his chance to remake civilization and human nature according to principles he believed to be enlightened but that most people, accustomed to relying on their own initiative and not government munificence, derided. One hopes some of the sting of his disappointment as a social reformer was removed by the continued success of the other great endeavor in which he had placed his faith and for which he had once been mocked as well. His accomplishment was not as significant a contribution to the advancement of civilization as he had hoped to make or, perhaps, all that important in the grand scheme of things, except for its revolutionary effect on the market for consumer goods, which, in a surpassing irony, Gillette's razor had made infinitely more competitive. But he could surely take pride in the praise he received from the man who had reluctantly agreed to manufacture his razor. The Gillette razor, William Nickerson argued, was unequaled "among the lesser inventions," and by making man master of his own grooming had earned the inventor the distinction he had yearned for. King Camp Gillette, Nickerson declared, was a "benefactor of his race."

"SHALOM, SALAAM, FOREVER"

On October 15, 1942, German soldiers had completely surrounded the Jewish ghetto in Brest-Litovsk. Many Jews had tried to hide, but the Germans managed to find them all, march them at gunpoint to the railway station, load them into cattle cars, and transport them to another village seventy miles to the northeast. A large trench had been dug there for the Jews of Brest-Litovsk. They were ordered to strip and then pushed into the trench. Machine guns opened fire, and the slaughter began. It lasted all day, until fifty thousand men, women, and children lay heaped together in a grotesque configuration. Thus ended the community that had welcomed the birth of Menachem Wolfovich Begin in 1913.

"The sighs of the condemned press in from afar and interrupt one's slumber," he wrote. "In these inescapable moments, every Jew in the country feels unwell because he is well."[1] He was born a Zionist. The local Zionist organization sent a cake to his bris. His father, Zev Dov Begin, an ardent Jewish nationalist and the secretary of the Jewish community, inspired in his third and youngest child a fierce and solemn

pride in his Jewish heritage. Zev Begin had once struck a Polish soldier who had tried to cut off a rabbi's beard, and he had been soundly beaten for his courage. Menachem had witnessed the incident and embraced his father as a hero. "I have never known a braver man," he later recalled. "I shall never forget how my father fought to defend Jewish honor."

The other great early influence in his life was Vladimir Ze'ev Jabotinsky, the Ukraine-born founder of the militant Alliance of Revisionist Zionists and its youth movement, Betar. Jabotinsky had formed a Jewish militia to defend Russian Jews during a wave of pogroms. During World War I, he organized five battalions of Jewish volunteers, the Zion Mule Corps, who fought with distinction in the Battle of Gallipoli. The corps served as the nucleus of a Jewish regiment in the British army established in 1917, which saw action against the Turks in the Jordan Valley in 1918. In 1920, Jabotinsky was stripped of his commission, arrested, and sentenced to fifteen years of hard labor for helping organize a Jewish self-defense force during the Nebi Musa riots when Arabs attacked Jews living in Jerusalem. International outrage over his sentence persuaded the British to release him. In 1925, he created the World Union of Zionist Revisionists to oppose

British policies in Palestine, encourage the mass immigration of Jews to Palestine, and support the underground Jewish militia, the Haganah. The British banned him from Palestine, which he was never to see again.

In 1935, with the rise of Nazism in Germany, Jabotinsky continued to lead opposition to the prevailing Zionist policy of self-restraint and compromise. As divisions among Zionists grew more acute, the Haganah split, and more militant fighters associated with Jabotinsky's Revisionists formed the Irgun Zvai Leumi (the National Military Organization).

An exceptional orator and gifted writer who wrote both poetry and prose in several languages under the pen name Altalena, Jabotinsky imbued the Revisionists' youth wing, Betar, with his urgent and unyielding dedication to the creation of the Jewish state, along with a reverence for their people's ancient and noble history. He was an elegant man with impeccable manners, which graced his impassioned leadership with great dignity. It was a style his young disciple, Menachem Begin, emulated all his life. Jabotinsky died suddenly in New York in 1940, as he campaigned for Jewish emigration from Europe to Palestine and the formation of a Jewish army to fight the Nazis.

Begin had first heard Jabotinsky speak in 1930 and was thrilled by his muscular advocacy of a Jewish homeland and the eloquence and intelligence of his arguments. Begin joined Betar at sixteen. After training as a lawyer in Warsaw, he worked for Betar in Czechoslovakia and Poland, where he was briefly imprisoned for leading protests against the British. At a Betar convention in 1938, he clashed with Jabotinsky over whether to take up arms against the British in Palestine, who were refusing to accept Jewish émigrés from Europe. Jabotinsky remained convinced that moral suasion would encourage a British change of heart. "The conscience of the world has ceased to react," Begin argued. "Our British partner leads us to the gallows and imprisons the finest of our nation."[2] Begin's convincing appeal for "the conquest of the homeland by force" increased his stature among Jewish nationalists. He became high commissioner of Betar in Poland, which organized the military training of its one hundred thousand members and the illegal immigration of Polish Jews to Palestine. Despite their differences, Jabotinsky traveled from London to Warsaw to attend his quarrelsome protégé's wedding to Aliza Arnold in May 1939.

In September 1939, Begin fled to Vilnius to escape the German advance on Warsaw. In 1940, after Soviet troops occupied Lithuania, Soviet secret police arrested him. Accused and convicted of being a British agent, he was sentenced to hard labor in a Siberian gulag, where he was tortured by the guards and assaulted by anti-Semitic inmates. Aliza Begin, with Menachem's encouragement, successfully fled to Palestine. He was released after the Wehrmacht invaded the Soviet Union in June 1941, and he enlisted in the Free Polish Army. In 1942, he was ordered to serve under British authority in Palestine. By then, he had located his sister, the only surviving member of his family. His mother had perished in the town's Jewish hospital. His brother Herzl had disappeared without a trace. His father had been arrested with five thousand other Jews from Brest-Litovsk, who had been taken outside the city and either shot or drowned in a river. "I had been taught by my father," he later recalled, "who went to his death at Nazi hands voicing his faith in God and singing 'Hatikvah,' that we Jews were to return to the land of Israel—not go, travel or come, but return."[3]

And so he returned to the land of Israel. He served as an interpreter in the British army, having learned English from listening to BBC broadcasts. When comrades tried to persuade him to desert and assume command of the Irgun, he initially declined. "I gave my word," he explained.[4] He managed to be discharged from the army in 1943 and as commander in chief of the Irgun began planning for the Jewish uprising that began in 1944. In 1946, he ordered the bombing of the King David Hotel, which served as the headquarters for the British army in Palestine. At Begin's instruction, a call was placed to the British to warn them, but it was ignored. Ninety-one British, Arabs, and Jews were killed in the explosion, and forty-five were injured. The attack provoked the ire of the Jewish Agency in Palestine, which claimed authority as the legitimate political representative of Jewish nationalists in Palestine. Its leader, David Ben-Gurion, denounced the Irgun as an "enemy of the Jewish people," and the Haganah ceased its cooperation with the harder-hitting insurrectionists. Haganah fighters apprehended many Irgun officers and turned them over to the British.

The British offered a fifty-thousand-pound bounty for the capture, dead or alive, of the Irgun leader. The Haganah attempted
to kidnap him. Begin went into hiding in Tel Aviv, sometimes disguised as a rabbi, where he continued to lead the Irgun. In May 1947,
he ordered his fighters, disguised as British soldiers, to attack the
prison at Acre, where hundreds of Jewish insurgents were held and
several had been executed. In July 1947, he had two British sergeants
seized and executed in retaliation for the executions of Irgun prisoners. The action dissuaded the British from executing any more Jewish prisoners and convinced them that they would have to relinquish
their authority in Palestine. In April 1948, in the early days of what
was to become the first Israeli-Arab War, Irgun forces destroyed the
Arab village of Deir Yassin. More than one hundred Arabs were killed,
including the elderly, women, and children. It was denounced as a mas-
sacre and condemned by Ben-Gurion. By May 1948, they announced
their intention to withdraw from Palestine, following a UN plan to
partition Palestine into separate Jewish and Arab states. Ben-Gurion
accepted the plan. Begin rejected it.

When the establishment of the State of Israel was announced on
May 14, 1948, with Ben-Gurion as the head of its provisional government,
Begin ordered the Irgun to lay down their arms and join the Haganah
in the new Israel Defense Force (IDF). In June, the Irgun awaited the
arrival of a shipment of arms on board the French freighter *Altalena*.
When Ben-Gurion learned of the shipment, he ordered that the arms
be turned over to the IDF. Begin attempted to negotiate with the government, but a confrontation ensued that ultimately resulted in the
government's order to fire on the *Altalena* as it approached Tel Aviv.
Begin was on board at the time and refused to leave the sinking ship
until the last of the wounded had been evacuated.

Despite the gravity of the crisis and its potential to provoke a civil war
between the rival Jewish factions, Begin insisted that the Irgun disband
and integrate into the IDF. After Israel's first parliamentary elections
in 1949 and the victory of Ben-Gurion's Labor Party, Begin entered the
Knesset in opposition as leader of the Herut (Freedom) Party.

He remained in opposition, except for one brief interlude, for
twenty-six years. In those years, he remained an unyielding nationalist, an advocate for Greater Israel, who demanded stern retaliation

for every attack by Arab guerrillas. In 1952, he incited a protest in the Knesset over a reparations agreement the government signed with West Germany, for which he was temporarily suspended from the Knesset. He was despised by Labor Party leaders as a reckless provocateur. Ben-Gurion could not bring himself to utter his name. Begin remained unaffected by the opprobrium and was as provocative as ever.

By the time of the 1956 war with Egypt and the ensuing Suez crisis— when Israel, in cooperation with France and Great Britain, invaded the Sinai desert—Herut, which backed the move, had become Israel's second strongest party and achieved a level of public approval it had never known before. During the Six-day War in 1967, Begin entered a unity government with his Labor Party rivals, which remained in effect until 1970, when Begin walked out in opposition to the government's consideration of territorial compromises with its Arab neighbors.

Herut continued to grow in strength, due in large part to the welcome it extended to the growing numbers of Sephardic Jews who were flooding into Israel from elsewhere in the Middle East. In 1973, Herut formed a political coalition, the Likud, with other smaller opposition parties. Under Begin's leadership, it remained stridently opposed to relinquishing any territory seized in war from the Palestinians and Israel's Arab neighbors. The October 1973 war saw Egypt and Syria catch Israel by surprise, making substantial early advances before Israel, resupplied by the United States, managed to push them back. Israelis' apprehension over the near disaster, and their disgust over recent political scandals, began to undermine the Labor Party's long dominance. Begin and Likud had sharply criticized the government's inadequate preparation for the war and resisted agreements over disengagement in the Sinai negotiated by U.S. Secretary of State Henry Kissinger. Begin assailed Kissinger's formulation of trading territory for legitimacy. "We don't need legitimacy," he retorted. "We exist. Therefore we are legitimate."

Likud approached the 1977 elections with the credibility it gained after the government's mistakes in 1973 and significantly strengthened by the support of recent émigrés. Nevertheless, when they won a parliamentary majority by a large margin, and Menachem Begin became prime minister, the world was stunned. Western statesmen dedicated to pursuing a resolution of the Arab-Israeli conflict, which had occasioned four wars to date and was an irritant in superpower relations, as well as those Arab leaders who were potentially receptive to peace negotiations, despaired that the hawkish new prime minister believed in anything other than Greater Israel and fighting.

Begin remembered the occasion of his elevation by reflecting on his long struggle: "I survived ten wars, two world wars, Soviet concentration camp, five years in the underground as a hunted man, and twenty-six years in opposition in the parliament. Twenty-six years, never losing faith in a cause."[5]

Despite the general view that Prime Minister Begin's uncompromising nationalism posed an insurmountable obstacle to the peace process, one Arab leader remained surprisingly undisturbed. "There are no doves in Israel," he observed dryly, "only hawks."[6] He understood if one was to make peace with such a country, it would be made with hawks, who wouldn't relinquish an inch of territory for a mere promise of peace but only if the security of the State of Israel was enhanced in the bargain.

That Anwar Sadat was the man who understood that reality and was bold enough to act on it was to be as big a surprise to the world as was the man who extended a hand of peace in return. He had been derided as a "poodle" and "Major Yes-Yes" for the obsequiousness observers saw in his loyalty to the charismatic Arab leader Gamal Abdel Nasser. But he was a more confident man than they gave him credit for and a rare combination of the romantic and the realist, with a shrewd sense of when circumstances gave him the opportunity to act boldly. He, too, was an ardent nationalist and champion of his country's ancient heritage. But it was Egypt that inspired his loyalty, not the chimera of pan-Arabism that gilded Nasser's reputation and deluded the Arab world into thinking that Israel, established by survivors of one of the greatest of all crimes against humanity, would ever yield to threats of extinction. He was a proud man and a proud patriot, but he knew the demands of Arab nationalism had precipitated events that, in the end, had only injured Egypt's pride. He would find means to recover that pride that didn't threaten the country's destruction or require Egypt to subordinate its interests to the schemes and ambitions of others.

He credited his self-assurance to his early childhood. "Everything made me happy in Mit Abuk-Kum, my quiet village in the depths of the Nile Delta," he remembered.[7] Muhammad Anwar el-Sadat was born in that quiet village forty miles north of Cairo in 1918. His modestly educated father, Muhammad el-Sadat, worked as a clerk in an Egyptian army hospital in the Sudan. Sadat's mother, the first of his father's three wives, was an illiterate Sudanese, from whom her second son inherited his dark skin. She lived with her husband in the Sudan, returning to Mit Abuk-Kum to deliver her children and leave them in the care of their paternal grandmother. Sadat revered his grandmother, who enjoyed the respect of the village for her wisdom and her skill as a local healer. From his grandmother he learned respect for the land and pride in his peasant heritage. "Nothing is as significant," she told him, "as your being a child of this land."[8] She saw to her grandson's early education, placing him first in the care of a kindly cleric in the local mosque who taught him the Koran and a love of learning, and then in a nearby Coptic Christian school. And at night she told him tales of Egyptian patriots who had lost their lives fighting the British occupiers, instilling in him, he claimed, his intense dislike of the British and the revolutionary zeal that was to bring him to national prominence.

After the assassination of the British commander of the Egyptian army, the army was ordered to return from the Sudan. In 1925, Sadat's father moved the family—three wives, thirteen children, and one grandmother—to a small house in a Cairo suburb, where he struggled to support them on his modest salary. School fees for his sons were more than Muhammad Sadat earned in a month, and had Anwar's older brother, Talat, not quit school, it is doubtful he could have continued to afford his second son's education.

Sadat attended school with the children of Cairo's elite, who made fun of his peasant dress and accent. But he dismissed suggestions that he had ever envied their advantages or felt any social insecurity whatsoever. Sadat's adult preferences for expensive clothes and elegantly furnished homes would seem to belie his claim of youthful indifference to class distinctions, but he insisted that his peasant heritage, his pride in working the land in his beloved delta, and belonging to a respected family in his village protected him from the taunts of wealthier schoolmates and inured him to his relative poverty. "We in the village took no notice of such things. A man of integrity was the ideal, whatever his poverty."[9]

He loved the theater, took acting lessons, and longed for a career on the stage, but his dark skin proved an impediment to his ambition. Yet his flair for theatrics in speech and action remained with him all his life. He saw the historical events of his time and place as a dramatic pageant, in which a smart, confident, and savvy man could have his chance, were he bold enough to seize it, to take a star turn.

Great Britain had controlled Egypt since the late nineteenth century, formally making it a protectorate in World War I. After the war, it sought to appease rising Egyptian nationalism by granting its colony nominal autonomy under an Egyptian king, but it retained effective control over the most important instruments of state control, particularly military power and the conduct of diplomacy. When King Farouk ascended to the Egyptian throne in 1936, the British, in negotiations with the principal nationalist party, the Wafd, ceded further responsibilities to the Egyptian government but maintained a significant military presence in the country primarily to protect its most important investment, the Suez Canal. As part of the agreement, the British promised to establish a royal military academy to train a new officer class for a larger Egyptian army that would not be restricted to the children of Egypt's most privileged families. Anwar Sadat was among the first to attend it. He enrolled in 1937, graduated a year later, was commissioned a second lieutenant, and married a daughter of one of the more prosperous families in Mit Abuk-Kum.

His first posting was to a signals unit in a Cairo suburb, but he was soon transferred to a remote post in Manqabad, in Upper Egypt. Raised on legends of Egyptian resistance to the "barbarous British oppressors who whipped and hanged our people," an admirer of Kemal Ataturk, Napoleon, Mohandas Gandhi, Adolf Hitler, and other notable enemies of Great Britain, Sadat was a committed revolutionary.[10] In Manqabad, he began working with other junior officers to form a revolutionary organization within the army that could drive the British from the country. In the beginning, the friendly and cheerful Sadat seemed to have been the main figure imparting revolutionary zeal to his fellow officers. But in time, the leadership of the embryonic movement, which became the Free Officers' Organization, would be assumed by "a serious-minded youth who did not share his fellows' interest in jesting," Gamal Abdel Nasser.[11]

World War II offered both motives and opportunities for Sadat, Nasser, and their compatriots to take often reckless chances to undermine the British position in Egypt. German successes early in the war encouraged Egyptians opposed to their country's involvement in the war to establish contacts with agents of the Axis powers. When Britain successfully demanded the resignation of Egypt's prime minister, who had advocated his country's neutrality and withdrawn troops from the field, and when British tanks surrounded King Farouk's palace and forced him to acquiesce in London's choice of a successor, Captains Sadat and Nasser seethed with hatred over this latest humiliation.

In 1941, Sadat attempted to organize a revolt. He planned an assault on Cairo, where the unit he commanded would rally on the outskirts of the city with other units led by dissident officers, quickly seize the government, and drive the British, demoralized by German General Erwin Rommel's successes, from their country. It was a poorly conceived plan and probably known to the British. On the appointed day, only Sadat's unit showed up.

Later that year, Sadat was arrested and detained briefly by British intelligence for his role in attempting to smuggle out of the country the former Egyptian army chief of staff, General Azis al-Masri, who was working with the Germans. In the summer of 1942, he was identified by two captured German agents as one of their local contacts and was again interrogated and released. With Rommel's army advancing relentlessly toward Cairo after his famous victory at El Alamein, the British had more important things on their minds than the disposition of one of many potential insurrectionists in the Egyptian army. That would soon change with the arrival in Cairo of General Bernard Law Montgomery as commander of the British Eighth Army. Through his previous carelessness, Sadat was now known to British intelligence. As Montgomery imposed his authority on the restive capital, Sadat was to pay a serious price for his revolutionary ardor: in the fall of 1942, he was arrested, dismissed from the army, and imprisoned in various Cairo jails for the next two years.

In 1944, he went on hunger strike and managed to escape while being transferred to a hospital. He remained in hiding until the war's end and the lifting of martial law, when he returned to plotting rebellion. By then, Nasser had assumed the leadership of the dissident officers' movement. Sadat later claimed that Nasser became the movement's leader only because he, imprisoned and a fugitive, had been in no position to claim authority. But Nasser's ascendancy was attributable to more than Sadat's misfortune. He was a more calculating revolutionary than the impetuous Sadat and a far more charismatic figure. Sadat was well liked for his good humor and exuberance for the cause, while Nasser was far more austere and distrusting, but Nasser was a more inspirational leader, with an aura of authority that the other officers deferred to. Sadat never betrayed any resentment over his subordinate role—on the contrary, he accepted it graciously.

In January 1946, Sadat was imprisoned again for his involvement in the assassination of a prominent Egyptian cabinet minister who supported the British presence. He spent the next eighteen months in a prison where conditions were much worse than he had experienced in his previous incarceration. In cell 54 in Cairo Central Prison, the only furnishings provided the prisoner Sadat were the floor mat he slept on and a dirty blanket to cover himself. It was a dark and dank hole, infested with insects. He was allowed very little time outside his cell for exercise or use of the unsanitary bathrooms, which spread disease among the inmates. The conditions were intended to break the prisoner's spirit so that he would confess or inadvertently betray himself during the frequent interrogations to which he was subjected.

Nevertheless, Sadat not only endured his travail with dignity but claimed the experience brought him a truer understanding of himself, and with it the peace of mind that proved to be his greatest strength in the years of trial and triumph ahead. "Suffering," he wrote, "crystallizes a soul's intrinsic strength; for it is through suffering that a man of mettle can come into his own, and fathom its own depths."[12] In prison, he claimed, all his faiths were strengthened: his faith in Allah; his faith in his peasant heritage; his faith in his own destiny and Egypt's. He never broke in prison, never fell for the blandishments or succumbed to the threats of his interrogators. And he counseled his fellow conspirators at Cairo Central Prison how to navigate interrogations without incriminating themselves or others. He emerged from cell 54 a man of mettle, hardened, more cunning, and more confident of his own judgment—a confidence that would inform the political flexibility for which he would become famous, as well as the acute sense of timing he possessed for making changes, changes that would often take friend and foe unaware. "My contemplation of life and human nature in that secluded place," he said, "taught me that he who cannot change the very fabric of his thought will never be able to change reality and will never, therefore, make any progress."[13] His first change was of a personal nature. He divorced his wife and soon after married Jihan Raouf, the beautiful Anglo-Egyptian daughter of a prominent Cairo surgeon.

He was brought to trial and acquitted in 1948 and somehow in 1950 managed to be reinstated in the army. By then, the Egyptian army had been humiliated, as had other Arab armies, by their defeat in the war with the new state of Israel in 1948. It was one more humiliation added to those imposed by the British and the weak and selfish King Farouk, who had ransomed Egyptian pride to the British in exchange for his throne. In the wake of the defeat, growing public disdain had finally forced the government to abrogate its treaty with the British. But the gesture to national pride was too late to save the regime. In 1952, the moment arrived for the Free Officers' Organization to rid its country of the disgrace of a corrupt king and his British advisors.

On the night of July 23, the Free Officers' Organization seized army headquarters, all government buildings, and radio stations. Sadat almost missed it. He had not been informed in advance of the hour for the coup and had taken Jihan to the movies. When he returned home, he found a written message from Nasser informing him that the revolution had begun. Sadat found Nasser at army headquarters, where Nasser was directing operations. Once he arrived, Nasser assigned him the responsibility to establish contact with the various rebel commanders and then instructed him to announce the coup on the state radio. He had missed the fighting but was a prominent figure in subsequent events. It was Sadat who persuaded a well-respected former prime minister, Ali Maher, to agree to become the head of a provisional government. And it was Sadat whom Nasser charged with giving an ultimatum to Farouk, demanding his abdication in exchange for safe conduct into exile. When the British chargé d'affaires and military attaché accosted Sadat and protested the rebels' treatment of the Egyptian royal family, he harshly rebuked them: "It has nothing to do with you. It is not a British royal family."[14]

The coup installed a popular general, Muhammed Naguib, as president, and Ali Maher as prime minister. Maher resigned a few months later to protest the policy of land redistribution and other reforms the socialist Nasser insisted on imposing. The monarchy was officially abolished at the same time, and Egypt was declared a republic. Sadat was a member of the twelve-man Revolutionary Command Council that Nasser formed in 1953, which held the real power in Egypt. In 1954, Nasser made his supremacy official, forcing Naguib's resignation and assuming the office of president of the republic.

Sadat held various offices during Nasser's fifteen-year reign, including speaker of the National Assembly. He was ridiculed as the most docile of Nasser lieutenants, and he was always careful never to provide the suspicious and ruthless Nasser with good reason to doubt his loyalty. No original member of the Revolutionary Council remained in Nasser's good graces for the duration of his regime, save one, Anwar Sadat. Sadat claimed that their nineteen-year friendship was the cement that held fast their bond, and that he could and did challenge decisions he felt were in error. It seems clear that Sadat, more than other Nasser lieutenants, could disagree with Nasser privately, and any resulting estrangement between them was always temporary. But few of their associates ever credited Sadat's temerity, and they attributed his political longevity to blind obedience. Sadat came to be perceived in Egypt and beyond as a weak figure, permanently overshadowed by Nasser, who dominated the politics of the Arab world and who, it was said, enjoyed insulting his unassuming subordinate. That impression of weakness was seriously mistaken.

Nasser had secured Britain's withdrawal from the Suez Canal and established Egypt's full independence. He solicited considerable sums of western aid and the promise of American support for building the Aswan Dam. When that support was withdrawn after Nasser signed an arms contract with Warsaw Pact member Czechoslovakia, Nasser nationalized the Suez Canal. Thanks to the intervention of the Eisenhower administration, Nasser successfully resisted the subsequent Anglo-French attempt to seize the canal. Israel's occupation of the Sinai Peninsula, in coordination with the French and British and in retaliation for frequent attacks Nasser launched from the Gaza Strip, ended when the Soviet Union weighed into the Suez crisis by issuing an ultimatum demanding the withdrawal of all foreign armies from Egypt. Though Nasser's "victory" over the Europeans and the Israelis was achieved by American and Soviet intervention, the lucky beneficiary became a hero to the Arab world, which was desperately short of heroes at the time. And he made the most of his acclaim.

He forged close relations with the Soviets, welcoming into Egypt thousands of Soviet technical and military advisors. With Soviet economic assistance and protection, Nasser was free to claim the mantle of leader of the Arab world. He was an advocate of Arab socialism and autonomy over Arab resources and a proponent of a pan-Arabism strong enough to confront the "imperialist" west and the "Zionist invaders" in Palestine. He formed the United Arab Republic with Syria in 1958, which proved to be a union in name only and not, as many hoped and many others feared, the first step toward a pan-Arab state. In 1961, Syrian dissatisfaction forced the dissolution of the UAR. Nasser's ambitions got the better of him in 1962 when he sent Egyptian troops to Yemen to stage a coup ostensibly in the name of Arab nationalism but in reality as a signal to the oil-rich Saudis, who weren't particularly interested in socialism or pan-Arabism. Within months, Egyptian forces in Yemen, which Nasser steadily increased, were bogged down and, after suffering many casualties, finally withdrawn in 1965.

The Egyptian economy, crippled by the disincentives of socialism and the burden of substantial and growing defense budgets, had weakened to the point of crisis, which Soviet aid was insufficient to prevent. Like other Arab leaders, Nasser suffered a serious blow to his prestige when Israel crushed Arab armies in the Six-day War in 1967. He felt obliged to announce his resignation of the presidency after the defeat, but millions of Arabs in Egypt and throughout the Arab world demanded he remain in office. For the last two years of his life, he led Egypt in an intermittent war of attrition to reclaim territory in the Sinai Peninsula that Israel had occupied. This venture, too, was unsuccessful, despite substantial Soviet military assistance, which vastly improved Egypt's air defenses. It ended in a cease-fire declared in August of 1970, a little more than a month before Nasser died of a heart attack. An ailing Nasser had appointed Sadat vice president in 1969, and when he died, Sadat became acting president.

Despite his many failures, Nasser at his death was still the most prominent and revered man in the Arab world. No one thought his amiable and obedient successor would prove to be anything other than a reminder of how great a loss Arabs had suffered with his passing. Sadat's elevation to the presidency aroused little jealousy among Nasser's other lieutenants, who, like their leader, were naturally suspicious men and distrustful of one another. None of them would trust any other with the power of the presidency. Reluctantly, they could agree to entrust it temporarily to Sadat, who they were confident would be easily pushed out of the way when a real successor to Nasser emerged.

By the summer of the first year of his presidency, Sadat, with the support of army loyalists, averted a coup by his war minister, Mohammed Fawzi, drove most of his rivals from power, and imprisoned a number of the most powerful figures in his regime, including his vice president, Ali Sabri, and the head of the secret police, Sharawy Gomaa. That unexpectedly decisive strike was the first of many surprises that the man mocked as "the donkey" was to spring in quick succession on the unsuspecting world. Among the most surprised were the governments of Leonid Brezhnev and Richard Nixon, who shared the view that Sadat was an ineffectual and transitional figure. Elliot Richardson, who had attended Nasser's funeral as Nixon's representative, reported when he returned to Washington that Sadat's government would last only several weeks.

One foreign leader had a more promising view of Sadat. Golda Meir, Israel's prime minister, judged the new Egyptian president to be a "reasonable man who might soberly consider the benefits" of peace with Israel.[15]

As Sadat faced the question and the challenges of resuming the war of attrition with Israel, he did consider accommodation with Israel rather than war. But in those first two years of his presidency, peace, he reasoned, would be achieved only through preparation for war. The Egyptian army had substantially recovered from the damage of the 1967 war. Egypt had not made any real progress in restoring its sovereignty in the Sinai during the war of attrition. Israeli occupation forces were still deployed on the east bank of the canal. But neither had the war entailed another humiliating defeat for Egypt. It had held its own.

Sadat knew Egypt was vulnerable to Israeli artillery and air strikes, and he was frustrated with the Soviets' refusal to supply Egypt, as promised, with surface-to-air missile batteries and combat aircraft required to pose a comparable threat to Israel. He traveled to Moscow in 1971, where, if his account is to be believed, the Soviets offered to provide modern MiG-25s and SAM batteries on the condition that Egypt not use them in an offensive without Soviet approval. Sadat rejected the condition. In the end, Moscow agreed to send some SAM batteries to Egypt—not as many as Sadat had requested, but enough for him to declare that Egypt would no longer be bound by the cease-fire agreement that had briefly suspended the war of attrition.

Nasser, too, had been frustrated with the inadequacies and delays of Moscow's support, but unlike Nasser, Sadat reacted to the Soviets' unreliability and interference by reconsidering their entire client-patron relationship. The coup plotters who had threatened his presidency in its first months were the most pro-Soviet figures in the regime, and Sadat suspected Moscow had played some role in their planning. He also began to address the decades of damage socialism had done by liberalizing the economy and opening Egypt to western investment. It seems that very early on Sadat had a more realistic appreciation than had his predecessor of the disparities between states that relied on U.S. friendship and support and those who had allied themselves with the east. It soon became clear that he was interested in improving his relationship with Washington.

It is probable that his announcement of a peace initiative in a speech before the National Assembly in February 1971 was intended, in part, to demonstrate to the United States that Egypt was reevaluating both its alliance with the east and its leadership of Arab hostility to Israel. He offered to negotiate a peace treaty with Israel through the offices of the UN secretary general for the return of the occupied territories, and to open diplomatic relations with the United States.

Sadat had declared 1971 to be "the year of decision," in which either war would resume or progress toward a negotiated peace would be achieved. Israel doubted Egypt could risk another full-scale military confrontation. Nor did it find his peace offer to be especially compelling. They correctly reasoned that Sadat, despite his declaration, was not yet in a position to make peace. A separate Egyptian approach to making peace with Israel rather than a comprehensive settlement that recovered all Arab territories and restored a Palestinian state would inflame the Arab world, outrage Egyptians who would view it as a concession made from weakness, not strength, and sacrifice Soviet support altogether. And when 1971 passed without either war or peace, Israeli derision of Sadat's "year of decision" seemed justified.

But in his "peace on the one hand or war on the other" posture, one finds the pillars of Sadat's strategy for resolving Egypt's quarter century of hostility with Israel and the disadvantages of Egypt's reliance on the Soviet Union. The Arab conquest of Israel was impossible. Militant pan-Arabism and the glorious vision of driving Israel into the sea were the most significant casualties of the Six-day War, whether Arab leaders admitted it or not. The burdens imposed on Egypt by those pipe dreams had proven unsustainable. As the largest Arab nation with the largest army, Egypt suffered disproportionately in the Arab-Israeli wars. In the 1967 war, they had had three times as many men killed in action as Syria and Jordan combined. Egypt's economy was a wreck and could not be repaired while burdened with huge defense costs, which represented more than one quarter of its national budget, and while receiving insufficient support from its superpower patron. Some accommodation with Israel would have to be reached. But to achieve it, Sadat would have to become the author of events that strengthened his hand both domestically and internationally, to make peace palatable to Egyptians, to impress the west with his sincerity, and to convince Israel to share the risks of peace by reevaluating the perils of war. It was an ambitious undertaking, and a risky one. But he knew the time was at hand to chance it.

During the superpower summit in Moscow in May 1972, U.S. and Soviet leaders issued a joint statement calling for a relaxation of mili-

tary hostility in the Middle East. Sadat took this as the last sign that
Moscow's interests in détente overrode their commitments to Egypt.
On July 18, 1972, he ordered fifteen thousand Soviet military advisors
and their families to leave Egypt within the week. Clearly, he hoped the
stunning move would convince the Soviets that he was serious about
holding them to their promises. But it was also intended to open the way
for rapprochement with the United States, Israel's benefactor. Turning
the largest Arab nation away from the Soviets was a tempting prospect
to the United States, and Henry Kissinger responded with a letter to
Sadat congratulating him on the move and suggesting high-level talks
between the two countries. He also warned Sadat that another Middle
East war would result in the same Arab defeat as the last one. Sadat
agreed to open a secret communications channel with Kissinger, but
by the time they commenced talking, the Egyptian leader had accepted
the necessity of one more wager on a military confrontation.

Within days of announcing the Soviet expulsion, Sadat began conferring with his generals and planning for war. He wrote a letter to the
Soviets at the end of August detailing the problems in their relationship and reiterating his demand that the Soviets provide the military
support they had promised. He had no illusion about Soviet good faith.
He suspected them, correctly, of encouraging plots against him and
supporting leftist demonstrations in Egypt ostensibly over the country's abysmal economic conditions. Neither did he believe the Soviets
seriously intended to supply the quantities of arms they had promised
him. But he believed that if he made a decision to go to war, they would
reluctantly go along and would recognize it was in their interest to do
what they could to make sure it didn't result in another humiliating
defeat for their client.

Sadat told his war council in December 1972 that he intended to
go to war with or without Soviet support, and preparations began in
earnest. Sadat secured Syria's commitment to launch a simultaneous
assault to recover the Golan Heights. He made sure not to repeat the
mistake of the Six-day War, when Nasser had given military commands
to his political allies. The Egyptian military that would cross the cease-
fire line to the east side of the Suez Canal would be commanded by
competent professional officers. As he expected, the Soviets eventually

began to cooperate, supplying Egypt with defensive and offensive missiles, antitank weapons, and other arms and insisting on modifications
to the operational plan. Egypt held four separate large-scale military
exercises in 1973 that put the Israelis on high alert, only to stand down.
When the real war began on October 6, Yom Kippur, with waves of
low-flying Egyptian aircraft bombing and strafing Israelis troops in
the Sinai as they rested on the Day of Atonement, Israel's leaders had
been caught by surprise.

Sadat had seen to it that his forces were better trained, better armed,
and better led than in past wars. They crossed the canal on the first
day with surprisingly few casualties. Egypt's air defenses had held back
the famously formidable Israeli Air Force from decimating the army.
Soviet antitank weapons were used to good effect. Hundreds of Israeli
tanks were destroyed in the first week of the war. More perilously, Syria
had quickly advanced well into the Golan and, with Israel's defenses
concentrated in the west to repel the Egyptians, for a moment looked
unstoppable. An alarmed U.S. government agreed to urgently resupply
Israel's depleted arsenal, and by October 13 the first shipments were
arriving. The next day, eight days into the war, a huge and decisive tank
battle was fought in the Sinai. Egypt was routed by Israeli tanks under
the command of Ariel Sharon. The tide had turned, and from that point
forward Israel began to roll back Egyptian and Syrian advances. By the
time a UN Security Council cease-fire was negotiated on October 22,
Israel had recovered most of the territory it had lost in the opening days
of the war. Fighting continued for another four days before all sides
accepted the UN cease-fire. In those last hours of the war, Israel had the
Egyptian Third Army trapped and was prepared to destroy it. Only U.S.
intervention stopped it from happening. Most alarming, the Soviets had
threatened to take unilateral action if Washington didn't agree to join
them in imposing a cease-fire. Both countries went on nuclear alert.
And it was with enormous relief that Washington and Moscow watched
as the cease-fire seemed to hold on October 26.

Sadat had started the war with realistically limited objectives, and
the most important of them were political, not military. He wanted to
prove to Egypt and the Arab world that the IDF was not invincible,
and with the early successes he had done so. Egypt had been defeated,

but it had not been humiliated. Sadat had restored the pride of the Egyptian people and was hailed as "the hero of the crossing." The war had also shown that Israel, with the support of a more generous and reliable superpower patron, could never be conquered. The State of Israel was a fact and would remain so. The time to make peace was approaching. Immediately after the cease-fire was in place, Sadat summoned a friend who ran a construction company and told him to begin building houses near the canal. "I want to rebuild those towns right within range of Israeli guns. I want to show the Israelis that I don't intend to make war against them again."[16]

The next two years saw Henry Kissinger's shuttle diplomacy result in two separate disengagement agreements in the Sinai, which Sadat would use to reopen the Suez Canal. Sadat joined the Soviets, the United States, and most of the Arab world in calling for a Geneva conference to negotiate a regional peace agreement that would include a settlement of the Palestinian question, with some form of participation by Palestinian representatives.

But he soon despaired of this approach to peace. Syria and other Arab states were proving obstreperous, and the Arab world had collapsed into another of its episodic feuds, this time over the civil war that had started in Lebanon. Israel rejected any direct involvement of the Palestinians in the conference, and Sadat soon abandoned any lingering hope that the Soviets would prove a more trustworthy ally than they had in the past. He detected Soviet complicity in massive riots over rising food prices that rocked Cairo in January of 1977, as he found himself in a perilously weaker position than he had been at the end of the war. The Egyptian military was growing impatient with him, as he had yet to find an arms provider to replace the Soviets. Egypt's economy, and the desperate poverty it produced, could not be repaired unless defense expenditures could be greatly reduced, perhaps with greater support from the west. Radical Islamic fundamentalists were becoming more active in opposition to Sadat's policies. Libya, under megalomaniacal strongman Muammar Qaddafi, was increasingly hostile to his regime. The Soviets were installing sophisticated surveillance equipment at Libyan airfields near the Egyptian border. He demanded they desist, and when they declined, he ordered the Egyptian Air Force to destroy the airfields.

Despite his continued public support for a Geneva conference, he expected only mischief from the Soviets there. Nor did he believe Arab rejectionists could be persuaded to negotiate in good faith or that Israelis could be persuaded to make concessions absent some bold move by one of their enemies that would both impress them and their indispensable ally, the United States.

The Soviet and American governments (the latter now led by the recently elected President Jimmy Carter) issued a joint statement in October 1977 reiterating their call for a Geneva conference and referring to the "legitimate rights of the Palestinians," which provoked bitter criticism from Israel and American Jewish organizations. Eventually, the Carter administration backed down and announced the U.S.-Soviet statement would not be the basis for Geneva negotiations. Sadat realized he would never recover the Sinai with so many conflicting interests at play in the tortured efforts to find a comprehensive settlement to the Arab-Israeli conflict. He knew his own impatience was surpassed only by his people's, who believed they had realized few tangible benefits from the 1973 war and were tiring of Egypt's sacrifices on behalf of the Palestinians. The prospects for peace, for which he had fought the war, were evaporating. If they were not saved, another Arab-Israeli war was inevitable. So he decided to act alone and offer his hand in friendship to the people of Israel and to the unwavering Israeli patriot who had promised never to surrender an inch of the biblical land of Israel. He knew any attempt to work bilaterally for peace with Israel would incur the wrath of other Arab states, the Palestinians, and Egyptian rejectionists. Many of his advisors warned against the idea. To gain the support of his people and his government would require a dramatic act that would seize the world's attention and could break through the unimaginative diplomacy, rigid animosities, and exhausted politics of the past.

In October 1977, Sadat met with Romanian leader Nicolae Ceauşescu, who despite Romania's affiliation with the Soviets maintained friendly relations with Israel. Ceauşescu had met with Menachem Begin earlier that year, and Begin had assured him he was ready to negotiate peace with any Arab country. Ceauşescu now told Sadat he believed the offer was sincere. Sadat responded positively to the assurance, and

Ceaușescu passed on the welcome development to Tel Aviv. In remarks
he delivered at the opening of the National Assembly in early November,
Sadat, in the kind of seemingly impulsive and unanticipated gesture that
characterized his unique statesmanship, declared he "would go even to
the home of the Israelis, to the Knesset, to discuss peace with them."

Begin thought the offer was simply posturing and didn't respond.
When Sadat repeated the offer on two other occasions, Begin casually
remarked, "I hereby invite President Sadat . . . to Jerusalem," betraying
the lack of seriousness with which he regarded the proposal. No Arab
leader had ever agreed to visit the State of Israel. Most of them couldn't
bring themselves to utter the name "Israel." Begin, with his scrupulous
formality, strict attention to protocol, and deliberative lawyer's mind,
couldn't imagine that any head of state would offer so casually such an
unprecedented and hugely significant gesture. But when Sadat repeated
the offer in an interview with CBS newsman Walter Cronkite, Begin
authorized his government to begin secret negotiations with Egypt to
determine whether Sadat was serious. To Begin's surprise, he was.

A few minutes before 8:00 p.m. on November 19, 1977, Menachem
Begin stood at attention as he watched a Boeing 707 with the words
"Arab Republic of Egypt" painted on its fuselage lower its landing gear
and touch the runway at Tel Aviv's Ben-Gurion Airport. When Anwar
Sadat emerged a moment later, smiling broadly and waving, a trumpet
blast greeted him, and the wild cheering of thousands of witnesses
drowned out the sharp gasps that issued from many Israelis present. To
think they had lived to see such a thing: an enemy had come to Israel to
make peace. When the applause died down as an Israeli military band
played the Egyptian anthem, many could be heard weeping.

No two men could have been more dissimilar, it was often remarked.
Unlike Sadat, Begin was not a man given to grand gestures. Sadat despised
detailed and exacting negotiations. Begin was a master of them. Sadat
was anxious for quick results. Begin was endlessly patient. To Sadat,
words weren't a substitute for action, they were intended to force action.
To Begin, words could mean the difference between life and death, and
they were to be weighed and constructed with great care.

But in the most important ways, in the ways of the heart, they shared
a kinship. Theirs was a pride derived from their faith in the causes they

served. They both were in thrall to the histories of their nations, both proud of their contributions to their countries' independence, both claiming the strongest attachment to their land as part of their personal identities and the historical identities of their civilization. They possessed the self-confidence of men who believed their every breath was drawn to defend and honor the civilizations they served. They were both brave men and self-assured. They could not be intimidated. They reacted poorly to threats. They had suffered sterner tests of their courage than most people ever face and survived more certain of their convictions and of the roles assigned to them by history.

They were warriors who unapologetically sanctioned violence in service to their causes. They had no bloodlust, but no doubts either over decisions they had made to make war, to sacrifice human life. They neither wanted to nor could have escaped the memories of their pasts. Both men had taken risks to fight for their countries, and both men perceived in the events of their time the moments when peace became possible and when it became their responsibility to take risks to achieve it. They shared a single concern in every negotiation, every decision, every call to arms, every offer for peace: was it right for their people? They took each other's measure, and believed they could create a peace that was right for their peoples, a peace that would endure for generations born long after their striving had ended, and they themselves had found the peace of a quiet grave.

In the Knesset, Sadat spoke words few of its members ever expected to hear in their lifetimes. "This corner is yours," he told them. "You want to live with us in this part of the world. We welcome you in sincerity. . . . People of Israel, teach your children what has passed is the end of suffering and what will come is a new life." He didn't shrink from insisting on what he believed was necessary to secure the peace he had come to promise, including a Palestinian state in the territories Arabs saw as occupied and Begin saw as liberated. Nor did Begin refrain from insisting on Israel's "eternal, undisputed rights" to the land in question: "We know how to defend ourselves, our wives, our children and our honor." But what began in Sadat's two-day visit to Israel changed forever the strategic equation in the Middle East. Without Egypt's participation, there could never be a successful Arab-Israeli war.

Sadat returned to a hero's welcome in Cairo, even more enthusiastic than the one he received in Jerusalem. Most of the Arab world and all the various feuding factions of the Palestine Liberation Organization immediately denounced him as a traitor. Begin and Sadat were to meet ten times in their lives, and their negotiations to achieve and maintain a formal peace were long, arduous, and often rancorous. There was often a coolness between them. But with President Carter as their mediator at Camp David over thirteen days of difficult negotiations in September 1978, which more than once appeared on the brink of failure, each man yielded something to reach a framework agreement for peace, because they believed that peace was more important to their countries than what they relinquished for it. Begin returned the Sinai and committed to removing the Israeli settlements there that he had sworn he would never abandon. Sadat agreed to terms that merely promised to negotiate the autonomy of the West Bank and Gaza, with a final decision about their status postponed for five years and a temporary—and as it turned out very brief—freeze on Jewish settlements there.

It took another six months of hard bargaining before the principles of the agreement were made into the details of the formal treaty, establishing peace between the two nations, signed in the White House Rose Garden on March 26, 1979. The unbending warrior for the Jewish people, Menachem Begin, ended his remarks at the signing by crying out, "No more war, no more bloodshed, no more bereavement. Peace unto you. Shalom! Salaam! Forever!"

In the Middle East, such dreams are hard pressed to survive. There are always more wars, more violence. The rest of the Arab world rejected the treaty and expelled Egypt from the Arab League. It was many years before another Arab country made a formal peace with Israel. A lasting peace between Arabs and Israel and a settlement of the Palestinian issue remains elusive. For Israel, there have been other wars, brief incursions, and long struggles. There have been intifadas, mortar attacks, and constant acts of terrorism. But the peace with Egypt has held, thanks in large part to the honorable Egyptian who gave his word and kept it and to the honorable Israeli who gave his in return.

Despite the scorn he received from other Arab states, Sadat was again hailed by Egyptians as a hero for the peace he achieved. But the acclaim would soon subside. When Begin submitted the treaty to a vote in the Knesset, twenty-nine out of forty-three Likud members voted against it. They argued that Egypt was sacrificing "strategic depth" and Jewish settlements for a piece of paper. "This is the first peace treaty Israel ever signed," Begin pleaded, "the first peace treaty after five wars in which we have lost twelve thousands of our people. Our . . . dream is to smash this helix of hatred. We must sign this treaty because it is a human act of the highest degree." He knew that piece of paper offered a just peace because a just man had signed it with him.

Sadat had anticipated that many in the fractious Arab world would resent his decision to make peace with Israel. But he believed most Egyptians would welcome it, and so they did. He never betrayed any doubts about the decision nor anxiety that he would face inordinate danger from fellow Egyptians for acting boldly in Egypt's best interests as well as Israel's. He did not expect to meet the end that the Middle East's hard and violent history accorded him.

On the anniversary of the Yom Kippur War in 1981, while attending a military review, Anwar Sadat was assassinated by members of the Egyptian Islamic Jihad who had infiltrated the army. His last words were "This is inconceivable." Yet violence is seldom inconceivable in that part of the world. The weak, the frightened, and the hateful seem to conceive of little else there. Conceiving peace is the rarer accomplishment. That Sadat and Begin achieved it, not despite their history but because of it, is a testament to the real truth of their lives: they were faithful tribunes of their people, and when they gave their word, they gave their nation's word. Sadat's commitment was his legacy. He had known when to make a peace that would outlive him. And so it has.

Begin was deeply moved by the murder of his peace partner and attended his funeral. It occurred on the Jewish Sabbath, and Begin, an observant Jew, could not ride in an automobile. So he asked to be lodged in quarters near the funeral site. The only rooms close enough to accommodate him were in run-down army barracks, which he accepted graciously. He walked in the funeral procession limping in pain from a leg injury. Egyptian soldiers lining the route returned his respect, saluting sharply as he passed them. Two years later, he was to abruptly resign from office, in despair over the death of his beloved wife, Aliza, and the protracted and bloody war in Lebanon he had authorized. "I can go on no longer," he explained, and spent the last ten years of his life in total seclusion.

In the year this chapter was written, Israel fought another war in Lebanon against terrorists supplied and trained by Iran, whose president regularly promises Israel's extinction and whose government is intent on developing the nuclear weapons that would pose a very serious strategic threat to the State of Israel. The United States is engaged in a long, anguishing war in Iraq. Both Syria and Iran seem intent on destroying the sovereignty and stability of Lebanon, which only recently has known a measure of peace and independence. The murderous extremism that killed Sadat has gained more adherents and even bloodier tyrants to lead it.

Sadat and Begin died having known little peace in their lives. But between Israel and Egypt there has been no more war, no more bloodshed, no more bereavement. Peace unto them who made it so. Shalom. Salaam. Forever.

CONFIDENCE

The most important distinction to understand about confidence is that it is not a conceit. When vanity is substituted for genuine confidence, it often has disastrous consequences. Some decision makers are blindly confident in their genius or so cherish their reputation for boldness that their pride always demands they act boldly in circumstances they might not fully comprehend, or despite available information that suggests caution. Conversely, there are people who work hard to convey the impression of confidence to mask their insecurity and reluctance to act responsibly in difficult situations.

When General George McClellan refrained from pressing his considerable advantages in men and arms during his army's offensive on the Virginia peninsula during the Civil War, his decisions were compromised by an insecurity in his own ability and an uninformed overestimation of the enemy's that he hid from himself and the public with excessive attention to his reputation and pridefulness, and sneering contempt for his detractors and his commander-in-chief, Abraham Lincoln. He fancied himself a self-assured commander, and much of the public perceived him as such. In reality—a reality he could not admit even to himself—he was grossly deficient in his responsibility to judge events on the battlefield, and he suffered from a timidity that bordered on cowardice. Yet no general ever seemed more confident than the man who reveled in the public's acclaim of him as the "little Napoleon."

Perhaps his worst mistake as a combat commander was his failure after the Union's narrow victory at Antietam to pursue and engage

General Robert E. Lee's retreating Army of Northern Virginia. Had he done so, and led competently in the ensuing battle, it is probable he would have inflicted a more decisive defeat on the Confederacy, possibly deprived the south of its greatest general, and hastened the end of the Civil War. Confederate general Joe Johnston wrote to Lee after Lee had escaped unbothered to Virginia, "No one but McClellan could have hesitated to attack."[1]

Typically, McClellan defended his failure to act by praising his own perspicacity and patriotism. He wrote after a night of anxious deliberation,

> and a full and careful survey of the situation and condition of our army, the strength and position of the enemy, I concluded that the success of the attack . . . was not certain. . . . [A] general is expected to risk a battle if he has a reasonable prospect of success; but at this critical juncture I should have had a narrow view of the condition of the country had I been willing to hazard another battle with less than an absolute measure of success.[2]

McClellan was a competent administrator and very skilled at organizing a well-trained, disciplined, and proficient Army of the Potomac from the disorganized, demoralized, and irresolute fighting force it had been before he took command. But he was a disastrous commander in the field. To McClellan, confidence was an attribute that enhanced his image. It was not an actual quality he possessed at all but merely an adornment. He possessed neither the confidence required in informed decision making nor the fortitude to see a decision through to its conclusion. His example is interesting because most often an excessive regard for one's own ability, exceptionality, or destiny breeds overconfidence. In McClellan's case, all it bred was pretense. Vanity, then, and the selfishness that is its source, can make a decision maker reckless or timid—but in both instances it renders him or her ill equipped for his or her responsibilities. In military commanders, such character flaws are exceedingly dangerous to the force and the cause they lead. For McClellan, the regard he possessed in his own superiority but lacked in his army or his own battlefield leadership—the "slows," as Lincoln called them—earned him history's contempt, summarized best, though harshly, by historian Kenneth Williams:

> Surely the verdict must be: McClellan was not a real general. McClellan was not even a disciplined, truthful soldier. McClellan was merely an attractive but vain and unstable man, with considerable military knowledge, who sat a horse well and wanted to be President.[3]

Confidence in making and executing a decision should be a quality derived primarily from a realistic perception of the situation and parties involved; your objectives; the risks; the quality of the information available; and past experience in similar situations. The decision maker's self-confidence is as important to the decision as is confidence in the information and advice used to make a decision. Self-confidence is often mostly, but not entirely, derived from a decision maker's previous successful decisions and, one hopes, a realistic appraisal of whatever reviews they received from people in position to judge the merits of those decisions. It should be attained not only from success but from learning the lessons of previous failure. It must be based in the author's preparation to make the decision, his or her acquisition of all relevant information in the time available, and the weeding out of extraneous information. Without this last quality, self-confidence can often lead a decision maker astray. It leads to complacency, overconfidence, and a sense of invulnerability. No matter how successful our previous decisions have been, we should never grow so confident that we invariably choose to "go with our gut" when faced with the choice between our gut and known facts that argue against our inclination. We should not, of course, be restrained from challenging facts or seeking additional information if our past experiences and instincts tell us they are inaccurate. But we must make the effort to know—and refrain at all times from dismissing the weight of the available evidence simply because it might prevent us from acting as boldly as we would like.

In one of the stories that follows, we examine General Douglas MacArthur's decisions in the Korean War because they offer such compelling examples of why such self-confidence is potentially harmful if not governed by more than self-regard. In the end, self-confidence is only a virtue when it is premised on the author's certainty that he has prepared himself, in the past *and* in the present situation, to make the best decision he can. All else is vanity, perhaps the worst attribute that anyone who is responsible for making important decisions could possess.

Confidence can be a difficult balancing act. Too little, and we become submissive, overly conforming, distrustful, and even depressed by the responsibility to decide. Too much, and we become excessively motivated, contemptuous of advice, inattentive, and rash. A little humility will go a long way to avoid either extreme. However anxious we become, few of us ever find ourselves in situations that lack any means but our own discernment to build our confidence. Knowledge and counsel and an acknowledgment of our own responsibility can at least prevent our concerns from paralyzing us. And however experienced or successful we are, we can all profit from remembering how yesterday's hero is tomorrow's goat. If it is a very hard call, with reasonable arguments on both sides, accept arguments and information contrary to the decision you prefer as instructive, not as challenges to your reputation. If there is no additional information available to settle the matter, weigh the experience, reliability, and humility of counselors on both sides of the argument and give the greatest weight to those who possess those qualities the most. When none of these factors obtains or are determinative, then and only then go with your gut, if you feel you are prepared and experienced enough to do so.

Once the decision is made, and its execution ordered, confidence should become fortitude. "What I essentially did was to put one foot in front of the other, shut my eyes and step off the ledge," Katharine Graham wrote. "The surprise was I landed on my feet."[4] She assumed the leadership of the Washington Post Company in 1963, after her husband Philip's suicide. She was, by her own admission, a shy and insecure woman, who few believed was capable of running a Fortune 500 company. She was devastated by her husband's death, and by his erratic and scandalous behavior in the last years of his life when he suffered from manic-depression. She was plagued by self-doubt. Yet, after she made her decision, she revealed a fortitude that was the equal of and quite possibly superior to that of her predecessor's. She kept her nerve through the Pentagon Papers and Watergate controversies, and a bitter and prolonged labor strike. While her self-confidence might not have approached the levels of a typical CEO, her resolve to make tough decisions and stick by them was as admirable as her humility and honesty. Her fortitude made her an exemplary decision maker and trailblazer for female executives.

If you believe you have taken care to make the best decision possible under the circumstances, and no new facts or early reactions to it have proved it unwise, then you must have the resolve to see it through to the end. Time pressures or a lack of immediate success or confusion or minor setbacks or unforeseen but not critical challenges will make you anxious. That is unavoidable. They will cause early second-guessing on your part or by others. But whatever doubts and worries might creep into your mind, you must not let them discourage you to the point that you reverse the decision or fail or unduly limit whatever actions are required of you or others to execute it. Only results or the obtaining of new and credible information you did not possess in advance of the decision should cause you to do that. And when results or new information reveal your decision was wrong, then you must have the confidence to reverse it, if it is still possible, or take some other compensating action.

During World War II, Winston Churchill often signed messages to subordinates and even to the president of the United States with the acronym KBO. It meant "keep buggering on," and it was the motto of his wartime leadership. Often, though not always, Churchill made his most critical decisions by applying his shrewd, informed, and experienced judgment to the known facts, and then he stuck it out unless he the results suggested failure. Worry and self-doubt help to lose wars. Persistence wins them. In war, more than any other endeavor, results are seldom achieved as quickly as we like them. Have the courage to be patient, the humility to recognize you could be wrong, but the confidence to wait until something more than anxiety over inconclusive results proves you so. Keep buggering on until facts and nothing else prove it imprudent to do so, and then have the confidence to stop.

MISS WHAT FOR

The 1924 summer Olympic Games in Paris featured so many memorable contests that they still hold an illustrious place in Olympic lore. Paavo Nurmi, "the Flying Finn," won five gold medals for long-distance running, setting an Olympic record for the 1500-meter race, and then another an hour later in the 5000. British runner Eric Liddell won a gold medal in the 400 meter, after declining to compete in his best event, the 100 meter, because the preliminary was scheduled on a Sunday. His teammate, Harold Abrahams, won the latter event, and a cherished story of British pluck and religious piety was born, memorialized fifty-seven years later in the film *Chariots of Fire*. Johnny Weissmuller, competing in his first Olympics, won three gold medals for swimming and a bronze for water polo, after nearly being ejected from the games for beating up a heckler. He was to win another two gold medals four years later in Amsterdam, before he achieved lasting fame as America's favorite Tarzan.

Americans dominated the games that year, winning nearly three times as many medals as the runner-up, France. American women won all three medals in the 100- and 400-meter freestyle swimming events, the gold and the bronze in the 100-meter backstroke competition, the silver in the 200-meter breaststroke, and the gold in the 400-meter relay.

Women's participation in the Olympic Games was still rather new in those days and limited to far fewer events than were open to the men's teams. The modern Olympics began in 1896, under the leadership of its autocratic founder, French aristocrat Pierre de Coubertin, who believed that women's role in competitive athletics should be limited to raising athlete sons. He grudgingly agreed to a few women's swimming events in the 1912 Olympics but insisted that women lacked the endurance to compete in any individual races longer than 400 meters, a restriction that remained in place until 1960. In 1924, women athletes were still barred from all track-and-field competition. The few female American athletes present that year were lodged in a Paris suburb, miles from the Olympic pool, in order to prevent their exposure to the lax morality of Parisian culture.

The success of the American women's team that year was a curiosity, but hardly on par with the thrilling, record-setting triumphs of the men's competition. And despite their success, they were disappointed with their performance, having come to Paris intent on capturing every medal in the individual swimming competitions. They attributed the failure to live up to their own expectations to fatigue caused by their transatlantic crossing and their difficult daily trek to and from the games.

One American in particular was dissatisfied with her performance. She had managed to win bronze medals in two events and was a member of the gold-medal relay team. That was less than she expected to achieve, but she had been hampered by a knee injury. Although, for reasons that are difficult to understand, she was not considered the best swimmer on the American team that year, she knew better than anyone else—except, perhaps, her sister Meg—that, in the water, she was the fastest woman alive. She was even better at long distances and intended to prove it. Gertrude Caroline Ederle, a shy, stocky, 142-pound girl, with broad shoulders, high cheekbones, and bobbed hair, swam because she loved it. She loved it so much there was nowhere she would rather be than in the water, competing with any swimmer, male or female. And in her brief but spectacular career as a competitive swimmer, she broke records, lots of them, men's as well as women's.

She had been, she later claimed, "a water baby," who was always "happiest between the waves." Born in 1906 to German-immigrant parents in New York City, where her father, Henry Ederle, owned a successful delicatessen and meat market, she grew to be a skilled swimmer, as did her five brothers and sisters. When she was still a little girl, she nearly drowned in a pond at her grandmother's house. The experience had made her afraid of the water, but, rather than succumb to her fear, she learned to swim. The next summer, near her family's summer cottage in New Jersey, her father tied a rope around her waist, tossed her into a river, and shouted encouragement to her as she furiously dog-paddled to stay above the water. She never wanted to be far from the water again. When the Ederles returned to the city, she often indulged her new infatuation, to her father's displeasure, by splashing around in the horse troughs near her family's apartment. Gertrude—or Gertie, as she was called by her family—had suffered a hearing impairment after contracting measles when she was five. Her doctor warned her parents that she could aggravate the condition if she continued to swim. But neither she nor her loving, indulgent family paid him any heed. Just four years after she had learned how not to drown, at the age of twelve she entered an 880-yard freestyle competition and won in thirteen minutes and nineteen seconds, becoming the youngest athlete in the world to hold a record.

Both her father and mother offered Gertie unstinting encouragement, but her sister Meg was her most ardent supporter. She gave Meg the credit for pushing her to enter swimming competitions, when Gertie had been content to swim for the pure pleasure of it. It was Meg who encouraged her eleven-year-old sister to join the Women's Swimming Association of New York, newly established in a rented pool in the basement of a Brooklyn hotel and dedicated to training girls for competitive swimming. Within the first few years its existence, it became the premier training organization in the new sport of women's swimming, and its members dominated national and international competition. The association trained many famous athletes, including future Olympic champion swimmer Eleanor Holm and Hollywood legend Esther Williams. But Gertrude Ederle was to become its greatest champion.

The genius behind the association's astonishing and immediate success was Louis deBreda Handley, an Italian immigrant who ran an import business. He had competed in amateur swimming events for years and had won two gold medals at the 1904 Olympics. He eventually became America's leading expert in the sport. He analyzed the techniques of competitive swimmers in four newspapers, wrote five books on the subject, and penned the entry for "swimming" in the *Encyclopaedia Britannica*. His friends called him Lou. The girls he trained without pay at the Women's Swimming Association referred to him as L. deB.

He taught them a new swimming stroke, the front crawl. It had been used for years by, among others, Native Americans, who demonstrated its superior speed to British colonialists. (The British refused to employ the stroke, thinking it uncivilized to thrash around so in the water.) But it was virtually unknown in the world of competitive swimming until Handley learned about the new stroke Australian swimmers were using and adapted it for his girls. He taught them to kick their legs three times for every powerful arm stroke and use the flutter kick, with the knees bent instead of straightened as in the scissors kick. The Australians used two kicks for every stroke. Handley's adaptation was the six-beat, double-trudgen crawl (named for an English swimmer, John Trudgen, who developed an early, less arduous form of the stroke), which soon came to be called simply "the American crawl." And he taught the girls to breathe by turning only their head slightly to the side, rather than rotating their entire body.

Until then, most competitive swimmers—who were men, of course—swam the breaststroke, using a scissors kick. Women, with more body fat, are particularly well adapted for the crawl. They are more buoyant and, thus, can kick faster and with greater ease. Handley knew it would prove a more efficient and less exhausting technique for women than the breaststroke. Yet most swimmers and their trainers assumed it was far too strenuous for men, much less women, to sustain in long-distance swimming and disliked what they considered its distinctly inelegant form.

Handley's first champion, Ethelda Bleibtrey, a polio victim who had joined the Women's Swimming Association to strengthen her atrophied legs, used the crawl to set world records in every event she entered at the 1920 Olympic Games. But it was Gertrude Ederle who popularized the American crawl and proved its superiority to all other strokes. A talented

competitor had made fun of Ederle early in her training as she practiced the stroke, only to find herself finishing a distant second to Ederle.
Ederle mastered the crawl easily and soon added a kick to each stroke.
She was the first of Handley's swimmers to use an eight-beat crawl, four
kicks for every arm stroke, which greatly increased her speed, without,
she soon discovered, significantly straining her endurance.

Just shy of her fifteenth birthday, she gained considerable public attention. She entered a three-and-a-half-mile race, the Joseph P.
Day Cup, from Manhattan Beach to Bergen Beach, with fifty other
swimmers, among them both the U.S. and British women's national
champions. Ederle was entirely unknown as a long-distance swimmer. But when the starter's gun fired that day, she plunged into the
water confident that with her eight-beat crawl she was the equal of
any competitor. And she was. She won the competition handily and
burst onto the public stage, where she was to remain for the rest of the
decade.

The 1920s, romantically remembered as the jazz age, are also considered by many sportswriters to have been the golden age of American
sports. It was the decade when heavyweight champion Jack Dempsey,
the Manassa Mauler, was perfecting his bob and weave and building
his unsurpassed thirty-two-fight winning streak, twenty-eight of them
by knockouts. It was the decade when an orphan kid from Baltimore,
Babe Ruth, became the biggest thing in baseball by hitting sixty home
runs in a single season and when he and Lou Gehrig and the rest of the
Yankees' "Murderers' Row" were terrifying opposing pitchers, winning three American League pennants and three World Series. It was
the era of Red Grange and the Four Horsemen of Notre Dame, "Big
Bill" Tilden in tennis, Bobby Jones and Walter Hagen in golf, and Man
o' War at the racetrack. And it was the era of Gertrude Ederle, who,
though she is dimly remembered today, was for a brief moment the
brightest star of them all.

She quickly followed her triumph in the Day Cup with a series of
wins that secured her national reputation. By the time she was seventeen and joined the women's Olympic team, she had broken eighteen
world records in distances from 100 to 800 meters. She had collected
dozens of trophies and held a number of national swimming titles. In

one summer afternoon in 1922, in a single 500-meter swim at Brighton Beach in Brooklyn, she broke seven world records. By 1925, she held twenty-nine amateur national and world records, more than any other woman in the world. And her greatest accomplishments still lay ahead.

After she returned from Paris, she began to train for her biggest challenge, one no other woman had ever accomplished. On June 14, 1925, she set a world record at Long Beach, Long Island, for the 150-yard freestyle, shaving a little under two seconds off the previous world record she had set three months before. The next day, she began her longest swim to date, seventeen miles from the Battery to Sandy Hook, New Jersey. Leaving on the ebb tide before dawn, she had fairly light work for a while as she left lower New York harbor, passed Governors Island, and crossed the main channel. As she swam past Staten Island and began pulling away from New York, the tide changed, and she had to struggle to finish. The saltwater stung her eyes, and she was weary from hunger, having decided not to provision the rowboat that accompanied her with food or water. But when she finished, with a time of seven hours, eleven minutes, and thirty seconds, she had shattered the previous record, the men's record.* The next morning, Gertrude boarded an ocean liner for France.

On July 11, 1925, *The New York Times* noted the passengers on the Cunard ocean liner, the *Berengaria:* "Miss Gertrude Ederle who swam from the Battery to Sandy Hook (a twenty one mile race which she won in record time) on Monday is also a passenger. She is going to try to swim the English Channel." That had been Meg's idea as well. "I thought she was crazy," Ederle remembered. But the more she thought about it, the more she liked the idea, and the more confident she became that she could succeed.

Swimming the English Channel was then, and remained until recently, the Mount Everest of marathon swimming. In an age before airplanes and car races and professional athletics, it had an almost

---

*The record remained intact for eighty-one years, until in 2006 an Australian marathon swimmer, Tammy van Wisse, who claims Ederle as her inspiration, beat it by two hours.

mythical quality. No one is known to have swum the Channel unassisted until 1875. That year, on his second try, Captain Matthew Webb, a British naval officer with a muscular physique and large mustache, managed to swim through a storm, huge seas, and stinging jellyfish to cross the Channel in twenty-one hours and forty-five minutes, while drinking coffee, beer, and brandy and nourishing himself with pieces of roast beef. (Seven years later, Captain Webb perished while attempting to swim the whirlpool rapids at the foot of Niagara Falls.) At a ceremony to celebrate his triumph over the Channel, the mayor of Dover predicted, "In the future history of the world, I don't believe any such feat will performed by anyone else."

No one else managed the feat for another thirty-six years until T. W. Burgess, from Yorkshire, wearing motorist goggles to protect his eyes, accomplished it on his thirteenth try in twenty-two hours and thirty-five minutes. Only three other men succeeded in the years between Burgess's crossing in 1911 and Gertrude Ederle's initial attempt in August of 1925. No women had ever conquered the daunting challenge. An American, Henry Sullivan, a robust if rather overweight thirty-four-year-old, successfully crossed on his seventh attempt on August 5, 1923, and still holds the record to this day for the slowest time, twenty-six hours and fifty minutes. Six days later, Enrico Tiraboschi of Argentina set the fastest record at sixteen and a half hours. Scores of others, even women, had tried. They had all used the breaststroke. Ederle's trainer, Jabezz Wolffe, a Glasgow native, enjoys the distinction of being the unluckiest Channel swimmer. He tried and failed on twenty-two occasions, once when he was only yards from the finish before heavy seas and fatigue defeated him.

The English Channel at its narrowest, between Calais and the white cliffs of Dover, is twenty-one miles as the seagull flies. But it is a treacherous twenty-one miles, with powerful tides and dangerous crosscurrents that can pull swimmers miles off course. Even in the height of summer, the water temperature seldom exceeds sixty degrees Fahrenheit. Swimmers face a real risk of hypothermia, particularly if they are slow and if the weather has whipped the sea into a fury, as the weather often does there. Even in summer, the weather in the Channel is often miserable, fogbound and windy, with prolonged gales and high seas moving in from the Atlantic and an abundance of stinging

Portuguese men-of-war and jellyfish to contend with. It is also home to the busiest sea-lanes in the world, another hazard to those who dare to swim it. There are, of course, longer marathon courses that swimmers have conquered, but few more daunting than the Channel.

Gertrude, like so many others before her, failed in her first attempt, to no one's surprise except her own. But she almost managed it and very well might have succeeded, had not her trainer, familiar as he was with the warning signs of failure, stopped her. She had completed twenty-three miles, in nearly nine hours of swimming, with only a little more than six miles remaining, when a great storm-tossed wave overwhelmed her. As she coughed out seawater and appeared in distress, the ever-alert Wolffe, on board the tugboat that accompanied her, shouted, "She's drowning." Another man reached out to touch her, which under the rules of Channel swimming is an immediate disqualification.

She was furious, and worried about what people back in the States would say about her. They didn't say much, as few people had expected her to succeed in the first place.

She vowed she would try again, and soon. She sacked Wolffe as her trainer and replaced him with Thomas Burgess, who unlike Wolffe had successfully crossed the Channel. She told her father that in her next attempt, no one—no one—was to bring her out of the water unless she told them to do so. The Women's Swimming Association had sponsored her first attempt, and Gertrude didn't want to burden it further as she pressed her luck a second time. Two newspapers, the *Chicago Tribune* and the New York *Daily News,* offered to finance her second attempt and pay her a small salary. If she succeeded, they would pay her a bonus, and she would give them the exclusive rights to her personal account of the experience. To accept the offer, she would have to forfeit her amateur status, which would make her ineligible to compete in the Olympics or any other amateur event. She accepted it. The Channel meant more to her than any future competition or honors.

She had not only to prepare herself for the arduous swim but to keep the memory of her first failure from affecting her confidence. She had been, as always, quite confident of success, but now that she had experienced defeat, she knew just how difficult a challenge she faced. And fear, as she later explained, is the greatest obstacle the Channel presents. But she knew, too, what she was capable of doing, and she was determined to do it. With Meg, her father, Burgess, and two reporters from the *Tribune* and *Daily News* accompanying her, she set out again in June of 1926 for the coast of France.

Three days before her second attempt, on August 3, Clarabelle Barrett, a schoolteacher from New Rochelle, New York, had tried to swim the Channel and had almost done it after swimming for nearly twenty-four hours. Two miles from the finish, she got lost in the fog and dark and was officially declared missing for a couple of hours before being rescued. Ederle was also aware that another American woman, Lillian Cannon, was preparing to attempt the feat in a few weeks.

The morning of August 6, on the beach at Cap Gris-Nez, France, the heavy gray skies and rising surf signaled an approaching storm front, and a posted warning advised small craft to stay at anchor. In anticipation of heavy seas, steamship crossings had been canceled for the day. In a black two-piece swimsuit, designed by her sister, with a small American flag sewn over her breast, a red swimming cap, and yellow goggles, Gertrude waited impatiently as Meg smeared her with Vaseline, olive oil, and sheep lard to protect her from the cold and jellyfish. "For heaven's sake, let's get started,"[1] she barked before she waded into the surf and offered a silent prayer, "Please, God, help me."[2] She had planned to swim a course that followed an S-shaped route, first to the west and then back toward the middle of the channel, before riding a favorable tide to the beaches of Dover. At 7:09, she said "cheerio," plunged into the cold gray water, and started swimming for England.

London bookies were giving six-to-one odds that she would not make it. The London *Daily News* published an editorial that morning predicting her failure and observing that "even the most uncompromising champion of the rights and capacities of women must admit that in contests of physical skill, speed and endurance they must remain forever the weaker sex."[3]

Just a few minutes out, battered by a big wave and feeling nauseous, Ederle gave a brief thought to turning back. "I nearly quit seven minutes after starting because of a rough swell," she remembered. "But I thought I had to make a showing . . . [and] when I got a few miles out I was confident I could make it."[4]

Two tugboats followed her. Written on one side of the *Alsace,* which carried her father, Meg, Burgess, and several other supporters, was the encouragement, "This Way, Ole Kid," with an arrow pointing toward the Dover cliffs. On board the other tug were the two reporters, husband and wife Westbrook Pegler of the *Tribune* and Julia Harpman of the *Daily News,* photographers, and a movie camera crew. They brought with them a phonograph, a few records, and wireless equipment to flash reports of her progress back to the States.

The seas were reasonably calm at first, and she plowed ahead in good time. But by ten o'clock, rain had started to fall, and the cold water numbed her left leg, making it difficult to kick. As the rain grew heavy, a strong southwesterly wind whipped up bigger swells and whitecaps. By early afternoon, the tide changed, and a squall kicked up. Powerful crosscurrents carried her farther off course. For every yard forward she gained, the sea pushed her two yards laterally. After six hours, as she struggled to make any progress, Burgess yelled for her to come out, and her sister urged her to keep swimming. She kept going.

To keep her spirits up, the reporters played "Let Me Call You Sweetheart" and "Sweet Rosie O'Grady" on the phonograph, though the needle jumped and scratched in the rough water. She sang along, timing her eight-beat stroke to the music and joined the reporters in repeated renditions of "Yes, We Have No Bananas," until her father warned her to conserve her energy. They read cables to her from her mother. And when they received no more cables, they invented them. Occasionally, they held up a sign to mark her progress, showing first one wheel and then two wheels, a reference to the red roadster her father had promised her if she made it. They fed her pineapple wedges, chicken legs, broth, chocolate, and sugar cubes, which they handed to her in a net on a long pole to avoid any disqualifying contact.

Sometimes the current pushed her nearly out of sight of the tugs, an "eerie feeling," she recalled. But she talked to the sea as if it were "a child that I've known for a long time." She never felt alone, she said, "when I'm out there." And she kept chopping through the waves. "I knew I would either swim it or drown," she remembered.

The storm worsened, and the swells rose to twenty feet, as she watched some of her companions lean over the lee sides of the tugs and vomit. Every time she paused for a moment to gather her strength, they looked anxiously at her and asked if she was able to continue. She turned away and resumed swimming. At six o'clock, she was clearly exhausted and swimming just to survive. The treacherous currents that whip around the English shore were trapping her in the pitching swells. Burgess had had enough. She had made a good showing, but the Channel was too daunting a challenge for any woman, even one as brave and strong as Gertrude.

Frantic with fear, he begged her to quit. "Gertie, you must come out," he shouted.

"No," she replied.

"You must come out," he repeated.

"What for?" she asked and swam away as the worried reporters wired the intrepid swimmer's response to her thrilled countrymen. If she gave any thought to heeding Burgess's pleas, she never admitted it. Even in the dark, she could see the Dover cliffs ahead of her, and every swell that had thrown her back was one less obstacle in her way. She was fighting for her life, and only she—and Meg, perhaps—still believed she could reach the shore.

The last several hundred yards were the worst, as her heavy limbs weakly slapped the water. But she could see the bonfires on the shore that had been lit by the thousands of people who were waiting to greet her, and she summoned her strength to make a good show at the finish: four swift kicks to each stroke of her tired arms until she cleared the current, reached the shallows, stood up, and waded ashore at 9:40 p.m. The wind, waves, and currents had added fourteen miles to the twenty-one that separated Cap Gris-Nez from Kingsdown, England. She had made it in fourteen hours and thirty-one minutes, beating Enrico Tiraboschi's record time by two hours. A relieved and immensely proud Thomas Burgess, whose own time had also just been surpassed by Gertrude's swim, declared, "No man or woman ever made such a swim. It is past human understanding." Henry Ederle, who had placed a bet with Lloyd's of London, had won $175,000, and he wired his delicatessen to hand out free hot dogs to any New Yorker who wanted one.

Her father joined the multitudes wading into the surf to greet her. He embraced her and wrapped a robe around her. Flares and spotlights guided her, ships blew their horns, and thousands shouted their acclaim as she walked toward the shore unassisted. The first person to greet her on the strand was a British customs officer, who asked for her passport. She was unable to produce one and had to wait a couple of hours on the *Alsace* before His Majesty's government relented and welcomed her to England. While she waited, the reporters asked where she had found the resolve to conquer the treacherous Channel. "I just knew it could be done," she answered. "It had to be done, and I did it."[6]

She returned to New York aboard the *Berengaria*. On her arrival, ships sounding their horns and sirens crowded the harbor, and a biplane dropped flowers on the ship's deck. The city gave her a bigger ticker-tape parade than it had given the returning heroes of World War I, bigger than any it had ever held, as two million people crowded the sidewalks and waved from office windows. New York's seldom understated mayor, Jimmy Walker, proclaimed her feat the equal "to Moses crossing the Red Sea, Caesar crossing the Rubicon and Washington crossing the Delaware." The always understated president, Calvin Coolidge, pronounced her simply "America's best girl." New Yorkers called her "Trudy, Queen of the Seas" and "little Miss What For."

Irving Berlin wrote a song for her, "Trudy." *The New York Times* proclaimed her triumph "the biggest thing in athletics ever done by a woman, or a man for that matter."[7] Westbrook Pegler wrote that he "would not have swapped my place in the tug . . . for a seat at the ringside of the greatest fight or at the arena of the greatest game in the world. For this, in my opinion, is the greatest sports story in the world."[8] Later that year, Ederle was voted "the most popular personage of our time," outpolling Babe Ruth for the honor.

She starred in a short film, *Swim, Girl, Swim,* and accepted an offer to join a touring vaudeville act. For months, the post office delivered bags of marriage proposals, but after one brief engagement ended when her intended got cold feet, she never considered another. By 1928, the shy girl who was happiest between the waves suffered a nervous breakdown from the strain of travel and public attention. Her Channel swim had severely worsened her hearing impairment, and within a few years she was almost completely deaf. That, too, frayed her nerves, as she struggled in public to hide her affliction. By the time she withdrew from public life, her star had already been eclipsed by Charles Lindbergh's solo flight across the Atlantic, a development that didn't seem to bother her at all.

In 1933, she slipped on loose floor tiles and fell down a flight of stairs, injuring her spine so severely that nineteen neurologists told her she would never walk or swim again. Six years later, she briefly reemerged in the public spotlight to swim in an exhibition at the World's Fair, "the Aquacade," staged by Broadway showman Billy Rose. Rose had asked her to give it all she had, but after she finished he acknowledged his surprise at her performance by explaining he hadn't meant his encouragement to make her swim "like a bat out of hell."[9] After her performance for the Aquacade, she slipped comfortably back into obscurity. Apparently, she had agreed to the performance only in order to show the world that she could do it.

LANDING THE EAGLE

They said good-bye on the far side of the moon. At 2:12 p.m. (ET), in their thirteenth lunar orbit, sixty-two miles above the lunar surface, Mike Collins pushed a button, triggering the springs that pushed the two spacecraft apart. "Beautiful," he exclaimed as he peered through the window of the command module, *Columbia*. Apollo 11 Mission Commander Neil Armstrong rotated the *Eagle*, giving Collins a good look at the lunar module so he could verify that its landing gear had extended and locked. "You're looking good," Collins confirmed.

"Roger," Armstrong responded. "The *Eagle* has wings."

"You've got a fine-looking flying machine, there, *Eagle*, despite the fact you're flying upside down," joked Collins.

"Somebody's upside down," Armstrong replied.

"You guys take care," Collins said as he bid good-bye to Armstrong and the lunar module pilot, Buzz Aldrin, before he fired a short burst of his thruster and drifted away from the *Eagle*.

"See you later,"[1] the laconic Armstrong responded, intent as ever on the job at hand. For the next twenty-seven hours, Collins remained alone, sixty miles above the moon, relaying communications from Mission Control in Houston to the two astronauts aboard the *Eagle*.

Back at Mission Control in Houston, Gene Kranz's White Team—the engineers, scientists, computer technicians, and astronauts who manned the rows of consoles in the crowded room, monitoring and directing Apollo's operations—had started their shift at eight o'clock that morning. They would see Apollo 11 through the day that culminated in the fulfillment of an eight-year dream, from President Kennedy's initial declaration in 1961 that Americans would try for the moon to the actual moment when an American placed his foot on the lunar surface. Now they were waiting to reacquire communications with the astronauts, who were out of radio contact while orbiting behind the moon. When the *Eagle* came around the moon, Houston gave Armstrong and Aldrin the go-ahead to begin their initial descent, which would lower their orbit to fifty thousand feet above the moon. They fired the *Eagle*'s descent engine for the first time and flew the spacecraft sideways, with their faces looking down at the moon. There were no seats in the crowded crew compartment, so the astronauts stood, with their feet in restraints.

The man with responsibility for communicating directly with Armstrong, Aldrin, and Collins, the capsule communicator (CAPCOM), was fellow astronaut and Air Force major Charlie Duke, a 1957 graduate of the U.S. Naval Academy and a fighter pilot with a master's degree in aeronautics from MIT. Three years later, he would be the tenth man to walk on the moon. While the *Eagle* made its descent, Duke's southern drawl became familiar to the world as he anxiously communicated the lunar module's fuel-consumption levels to Armstrong and Aldrin, while Armstrong silently steered the craft to a suitable landing spot.

Gene Kranz, the flight director, called "Flight" by his team, and boss of the entire mission operations, sat behind Duke, in the third row. He was wearing his trademark white vest, listening in his headset to the buzz of communications among his chattering team, and somehow making sense of it all. In the nearly fatal disaster that befell a subsequent mission to the moon, Apollo 13, his steady resolve and unyielding determination to bring his three astronauts home made him a hero in the eyes of the American public and a symbol of the remarkably resourceful engineers and scientists at Mission Control during the Apollo years.

Sitting at the middle console in the front row, "the trench," was an earnest, focused, and whip-smart young man, Steve Bales, who had been hired by NASA in 1964, shortly after he had graduated from Iowa State University with a bachelor of science degree. Bales served as the guidance officer (GUIDO) in charge on July 20, responsible for monitoring the computer guidance systems on board Apollo 11. He had been a backup controller for early Gemini missions but had worked as a flight controller for the first time only three years before. Now, when Kranz or the astronauts demanded information from "Guidance," Steve Bales was responsible for answering them, as authoritatively and quickly as he could.

Born in Ottumwa, Iowa, where his father worked as a janitor and his mother as a beautician, Bales had been a college freshman majoring in aeronautical engineering when President Kennedy committed America to "landing a man on the moon and returning him safely to earth" before the decade was out. But he traced his obsession with space travel to an earlier experience. "It was about 1956 when I saw that Disney program," he remembered. The program he referred to was a series of television shows that Walt Disney had produced, working in collaboration with Wernher von Braun, to promote von Braun's vision of manned space exploration to the moon and Mars. The program used cartoons to illustrate how such a feat could be accomplished within the lifetimes of most of its viewers. "At the time, one of the big unknowns was what the back side of the moon looked like," Bales recalled. "And they were doing radar mapping of the moon. And then they had another flight and actually did the landing . . . and it made a very big impression on me. It was outstanding."[2]

Twenty years after Apollo 11 made history, Bales described his emotions on the day when a manned mission, which he played a critical part in directing, actually landed on the moon. "It was the Walt Disney cartoon come to life. It was like everything you had ever read about when you were a kid about going to another place other than Earth. And yet it was real."[3]

On July 20, 1969, Bales was only twenty-six years old, and before the day was out he would be hailed as exactly the right man in exactly the right place at exactly the right time by his colleagues at Mission Control and by the three Apollo astronauts, whose fate, and the fate of their mission, he would hold in his hands.

Neil Armstrong was born in 1930 and raised in Wapakoneta, Ohio. A quiet, serious boy and Eagle Scout, he fell in love with airplanes after his first ride in one at the age of six. He built a wind tunnel in the basement of his family's home to test the aerodynamics of his model airplanes. At fifteen, he started flying lessons, and on his sixteenth birthday he received his pilot's license, before he earned a license to drive a car. He attended college at Purdue University on a scholarship that required him to serve three years on active duty in the U.S. Navy after finishing his sophomore year.

He reported for flight training at the Naval Air Station in Pensacola, Florida, in 1949. After earning his wings, he received orders for Korea and flew his first combat mission on August 29, 1951. Five days later, he was shot down on a reconnaissance flight and ejected safely. He flew seventy-eight combat missions in Korea and earned three air medals before retiring from active duty in August 1952 and returning to Purdue to finish his degree in 1955. The next year, he was accepted as a civilian test pilot at the National Advisory Committee for Aeronautics High Speed Flight Station at Edwards Air Force Base in California. In the seven years he remained at Edwards, he flew the Bell X-1B rocket ship to an altitude above eleven miles and flew seven missions as a project pilot for the X-15, once reaching an altitude of nearly forty miles. In 1962, he was chosen as one of six pilot-engineers for the X-20, a "space plane" then under development by the Air Force. But in the autumn of that year, he was selected as an astronaut in NASA's new Apollo project.

Armstrong had a quiet air of command. He indulged in little if any small talk, even with his family, and never gave any outward sign of his emotions. He appeared to be all business, all the time, and kept his opinions on matters unrelated to his work or outside his authority to himself. He had a very dry sense of humor, which was often undetected by those who didn't know him well. Unlike his fellow astronauts on Apollo 11, and with the exception of his one memorable observation upon setting foot on the moon, he never felt an urge to describe the spectacular experience of flying to and landing on the moon beyond the matter-of-fact communications he used to check off this or that task. It was not in Armstrong's nature to wax poetic about his experiences and the emotions he felt during them. That doesn't mean he didn't have any emotions. He just kept them to himself. Shortly before Apollo 11 launched, a NASA administrator, George Low, asked him if he had thought about what he would say when he reached the moon. "Sure, George, I've thought about it," was all the enigmatic Armstrong volunteered.[4]

Air Force colonel Edwin Eugene "Buzz" Aldrin Jr. was born in 1930 in Montclair, New Jersey. His father, Edwin Eugene Aldrin Sr., had been a student of Robert Goddard and an aide to the man whose will and vision created the U.S. Army Air Corps, legendary general Billy Mitchell. Aldrin Jr. graduated third in his class from West Point in 1951 and flew F-86 "Sabre" jets in sixty-six missions during the Korean War, with two confirmed MiG shootdowns to his credit. After the war, he served as an aerial-gunnery instructor at Nellis Air Force Base and later as an F-100 squadron commander in Bitburg, Germany.

Aldrin temporarily stopped flying in 1959, intending to earn a master's degree at MIT in aeronautics and astronautics. He stayed long enough to earn a Ph.D. and successfully defended his thesis, a study of manned space rendezvous, in 1963. He dedicated his thesis to "the men in the astronaut program. Oh, that I were one of them." The techniques he devised in his thesis for bringing piloted spacecraft into close enough proximity to dock were used in all NASA rendezvous and docking flights, including the first docking between American astronauts and Russian cosmonauts. Not long after earning his Ph.D., Aldrin was accepted into the Apollo program, making him the first astronaut with a doctorate. His NASA colleagues nicknamed him "Dr. Rendezvous."

Aldrin was notably more voluble than Armstrong—most people were—and seemingly more comfortable in the public spotlight. He lobbied hard to be the Apollo 11 mission commander and the first man to walk on the moon, and he was disappointed when the assignment was given to Armstrong, reportedly because NASA and the Nixon administration believed a civilian commander would better represent the peaceful intentions of the American space program. But he took the disappointment in stride, performing admirably throughout the mission and with more obvious joy that he was one of the two luckiest men in the world. "Beautiful, beautiful," he exclaimed upon setting foot on the moon, "magnificent desolation."

Air Force lieutenant colonel Michael Collins was born into military service, in Rome, where his father, Army major general James Lawton Collins, was stationed in 1930. He took his first ride in a plane when still young, while his family resided in Puerto Rico. He followed his father, brother, two uncles, and a cousin into the military when he enrolled in the U.S. Military Academy's class of 1952. But to avoid charges of nepotism, he chose to enter the Air Force upon graduation from West Point. After earning his wings, he was chosen for advanced fighter training at Nellis and eventually assigned to the Twenty-first Fighter-Bomber Wing, where he learned to fly and deliver nuclear payloads. He transferred with the wing in 1954 to a NATO base in France. While serving in France, his bomber caught fire during an exercise, and he and his copilot ejected safely.

A highly skilled pilot, he was accepted as test pilot at Edwards AFB, where he amassed four thousand hours of flight time. But after John Glenn orbited the earth in 1962, Collins applied to join the exclusive ranks of American astronauts. He was not accepted for the class of astronauts chosen that year. Undeterred, he enrolled in a class that offered instruction in spaceflight, reapplied to NASA, submitted to a second round of evaluations, and was accepted into the program in October 1963.

He had been selected as command-module pilot for Apollo 8 in 1968 but suffered a herniated disc. After surgery to fuse two of his vertebrae and three months in a neck brace, he was scrubbed from the flight. When fire broke out in the capsule of Apollo 1 during a training exercise in 1967, killing all three astronauts aboard—Virgil Grissom, Ed White, and Roger Chaffee—Collins volunteered to tell Martha Chaffee of her husband's death.

Good-natured, easygoing, and self-effacing, Mike Collins never seemed to resent having to remain sixty miles above the moon while Armstrong and Aldrin enjoyed the privilege of walking where no man had ever been before. In his autobiography, he wrote that the mission "has been structured for three men, and I consider my third to be as necessary as either of the other two."⁵

During his nearly twenty-eight hours of solo flying around the moon, with forty-eight minutes of each orbit out of radio contact with earth, utterly alone, he said he never felt loneliness but "awareness, anticipation, satisfaction, confidence, almost exultation."⁶ He designed most of the famous mission patch for Apollo 11, with an eagle about to land on the moon, its talons open, and a partial view of the earth in the background. Someone complained that the image was too warlike and suggested placing an olive branch in one of its claws. The recommendation was accepted, and Collins dryly noted that he hoped the eagle "dropped that olive branch before landing."⁷

Armstrong, Aldrin, and Collins all had previous spaceflight experience. Armstrong had served as the command pilot in Gemini 8, in 1966, when he and fellow astronaut David Scott executed successfully the first docking of two spacecraft in orbit. During the last Gemini mission, Gemini 12, Aldrin proved in a two-hour-and-twenty-minute space walk that astronauts could work outside the vehicle— EVA (extravehicular activity) in NASA nomenclature. Collins had flown with astronaut John Young in Gemini 10 and performed two EVAs, during one of which he fixed a serious problem that was affecting the docking mechanism.

Despite their extensive training for and experience in earlier missions, the astronauts chosen for Apollo 11 had to undergo a full year of additional training. No training for any space project had been more detailed or rigorous. It included flying simulators for both the command and lunar modules. The astronauts traveled to the factories where both modules were built and were briefed on every detail of their spacecraft. They sat through lectures on subjects as far afield from their expertise as geology and volcanoes. They trained for launch, reentry and splashdown, rendezvous, docking and undocking, lunar descent and ascent, moon walks. They were measured for pressure suits, endured centrifuge training to experience the g-forces they would have to withstand, and pored over dozens of scenarios for every phase of the mission. Collins's training focused on the command module, and sometimes he trained alone, to prepare him. Armstrong and Aldrin practiced flying the lunar module in an ungainly machine called the lunar-landing training vehicle (LLTV). It was built to replicate as much as possible all the controls they would use and the feeling of handling the module in the last stage of its lunar descent. With its powerful thrusters, it was difficult to fly. Armstrong had to eject during one practice flight, when the LLTV flew out of control and crashed.

Most important, NASA trainers and the astronauts tried to conceive of every possible thing that could go wrong, devise a procedure to correct it, and rehearse it over and over and over again, keeping a lengthy log of each contingency and response. They were as prepared as anyone could be for their historic mission. Whatever natural confidence they had in their own abilities and capacity to function under duress, nothing beats preparation and experience, as any pilot will tell you, to give you the confidence to make real decisions under real stress. Some decisions, even life-and-death ones, must be made instantly in certain situations, which don't afford time to consult widely or consider at length your reaction to an unexpected problem. A manned mission to the moon qualifies as one of those situations. Training and experience are all that can prepare you for making such decisions, no matter how fateful, with a confidence that isn't reckless but sure. You learn instincts. You're not born with them. And any confidence you possess that isn't derived through testing yourself and preparing for an experience isn't confidence. It's a conceit, and a dangerous one at that.

Mission Control trained as well. Dick Koos ran the computer simulations for the Mission Control teams, and he took his work seriously. He had worked as a computer guidance specialist for the army's Missile Command at Fort Bliss. During the Mercury and Gemini projects, he became expert at programming simulated spaceflights and was rightly proud of his ability to devise problem scenarios to throw at his astronauts and controllers. Eleven days before Apollo 11 launched, he threw "Case No. 26," at Gene Kranz's White Team, a particularly obscure program alarm he was confident the controllers wouldn't recognize. Koos wasn't concerned about whether they knew what the alarm meant. He wanted to observe whether they followed procedure for handling an unknown program alarm: unless you had two cues for a problem or could see that there was some malfunction in an important task, you were not to decide to abort the mission.

That, however, is exactly what Steve Bales, the GUIDO, decided to do. Three minutes into the landing simulation on July 5, Koos told his technicians to load alarm 1201. Neither Bales nor anyone on the team knew what it meant. Bales was the team's expert on the *Eagle*'s computer system, and he had to quickly page through a handbook to determine its import. Before Kranz or Koos demanded an answer, Bales had found that alarm 1201 signified that the *Eagle*'s computer was overloaded with tasks. But Bales hadn't any idea what would be the probable upshot of an overload. All systems seemed to be working. Then Koos ordered another series of alarms, and Bales quickly consulted with a backroom software engineer, Jack Garman, for an explanation. "It's a BAILOUT alarm," he said. "The computer is busier than hell for some reason, it has run out of time to get all the work done."[8] Bales had no idea what task was being neglected. Other than the alarms Koos kept firing into his console display, everything appeared to be functioning normally. Worried that something critical was being overlooked, Bales told Garman he thought it was time to abort the mission. He so informed Kranz, and Kranz called the abort.

Koos marched into the Mission Control room to blister the controllers for the decision. "This was not an abort. You should have continued the landing."[9] If everything else appears to be working, he explained, you need another reason to abort. "You must have two cues to abort," he scolded. "You called for an abort with only one." Over the next six days, Koos drilled the controllers with flurries of program alarms until Bales and Garman knew which ones were serious and which ones probably weren't. Bales made a list of all the program alarms that would require an order to abort the landing. Alarm 1201 wasn't among them.[10]

———

ON THE DAY of the lunar landing, while Mission Control waited to reacquire communications with the *Eagle,* Gene Kranz gave his controllers a final pep talk.

Hey gang, we're really gonna go and land on the moon today. . . . We're about to do something that no one has ever done. Be aware that there's a lot of stuff that we don't know about the environment that we're ready to walk into, but be aware that I trust you implicitly. . . . I know we're working in an area of the unknown that has high risk. But we don't even think of tying this game, we think only to win, and I know you guys, if you've even got a few seconds to work your problem, we're gonna win. So let's have at it."

The *Eagle*'s engine burn to bring it into a lower lunar orbit began at 3:08 p.m. (ET) and lasted a little less than half a minute. When both *Columbia* and *Eagle* reemerged from the far side of the moon, CAPCOM Charlie Duke asked for a report on the Eagle's initial descent. Since *Columbia* was now flying in an orbit fifty miles higher than the lunar module, Houston received radio communications from Collins sooner than it received them from Armstrong and Aldrin. Additionally, communications with the *Eagle* were occasionally interrupted due to problems with the lunar module's antennae. Aldrin had relayed to Collins that they had reached their orbit of fifty thousand feet, and Collins now reported to Duke that "everything is going just swimmingly. Beautiful."[12] Ninety seconds later, Aldrin's voice reached Houston, and he confirmed that the *Eagle* was in position to begin its final powered descent to the moon. The astronauts ran a check of their computer guidance and navigation systems and waited for Mission Control to give them the order for powered descent initiation (PDI). It was critically important that PDI occur at a precisely determined place in their orbit. If they began too soon and too high, they would run out of fuel before landing.

The astronauts had to determine their location by sighting landmarks on the moon. The *Eagle* was still flying horizontally, and the radar the module was to use to determine its exact distance from the moon's surface faced upward and could not provide any usable data. As they flew facedown, Armstrong and Aldrin sighted lunar mountains, noted their own velocity, and, using a mathematical formula Armstrong devised, determined their angle and rate of descent and thus calculated their location and altitude. Around 4:00, Collins radioed Armstrong and Aldrin that Houston had given them a go for PDI. At 4:05, the *Eagle* fired its engine at 10 percent of maximum thrust and began its final descent to the moon. Not long after, Armstrong noted that they were passing landmarks a few minutes ahead of schedule. He assumed that they had begun powered descent a little late and might overfly their landing target, a ten-mile-long and three-mile-wide "footprint."

Looking back at the experience twenty years later, Neil Armstrong explained how the astronauts managed to remain such a picture of coolheaded self-assurance in the exacting enterprise: "Although confident, we were certainly not overconfident. In research and in exploration, the unexpected is always expected. We were not overly concerned with our safety, but we would not be surprised if a malfunction or an unforeseen occurrence prevented a successful lunar landing."[13] They had prepared for the unexpected. And they were ready to respond when it happened.

At Mission Control, Steve Bales was worried. The *Eagle*'s velocity was too great. It was flying twenty feet per second faster than it should have been. He told Kranz that the module's speed and low altitude indicated that the module's navigation system was in error, which would affect the *Eagle*'s trajectory. He was close to calling an abort, but it could not be called too late in the descent or the engine burn might severely damage the module's ascent stage. Still, Bales told Kranz that he would wait a little while longer to see if the problem continued. Minutes later, Armstrong swung the *Eagle* around to get in position for landing. Once the module was no longer flying horizontally but upright, its landing radar found the moon's surface, calculated the *Eagle*'s altitude, and signaled the onboard computer guidance system that the rate of descent was too fast. The computer caught the problem and reduced the module's velocity.

"For the first three minutes of the descent," Bales recalled, "I was just praying this thing wasn't going to grow because I didn't want to stop the landing." After his patience was rewarded by Armstrong's timely maneuver, Bales thought, "The worst thing that could happen to me has happened to me. . . . Things will be OK now."[14]

Charlie Duke advised the astronauts they were a go to continue powered descent. Minutes later, as the burn pitched the module violently from side to side, the *Eagle*'s display console flashed a yellow computer alarm. Armstrong radioed Houston, "program alarm . . . It's a 1202." Not knowing what a 1202 signified, Armstrong asked Mission Control to explain it. Steve Bales didn't know what a 1202 meant either, but he knew it wasn't among the major alarms he had listed after Dick Koos's simulation drills. Gene Kranz needed an answer immediately.

Bales consulted with Jack Garman. Only seconds had passed since the alarm first flashed when Kranz pounded his console, demanding guidance from his GUIDO. In a controlled but clearly urgent voice, Neil Armstrong demanded a "reading on that 1202 program alarm." Armstrong later recalled that he wasn't particularly worried about the alarm, knowing that alarms flash frequently that don't amount to serious problems. But for a few anxious seconds, nineteen to be precise, Houston sensed a potential abort, which—in addition to being a crushing disappointment for the astronauts, everyone involved with the mission, and virtually the entire world—was a dangerous maneuver, as the two stages of the module violently separate, and the ascent stage guns its engine at maximum thrust to race back toward *Columbia*. "It was a heart stopper," Charlie Duke recalled.

No one panicked. Bales would have liked more time to make such a fateful decision, but he and Garman quickly decided that 1202 indicated the same problem as 1201: the computer was simply signaling that it had too much work to do. If the *Eagle* was flying well, and Armstrong and Houston could see that it was, and as long as the alarm remained intermittent and not continuous, they should be fine. So as every controller in Houston waited for word on whether the mission would be aborted minutes before it made history, twenty-six-year-old Steve Bales, after conferring with his twenty-four-year-old associate Jack Garman, gave the order: "We're a go on that, Flight. If it doesn't recur, we are go." Kranz repeated the order to Charlie Duke, who radioed the astronauts, "we're a go on that alarm."

Moments later Aldrin reported another 1202. Without hesitation, Bales responded that they are still a go. Twice again, Aldrin radioed that the 1202 alarm had flashed, and twice again Bales told Kranz to proceed. At three thousand feet, the astronauts received the order from Duke that they were a go for landing. "Roger, understand," Aldrin responded. "Go for landing." In the same instant, the computer sent a 1201 alarm. Bales dismissed it, and Charlie Duke told Aldrin, "Roger,

1201 alarm. We're go. Same type. We're go." When a 1202 flashed at two thousand feet, Bales waved it off again. In all, seven program alarms flashed during the *Eagle*'s descent. Whatever anxiety Bales must have suffered, he betrayed no doubts. "Go," he repeated, "go."

The astronauts aboard the lunar module showed no panic either. But they were distracted. Armstrong was searching the lunar landscape for a suitable place to land the *Eagle,* and his concentration was interrupted repeatedly by the shrill alarms. Now, as they approached five hundred feet, he didn't like what he saw. The guidance and navigation system was flying the *Eagle* toward a crater surrounded by immense boulders. He thought if he could stop the module just short of the crater, they would be all right. But it soon became obvious that they wouldn't be able to stop in time to avoid a potentially disastrous impact with one of the threatening boulders. He took control of the *Eagle* and flew it manually, as if he were flying a helicopter, looking to "land long," in a pilot's vocabulary. At that point, the module was pitched slightly forward.

Armstrong brought it fully upright to slow its rate of descent. As Aldrin called out various readings of their altitude and velocity, Armstrong—standing, peering out of a small triangular window, gripping the hand controllers—scanned the surface for a safe place to land. For agonizing minutes, he could not find one. But the experience and steady calm of the pilot and his hours of training in the LLTV made him well suited to the challenge.

In Houston, they didn't know what was happening. Their computers told them that Armstrong had assumed manual command. But they didn't know about the crater. And they didn't know why the *Eagle* hadn't landed. All they could hear was Buzz Aldrin reading out numbers. From the sensors attached to the astronauts' bodies, they could see that Armstrong's heart was racing at 156 beats per minute, twice its normal rate. They also knew that the *Eagle* was nearly out of fuel.

At 260 feet, Aldrin glimpsed the *Eagle*'s shadow. Between 200 and 160 feet, Armstrong saw where he wanted to land, just past another smaller crater. A little below 100 feet, however, their engine blast began to kick up clouds of lunar dust that obscured surface visibility. At 75 feet, Duke told the astronauts they had sixty seconds of fuel remaining.

Fully occupied with flying the module, the astronauts did not radio any response, and everyone in Houston was becoming seriously worried. With still no idea what Armstrong and Aldrin were doing, Kranz told Duke to remind them that "there ain't no gas stations on the moon." Duke informed them that they had thirty seconds before their fuel was exhausted. Again, no response, just Aldrin continuing to report the numbers: "Forty feet, down two and a half. Picking up some dust. Thirty feet, two and a half down. . . . Four forward, four forward. Drifting to the right a little."

"You could hear a feather drop," Kranz said.[15] He and everyone else at Mission Control knew that, for the time being, they were no longer part of the decision making for Apollo 11. Neil Armstrong had assumed sole authority for landing the *Eagle*. Houston, in a state of unbearable anxiety, waited to learn if he had made the right decisions, as did an anxious Mike Collins, quietly flying alone, sixty miles above them.

At fifty feet from the moon's surface, it was too late to abort. Still, Armstrong hadn't reached a safe place to land. But at this point, Armstrong believed the *Eagle* was close enough to survive even a crash landing intact. "I knew we were getting short. I knew we had to get it on the ground. . . . But I wasn't panic-stricken about the fuel."[16]

After they had cleared the crater, Armstrong banked a little to the left to avoid boulders, and moments later saw a smooth and level space, about two hundred feet square, on which to land the *Eagle*. As he slowed the module's descent, the swirling dust confused his perception of depth and speed. The *Eagle* began to drift first backward and then sideways, as a frustrated Armstrong pumped the hand controllers to correct it. The *Eagle* handled more easily than the LLTV, but the poor visibility, as well as the worry over the nearly exhausted fuel, made it as stressful a landing as most pilots could bear.

Armstrong was so intent on his job, he didn't hear Aldrin report that the light signaling contact with the surface had flashed on, with fifteen seconds of fuel left. And he had settled the *Eagle* down so gently that he hadn't felt it make contact with the moon. He intended to kill the engine at contact to prevent pressure from its exhaust from damaging the module. As soon as he realized a moment later that he had managed to land the *Eagle* safely, he shut off the engine. In Houston, the controllers, to their intense relief, had heard Aldrin affirm contact and state "engines stop." Almost as if he were querying the astronauts, Charlie Duke radioed, "We copy you down, *Eagle*."

A second later, Armstrong announced, "Houston, Tranquility Base here. The *Eagle* has landed."

"Roger, Tranquility," a delighted Duke responded. "You got a bunch of guys about to turn blue. We're breathing again. Thanks a lot."

———

I WAS IN prison the day Americans walked on the moon. The Vietnamese were always careful to provide us only information from the outside world that would discourage us. They kept us apprised of antiwar protests, international opposition to America's continued involvement in the war, and military setbacks in the hope that we would believe their repeated assertions that America was losing the war and that our government had abandoned us. It seldom worked, and we managed to get a more accurate picture of the war's progress and events back home from newly arrived POWs. But I didn't learn about Apollo 11's momentous success until I caught a reference to it in a radio broadcast of a speech by a prominent American opponent of the war. If memory serves, he said something to the effect that "if America can put a man on the moon, then we ought to be able to withdraw from a losing and unpopular war." Not long after, I received one of the infrequent and short notes from my family that our captors permitted us. About the size of a small postcard, it bore on its back a stamp with a picture of an astronaut standing near an American flag on the moon. That was a good day in Hanoi.

THE SURGEON SCIENTIST

There are more than twenty thousand proteins in blood. Judah Folkman was looking for one. If he found it, he might unravel the mystery he had discovered and maybe someday help treat successfully and more humanely that most feared human disease, the one no one ever wants to hear their doctor diagnose: cancer. Folkman had a theory that his critics dismissed as controversial, highly speculative, and dubious. And he had observed a phenomenon that they termed circumstantial and irrelevant, if even real.

In October of 1971, a colleague, the head of endocrinology at Beth Israel Hospital in Boston, had offered him the opportunity to present his theory to his fellow Harvard Medical School physicians at a weekly seminar. He welcomed the opportunity, eager as always to discuss his ideas and share his enthusiasm for the work that had consumed much of the previous ten years of his life. His colleague promised to arrange for his presentation to be published in the prestigious *New England Journal of Medicine,* an offer appealing to Folkman, who had grown accustomed to, although never defeated by, rejections from scientific journals. Perhaps, at last, he would be able to impart to the broader medical community some of the excitement he experienced on those all-too-rare occasions when his experimentation led to what he called the "aha!" moment, when years of laborious trial and error yielded the one clarifying insight that would drive research forward. As most researchers will tell you, to experience just one such moment is a cherished exception to the frequent moments of failure that characterize life in a laboratory. Folkman has known several such moments. That probably explains as well as anything why, despite all the criticism and setbacks he has endured in his now forty years of research, he remains such a voluble, unguarded, and impassioned believer in his work and himself.

On this occasion, however, his expectations crashed once again into the brick wall of skepticism and indifference that the scientific establishment raised to keep troublesome nonconformists from infecting respectable medical research with their intuitive hunches, their grand obsessions. Judah Folkman told his audience four things most of them either didn't know or wouldn't believe. First, the blood vessels that nourish cancerous tumors are newly created, and the tumor plays the critical role in generating them. Second, the tumor must be producing some mysterious substance, diffusing some unidentified proteins, which he labeled TAF (tumor angiogenesis factor). Third, these diffused proteins trigger the growth of new blood vessels to the tumor. Last, most provocatively, if you could find a way to shut this process off, you could starve the tumors and prevent their growth.

Folkman termed the process of tumor-stimulated blood-vessel growth "angiogenesis" and called his speculation that the process could be blocked "anti-angiogenesis." Today, he is credited with inventing what has become a crowded field of cancer-therapy research. But that October morning in 1971, he was a heretic.

The doctors who listened to him asked few questions after his presentation and filed out of the auditorium without any sign that they had just heard something brilliant. They might have thought this radical departure from conventional cancer therapies an imaginative concept. It was certainly a new one. But they were doctors who had patients to treat, patients with cancer. And cancer therapy at the time involved killing cancer cells with chemical poisons and radiation and removing tumors surgically. The science was evolving every day, and promising new chemotherapies would be available long before anyone knew for certain whether Folkman's ideas were viable. It wouldn't do their patients any good to join Judah Folkman on his improbable journey to find a way to starve tumors to death. They would stick with poisoning them, burning them, or cutting them out, despite the unavoidable damage such therapies did to healthy cells and to their patients' quality of life.

Neither did his presentation's publication in *The New England Journal of Medicine* prompt anything other than the same criticism and apathy that had greeted his research before. Folkman would have to proceed as he always had, struggling for funding and recognition and trying to recruit a few more brilliant disciples who saw the genius in his idea.

He was not the first researcher to discover that as tumors grew, new blood vessels formed to feed them. But he was the first not to dismiss the phenomenon as irrelevant. And he was certainly the first person to devote his entire medical career to finding a practical application for his discovery.

The U.S. Navy had drafted Judah Folkman in 1960 and made him a lieutenant. The navy had just entered the nuclear age with the commissioning of the USS *Enterprise,* the first nuclear-powered aircraft carrier. Because it had no need to come into port to refuel and could carry sufficient stores of supplies, the carrier and the four thousand sailors aboard it could remain at sea for as long as a year but for one unforeseen problem: the inability of the carrier's four operating rooms to preserve fresh blood supplies. Blood deteriorated after three weeks. The twenty-eight-year-old Folkman, who had graduated cum laude from Harvard Medical School in 1957 and was three years into a prestigious surgical residency at Massachusetts General Hospital, and another new lieutenant, Fred Becker, a promising young pathologist in residence at New York University, received orders to report to the Naval Medical Research Institute in Bethesda, Maryland. There they were assigned to develop a blood substitute that could be stored for long periods. They experimented with hemoglobin to determine whether it could be dried and reconstituted without losing its capacity to supply oxygen to human organs. Once they developed a technique to dry hemoglobin, which could be reconstituted in a saline solution, they tested the product on thyroids they had removed from rabbits. It worked.

Once they had completed their project, the two doctors were given leave by their commanding officer to keep themselves busy in the lab in whatever way they thought useful. They conceived of exploring whether the perfused rabbit thyroids could grow new cells, and they selected the fastest-growing cells, malignant cancer cells, to test their hypothesis. They transplanted melanoma cells from mice into the rabbit thyroids and perfused them with their blood substitute. The cells divided, and the little tumors grew . . . for a few days. Then they stopped at exactly the same size, about a millimeter in diameter—very unusual behavior for malignant tumors, which don't grow to a uniform size.

Why? Had they inadvertently killed the cancer cells? Were they dead or just inexplicably dormant? They transplanted the cells into live mice, and they sprang back into action instantly and quickly grew into large tumors. Why? Obviously, the cells hadn't been killed by being injected into thyroid glands, but they had become inactive. What substance was present in the animal and not in the removed thyroid glands? They soon discovered the answer. When they removed the large tumors from the mice they noticed they were full of blood vessels. The tiny, uniform tumors extracted from the thyroid glands had none. Immediately after the tumors had been injected into the mice, new capillaries began to grow from the surrounding tissue and encircled them. Their experiment had revealed a previously undiscovered biological phenomenon. Judah Folkman's odyssey to understand and make his discovery serve a great humanitarian end began in that moment.

For the next forty years, he decided, again and again, through success and setback, rejection and acceptance, to bet everything—his career, his reputation, his peace of mind—on what he might have glimpsed in that very instant of discovery: that there might be a more effective and humane way to treat cancer than conventional therapies offered.

Both doctors realized they had stumbled onto something more than a curiosity. But as, Becker recalled, "I thought it was interesting. Judah thought it was terrific."[1] Another draftee doctor, David Long, who worked with Becker and Folkman, was stunned by how quickly and completely Folkman grasped that their experiments had revealed something that the scientific community was oblivious to and that had potentially huge implications. "He knew it right away. He could grasp things, he could see right through them. He was standing there, and he told me what was happening. And I believed him."[2]

He had wanted to be a healer from the age of seven, when he accompanied his father, Rabbi Jerome Folkman, to visit the sick. His father, a compassionate and gentle man, whispered prayers for patients through the thick plastic of their oxygen tents. Young Judah noticed that the doctors caring for them worked within the tents and played a more direct role in caring for the sick. He told his father he thought he would rather be a doctor than a rabbi. "Then be a rabbi-like doctor," his father counseled.[3]

He became a boy who preferred laboratories to playing fields, a good student with an aptitude for science. He had two teachers who went out of their way to teach him important lessons that informed his adult vocation: a geometry teacher, who taught him there were different ways to solve the same problem, and a chemistry teacher, who encouraged him to further knowledge in one field of science by using knowledge acquired from other disciplines.

While in high school, he worked as an orderly in the operating rooms of Ohio State University Hospital. The chief surgeon invited him to work in the laboratory where surgical residents trained by operating on dogs. Every afternoon for three years as an undergraduate at Ohio State, Folkman worked as an assistant to the residents and became so adept at the work that he was often allowed to begin and finish operations. By the time he was admitted to Harvard Medical School, he had already acquired the basic skills of a surgeon. As a medical student, he developed the first atrioventricular implantable pacemaker, for which he won several awards. Two years after he returned to Massachusetts General Hospital after his stint in the navy, he was made chief resident surgeon. In 1965, he joined Harvard's surgical service at Boston City Hospital and was made an instructor at the medical school.

In 1968, within five years of his discharge from the navy, he was given a full professorship and appointed chief of surgery at Boston's Children's Hospital. He was the youngest doctor ever to hold the position, and yet he lacked any training in pediatric surgery, an omission that was remedied with a six-month training course in Philadelphia, under the supervision of C. Everett Koop, the future U.S. surgeon general. He was perhaps the fastest rising star in his profession, with unlimited prospects. Yet the prospects Folkman envisioned for himself were not restricted to those his profession assumed he would pursue—eminence in his chosen field, surgery. He intended to be a surgeon scientist, at a time when the medical establishment scoffed at surgeons who had research ambitions beyond improving standard surgical procedure. His ambitions were much grander than that. Whenever he removed a tumor from a patient and held it in his hand, he could see the new blood vessels that had formed to feed it, and he couldn't stop wondering if that unexplained phenomenon held the answer to why tumors grew and how they could be stopped.

"If Folkman wanted to study the relationship between tumors and blood vessels, he would have to invent an entire new field of research. . . . It signaled the beginning of what for Folkman would be a kind of double life."[4] At both Boston City Hospital and then at Children's, Folkman set up his own one-man laboratory, where he spent his nights and weekends exploring his new theory of angiogenesis. He began by reconstructing his Bethesda experiments and confirming their results. For the first two years, using the proceeds from a small grant he received from the National Cancer Institute, he worked alone. In 1967, a second-year Harvard Medical School student, Michael Gimbrone, volunteered to join his research. Soon a few other aspiring scientists, taken with Folkman's vision and enthusiasm, joined the team. But their research was always hindered by the modest amounts of the few research grants Folkman managed to procure, the limited accommodations of their small laboratory, and the reaction of the scientific community, which ranged from disdain to outright hostility.

Graduate students interested in joining Folkman's lab were discouraged by their professors, who warned that his research was controversial and potentially career destroying. During public presentations, audience members would walk out before he had concluded—an intentional display of disrespect. Scientific journals routinely refused to publish his research papers, dismissing the theory of angiogenesis and the results of their experiments in coldly disparaging terms. Fellow Harvard professors ridiculed his work. Surgical colleagues worried that Folkman was throwing away a brilliant surgical career to pursue his curious obsession. Many of his grant proposals were rejected with expressions of incredulity that Folkman would waste his time on an intuition that didn't just cut against the grain of considered scientific opinion but entirely departed from the direction of the fast-growing field of cancer research. In one small grant award given by the National Institutes of Health, a member of the review board indiscreetly scribbled a note in the margins of the papers informing Folkman of the decision: "This is the limit. We do not want Folkman to build an empire."[5]

The criticism that inundated Judah Folkman, impeded his research, and sorely tested his confidence seemed to be incited by three unfavorable perceptions. First, the scientific consensus formed in the second half of the twentieth century held that the key to understanding cancer would be found in studying cancer cells, not healthy blood vessels. Second, his research was driven by intuition, not solid scientific evidence. And, third, Folkman was a surgeon, an occupation that was not held in particularly high esteem by the scientific community. He had no training in molecular biology or biochemistry. His job was to remove tumors from his patients, not follow a hunch about why they did what they did. That was the province of scientists, who built years of data to prove their hypotheses before they unleashed them on an unsuspecting and naturally conservative scientific community.

Only the criticism of proceeding on intuition partly bears some truth. Folkman's theory was backed by observations he made in the laboratory. But the mind that so impressed Fred Becker and David Long with its quick insights did race ahead of the evidence and the grasp of established science. Eventually, Folkman's mind would seize on a stunning counterintuitive idea: if tumors were secreting some substance to attract new blood vessels, then, because in nature there is usually a contrary force, they must also possess the means to prevent angiogenesis and to starve themselves. Folkman knew that some patients with tumors that had metastasized often had dozens of small dormant tumors in other organs that seemed to become malignant only when the original tumor was surgically removed. Physicians attributed such incidents to something unnoticed about the surgery, perhaps a reaction to some problem with the incision. Folkman intuited that just as the tumor contained the means to nourish itself, it might also contain the means to deny nourishment to the metastases; once it was removed, the metastases were free to grow.

Judah Folkman didn't believe that he was handicapped as a scientist by his training as a surgeon. On the contrary, he thought it his great advantage over his critics. Biochemists and molecular biologists only examined white and bloodless tumors in petri dishes. Oncologists, strangers to an operating room, examined tumors in X rays. The surgeon held in his hands the warm, bleeding, still living tumors, encircled in blood vessels. "You could operate on a kidney, a liver . . . and if you lost blood the organ would stop bleeding," Folkman observed. "All the vessels would clamp down and the anesthetist would say, 'stop, we've got to give a transfusion.' But in a tumor . . . [it] could just keep bleeding and bleeding, . . . and you would use up pints of blood, and all surgeons know that. I knew there was something different about these blood vessels."[6] Folkman took his inspiration from experience, from life, not from conventional wisdom in a petri dish.

As discouraging as it must have been for a man who was only trying, after all, to help medicine save lives, Folkman never yielded to his critics' doubts or to frustration with the slow, painstaking process of discovery needed to overcome them. "I had one advantage," he remembered. "I kept saying, 'I'm pretty sure these people are wrong.'" Still, he had his moments of doubt.

"In research there is a very fine line between persistence and obstinacy. You don't know whether if you're persistent a little while longer you'll make it, or whether you're just being obstinate. . . . I was beginning to think we had crossed that line."[7] But Folkman persisted.

He credits his wife, Paula, with giving him the encouragement he needed to withstand the abuse and disappointment. And his father's advice, remembered through the years, still compelled him to persist through all the vicissitudes of his singular career. When in time his fortunes changed with success, he remembered their assistance, as well as the indispensable contributions of the brave and resourceful few who shared his research and his vision, and those institutions that had, despite all the criticism, funded his research. For Folkman, whose enthusiasm for his work never became boastful, the only thing approaching self-praise he now permits himself is the observation that, despite it all, he knew he was right.

The assault on his theories before his 1971 presentation showed little sign of abating in the months following its publication in *The New England Journal of Medicine*. Funding was still modest, although in 1971 Folkman was given the entire tenth floor of a brand-new research facility, affiliated with Children's Hospital, named for the resident Nobel laureate, Dr. John Enders. Folkman received prophetic advice from Enders, whose own lab was next door, about a grant proposal he was preparing to submit that would outline his entire field of inquiry. Folkman worried that he was disclosing too much information about the nature of his research, which an unethical researcher might be tempted to expropriate. Enders read the proposal carefully, looked up from the papers, and answered thoughtfully, "It is theft-proof. You'll be able to work at your own pace I figure ten years before anybody is going to believe this."[8] Folkman often turned to Enders for encouragement when his grant applications were rejected or another critic had assailed him, and Enders would observe that "this just proves that there are no experts of the future. There are only experts of the past, and they sit in the study section."[9] Folkman, like the wise man who counseled him, intended to be an expert of the future.

The most common criticisms made against his work in the early 1970s were that his experiments were not done in situ, inside the body that hosted the tumor, and that angiogenesis was likely no more than inflammation—the body's natural reaction to an injury, like pus in a wound. With Michael Gimbrone, Folkman devised an experiment to answer the charges. They transplanted growing tumors from lab rabbits into the rabbits' own corneas, a delicate operation that Gimbrone mastered. The cornea, the transparent front part of the eye, has no blood vessels of its own and served as the ideal and easily observable place to test the theory that tumors need access to their own blood supply to thrive. The transplanted tumors barely grew and became dormant. When they removed a tumor from the rabbit's cornea and transplanted it deeper in the eye, into the iris and closer to a blood supply, they watched angiogenesis in action as new capillaries quickly grew from the iris and encircled the tumor, which then grew to be thousands of times greater than its original size. Here was an "aha!" moment that Folkman remembered long after as one of his most exciting discoveries.[10]

Next, they worked an experiment, devised by Gimbrone, to support Folkman's contention that the tumor itself diffused a substance that triggered new blood-vessel growth. They implanted some pieces of tumor in rabbit corneas far from the nearest blood vessels and other pieces at various distances from the corneas, closer to the iris. They surmised that if the tumors were diffusing a substance with large molecules, those diffused farthest from the iris wouldn't reach it. They watched capillaries shoot from the iris to reach the tumors close to it, while the tumors implanted in corneas caused no angiogenesis.[11]

Excited by their results, Folkman submitted their findings in a peer-reviewed article for a prestigious medical journal. But if they expected any greater respect for this latest discovery, Folkman was quickly disabused of his optimism. A young biochemist published her experiment contradicting Folkman's conclusions. She had deposited a small amount of uric acid into a rabbit's cornea and gotten the same result, rapid blood-vessel growth, confirming the chief criticism against Folkman: that he had discovered nothing more than inflammation. A grant-review committee used the experiment to reject an application from Folkman, and an eminent Chicago pathologist on the committee cut Folkman with a dismissive remark he has never forgotten: "If uric acid can do it, what's so special about a tumor?" Folkman, he dismissed, was "just working on dirt."[12]

The next years proceeded in much the same way. Extraordinary advances in his laboratory were followed by fresh criticism and challenges.

In 1972, he was persuaded to address an American Cancer Society press seminar and to show a film he had made through a microscope of tumor-stimulated blood-vessel growth. The press reaction was excited and positive. But the press did not represent the scientific establishment, which remained ever skeptical and reacted scornfully to Folkman's presentation, accusing him of promoting false hope for new cancer treatment. Other surgeons at Children's Hospital complained that their gifted chief surgeon should spend more of his time in the operating room instead of playing the biologist in his laboratory. The criticism from the cancer research establishment was, of course, even more contemptuous. To them, Folkman was a fraud who only rarely dared to submit his findings in peer-reviewed articles to respectable scientific journals, where they could disparage them from on high.

He spent as much time in his lab as his surgical duties permitted, assisted by a small but reliably replenished corps of young grad students and doctors who were convinced by his enthusiasm and his findings to join his quest for a while. Much of their work would lead to their most important discoveries, and their contributions, one hopes, have been sufficient compensation to Folkman for the abuse he has suffered elsewhere. Together they searched for the elusive substance they believed tumors diffused to create their blood supply, as well as for the even more elusive protein that could shut the process down.

In 1974, Folkman's fortunes turned considerably when the Monsanto Company offered him a twenty-three-million-dollar grant to be used to further his search for the substance that induced angiogenesis. Though Harvard president Derek Bok approved the grant, the university faculty and students erupted in criticism for Bok's taking such a huge sum of research money from a corporation, which would hold the rights to license patents that Folkman and a fellow researcher, Bert Vallee, would retain for any of their discoveries. Prior to that arrangement, Harvard forbade its researchers to hold patents on their discoveries. Folkman and Monsanto were accused of self-dealing, and worse. Still, Bok defended him, and he was allowed to use the grant.

In 1977, an article in *Science,* a highly respected venue for peer-reviewed articles, reopened the Monsanto controversy, repeating all the charges leveled against the grant and casting fresh doubt on angiogenesis. The mystery factor in tumors that triggered angiogenesis, which Folkman had yet to identify, "may or may not exist," the reporter declared before quoting one skeptical scientist: "I believe anyone who has a 'factor,' which means they don't know what it is, has five or six years to prove it. After that, I stop reading about it."[13]

The article reignited criticism of Folkman from the Harvard community, fueled more animosity from his fellow surgeons, and eventually caused the board of the Children's Hospital to tell their chief surgeon, who had never neglected his responsibilities as a surgeon and who was held in high regard by his legions of patients and their families, that he must choose between his position and his research. If he chose to continue his research, he would have to find his own grant money to support it. Regretfully, but with confidence that he was right, Judah Folkman relinquished his position as chief of surgery and in 1981 performed his last operation.

Despite Folkman's trials, by the end of the 1970s the medical establishment had finally accepted that angiogenesis was real, but they dismissed it as a side effect of dying tumor cells. A young scientist working with Folkman, Robert Auerbach, put live tumor cells in one eye of a rabbit and dying ones in the other. The dying cells recruited no new blood vessels. The live ones did. Angiogenesis was finally becoming a respectable topic of scientific inquiry. But it seemed as if every advance in Folkman's research was countered with a new round of attacks. The establishment's disdain was proving harder to eradicate than angiogenesis was to prove.

Then, in 1983, Folkman's persistence paid off. Two of his associates, biochemists Michael Klagsbrun and Yuen Shing, located in the complex soup of protein molecules in tumor fluids the growth factor that had eluded Folkman for two decades. They spent several more months trying to isolate and purify the factor using hundreds of rat tumors until they finally had a molecule that triggered angiogenesis. They published their findings in *Science* in 1984, and almost instantly, Folkman observed, "many, many, many critics were transformed into competitors."[14] Angiogenesis and the search to shut it down became one of the fastest-growing fields in medical research.

In November of 1985, Dr. Donald Ingber, who had joined Folkman's team the previous year, fortuitously stumbled on a discovery. He found a strange fungus, accidentally caused by some airborne organism, growing in a culture dish containing the blood cells that angiogenesis activates to form new blood vessels. The rule in Folkman's lab was to discard any cultures contaminated by fungus, but Ingber decided to examine the contaminated cells under a microscope. What he found resulted in an enormous leap forward in Folkman's search for an angiogenesis inhibitor. He observed that when the blood cells were exposed to the fungus, they seemed to stop growing. This discovery, made while Ingber was working with a Japanese chemical company, resulted in the manufacture of the first anti-angiogenesis drug, TNP-470, proven to slow tumor growth in lab animals, which has shown promise in clinical trials when used in combination with chemotherapy.

In 1991, a young surgeon, Michael O'Reilly, joined Folkman's lab to study how tumors seemed to inhibit secondary metastases. He implanted tumors into mice and then collected their urine, gallons of it, for three years, before locating the agent that Folkman had always suspected existed, an angiogenesis inhibitor residing in tumors. O'Reilly had located and purified a protein fragment called angiostatin. Soon after, he and Folkman found another one, endostatin. And in subsequent experiments, the two proteins proved shockingly adept at shrinking tumors in mice.

Word of the discoveries circulated for several years, and cancer patients, many of whom personally called Folkman, inquired excitedly about when this promising new treatment might be able to save their lives. In 1998, the buzz became feverish speculation, and controversy ensued. On May 3, 1998, *The New York Times* published a front-page story in its Sunday paper trumpeting the success of the new anti-angiogenic compounds, quoting Nobel laureate and codiscoverer of DNA James Watson promising, "Judah is going to cure cancer in two years." The reaction was swift and uncontrollable. To many, especially cancer patients, Judah Folkman was a folk hero. To many in the cancer research establishment, he was the same old irresponsible grandstander they always said he was. Proving that the proteins reduced mice tumors did not prove they would be effective in combating tumors in human beings. Nowhere in the article was Folkman quoted as suggesting they would. He took care to keep his optimism in perspective and not to incite false hopes among cancer patients. All he promised was "If you have cancer and you are a mouse, we can take good care of you." He was enthused by their success, but "going from mice to people is a big jump," he warned.[15]

The article was swiftly followed by others casting doubts on his data and its potential use in cancer therapy, as well as criticizing all involved for raising false hopes. Watson claimed he had been misquoted. In November, *The Wall Street Journal* ran an article asserting that other labs were unable to repeat the experiments successfully. But others had been able to, Folkman fumed, and the trouble with some seemed to be caused by the difficulty in transporting the proteins long distances. Always, always, when Judah Folkman, against the odds and in the teeth of persistent criticism, made an important discovery, his detractors, people he was "pretty sure were wrong" tried to deny his progress.

Angiostatin and endostatin have proved difficult to manufacture. The small drug company that had the license to manufacture endostatin gave up in 2004 after years of trying, citing the costs involved and disappointing results in clinical trials. But in 2005, *The Wall Street Journal* reported that a Stanford-educated biochemist working in China had successfully tested an improved version of an endostatin drug, which has yet to be licensed or tested in the United States.

And in 2004, after clinical trials, the Food and Drug Administration approved the drug Avastin, made by Genentech, for use by patients suffering from colorectal cancer. It was the first drug approved for cancer treatment that works by choking off new blood-vessel growth that feeds tumors. Forty years after Judah Folkman glimpsed the possibility, the medical-research establishment that had scorned him now devotes much of its attention to the field of research he labored so diligently to make respectable.

A doctor reviewing a recent biography of Folkman, which we have relied on in this chapter, described it as a tale of "one man's magnificently obsessive quest for the truth." It was surely that, and though, in his darker days, he worried whether he had crossed the line from persistence to obstinacy, Judah Folkman never let himself become another of history's examples of when an important discovery was delayed because the person searching for it couldn't bear the challenges any longer.

"You can tell a leader by the number of arrows in his ass," he said, a small, self-delivered pat on the back, for which he can be readily forgiven.[16] For the most part he has remained the compassionate, determined, and confident rabbi-doctor he promised his father he would be. And someday, hopefully, no one will ever doubt it.

IN COMMAND

G eneral of the U.S. Army Douglas MacArthur, liberator of the Philippines, shogun of occupied Japan, and commander of UN forces in Korea, arrived at tiny Wake Island in the north Pacific Ocean as he preferred to arrive for any important occasion: fresh from another glorious triumph. The meeting had not been his idea. President Truman had wanted to meet with him "for a personal talk." It was, of course, an imposition. X Corps had liberated Seoul on September 26, 1950.* The Eighth Army had broken out of the Pusan perimeter and was chasing the enemy, who was in full retreat, into its own territory. After three months of besiegement, the Eighth Army was now the hammer, striking the enemy against the anvil, X Corps, which had, following a daring amphibious landing at the Port of Inchon, outflanked the North Koreans. American soldiers, advance

---

*Or so MacArthur declared. Serious fighting against pockets of resistance in the capital continued for several days.

elements of the Eighth Army's Twenty-fourth Infantry Division, had crossed the thirty-eighth parallel in Korea on October 7. What remained of the North Korean army was scattered and disorganized. On October 1, MacArthur had demanded North Korea's surrender and had yet to receive a reply. He was planning another amphibious landing for X Corps at Wonsan, on the east coast of the peninsula. He was confident the end was in sight for the first major war of the post–World War II era and expected to have most of his soldiers and Marines back in Japan for Christmas, but there was still some fighting left to do. He was a very busy man.

After Secretary of Defense George C. Marshall informed him that the president wished to meet with him at Wake Island, if that was more convenient for the general than Hawaii, MacArthur griped privately to his aides that he was being unnecessarily diverted from his duty for what appeared to him to be a public-relations stunt. Nevertheless, he closed the conversation with Marshall with the assurance, "I would be delighted to meet the President on the morning of the 15th at Wake Island." When the meeting occurred, *Time* magazine likened it to an encounter between "two sovereign rulers of separate states, approaching a neutral field with panoplied retainers to make talk and watch each other's eyes."[1]

MacArthur always appeared the most self-assured of men. He had his insecurities and was obsessed with delusional conspiracies in which he was assailed on all sides by jealous rivals and incompetent superiors, military and civilian, but he affected the sublime outward indifference of a man ever focused on his duty: the defense and glorification of his civilization and not himself. He was particular about that image and went to considerable lengths to protect it. Whatever doubts he had, they were not self-directed. He believed in his destiny and was sure of his genius. But then, even a cynical observer would have to concede that he was a superb general—daring, assured, demanding, and brilliant. His genius had helped win many an astonishing victory. His daring conception of an amphibious landing at the enemy's rear had completely changed the course of the war in Korea. But the same daring and self-assurance would also produce, in the same war, a catastrophe.

In 1950, the U.S. armed forces were much reduced and in a poor state of readiness, a peacetime military with commanders who were focused on threats in Europe from the new enemy, the Soviet Union, and not in Asia. The Marine Corps had a half-million men under arms at the end of World War II. Five years later, only seventy-four thousand Marines were on active duty, with further reductions planned. The communist conquest of China and the threat to the Chinese Nationalists in Taiwan was a worry, but not one that suggested a military solution at the present time, beyond showing the flag with the Seventh Fleet. The Americans on garrison duty in occupied Japan, constituting four understrength divisions of the army's ten active-duty divisions, were mostly new conscripts, ill trained and poorly equipped, their duty enjoyably easy and their discipline alarmingly lax. They were in no shape to fight a war on short notice. MacArthur, their commander, was keeping a watchful eye on the Taiwan Straits but spent the bulk of his time on the complex and exhausting task of rebuilding Japanese society, transforming it from a militaristic autocracy to a pacific, liberal democracy. When the North Korean People's Army, the In Min Gun, crossed the thirty-eighth parallel on June 25, 1950, the United States was as surprised and nearly as ill prepared as was the outnumbered South Korean army (ROK).

The UN Security Council had authorized member states to help repel the invasion, and Washington ordered MacArthur to come to the aid of the beleaguered ROK forces. He shipped supplies and weapons

to Korea and ordered naval and air support, but within days of the outbreak of the war he was receiving reports that the situation appeared to
be a rout, with the ROK, deficient in armor and artillery, its command
structures deteriorating, stumbling south in retreat from the overpow-
ering In Min Gun onslaught. A South Korean general had given the
order to blow up the bridges over the Han River, which marked Seoul's
southern boundaries, to slow the advance of the North Koreans.
Unfortunately, most of his own soldiers were still north of the river
and were trapped and destroyed. On the fourth day of the war, MacArthur, in a typical display of his zest to show himself a fighting general,
leading from the front and exposing himself to danger, took several
reporters to the front lines of the war. They flew in bad weather with
light fighter cover to an airstrip at Suwon, twenty miles south of the
captured capital, Seoul, where he met with the desperate South Korean
president, Syngman Rhee. From there, he drove to the front and spent
eight hours touring the lines. Swarmed by retreating soldiers and panicked refugees, he surveyed the disaster. Death, destruction, and fear
were all he saw. When he returned to Tokyo, he informed Washington
of the situation and advised that only the immediate deployment of
American combat troops could hold the present lines until a counteroffensive could be organized. Truman gave the order twenty-four
hours after receiving MacArthur's report.

The first American units ordered to Korea deployed by air from
Japan on July 1, with orders from MacArthur to demonstrate "an
arrogant display of strength." Elements of the Twenty-fourth Infantry Division, an artillery battery with six 105-mm howitzers, and Task
Force Smith—named for its commanding officer, Lieutenant Colonel Charles B. Smith—reached the southeastern Korean port city of
Pusan and reported to their division commander, Major General William Dean, who ordered them to march at once for Osan. Smith had
four hundred men, mostly teenagers, under his command, only one
sixth of whom had combat experience. Each man was armed with a
rifle, 120 rounds of ammunition, and two days' worth of C rations.
The task force had a couple of 75-mm recoilless rifles, several mortars,
and six bazookas. Five days after they arrived in country, they were
dug in on a ridge along a mile-wide front between Suwon and Osan to
the south. In the early morning of July 5, a column of North Korea's

Russian-built tanks approached. The Americans' bazookas and recoil-less rifles, as well as the howitzers firing from their rear, were ineffec-tive at checking the armored advance. The tanks ignored them and rumbled on south. More tanks followed in their wake, and after giv-ing brief battle to Smith's men and the supporting artillery battery, kept going. Within the first hours, Smith had lost twenty men, dead or wounded. Some of the soldiers with the artillery battery had bugged out, and their commanding officer had been wounded.

An hour after the last tanks had passed, a large infantry column approached. Smith's men—under artillery barrage and heavy machine-gun fire and facing superior forces, their lines of communication with their own supporting battery destroyed—held their position until early afternoon, when Smith ordered his two understrength rifle companies to retreat. Machine guns tore into them, inflicting heavy casualties and fragmenting unit cohesion. They abandoned their heavy weapons and equipment and disabled the howitzers when they reached the battery. The dead and many wounded were left where they lay. The soldiers struggled back to Osan, only to find it invested by North Korean armor. The retreat became a disorganized rush to safety. When all were finally accounted for, Smith had lost around 150, killed, wounded, or missing.

Several regiments of the Twenty-fourth Division were sealifted to Pusan during the first week of July, and other reinforcements includ-ing regiments from the Twenty-fifth Division quickly followed. General Dean, whom MacArthur had appointed temporary commander of U.S. forces in Korea, had established his headquarters at Taejon, one hun-dred miles south of Seoul, where he hastily organized his lines to check the North Korean advance at the Kum River. On July 7, the UN Secu-rity Council had approved a unified command for all military forces in Korea, and President Truman gave the command to MacArthur. Lieutenant General Walton "Johnnie" Walker, the Eighth Army's com-manding general, arrived in Pusan on July 13 and assumed operational command of U.S. and ROK forces. Dean's line of defense at Taejon consisted of three understrength infantry regiments, the Thirty-fourth, Nineteenth, and Twenty-first—about four thousand men.

The North Koreans advanced along a wide front with eight full divisions, two half-strength divisions, two separate regiments, and an armored brigade. Two North Korean divisions overwhelmed Dean's forward defensive positions by July 16, and Dean consolidated his forces in a tighter defensive perimeter around Taejon. The North Koreans struck on July 19, enveloping Dean's lines, and by the next day the Americans were in full retreat. During the retreat, General Dean, traveling by foot with his headquarters' party, slipped down a ravine while fetching water for the wounded. Knocked unconscious and presumed lost, he was left behind. He regained consciousness and for over a month tried to reach the American lines, until he was captured by the North Koreans and held prisoner for the remainder of the war. He was to be awarded the Medal of Honor when he returned to the States in 1953.

Other attempts by the Eighth Army—now comprising regiments of the Twenty-fourth, Twenty-fifth, and First Cavalry divisions—to stop the southward rush of the North Korean armies failed, and the Americans were pushed relentlessly toward Pusan and the sea. MacArthur arrived in Pusan in late July to confer with Walker, and both men agreed there would be no Dunkirk-like evacuation of American forces. On July 26, Walker issued orders to withdraw to defensive positions behind the Naktong River. A tough Texan who had commanded a tank division in World War II and whom George Patton called his "fightingest sonofabitch," Walker visited his division HQs and gave the order to "stand or die." On August 1, his army crossed the Naktong, blew up the bridges, and dug in. Fifty miles from the sea, they held the 145-mile Pusan perimeter for the next six weeks. The In Min Gun threw thirteen infantry and one armored division against the perimeter. With reinforcements arriving steadily, and aided greatly by American airpower, the Eighth Army held fast. Walker was a master of improvised defense, while his North Korean counterparts were inept tacticians in comparison. The North Koreans probed the perimeter in uncoordinated, small assaults. Walker shuffled his forces here and there to plug gaps in the line, inflicting heavy casualties on the enemy and draining the vitality out of the North's offensive.

On August 6, North Korea's Fourth Division successfully crossed the Naktong, creating a salient inside the perimeter, the Naktong Bulge. The Battle of the Naktong Bulge, which continued into September, saw some of the fiercest fighting of the war to date. The Americans took a lot of casualties but not as many as they inflicted. The North, its supply lines stretched many hundreds of miles and its forces considerably diminished, was being bled dry along the perimeter, while MacArthur sent another army division, a Marine brigade, a regimental combat team, and four tank battalions into battle. ROK forces had regrouped, and Great Britain had committed the Twenty-seventh Commonwealth Infantry Brigade to the fight. The tide of the war was poised to turn, waiting for just one bold move to throw the North off the initiative and onto the defensive. MacArthur made that move on September 15.

As early as Task Force Smith's misadventure on the Seoul-Osan highway, MacArthur had been contemplating how to use his naval and airpower advantage to release his army from the restricted space they had been forced to occupy, in which they had little room to maneuver. He ordered his chief of staff, Major General Ned Almond, to plan an amphibious operation on the west coast of Korea, landing U.S. Marines well behind the front and severing the enemy's supply and communication lines. The rapid retreat of American forces and the necessity of sending reinforcements to defend the shrinking perimeter frustrated the planners, but by July 20 MacArthur had chosen the port city of Inchon, eighteen miles west of Seoul, as the site of perhaps the most brilliant and boldest gambit of his remarkable career.

As a landing site for an amphibious assault, Inchon offered few attractions. It was believed to be lightly defended because the North Koreans couldn't imagine anyone would choose the place to land an invasion force. With its extreme tides and expansive mudflats at low tide, landing craft could enter the harbor only during a few daylight hours. Its narrow channels and swift currents, almost nonexistent beaches, and sixteen-foot-high seawalls were such daunting obstacles that a massive amphibious assault would have dubious prospects of success, no matter how lightly the beaches were defended—hence, its attraction to MacArthur. Like General Montcalm at Quebec, surprised and unprepared when General Wolfe's soldiers scaled the high bluff of the walled city and brought the war effectively to an end,[2] the North Koreans would assume their position impregnable.

MacArthur gave command of X Corps to his favorite subordinate, General Almond. Almond might have been the only one of his flag officers who believed the plan feasible. His navy, Marine, and army commanders argued against it. The Joint Chiefs dispatched two of their members to Tokyo to try to dissuade him. They urged him to choose another site, perhaps near Osan, south of Seoul. But MacArthur countered that Inchon gave him the opportunity to strike at the enemy's nerve center in the captured capital. A landing too far to the south and near the front wouldn't permit the wide envelopment of the enemy he planned and would serve only, in effect, to reinforce Walker's Eighth Army on the perimeter. The navy explained that the natural challenges at Inchon posed insuperable obstacles, and an assault would violate nearly every rule of amphibious landings. But MacArthur was confident it would succeed and confident that it would bring an early end to the war and avoid the necessity to grind out an offensive from the perimeter, fighting for every long mile north. After debating his commanders, and after an extended back-and-forth by cable with the Joint Chiefs, he informed the Joint Chiefs that the operation would commence on September 15. On September 6, the chiefs cabled him to reconsider, and he replied, "There is no question in my mind as to the feasibility of the operation and I regard its chance of success as excellent." Permission was granted in a terse reply: "We approve your operation and the President has been so informed."[3]

X Corps's ground forces would consist of the army's half-strength Seventh Infantry Division and the hurriedly assembled First Marine Division. To bring the divisions up to combat strength, MacArthur diverted reinforcements from the Pusan perimeter and took a Marine regiment away from a bitterly protesting Johnnie Walker. On September 13, the Seventh Division, First Marines, and the Fifth Marine regiment from Pusan rendezvoused in typhoon-roiled waters in the Yellow Sea and steamed in a convoy of 261 ships for Inchon. MacArthur, on board the USS *Mount McKinley,* was commanding from the front. The following description is taken from T. R. Fehrenbach's definitive study, *This Kind of War*:

> The X U.S. Army Corps, 70,000 men, was at sea. It had been formed from scratch, operating against time, manpower, and every known logistic difficulty, and its very conception embodied the best of American military capability. No other

nation in the world had the means and knowledge to put such a force together in so short of time. No other nation would have attempted what MacArthur had planned from the first.[4]

The assault had to proceed in two phases. Wolmi-do Island guarded the entrance to the harbor with troops and artillery. A Marine battalion landed to secure the island early on the morning of the fifteenth. Wolmi was connected by a causeway to the mainland, and the Marines would have to fight unsupported by other ground troops. Because of the ebbing tide, the fleet had to withdraw from the harbor after the Marines had landed or be stuck in the mud. Then it would wait until the late afternoon to ride the flood tide back into the harbor, when landing craft carrying the rest of the assault force could reach the sea-walls, giving the Marines two hours of daylight to secure their beach-head. In the interim, ships' guns fired incessantly from off shore, while naval and Marine air support provided cover to the Marines on Wolmi. It took the Marines around ninety minutes to take the island from four hundred North Korean defenders, at the cost of seventeen Marines killed. Aboard the *Mount McKinley,* MacArthur dictated a dispatch to the Pentagon: "First landing phase successful with losses slight. All goes well and on schedule."

The main amphibious-assault force landed on three separate beaches. The first detachment came ashore at about 5:30 in the afternoon. Within twenty minutes, they had seized their initial objective and were fighting in the streets of Inchon. By 1:30 the next morning, they had completely overwhelmed the two thousand North Korean defenders and surrounded the city. Later on the sixteenth, the Fifth Marines and Colonel Lewis "Chesty" Puller's First Marines headed toward Seoul, while elements of the army's Seventh Division came ashore. A North Korean division, headed for the Naktong River, turned around and raced north to defend Seoul from the invaders. They were met, engaged, and defeated by the First Marines. MacArthur had come ashore on seventeenth. By the next day, Kimpo Air Field was in American hands, and the troops could now be resupplied by air. By the twentieth, Marines had crossed the Han River. Heavy fighting on the western outskirts of Seoul lasted four days. By the twenty-fifth, the

Marines were in the capital, with the Seventh Division protecting their flank. Although heavy house-to-house and often hand-to-hand combat continued for several days in Seoul, MacArthur declared it taken on the twenty-sixth. In a ceremony on the twenty-ninth, he gave the capital back to an emotional Syngman Rhee.

A little over two weeks later, MacArthur was on Wake Island waiting on the tarmac to greet his commander-in-chief as the president's plane landed. Dressed informally, as was his habit—and, the president himself later wrote, disrespectfully, in an open-necked khaki shirt and a crushed and dirty cap—he did not salute as the president emerged from the plane. Instead, he warmly extended his hand and smile to the man who had flown halfway around the world to see him. The great MacArthur, seventy-one years old, had just added another stunning victory of American arms to his country's and his own glory. The landing at Inchon, which he had conceived of and alone believed would succeed, had, as he had promised, brought the war's end within prospect. General Matthew Ridgway, who was to succeed Johnnie Walker in command of the Eighth Army and eventually MacArthur himself, remarked that the victory the Joint Chiefs had doubted possible so elevated MacArthur's stature and influence that if the general next ordered that a battalion "walk on water, there might have been someone ready to give it a try."[5]

But what neither MacArthur nor his president knew at the time was that the same self-confidence and sense of invincibility was to lead to the greatest blunder of Douglas MacArthur's career and to his downfall. The People's Republic of China had been issuing warnings that U.S. forces should not drive too deeply beyond the thirty-eighth parallel and that all forces, ROK and American, should keep well clear of the Yalu River, which formed the border between China and Korea. Americans had intelligence reports and found considerable supporting evidence to suggest that Chinese soldiers were already in Korea. MacArthur and his intelligence chief, Major General Charles Willoughby, had dismissed the reports, believing that the moment for Chinese intervention had passed, that any Chinese incursion now, after Inchon, would be slaughtered by American airpower and that any Chinese soldiers found in the country were from a few, insignificant volunteer units. When President Truman asked the supreme commander, "What are the chances of a Chinese or Soviet intervention?" MacArthur replied, "Very little." No one disagreed.

At that moment, there were as many as 120,000 Chinese soldiers in Korea. And no one knew it.

In late October 1950, there were only scattered remnants of the In Min Gun in the field, and there were no apparent efforts to reorganize and resupply them. Army intelligence took that as a sign that their Chinese and Soviet patrons were cutting their losses. China had a massive army on the border. The United States estimated at least twenty-four divisions were stationed north of the Yalu.* But without much of an air force to protect those divisions, the Chinese, MacArthur and his staff believed, would be suicidal to order them into the field against the victorious UN forces in Korea. They would be chewed to pieces from the air. The warnings China gave, that incursions deep into North Korea by UN forces would be perceived as having hostile intent toward China, were ignored by MacArthur and by much of the American government as a "diplomatic bluff."

When the Eighth Army reached the Han River, General Walker expected that X Corps would now come under his command. X Corps and the Eighth Army reported separately to MacArthur, who oversaw their operations from Tokyo. It is a dangerous thing for a general to divide his forces, and once X Corps had successfully completed its daring maneuver to outflank the North Koreans and the Eighth Army had broken free of the perimeter and was destroying the In Min Gun in detail, the prudent commander would have unified his armies under one command. But MacArthur had other plans. He devised another amphibious landing for X Corps on the east coast of the peninsula at Wonson and felt confident he could supervise the progress of both forces from Tokyo. By the time X Corps reached the port city on the Sea of Japan, ROK units had already liberated Wonson. The danger in dividing his forces in two was made graver by the cruelest feature of Korean geography, the Taebaek mountain range. The Taebaeks divide

---

*In fact, by June 1950, 600,000 peasant soldiers under the command of Lin Piao had begun to march south to the border.

Korea east from west. They are a formidable barrier to armies—a vast, cold, lofty, and mostly impassable wasteland. They reach their highest altitudes north of the North Korean capital, Pyongyang, where there were no roads or rail lines to move armies through the passes. Should the Chinese invade and escape destruction by air, they would confront X Corps to the east of the Taebaeks and the Eighth Army to west, entirely isolated from each other, with no means for one American force to come to the aid of the other.

Not long after U.S. soldiers and Marines crossed the thirty-eighth parallel, just a day before MacArthur left for Wake Island, elements of China's Fourth Field Army crossed the Yalu. By the twenty-fifth, six more Chinese divisions were in Korea, undetected. Five Chinese armies now lay in the path of Walker's Eighth Army, and one was in the east, waiting for X Corps. Pyongyang fell to the Eighth Army on October 19. After the Eighth Army crossed the Chongchon River north of Anju, it was no longer possible to maintain a solid front in the hills and valleys of the rugged terrain. Within battalions, infantry companies were scattered and operating almost in isolation of one another, and Walker's supply lines were dangerously stretched.

All this time, Chinese forces were streaming across the Yalu west and east of the mountains. They marched at night and stayed in cover during the day. Hiding in forests and deep ravines or simply covering themselves with their white ponchos and tarps as they lay in the snow on mountain plateaus, their presence was undetected by American air reconnaissance. In contrast, the disposition of UN forces was not only observable but broadcast by news reports.

By late October, UN forces had begun capturing enemy soldiers who were clearly Chinese, but intelligence still dismissed their presence as small numbers of volunteers that Mao Tse-tung had already announced were fighting in Korea. The Chinese were prepared for winter warfare, dressed in quilted winter uniforms and marching in fur-lined boots. Many American soldiers wore summer uniforms and slept in summer-weight sleeping bags. By November, the first bite of Siberian winds could be felt. The discomfort was easier to endure with the prospect that they would all be in Japan for Christmas.

The American advance was proceeding rapidly. Advance elements of the Twenty-fourth Division were already near the mouth of the Yalu. Lin Piao felt obliged to fight ahead of schedule and launched China's "First Phase Offensive." In the last week of October, U.S. and ROK units were reporting their first contact with Chinese soldiers. On November 1, the Chinese surrounded a battalion from the Eighth Cavalry Regiment and nearly destroyed it. Throughout the first week of November, Eighth Army battalions were reporting almost nightly engagements with a well-led, well-armed, and obviously professional Chinese enemy, attacking from all sides to the blare of bugles.

On the night of November 5, E Company of the Nineteenth Infantry Regiment's Second Battalion, protecting the Chongchon bridgeheads, bedded down for the night on a low hill that the United States had numbered 123. They were dug in on the regiment's extreme left flank. Five miles of mountainous terrain separated them from the British Twenty-seventh Commonwealth Brigade. They were isolated and nervous. They had been in firefights with the Chinese the previous two nights. They expected another that evening. Still, when a Chinese battalion enveloped them, striking first from the front and then from behind, most of the Americans were killed in their sleeping bags. The heroics of two men, who covered the company's retreat, saved E Company from being wiped out to the last man. Only eighteen of the soldiers who had been with the company since its arrival in Pusan in July survived the night.

An alarmed Johnnie Walker considered the Eighth Army's perilous disposition. His divisions were strung out, fragmented, and far ahead of their supply lines. The Chinese were clearly fighting in Korea in greater numbers than previously believed. He gave the order to halt the advance and pull his forces back to the Chongchon. MacArthur wasn't happy with the order and agreed only reluctantly to allow Walker to consolidate his confused and tired army. In the east, the Marines of X Corps found themselves fighting a new enemy as well, but they were taking less punishment than Eighth Army, and their advance, while slowed, proceeded to the Yalu.

As suddenly as it began, the Chinese First Phase Offensive halted by the end of the first week of November. Again, Lin Piao's soldiers disappeared into the woods, valleys, and mountains. As the days passed with no further contact, MacArthur and his staff, which now estimated that no more than seventy thousand Chinese had entered Korea, regained their confidence that the incursion was a limited one, intent on bluffing the UN forces into discontinuing their advance and completing the reunification of Korea. That they had disappeared and were assumed to have returned to Manchuria reaffirmed MacArthur's initial (albeit wrong) judgment and strengthened his determination to bring the war to a swift conclusion. He did not intend to make his soldiers and Marines hold their present positions throughout the long and bitterly cold Korean winter. He ordered the advance of the Eighth Army and X Corps to resume. He was certain his divided forces would achieve a "massive, compression envelopment," which would "close the vise" at the Yalu within weeks.[6] Once a defensive line was established from west to east just south of the Yalu, he would hold all of Korea. Were the Chinese to send in massive reinforcements, his Air Force would annihilate them as they crossed the river. Typical, he thought, of their tentativeness and meddling, the Joint Chiefs were worried and recommended to MacArthur that he allow only ROK units to reach the Yalu. He dismissed their concerns. "Get to the Yalu," he urged the Eighth Army, "and I will relieve you."[7] In a message to the troops enjoying their Thanksgiving dinners, he assured them that this last offensive would have them off the line by Christmas.

The offensive commenced the day after Thanksgiving, with MacArthur on hand to celebrate the holiday with the Eighth Army and observe its resumed operations. Unbeknownst to MacArthur or General Walker or General Almond, commanding X Corps, they were walking into a trap. Hundreds of thousands of Chinese soldiers were waiting. Their numbers were to quadruple in the days and weeks ahead, as hundreds of thousands more swarmed the bridges over the Yalu River to join the fight. They struck on November 26, hitting the Eighth Army and the ROK II Corps in the west first. The Eighth Army's Second and Twenty-fifth Divisions were defeated in four days of heavy fighting, and the Eighth Army began its retreat south, which soon became a disorganized rout. On November 27, the Chinese hit the First Marine Division and Seventh Infantry Division at the Chosin Reservoir. Chesty Puller, in command of the First Marine Regiment at Chosin, surveyed the calamity and remarked: "We've been looking for the enemy for some time now. We've finally found him. We're surrounded. That simplifies things." For his heroic leadership in the battle that commenced that day, Puller was awarded the Navy Cross, his fifth.

The Marines did not bug out. They fought a fierce retreat from the hills surrounding the reservoir, bringing their dead and wounded and their equipment with them, inflicting heavy casualties on the Chinese, and writing perhaps the greatest chapter in the storied history of the U.S. Marine Corps. The Seventh Infantry Division suffered fifteen thousand casualties, but it, too, fought its way to the port of Hungnam and safety. The seven Chinese divisions that had entrapped Marines and soldiers at "Frozen Chosin" were so badly mauled by the retreating Americans that they were unfit for further service. But by Christmas Eve, the last of X Corps had been evacuated from North Korea.

In the west, the Eighth Army was stumbling south in the longest retreat in U.S. military history. On December 23, General Johnnie Walker was killed when the jeep he was riding in collided head-on with a truck. General Matthew Ridgway assumed command of the Eighth Army. On the third of January, Seoul was abandoned to the Chinese. Two weeks later, Ridgway stabilized his lines near Osan. In March, he led the counteroffensive that liberated Seoul and pushed the enemy back to the thirty-eighth parallel, the border between North and South Korea. There, a stalemate continued for almost three years, before a negotiated settlement ended the war. MacArthur had long since departed by then.

The president had announced his intention to begin cease-fire negotiations on March 20, 1951. Four days later, MacArthur, who had been expressly instructed to refrain from any public statements that contradicted administration policy, issued an ultimatum, threatening to expand the war to China. He felt certain the war would yet yield another historic triumph achieved by daring, brave men, undeterred by the timid counsel of nervous politicians and uninspired generals. The president believed otherwise. After having come home in April 1951 to a hero's welcome, MacArthur was fired by President Truman for rank insubordination.

LIEUTENANT COLONEL Fred C. Weyand took command of the depleted First Battalion, Seventh Regiment, Third Infantry Division (the Third

I.D.) in January 1951. The men had seen hard fighting when they covered the retreat of the First Marines and Seventh Infantry from the Chosin Reservoir and their evacuation from Hungnam, the most massive beachhead evacuation in U.S. military history. Their ranks were reduced to 162 Americans. The rest were South Korean replacements, civilians who had been pressed into military service with undermanned American units. "The battalion was all that a commander could wish for," he recalled years later.[8]

From March 7 to April 4, the Third I.D. and Weyand's battalion had participated in Operation Ripper, which had liberated Seoul and pushed the Chinese and North Koreans back to the thirty-eighth parallel. By the third week of April, UN forces, having seriously bloodied the numerically superior Chinese, had again crossed the parallel. China rushed more troops into Korea until their numbers reached three quarters of a million. Weyand's battalion was deployed thirty or so miles north of Seoul, along Route 33, where they were when the Chinese launched their first spring offensive to retake Seoul, the largest single battle of the Korean War.

The Chinese hurled nine field armies with twenty-seven divisions and 250,000 men against the UN front along the Imjin River. The Third I.D., which took the brunt of the attack, was known as the Rock of the Marne for its heroic action in France during World War I. In Korea, the division was hailed as the Rock of Seoul for its stubborn and costly defense of the approaches to the South Korean capital in seven days of brutal fighting. Weyand's battalion received a Presidential Unit Citation for its bravery and was credited with killing more than three thousand enemy soldiers. Two of his men received the Medal of Honor posthumously. Weyand received the Silver Star for gallantry in action, and his corps commander described First Battalion as his finest.

The Chinese were pushed back again, and First Battalion with the rest of the Third I.D. settled into front-line duty, where they fought off another Chinese offensive three weeks later. Weyand was relieved in 1952 and returned to the States. He remembered his Korean War service as a time "when you commanded your battalion from the lead platoon. If you succeeded, it was because you were there."[9]

He had been commissioned a second lieutenant through the ROTC program at the University of California–Berkeley in 1938. A tall, infor-mal, and good-humored Californian, Weyand served in the China-Burma-India theater in World War II, as an intelligence officer on the staff of General "Vinegar Joe" Stilwell. He remained in intelligence after the war, serving as the army's chief of staff for intelligence at the Middle Pacific Command in Hawaii until a general advised him that if he wanted to get ahead in the army he would need to transfer to the infantry. He had just graduated from infantry school at Fort Benning, Georgia, when the North Koreans crossed the thirty-eighth parallel.

Having proved himself an exceptional combat commander in Korea, he was given several assignments that advanced his career, graduated from the Army War College in 1958, and was selected to command an infantry battalion in Germany. He received his first star in 1960 and his second in 1962. Two years later, he took command of the Twenty-fifth Infantry Division, stationed in Hawaii, and led it to Vietnam after President Johnson's decision to introduce American combat forces there. Under his leadership, the division distinguished itself in combat. In recognition of his battlefield successes General William Westmoreland put Weyand in charge of II Field Force, the headquarters command for III Corps, the largest corps command in Vietnam, which included the eleven provinces around Saigon, from the southern boundaries of the Central Highlands to the Mekong Delta and Cambodian border.

Nguyen Chi Thanh, senior general of the North Vietnamese Army (NVA), Politburo member, and rival of General Vo Nguyen Giap, died in July 1967. He had been a leading proponent of large-scale offen-sive operations to win an early and decisive victory in the South. But as North Vietnam's senior commander in South Vietnam, he should have seen the futility of conducting a conventional campaign against the Americans' superior firepower and mobility. Since the Battle of the Ia Drang Valley, massed engagements with the Americans had proved disastrous to the NVA. There remains some debate over who deserves credit for being the architect of the Tet Offensive. Many his-torians claim Thanh was the senior proponent of the plan and that Giap inherited the responsibility for implementing it. Hanoi's official accounts of the offensive's planning substantiate that view, and Giap himself has been reported to have claimed he opposed the idea. Others have disputed that assertion. Whatever the case may be, by the summer of 1967 Hanoi was clearly planning to confront the American and South Vietnamese armies in a general offensive throughout the South in both small- and large-scale operations targeted primarily at urban areas.

The offensive was timed to coincide with the Tet holiday, the beginning of the lunar New Year in late January 1968, during a temporary cease-fire declared by the U.S Military Assistance Command, Vietnam (MACV). It had two strategic components: a general offensive launched in almost every town and city of note, which to succeed would have to be followed by the general uprising of the South Vietnamese people. Hanoi and the senior leadership of the Viet Cong expected their daring throw of the dice to reveal that the South Vietnam Army (ARVN) was unable or unwilling to fight, to encourage the South Vietnamese people to rally to the banner of Vietnamese nationalism, to destroy the puppet regime in Saigon, and to drive the discouraged Americans from their country. That was a critical misjudgment. Most South Vietnamese had no desire to be governed by Hanoi, nor would they be moved by appeals to their patriotism to take up arms against the powerful American military.

Despite the plan's strategic misconceptions, Giap's staging of the campaign was brilliantly deceptive. To that end, he was unwittingly assisted by General Westmoreland, a fine and honorable officer whose desire to find, engage, and defeat the enemy in conventional battle—in the belief that Hanoi's will could be broken—was as strategically misguided as were Hanoi's attempts to do the same. The Vietnam War was fought south of the Demilitarized Zone (DMZ), and only American airpower was allowed even intermittently to take the war to the enemy's territory. Air superiority is an invaluable weapon in war, but it cannot hold real estate. Only the infantry soldier can do that. The Johnson administration feared an American offensive in the North would trigger a conflict with the Chinese and Soviets. At the time of the Tet Offensive, the administration had refused to authorize U.S. ground operations to attack the enemy's supply lines in Laos. Without confronting the enemy on his territory, denying him sanctuary, and threatening the conquest of his capital, success in destroying his will to wage a protracted war would have to be achieved through classic counterinsurgency tactics—securing, holding, and economically developing ever-greater parts of your own territory—rather than the search-and-destroy tactics employed by General Westmoreland. The former tactics were to be employed by General Westmoreland's successor, General Creighton Abrams, and they yielded considerable success. But by then it was too late. The American people had lost confidence in the military's ability to win the war.

Westmoreland hoped North Vietnam would give him further opportunities to destroy its forces in large-scale battle, and in the late fall of 1967 and early winter of 1968 Vo Nguyen Giap seemed prepared to oblige him. Beginning in late October, Giap ordered a number of battles with U.S. forces near the DMZ and the Cambodian border. While they were all repelled, with heavy casualties inflicted on the enemy, and gave the appearance of futile probing attacks, they were in fact part of Giap's "peripheral campaign," an attempt to deceive American forces into leaving urban centers to confront the enemy on the borders. This squared nicely with Westmoreland's belief that the enemy was in retreat and able to make war only from his sanctuaries in Cambodia and Laos. He had transferred the defense of Saigon to the ARVN and planned to use the American units released from Saigon in a massive search-and-destroy campaign early in 1968. He had already given orders for a buildup along the Cambodian border, in the sector under Fred Weyand's command.

In early January, several North Vietnamese divisions marched toward Khe Sanh, an isolated Marine base at the western end of the DMZ. Westmoreland believed Giap was trying to re-create his greatest battlefield success, the one that had broken the will of the French colonialists. Westmoreland knew the French at Dien Bien Phu did not have the airpower, ground firepower, or mobility that the Americans possessed. A pitched battle at isolated Khe Sanh would allow him to use all those advantages to their fullest violent extent. He rushed reinforcements and equipment to the base and other border areas in anticipation of a climactic confrontation. Giap, however, had thought this through. And though the seventy-seven-day siege of Khe Sanh was to occasion great heroics on the part of the Marines defending it, it was another feint intended to draw the Americans away from the cities of South Vietnam, leaving those places vulnerable to fresh attacks.

Fred Weyand was worried. He suspected the enemy's border attacks were feints. He was a cool and capable combat commander and not given to overreaction. He was also a perceptive commander who knew how to read warning signs of the enemy's true intentions. His long experience as an intelligence officer and the disastrous misjudgments he had observed in the Korean War had sharpened his senses and given him the special instinct that is characteristic of all great warriors: a feel for what the enemy is doing and why. Early on, he was skeptical about Westmoreland's war of attrition in the remote outreaches of the country, and, like his deputy, the already legendary John Paul Vann, he believed the key to success in Vietnam was securing and pacifying the towns and villages of South Vietnam. Now he became increasingly concerned that Westmoreland was letting his own preferences for how he wanted to wage war blind him to evidence of how the enemy planned to wage it. Vann, by contrast, was a man who "worried about being too conventional in his thinking."[10] Weyand was willing, as MacArthur in Korea had not been, to look to the enemy's operations for evidence of his real purpose and to weigh that evidence objectively. The fact that Americans had soundly defeated the North Vietnamese and Viet Cong in every major encounter of the war had not bred in him an overconfidence.

Enemy attacks along the Cambodian border had ceased as suddenly as they had commenced, and Weyand's soldiers deployed at the border were not finding much additional evidence of enemy strength in the area or that the North Vietnamese were planning a serious offensive there. Weyand also believed that MACV was underestimating the ability of Viet Cong units to strike in the interior of his sector if given the opportunity. The VC had been very active in III Corps sectors in the first three weeks of January. One of the battles Giap had ordered as part of his peripheral campaign had been at Loch Ninh, sixty miles northwest of Saigon. Enemy documents captured there included information revealing that VC units were changing their locations and the ways they aligned with one another. When the new locations of VC battalions were plotted on a map, it seemed that no single unit had responsibility for operations in the Capital Military District; rather, "all the unit sectors included Saigon, like daggers pointing at the heart."[11] Intercepts of increased VC radio traffic around Saigon and interrogation of defectors and recently captured VC prisoners indicated to Weyand that the enemy was planning a major offensive, with as many as three divisions threatening the capital as well as the sprawling military complex in the Long Binh–Bien Ho area northeast of the capital. That area included the second-largest American air base, the ARVN III Corps, a POW camp, and the headquarters for II Field Force and III Corps.

As the Tet cease-fire, scheduled to begin at 6:00 p.m. on January 29, approached, Weyand knew "something was coming that was going to be pretty goddamn bad and it wasn't going to be up on the Laotian border somewhere, it was going to be right in our own backyard."[12] Military intelligence discounted the threat to the Saigon Circle, the twenty-mile radius around the capital, more out of conformance with Westmoreland's preconception than from an objective evaluation of data. With ARVN troops in command of the city and many of Weyand's battalions on the Cambodian border, only fourteen of III Corps' maneuverable battalions remained within the Saigon Circle. On January 11, Weyand asked Westmoreland to postpone the offensive and allow him to reposition battalions to block the approaches to the city. Westmoreland considered Weyand's concerns to be based on "various bits" of intelligence that were "tenuous," even though "disturbing."[13] Still anticipating the brunt of the attack would be in the north, Westmoreland had canceled the Tet cease-fire in the two northernmost provinces and considered shortening the cease-fire in other areas. He also issued a general alert for all U.S. forces, but such alerts were fairly common and often disregarded. Nevertheless, he agreed to his corps commander's request. Weyand immediately ordered the deployment of an additional thirteen maneuverable battalions back inside the Circle. Historians have judged this "the single most decisive decision of the entire battle."[14] To clear for action at Long Binh and Bien Ho, Weyand ordered bulldozers to cut down all vegetation around the military installations in the area. And he put his armored cavalry on full alert.

Weyand's own intelligence analysis had convinced him that the attack on Long Binh and Bien Ho would come in the early morning of January 31, 3:00 to be precise. Giap had staged his forces carefully, and while his units had been briefed on their objectives, he had kept the exact time of the operation a secret from his unit commanders until very near Tet Eve. They were ordered to begin the attack on January 30, but the order was subsequently changed, and the attack postponed until the following day. There was insufficient time to get word of the change to all his units, and some of them jumped the gun and attacked at Da Nang, Pleiku, and ten other cities on January 30. Westmoreland and MACV intelligence suspected these sporadic attacks were a diversion from the main attack at Khe Sanh, but they were convinced that other attacks would be forthcoming the next day. Westmoreland canceled the cease-fire for the rest of the country. The main offensive of VC guerrillas who had infiltrated urban areas throughout the South commenced the following morning. The attack at Long Binh and Bien Ho occurred right on schedule at 3:00 sharp on January 31, just as Fred Weyand had predicted.

Thousands of VC had used the holiday's festivities and the leave granted many ARVN units to infiltrate their target areas disguised as soldiers returning home for the holiday. By the evening of the thirty-first, almost every city and every provincial and district capital in South Vietnam had been attacked, with American and ARVN units scrambling to repel the invaders in some very serious firefights. But much of the element of surprise, as critical to the success of the operation as was the expected general uprising, had been lost. Fred Weyand and III Corps were prepared.

The attacks on the Saigon Circle were commanded by Lieutenant General Tran Van Tra, the second-highest-ranking officer in the NVA, who had established his headquarters on the outskirts of the city. He had one NVA division and two VC divisions at his command, aimed at eight major objectives in the Saigon Circle that Hanoi believed were critical to produce the general uprising. He failed to achieve a single one. Weyand gave command of all U.S. forces in the city to his deputy, Major General Keith Ware, a World War II Medal of Honor recipient. General Ware and the Americans under his command fought tenaciously in defense of the city. Similarly, the ARVN, which the North believed wouldn't fight, while broken in a few bloody encounters, performed quite well on the whole. And the enemy's decision to wage a widespread assault, "attacking everywhere at once," as Weyand observed, "fragmented their forces and laid themselves open to defeat in detail."[15]

Despite the sensational assaults on high-profile targets in the city, including the American embassy, the Battle for Saigon ended in a few days in a devastating defeat for the enemy, as did most of the fighting in the Tet Offensive. Only at Hue, the old imperial capital and the only city captured in the offensive, and at Khe Sanh did major operations continue longer than a week. Out of eighty-four thousand enemy soldiers committed to the offensive, fifty thousand are believed to have been killed. Tet had been a calamitous failure for the enemy. The Viet Cong were never again a serious factor in the war. There were too few left alive to present much of a threat to anyone. Henceforth, the NVA alone would continue the struggle.

The press, however, having been assured that the war was well within hand, interpreted the sensational and widespread nature of the offensive—Viet Cong in the American embassy compound, the costly sacrifices at Khe Sanh and Hue—as proof that the war was far from over and that the enemy was in a position to fight on for years. Walter Cronkite pronounced the war a stalemate, and much of elite opinion in the press and in Washington concurred. Senior North Vietnam general Tran Do, a legendary and much decorated hero who had fought against the French alongside Ho Chi Minh, aptly described the paradox of the Tet Offensive.* "In all honesty," he said, "we didn't achieve our main objective, which was to spur uprisings throughout the south. . . . As for making an impact in the United States, it had not been our intention—but it turned out to be a fortunate result."[16]

Contrary to popular belief, the American public did not immediately abandon support for the war. Public-opinion polls showed most Americans rallying to the cause in the days and weeks after Tet; the

---

*Tran Do died in 2002, after becoming near the end of his life a prominent dissident opposed to the endemic corruption and political repression of his government.

precipitous decline in public support for the war did not occur until much later. But it did occur, and as Fred Weyand observed,

The American Army really is a people's army in the sense that it belongs to the American people, who take a jealous and proprietary interest in its involvement. When the Army is committed, the American people are committed; when the American people lose their commitment, it is futile to try to keep the Army committed.[17]

The seeds of American disapproval of the war may have been planted in the pronounced change in elite opinion following Tet. Despite Creighton Abrams's best efforts and considerable success (according to Weyand, American tactics changed "fifteen minutes" after Abrams succeeded Westmoreland), when America turned against the war there simply wasn't sufficient time left to change hearts and minds in this country. And where the people lead, their Congress inevitably follows.

Fred Weyand succeeded Abrams as MACV commander and oversaw the withdrawal of the last American combat troops from Vietnam, following which he was selected chief of staff of the army. In that capacity he traveled to Vietnam in 1975 at President Ford's request to ascertain what the United States should do to support the government and military of South Vietnam after Hanoi violated the terms of the Paris Peace Agreement and launched a conventional invasion of the South. Weyand recommended that American honor and interests required that we provide South Vietnam with $750 million worth of support. Congress declined to appropriate the funds. Nor would Congress allow the U.S. Air Force and Navy to come to the defense of the beleaguered ARVN, as the U.S. government had promised it would when it signed the Paris accords. It was too late for all that, even though the resulting humanitarian catastrophe in Vietnam, Laos, and especially in Cambodia occasioned by North Vietnam's total victory suggests that Fred Weyand, the clear-eyed commander, had once again been right.

HUMILITY

F ew afflictions were more dreaded or had a more pronounced effect on the history of the Americas before the twentieth century than yellow fever, the viral disease that attacks the liver, causing internal bleeding and the jaundice that gives the disease its name. One in five of its sufferers perished. Periodic and devastating epidemics of yellow fever incited panic and sent the inhabitants of entire cities fleeing for the countryside to escape what they wrongly believed was a contagion. In 1793, a yellow-fever epidemic struck Philadelphia, the capital of the new American republic, killing 10 percent of its population and causing many of the city's most prominent residents, including President Washington and Secretary of the Treasury Hamilton, to temporarily abandon the seat of government. In 1802, yellow fever decimated a French army sent to Haiti by Napoleon Bonaparte, influencing Napoleon's decision to sell the Louisiana Territory to the United States. At the time, the disease was believed to be communicated by contact with its sufferers or with their bedding and clothing. Many cities in tropical regions of the western hemisphere, where the disease occurred most often, were considered almost uninhabitable by Americans. In Cuba, which American forces occupied following Spain's defeat in the Spanish-American War, and Panama, where the United States built a canal across the Central American isthmus, yellow fever was endemic and threatened not only Americans in residence there but any American port that received goods and people from the afflicted cities.

The U.S. Army, recognizing that in Cuba the disease often caused more casualties than enemy fire, established a medical-research team to conduct experiments there to ascertain its cause and devise more effective means of protecting soldiers. To head its Yellow Fever Commission, the army chose Dr. Walter Reed, a brilliant and prominent physician who earned his first medical degree at eighteen. A Cuban doctor's recent research into the disease hypothesized that it might be spread not through contact but through the bite of infected mosquitoes. The hypothesis was considered dubious at the time by most medical researchers, but Reed's team eventually decided to test it through experimentation with subjects who volunteered to be bitten by infected mosquitoes. In addition to Reed, three other doctors traveled to Cuba as part of the commission: U.S. Army physician James Carroll; Cuban-born Aristides Agramonte, who had acquired immunity from yellow fever following a mild childhood bout with the disease; and the head physician of clinical research at the Johns Hopkins School of Medicine, Jesse Lazear. Of the four, only Lazear strongly suspected that the theory of mosquito infection offered the key to understanding how the disease was spread.

The commission initially conducted its experiments at Columbia Barracks in Quemados, Cuba, where there had been a recent outbreak of yellow fever. They subjected dozens of volunteers, mostly drawn from the army hospital detachment there, to bites from infected mosquitoes. Three of the commission members—Carroll, Agramonte, and Lazear—also volunteered to be infected. All the volunteers who subsequently contracted the disease ultimately recovered except one, Lazear, who died from the disease after seven days of suffering. The experiments continued in a new location near Havana, Camp Lazear, named for the man who sacrificed himself to spare others.

Walter Reed is credited with proving the cause of yellow fever, which led to efforts to eradicate mosquito populations and ultimately to a vaccine for the disease. The army hospital and medical-research center in Bethesda, Maryland, is named for him. Yet as estimable as Reed was, he was the only one of the four doctors on the commission who did not choose to infect himself with the virus. Humanity owes a greater debt to Jesse Lazear for the discovery that would eventually prevent the epidemics that had terrorized cities of North and South America as well as the islands of the Caribbean.

The humility evident in Jesse Lazear's decision to risk his own life to advance medicine is a deeply admirable quality of certain decisions. We do not use the term as a synonym for modesty or to describe decision makers whose personalities are self-effacing and retiring. Rather, the humility we write of is the quality of a decision that has as its primary objective the well-being of others.

The soldiers who reenlist after a combat tour not because they have decided to make a career in the military—perhaps not even because they believe they have yet to discharge completely a patriotic obligation to defend their country—but because they cannot bring themselves to leave their comrades to face the sacrifices and deprivations of war without them. The mother who leaves a rewarding professional career to give her children her full attention at home. The father who takes a second job so his children can attend a better school. The doctor who remains at an Indian reservation clinic after her requisite service is completed and her obligation to the government for helping finance her education has been discharged, because she has come to love the people for whom she cares more than she values the rewards of a comfortable and better-paid position. These are everyday examples, not as heroic as Lazear's but truly admirable, of people who have made decisions not to benefit themselves but others.

The decision makers whose humility characterizes their decisions are those who act not for themselves primarily. They consider the potential consequences of their decision, its success or failure, as less important to them than to people they are trying to serve. In 1988, Aung San Suu Kyi decided to abandon a comfortable and happy life in the west and return to her country, Burma, where she has braved threats, imprisonment, and isolation to lead her people's struggle for freedom. She has remained there ever since, separated from her family, beloved by her people, and determined to meet any cruelty, any adversity for the sake of the Burmese people who chose her as their leader, and who rely on her courage as their only hope. When her husband, Michael Aris, was dying of cancer, the Burmese regime refused to let him into the country for a last reunion with his wife. Had Suu Kyi left the country to visit him, she would not have been allowed to return. So husband and wife chose to remain apart in the sad last days of Michael's life because both were committed to a cause greater than themselves.

MA ELLEN

T he Republic of Liberia was conceived in conflict. The Americans who sponsored its creation shared a common purpose but conflicting motives. Some were intent on liberating slaves from bondage, others on preventing a slave insurrection from plunging the young American republic into violent chaos. The American Colonization Society (ACS) was founded in 1816 by Quakers who detested the institution of slavery and by southern slave owners who had watched with dread as a bloody 1791 revolt in the most prosperous French slave colony in the Caribbean, St. Domingue, led thirteen years later to the establishment of the Republic of Haiti. Both parties agreed their opposite interests would be best served by the repatriation of emancipated American slaves to Africa.

Although many abolitionists and prominent emancipated African Americans opposed the idea, the ACS attracted sufficient subscribers to establish the first settlement in the British West African colony of Sierra Leone. It failed. Two years later, they made another attempt. In 1822, eighty-six former slaves and white agents of the ACS, who were to govern them for the first twenty-five years of the colony's existence, arrived at Cape Montserrado on the west coast of Africa and settled on land expropriated from indigenous Africans with a small sum of money and the threat of force. Other émigrés, sent by slave states wishing to rid themselves of emancipated slaves, soon followed and established their own settlements nearby, which eventually joined the growing ACS settlement.

They had a hard time of it. Afflicted by endemic diseases and confronting violent opposition from displaced natives who resisted the settlers' attempt to spread Christianity and ban the slave trade, which many indigenous tribes profited from, the colony's early years were a severe trial. Yet they persevered. In 1824, they named their settlement Monrovia, after the fifth president of the United States and charter member of the ACS, James Monroe, and declared it the capital of the Republic of Liberia.

Over the next forty years, nearly twenty thousand Americans arrived to establish a society that was to replicate the religious practices and social customs of the only culture they had known: the antebellum American south. They lived on the coast in plantation-style mansions; worshipped in churches much like those where their former masters had knelt in prayer; and spoke English flavored with southern idioms and diction. They made some attempts to assimilate natives into their transplanted American society, mostly through intermarriage, but on the whole the settlers, who referred to themselves as Americans, sought to dominate the far more numerous native peoples by depriving them of social, economic, and political rights.

In 1847, the colony severed its colonial relationship with the United States, bid good-bye to the ACS agents, and became the first independent African republic. A Virginia native of mixed African and European ancestry, Joseph Jenkins Roberts, was elected by Americo-Liberians (native peoples were not enfranchised until 1946) as Liberia's first president. The newly independent republic adopted a flag that resembled the American flag, with eleven red and white stripes, and a single white star on a blue background. It modeled its constitution on that of the United States, establishing three branches of government: a chief executive, a bicameral national legislature, and a supreme court.

Liberia's currency, then and now, is the American dollar. The national motto is "The love of liberty brought us here."

But Liberia also borrowed from the United States the social and political customs that in time threatened its destruction, just as they threatened, sooner and more decisively, the constitutional order of its mother country. Mutual distrust between settlers and their descendants and the oppressed indigenous population persisted for most of Liberia's history. Animosity between the Americo-Liberian ruling class, which would never constitute more than 10 percent of the country's population, and the country's sixteen different ethnic groups—most of whom lived in the rain forests of the interior, spoke different dialects, and worshipped spirits according to animist practices—posed, along with economic hardship and the imperial ambitions of European colonial powers, the primary challenge to Liberia's survival. The hostility was to erupt periodically in tremendous violence.

In 1943, Americo-Liberian William Tubman, son of a Liberian army general and Methodist minister, was elected president. He retained the office until his death in 1971. He was prowestern and, upon his inauguration, declared solidarity with the Allied powers in World War II. He was generally considered by the west to be a force for stability and moderation in Africa. He granted suffrage to all Liberians, including women and members of the rural tribes, who had been discriminated against since the first settlers arrived. But his political reforms were limited and self-serving. He effectively used the purported expansion of civil rights to concentrate power in his own hands. Rural, indigenous Liberians were allowed to elect local officials, but the candidates had to be approved by the president. Systemized fraud of election results was achieved through the True Whigs' complete control of the electoral process. A failed assassination attempt in 1955 reinforced Tubman's antidemocratic instincts and triggered pervasive and severe reprisals against opponents to his rule. He subjected the press to severe restraints and censorship, making them little more than government organs. He built an extensive network of political spies and enforcers to intimidate his opponents. And he ordered constitutional term limits to be dropped to permit him to remain in office for seven consecutive terms. The culture of fear that worsened over the course of Tubman's twenty-seven-year presidency terrorized Liberians even in the last two decades of the twentieth century.

Tubman, however, did manage to significantly expand the Liberian economy with liberal trade and foreign-investment policies. Liberia is a relatively well-advantaged African country, with adequate water, considerable mineral resources, and vast tracts of timber. Its climate is conducive to agriculture. The country was a major exporter of timber, rubber, and iron ore, the latter constituting more than half of its export earnings. By the mid-1950s, Tubman's policies produced an economic growth rate among the highest in the world and attracted significant foreign investment. Liberia possessed the largest mercantile fleet in the world.

Corruption, of course, thrives in fast-growing economies when political freedoms and the rule of law don't accompany free-market principles. And Tubman and his cronies took their share of their country's prosperity. What followed his rule, after a nine-year interregnum— when the seeds of political, social, and economic inequality planted in the first days of the American settlement bore full and bloody flower— was an infinitely worse political order, marked by two extraordinarily brutal regimes, and thirteen years of intermittent civil wars, which featured almost apocalyptic violence. Liberia became a textbook example of a failed state, with the worst imaginable consequences. Liberia's economic health was among the casualties, though it was certainly not the only or the most wretched victim. Today, Liberia's hope of a better future, tenuous as it is, rests not exclusively but to a very significant extent with the short, professorial, and determined grandmother who occupies the office of president after winning a mandate in Liberia's first truly fair and free elections.

Near the end of William Tubman's long rule, he might have taken note of and exception to the accusation of his future successor—then a thirty-one-year-old American-educated civil servant—that his regime was guilty of kleptocracy. The young woman in question, Ellen Johnson Sirleaf, was advised by a visiting Harvard professor, alarmed by her intemperance, to continue her education in the United States, where her outspoken opposition to the regime was unlikely to get her into trouble. That she accepted his advice and his offer to help enroll her

at Harvard is hardly surprising. Far more surprising was her decision
to come back, a decision she made several more times, after suffering
extremely harrowing experiences. Most surprising of all, she survived.

She was not born into the Americo-Liberian ruling class. Her
father, the son of a chief of the Gola tribe, was the first native Liberian
to be elected to the national legislature. Her mother, the daughter of
a German trader and a rural Liberian woman, was a Methodist circuit
preacher who traveled by canoe to remote congregations. Sirleaf credits her parents for her steadfastness and probity. "The things we did as
kids instilled hard work and honesty," she explained. "We did chores
before and after school, we said prayers every morning. We understood
the sanctity of 'do not steal.'"[1]

As children, both of her parents were taken in by Americo-Liberian
families, a common practice in Liberia, where promising children of
indigenous tribes were sent to Monrovia, where elite families usually employed them as domestic servants but could also see to it that
they were provided a decent education. Sirleaf has often spoken of the
"humiliations and indignities" her parents suffered in the households
of wealthy Monrovians. Her father adopted the name of Johnson, in
honor of Liberia's president, Hilary Richard Wright Johnson, a friend
of his father.

Ellen, their third child and first daughter, was born in 1938 and
was raised in Monrovia by her parents, who had assimilated into the
dominant Liberian society. But she spent her summers at her father's
ancestral village in the interior. When her father suffered a stroke at a
young age, her family had to rely on her mother's modest income. She
received a decent education, attending a Methodist high school, the
College of West Africa, where she excelled at economics and accounting. While a student there, she witnessed an incident in President Tubman's crackdown on political dissent following a failed assassination
attempt. Liberian soldiers violently broke up a student demonstration
on the school grounds. "It was the first time I had seen active violence," she remembered.[2] She was to see more and far worse in the
years to come.

She married James Sirleaf just after her high school graduation and
gave birth to four sons over the next four years. In 1961, her husband

accepted a scholarship to continue his education at the University of Wisconsin. Ellen accompanied him on her first trip outside Liberia, leaving her four young children in her mother's care. While her husband pursued his master's degree in economics, she enrolled at the Madison Business College, where she studied accounting and obtained a B.B.A. in 1964. To support them, she waited tables and swept floors at a drugstore lunch counter.

After she and James returned to Liberia, she managed to secure a position in President Tubman's planning ministry, and it was in that capacity that she attended the development conference where she attracted the attention of the visiting professor of economics at Harvard, Gustav Papanek, for denouncing the "big man" who ruled Liberia and who was, at that time, the hand that fed her. She left Liberia again in 1969 to pursue an economics degree at the University of Colorado and, with Papanek's help, a master's degree in public administration from Harvard's Kennedy School of Government. While at Harvard, she was divorced from James Sirleaf.

She returned to Liberia in 1971. William Tubman was dead, and his long-serving vice president, William Tolbert, had succeeded him. Sirleaf joined his government and eventually rose to the position of assistant finance minister, and in the last year of his presidency, she joined his cabinet as minister of finance. Tolbert's administration was comparatively enlightened. He instituted political and economic reforms, even allowing the first opposition party since 1877 to organize. For some members of his government, he was moving too swiftly. But for many of the majority of Liberians, those who were not descendants of American settlers, nothing the ruling party proposed would satisfy their desire for change. The entire socioeconomic system would need to be destroyed to redress the ancient disparities between the 5 percent who ruled the country and the 95 percent who depended on their unreliable benevolence, most of whom were consigned to the same standard of living—poor, uneducated, hopeless—that their ancestors had suffered. Thus, the unresolved original conflict of Liberian history, with its antecedents in the American south, finally bore its awful fruit, and the great ironic tragedy of Liberia commenced. Systemic change was to come. The 133-year dominance of the Americo-Liberians was to end.

And the results were infinitely worse for nearly all Liberians than the inequities and injustices suffered by so many of them for so long.

Matters came to a head when Tolbert proposed to increase the price of imported rice, a staple of the Liberian diet. He intended to encourage domestic production, but Liberians reacted to this new economic burden by taking to the streets in demonstrations that soon turned violent. In April 1979, Tolbert instructed Liberian soldiers to fire on a crowd of protestors, killing seventy, and ordered the arrest of opposition leaders. The riots spread throughout Liberia and became more violent. Some soldiers in the Liberian army sympathized with the protests, particularly enlisted men who were not drawn from the Liberian elite, as were most of their officers. Some of them, however, had more than social equality on their minds.

On April 12, 1980, a gang of soldiers from the small and impoverished Krahn tribe—led by an illiterate twenty-eight-year-old master sergeant, Samuel K. Doe—stormed the presidential mansion and bayoneted William Tolbert to death in his bed. A few days later, Doe ordered thirteen members of Tolbert's cabinet arrested, taken to a public beach, and machine-gunned in front of a stunned international press corps and a large and enthusiastic crowd of native Liberians. Ellen Johnson Sirleaf was one of four senior members of Tolbert's government whose life was spared. Her relationships in the west, where she was respected as one of Liberia's few honest and capable public officials, probably dissuaded Doe from ordering her death.

Proclaiming himself chairman of the People's Redemption Council, Doe inaugurated a ten-year military dictatorship, dominated by ethnic Krahns, the least assimilated of Liberia's tribes. Doe's regime was to boast a reputation for brutality and greed exceeding the corruption and injustice of any previous Liberian government, but it was not, as it turned out, as incomparably cruel and grasping as the dictatorship that succeeded his. Sirleaf fled the country to Nairobi, where she found employment as a vice president of Citibank's African regional office.

Ever paranoid, Doe surrounded himself exclusively with fellow Krahns, which sparked the resentment of Liberia's other ethnic groups and fomented the rebellion of former allies that would lead ultimately to his downfall. Intent on developing a relationship with the west that best served his interests, Doe dispatched potential opponents to his rule by accusing them of socialism, a crime typically punished by imprisonment or death. (He had severed Liberia's relations with the Soviet Union to curry favor with the United States.) He eventually made a show of permitting heavily restricted opposition parties to organize, had a new constitution adopted by referendum in 1984, and stood for election as president in 1985. The election was a farce. Doe ordered the murder of scores of his political opponents, and, when it looked as if a rival had won the election, he assigned fifty of his agents to count the ballots in secret.

Despite the dangers apparent to any informed observer of Liberian politics, Ellen Johnson Sirleaf decided to return to Liberia in 1985 and campaign for election to the Senate. She rejected precautions to fake a little deference to the "big man" who now misruled her country and ran as an avowed critic of Doe. She was briefly imprisoned along with several university students for protesting the regime's refusal to register her political party for the election, but she was released following official protests from the United States.

Four weeks after Samuel Doe claimed a 51 percent majority in the election, a former commander of the Liberian army who had fallen out with Doe, Thomas Quiwonkpa, led a small band of guerrillas in an attempted overthrow of the regime. The insurrection was quickly put down. Quiwonkpa was captured, tortured, and reportedly devoured by Krahn soldiers. The failed coup gave Doe an excuse to go on a rampage. He ordered his soldiers to slaughter thousands of innocent Liberians in Nimba County, where the villages of Quiwonkpa's Gio tribe were located, and initiated a campaign of political murders in the capital. The new wave of bloody repression intensified ethnic hostilities that eventually plunged Liberia into a more or less continuous state of civil war.

In the immediate aftermath of the coup attempt, Ellen Johnson Sirleaf was among hundreds of Doe's political opponents rounded up and imprisoned, most of whom were subsequently murdered. Two soldiers came for Sirleaf and debated whether to take her to prison or summarily execute her. Somehow she managed to persuade them to spare her life. They brought her to a Monrovia jail, where she was

locked in a cell with twelve men. The men were soon taken away and
executed. Other imprisoned women were raped by the guards, and after
one victim was thrown naked into Sirleaf's cell, she prepared herself
for a similar fate. A sympathetic guard from her own tribe asked her to
prove her ethnic origins by speaking a few words in the Gola dialect.
When she complied, he remained at her side and prevented another
guard from molesting her.[3]

She recalled the terror of that night years later in an interview. In
time, the experience strengthened her resolve to alleviate the suffering
of her people:

> At that moment, all I could think of was to pray for life.
> However, once I had passed that and had been released, my con-
> viction in the course I was pursuing was reinforced, because
> I knew then, more than ever, that we had to work to bring
> change to our country, so that my experience would never be
> something that would be experienced by anyone else. . . . [I]t
> emboldened me.[4]

Tragically, for many years, her experience and much worse would be
suffered by hundreds of thousands of her countrymen. Liberia, conceived
in liberty, modeled on the political values and contradictions of the distant
republic that had dispatched victims of its moral transgressions to secure
their freedom in a wilderness, slipped into a long nightmare of horrific
violence from which, for a time, it seemed it might never awake.

Ellen remained in prison, her fate uncertain, for another six months.
She was sentenced to ten years, but support for her in the west, particularly in the United States government, eventually persuaded a reluctant
Doe to allow her to leave the country. Years later, in Washington, D.C.,
she attributed her deliverance to "the grace of Almighty God and the
mercy of others."[5]

While in Washington, she worked for a bank with branches in
Africa before accepting a position with the UN Development Program.
She remained engaged in resistance efforts to Doe's dictatorship, but
the extreme violence his regime employed prevented her from returning to the country and to the mission she accepted as her personal

responsibility: to rescue Liberia, all of it, from the carnage and injustices of its benighted history.

One of Doe's many former allies who became his opponents, Charles Taylor, a Liberian of mixed heritage (his mother was a native of the Gola tribe, his father an Americo-Liberian), had also sought refuge in the United States. Doe's regime had accused him of embezzling government funds, and Taylor was briefly held in a Plymouth, Massachusetts, jail, pending extradition. He escaped with four other inmates by sawing through the bars of a prison laundry room window and climbing down a knotted sheet. His fellow escapees were soon apprehended, but Taylor managed to get out of the country and make his way first to Libya, and then to the Ivory Coast, where he raised a rebel army, proclaimed them the National Patriotic Front of Libya (NPFL), and invaded Nimba County on Christmas Eve 1989. Joining the NPFL was an allied rebel force of Gio tribesmen, led by an illiterate and insanely bloodthirsty warlord who called himself Prince Johnson.

Doe's soldiers responded to the insurrection with their usual violent indiscretion, destroying everything and everyone they encountered in Nimba County, causing a tidal wave of refugees to flood across the border into the Ivory Coast and Guinea. Within six months, the civil war had spread throughout the country. Soldiers on all sides of the conflict, many of them children, committed so many gruesome atrocities, indiscriminately raping, torturing, and slaughtering thousands of combatants and noncombatants alike, that the rest of the world could scarcely comprehend who was fighting whom, and for what, and looked on with horror as Liberia descended into what appeared to be an earthly kingdom of hell. Taylor's soldiers were soon in control of much of the country but were prevented from entering the capital when soldiers from neighboring West African nations intervened. But they failed to prevent Prince Johnson's forces from taking Monrovia. Doe, garrisoned in his presidential palace, was soon apprehended by Johnson's forces. Before they killed him, they tortured him at length, cutting off both his ears. Reportedly, their leader, sitting in a chair and sipping a beer, watched the gruesome spectacle while one of his soldiers fanned him.[6]

Sirleaf originally supported Taylor and traveled secretly to Liberia in

1990 to meet with him. When a reporter questioned her years later why she hadn't recognized Taylor's brutality earlier, she argued that her purpose in their clandestine 1990 meeting was to confront him about the "tribalistic killings."[7] "So many supported him in the early days," she explained. "But he betrayed everybody. He was hungry for power."[8]

Taylor and Prince Johnson had parted ways prior to Doe's assassination, and Johnson had formed the rival Independent National Patriotic Front of Liberia. Taylor's soldiers eventually forced Johnson to flee Monrovia. The war to liberate the country from Samuel Doe's tyranny became nationwide tribal war in which seven different warlords vied to become Liberia's next big man. Taylor's soldiers, some as young as ten, wearing fright wigs and dosed with narcotics, were the authors of some of the greatest atrocities, but all sides competed to terrorize their way into power.

By October 1990, the Economic Community of West African States (ECOWAS) declared a transitional Liberian government, headed by Amos Sawyer, an American-educated political-science professor. Prince Johnson initially supported the interim government, but Taylor refused to recognize its authority and kept fighting. Taylor attacked Monrovia again, but ECOWAS soldiers reinforced the city, and in 1992 Taylor agreed to join in a coalition government. For the next five years, however, ECOWAS and successive international peace efforts ultimately failed to bring the civil war to a conclusion, as hostilities perpetually reignited between Liberia's various warlords, intent on power no matter what the cost to their country. In 1996, widespread fighting resumed in Monrovia. Finally, in August 1996, a settlement was achieved, and elections were scheduled for the following year.

Taylor was clearly the most powerful warlord contending for the presidency. His forces were largely in control of Monrovia. And despite his agreement to a cessation of hostilities and a free election, it was clear by now to everyone that he was not a man much interested in the welfare of his nation or its progress toward political reconciliation. Most Liberians feared his response should he lose the election, but Ellen Johnson Sirleaf didn't. She returned again to her country and challenged him for the presidency. During the campaign, children chanted a succinct summary of Taylor's electoral appeal: "He killed my ma.

He killed my pa. If he's President, he won't kill me."⁹ In the elections, which former U.S. president Jimmy Carter pronounced free and fair and Sirleaf denounced as fraudulent, Taylor claimed 75 percent of the vote. Sirleaf had won only 10 percent. Taylor's party claimed majorities in both houses of Liberia's Congress, and he assumed the presidency in August. Angry at her determined opposition and her refusal to sanction his election, Taylor accused Sirleaf of treason. Given the circumstances and the nature of her accuser, it was not a charge she dared take lightly, and she was again forced into exile.

The seven years of civil war had decimated the country. Its infrastructure was in ruins, and the vast majority of Liberians who had survived the savage fighting were desperately poor. The new president was little interested in the suffering of his people. His efforts to restore Liberia's economic fortunes were limited to producing wealth in sufficient quantity to make his own systemic looting of the country's resources worthwhile.

Although the civil war had officially ended with his election, in reality the contest for Liberia was far from over. Two of the largest rebel armies were forced to relocate to neighboring countries but remained intent on replacing the new big man with one of their own. Taylor's government fought intermittent actions with rivals even before the civil war resumed in full several years later. In 1998, his soldiers fired on the American embassy, where a rival warlord had taken refuge. The United States dispatched a Marine force to Liberia to protect embassy personnel before evacuating them.

Fighting began again in 1999, after neighboring countries and the United States accused Taylor of fomenting civil war in neighboring Sierra Leone (which claimed hundreds of thousands of lives there), and became widespread by 2001. The UN imposed sanctions on Liberia for its continued meddling in Sierra Leone. Yet again, Liberians were subjected to ever-intensifying and truly horrific terror that had few precedents in modern times except in Sierra Leone and in the even more tragic country of Rwanda. Drugged and demented children were again employed as the soldiers. Rape, torture, and mass murder were commonly used tactics. Civilian areas were shelled indiscriminately. What remained of the country's fragile infrastructure was destroyed as rival big men fought with abandon for the privilege of looting Liberia's natural wealth.

Throughout the tragedy, and in defiance of Taylor's threats, Ellen Johnson Sirleaf worked with an NGO to alleviate her people's suffering. She organized peaceful political opposition as head of the Unity Party. She believed her impeccable international credentials as an honest administrator, her stubborn courage, and her desire to rescue Liberia from its nightmare made her the ideal candidate to lead her nation. But she had to await events on the ground, as did all Liberians, before she could seize her opportunity.

By 2003, rebel forces were within a few miles of Monrovia. That summer, another attempt at a negotiated settlement failed, and initial plans to deploy an international peacekeeping force collapsed. A UN-supported special tribunal indicted Taylor for war crimes, and the U.S. government called for him to resign. In August, with rebel forces closing in, Nigerian peacekeepers and U.S. Marines arrived, and Taylor was persuaded to flee to exile in Nigeria, promising, "God willing, I'll be back."

An interim coalition government was established to manage what remained of the country until elections could be held in 2005. Sirleaf joined it, chairing the Commission on Good Governance. In reality, UN administrators and fifteen thousand international peacekeepers actually ran the country. It was and remains a formidable task. The once-prosperous country, founded in the name of liberty, was a wreck. The capital had been reduced to a city of slums, with no electricity or running water. Ninety percent of adult Liberians were unemployed. More than 60 percent were illiterate. Schools, hospitals, and other local institutions barely functioned. Members of the transitional government quickly proved themselves worthy of their predecessors. Official corruption remained as a common as ever. The National Assembly was stripped bare of any furnishing of value by outgoing parliamentarians in advance of the 2005 elections. Donor countries withheld promised aid to Liberia out of the well-founded concern that it would just line the pockets of another gang of government thieves. Taylor's supporters, many still armed, roamed the country, as did the unemployed warriors of rival factions. Well over two hundred thousand Liberians perished during the long years of civil war. Millions were refugees in other countries or lived in awful circumstances in hastily established relief camps.

In the face of this probably insurmountable dysfunction and despair, Sirleaf offered her services as president. Along with twenty-three other candidates, she declared her candidacy in elections scheduled for October 11, 2005. George Weah, an international soccer star and UN goodwill ambassador, was the favorite, but when no candidate in the crowded field could claim a majority, a runoff election was scheduled for November 8 between the candidate who had won the largest share, Weah, and the first runner-up, Ellen Johnson Sirleaf. The sixty-seven-year-old grandmother won, handily.

Her courage and the indomitable spirit she had shown in her lifelong opposition to the brutal dictatorships that had ruined her country had earned her the nickname Liberia's "Iron Lady." But to the thousands of Liberians who flocked to the polls to vote for her—the majority of whom were woman who had, with cause, despaired of the male-dominated world of Liberian politics—she was known more affectionately as "Ma Ellen." And despite her reputation for toughness, which she is not a little proud of, she knows and has said that the best she can now offer her wretched country is a little motherly care.

She has won many admirers abroad and has encouraged the hopes of her people, who, one would think, had long ago accepted that hope had been banished forever from Liberia. Her inauguration in January 2006 was attended by First Lady Laura Bush and Secretary of State Condoleezza Rice, as well as many other foreign dignitaries. Many foreign governments have also placed their trust in Sirleaf and have promised to help her repair Liberia. She faces staggering odds, though. While Sirleaf has made fair progress in restoring some semblance of normalcy to her country, Liberia is barely removed from the status of a failed state. In addition to the manifold economic challenges confronting it, the specter of a return to violence remains. Many representatives of the factions that had looted and destroyed the country during the civil war currently sit in the Liberian parliament, including Charles Taylor's wife and the man who had enjoyed watching Samuel Doe tortured to death, Prince Johnson. Out of inescapable political necessity, the new government has had to reach some tenuous accommodations with several of the big men who would like another turn at profiting from Liberia's misery. Thousands of their soldiers, children hardened by war, remain unemployed and uneducated. The injustices that had made such a mockery of the motto and political values of Liberia's founders may never be reconciled. But President Sirleaf, Ma Ellen, believes they can be, and she is, as ever, intent on her purpose.

She believes she understands Liberia's contradictions better than many do. She once explained to a reporter that her experience in Liberia's two conflicting worlds, the elite and the disadvantaged, her personal exposure to human cruelty, and her privileged life in the west qualified her to "represent the whole zodiac of the Liberian contradictions, and I know the Liberian potential. If there is anybody who can bring change, it's someone whose life experience represents all the good *and* the bad."[10]

Her confidence in herself as an agent of change and a beacon of hope to a forlorn country might seem grandiose, but it gave her the strength to brave great dangers, to recover from her own experiences with terror, and to return again and again to Liberia, when she could have lived a life of comfort and ease abroad. She did so not to elevate herself but to be of service to others. Perhaps her decisions reveal that she knows the very secret of life is just that: to be of service to others. It is that kind of humility that is the source of genuine self-respect, the opposite of vanity. And it is the value common to the noblest decisions.

TO SECURE THESE RIGHTS

O n February 13, 1946, Sergeant Isaac Woodard Jr. was honorably discharged from the U.S. Army at Camp Gordon in
Augusta, Georgia. That evening, he boarded a Greyhound
bus bound for Winnsboro, South Carolina. At a stop outside Augusta,
he asked the driver to wait while he used the restroom. The driver,
A. C. Blackwell, refused, and an argument ensued. Woodard apparently resented the belittling expressions Blackwell used to rebuff his
request and told the driver so. Eventually Blackwell relented, and the
bus waited while Woodard relieved his bladder.

What occurred next is disputed. The driver claimed Woodard and
several other soldiers were drunk and disruptive and that Woodard's
behavior had offended a female passenger. Woodard claimed he was
sober, a fact attested to by some of his fellow veterans, and that his
only offense had been talking back to the driver who had treated him

disrespectfully. When he returned from the restroom, he had taken his seat without any further exchange with Blackwell and sat quietly until the bus stopped in Batesburg, South Carolina.

Blackwell left the bus for a moment and returned with the town's chief of police, Lynwood Shull, and another officer, Elliot Long, who took Woodard off the bus and struck him. Shull later claimed that Woodard had been drunk and profane, and he had to threaten him with his blackjack but had not, at that point, felt it necessary to use violence. Several passengers who witnessed the incident contradicted him. Both Shull and Woodard agreed that violence was used moments later.

Shull dragged Woodard into a nearby alley, out of the other passengers' sight. Woodard admitted that he had tried to wrest the blackjack from the 210-pound Shull, after the police chief assaulted him when he had answered a question with "yes" instead of "yes, sir." Shull claimed that he had acted in self-defense. After Officer Long arrived on the scene, the struggle, however it started, became a beating. Shull later admitted he struck Woodard with his nightstick but couldn't recall how many times. Woodard claimed that he was beaten repeatedly about his head and that Shull jabbed at both his eyes with the stick. When the beating subsided, Shull and Long took the bleeding Woodard to jail and dumped him in a cell, leaving his wounds untreated.

When he awoke in the morning, Woodard's sight had begun to fail. He was taken before a local judge, tried and convicted of drunk-and-disorderly conduct, and fined fifty dollars. Returned to his cell, he asked for a doctor. Two days later, a doctor arrived, who advised that he be removed to the veterans' hospital in Columbia. The army located him there three weeks later, after his family had filed a missing person's report, and immediately transferred him to an army hospital in Spartanburg, where doctors pronounced him completely blind. Both his eyes had been ruptured in their sockets by blows from Lynwood Shull's nightstick.

As outrageous as it was, the savage beating inflicted on Sergeant Woodard was not unusual for the time and place in which it occurred. Isaac Woodard was black. His antagonists were white. In the completely segregated south of the 1940s, an African American's civil rights were not, as a matter of course, viewed as an obstacle to any form of abuse.

Sergeant Isaac Woodard, a twenty-seven-year-old decorated veteran, just returned from the Pacific theater and discharged from the army for only a few hours, might have expected a better welcome from fellow citizens who had managed to avoid military service. He should have known better. He had been born in South Carolina and raised in North Carolina. He knew how resistant racist culture was to change, to any African American's aspirations for justice, veteran or not. But war changes a man. His service, as it had for thousands of African-American soldiers, had apparently given him the idea that white Americans, even below the Mason-Dixon line, owed him more respect than they had shown him before he had put on a soldier's uniform and risked his life for his country. Southern defenders of white supremacy were offended by this notion. And they resolved to disabuse the veterans of these presumptions, immediately.

The first postwar months saw a marked rise in Ku Klux Klan activity, as it thrived from white southerners' concerns that the war had empowered black soldiers to upset the existing social order. And the Klan's revival was not only a southern phenomenon. In the State of New York, Klan membership had increased and its public demonstrations had become more frequent and well attended. But in the south, more drastic action was taken to express old hatreds.

In February 1946, a white man in Columbia, Tennessee, struck a black woman. Her son, a recently returned navy veteran, James Stephenson, threw him through a plate-glass window. A lynch mob headed for the black section of town, intent on killing Stephenson, only to encounter a group of armed black veterans. In the ensuing violence, several of the mob were killed or wounded, including four white policemen. The governor dispatched five hundred state troopers to the scene, who fired indiscriminately at people, destroyed everything in their path, arrested more than one hundred men, and murdered two of them while they were in jail. An attorney for the NAACP, who served as counsel for the defendants, future Supreme Court Justice Thurgood Marshall, likened the state's action to the behavior of "German storm troopers."

On July 25, army veteran George Dorsey, his wife, May, his sister-in-law, and her husband were stopped on a bridge in Walton County, Georgia, by a gang of more than twenty men and pulled from a car driven by the white farmer who employed them as sharecroppers. Their unrecognizable bodies were found by the bank of the Appalachian River, riddled with more than sixty bullet wounds. The man who had driven them to their terrible fate remarked that "before George went into the service he was a pretty good nigger, but after he got out he thought he was as good as any white man."[1]

The same night, Maceo Snipes, another decorated veteran, answered a knock on the door of his mother's house in Butler, Georgia, and was shot dead. He had voted that day in a Democratic primary election, the only African American in his district to exercise his franchise.

In August, a white mob tortured to death, with a blowtorch and meat cleaver, another veteran, John C. Jones, and dumped his body in a swamp near Minden, Louisiana.

These were some of the worst but hardly the only incidents in a wave of white violence against black veterans. Their tragedies outraged decent Americans and galvanized civil-rights organizations to protest the shameful treatment of black veterans in the south and the unyielding injustice of Jim Crow laws. The executive secretary of the NAACP, Walter White, discussed the shocking stories with a friend who was himself a decorated veteran of World War I and whose affection for his brothers in arms had ever remained boundless.

Certainly, White knew the background of the man with whom he shared his outrage. He was an eminent citizen of a segregated border state, born just two decades after the Civil War, whose family, former slave owners, still nursed resentment for the rough treatment they had received from Union forces. He had long harbored racial prejudices common to the family and culture that had raised him. He used the word "nigger," not maliciously but as one of the conventions of white conversation in that day. He was not known to have lately developed any radical sympathies for the cause of racial justice. White knew him to be a good man and respected him. He knew him to be a man of proven integrity who, though he had stayed loyal to the boss of a corrupt political machine who had been his patron, was scrupulously honest himself. The machine had relied on the votes of urban blacks and had taken care to show some concern for their welfare. And the man to whom White now turned had always showed himself to be an instinctively courteous and concerned man to people of color. But he surely wasn't a rabble-rouser when it came to race relations. On the contrary, he was a well-intentioned fellow, with a basic instinct for fairness and supporting the underdog, who tried to do right but who had not transcended the deeply embedded biases of American culture in the mid-twentieth century.

In a speech six years before, he had pledged his concern for the treatment and condition of African Americans but cautioned his all-black audience that he was not "appealing for the social equality of the Negro. The Negro himself knows better than that, and the highest type of Negro leaders say quite frankly they prefer the society of their own people. Negroes want justice, not social relations." But he continued by offering "a note of warning. Numberless antagonisms and indignities heaped upon any race will eventually try human patience to the limit and a crisis will develop. We all know that the Negro is here to stay and in no way can be removed from our political and economic life, and we should recognize his inalienable rights as specified in our Constitution. Can any man claim protection of our laws if he denies that protection to others?"[2]

He was a good man, a just one, though only a little ahead of his times. But he was something else, as well, to the black veterans who suffered atrocities in the south. He was their commander-in-chief, and Harry S Truman took the responsibilities of his job very seriously.

When Harry Truman first ran for political office in 1922, an army buddy suggested that he get in the good graces of the Klan, which was growing in influence in Jackson County, Missouri, and could help secure his election in a difficult, crowded Democratic primary. He balked at the suggestion at first but was eventually persuaded to pay a ten-dollar membership fee and to agree to meet with a Klan organizer. But when the Klan official told Truman he must promise if elected never to hire Catholics, Truman asked for his ten dollars back. He had commanded in World War I a battery made up of Irish Catholics from Kansas City, whom he affectionately referred to as his "Irish bunch." Ever since, he had insisted that his "comrades in arms are closer than brothers to me."[3] The Klan opposed Truman in that campaign and every one of his subsequent campaigns. He didn't much care. He had never liked them.

Truman first met Walter White only a few weeks after he had become president, and both men emerged from the meeting considering each other friends. In a symbolically important move, the new president had invited the NAACP leader to the White House, where they discussed, among other things, making permanent the Fair Employment Practices Committee (FEPC), which President Roosevelt had created by executive order. Its mandate was soon to expire, and Truman needed congressional approval to make it permanent and to secure funding for its operations. Roosevelt had not been willing to push Congress for the legislation, but Truman was. On June 5, 1945, he wrote the chairman of the House Rules Committee, where the bill had been buried, warning that "discrimination in the matter of employment against properly qualified persons is not only un-American in nature, but will lead eventually to industrial strife and unrest." A week later in a press conference, he urged Congress to move the legislation forward.

Southern Democrats in the Senate reacted predictably, in words that would shock most Americans three generations later. Senator Theodore Bilbo of Mississippi warned his colleagues that "the niggers and the Jews of New York are working hand in hand. . . . This is a damnable, Communist, poisonous piece of legislation." Mississippi's other senator, James Eastland, concurred and disparaged the people whom the legislation was intended to protect. "We are dealing with an inferior race. . . . Negro soldiers have caused the U.S.A. to lose prestige all over Europe. . . . They will not fight. They will not work."[4]

Ultimately, though Truman continued to push for a permanent FEPC for more than a year, a Senate filibuster killed the legislation. All he had to show for his efforts was a small appropriation that allowed the commission to finish its last report before going out of business.

Truman and White's meeting occurred years before the landmark Supreme Court decision in *Brown v. Board of Education* accelerated the great struggle for racial justice in the fifties and sixties. Although the abuses inflicted on black veterans in the south had mobilized civil-rights organizations and attracted the activism of prominent white citizens, there was no widespread clamor in the country, and certainly not in the comfortably bigoted offices of Congress, to restore to African Americans their constitutional rights. Washington itself was a segregated town, where black citizens weren't treated any better than they were in Kansas City and probably worse.

Neither was Truman in much of a position to be politically daring. He had only five months before succeeded the beloved Franklin Roosevelt and was believed by much of the country and official Washington to so lack the skills, intelligence, and charm of the late president as to make any comparison between them absurd. He was well liked in Washington and back home, and for the most part he was respected on Capitol Hill, where he had served ably as a senator. But no one, except his closest friends (and not all of them), thought he was the right man for the job. His popularity, as measured in public-opinion polls, was low, and his prospects were poor for being anything other than a caretaker of the federal government until a more suitable chief executive could be found.

When Truman inherited the presidency, he was seen to be an inconsequential man in charge during hugely consequential times. The war had yet to end. The decisions he was required to make to end the war and to establish the basic structure and institutions of the postwar world order were immensely difficult and burdensome. The Potsdam Conference where Truman had met with those formidable and experienced players on the world stage, Winston Churchill and Joseph Stalin, occurred only a few months after he had been sworn in. The decision to drop the first atom bomb on Japan awaited him. Negotiations to establish the United Nations were ongoing. After Japan's surrender, Truman led the free world in the opening days of the Cold War with our former ally, the Soviet Union. His administration was to launch the Marshall Plan and announce the Truman Doctrine, which became the basic strategic doctrine of the Cold War, providing assistance to Greece and Turkey to prevent the Soviets from turning them into satellite states. These and many other monumentally important decisions were the responsibility of the modest former haberdasher with a high school education. Few would have advised him that this would be a good time to launch a groundbreaking initiative on civil rights.

Yet after Walter White and his associates shared with Truman on September 19, 1946, the details of southern atrocities against veterans,

Truman took immediate action. He was not a man to ignore a shocked conscience or let actions so vile to his sound moral code go unanswered. These men were soldiers who had defended their country. They had a right to decent treatment from their fellow citizens, wherever they might live.

In his memoirs, Walter White recalled a stunned Truman reacting to the information he had just received. "My God," said Truman, "I had no idea it was as terrible as that! We've got to do something."⁵ He told his attorney general, Tom Clark, to investigate federal crimes committed against veterans in the south and to apprehend and prosecute the culprits. This Clark did, with mixed success. Six days after Woodard's beating, federal agents arrested Lynwood Shull, but an all-white jury subsequently acquitted him. Clark was a good man, with notably liberal sentiments about civil rights for a southerner from a family with a slave-owning past. He tried his best. But J. Edgar Hoover, whose agents did the investigating, decidedly did not share those sentiments. And southern white juries were surely not the hanging kind in trials where white men were accused of abusing the rights of African Americans. The day after his meeting with Walter White, Truman ruminated in a note to Clark about appointing on his own authority a federal commission to examine racial injustice and report to Congress recommendations to improve the situation.

It would be a mistake to suggest that the decision to create a presidential civil-rights commission was motivated solely by Truman's outrage over the treatment of veterans. It greatly upset him, indeed. But in this decision, as in so many others, he was impelled to act by more than his innate sense of fairness or respect for the sacrifices of American fighting men. Although Truman had less formal education than most of his predecessors, he was an extraordinarily well-read man, who, as a boy growing up in the hard and often lonely environment of a small family farm, had read all the texts of a classical liberal education. He could quote "old Cicero" or Plutarch or Marcus Aurelius as correctly and aptly as could a Harvard scholar. And he was very well versed in the philosophy and history of the American republic. He had a genuine and animating devotion to the country's founding texts, the Constitution and the Declaration of Independence. He was now a constitutional officer, and he took his oath to uphold the Constitution as seriously as he took his responsibilities as a husband and father.

Truman also knew that racial injustice at home exposed Americans as hypocrites and weakened our moral standing and our ability to establish a new world order based on the principles of democracy and justice. He knew that our new enemy, the Soviets, was quick to point to that hypocrisy as they prepared to draw an iron curtain over half of Europe.

So, on December 5, 1946, Truman issued Executive Order 9808, creating the first Presidential Committee on Civil Rights, comprised of fifteen eminent Americans of European and African descent, with a mandate to examine all areas of racial and religious discrimination and to report what actions, either by legislation or presidential directive, were required to remedy the injustices. One month prior to the announcement, the voters had handed Truman a humiliating setback. The midterm elections of 1946 produced Republican majorities in both houses of Congress. Truman's own popularity had sunk to the mid-thirties in public-opinion polls, which also showed that an overwhelming majority of Americans did not support any new federal civil-rights policies. Truman knew that the new Republican majorities on the Hill, working with southern Democrats, would not provide the funds for his new committee's operation, so he paid for it out of the presidency's contingency fund.

The fifteen eminent citizens he appointed made up, in the words of one aide, "a Noah's Ark Committee."[6] He asked the respected president of General Electric, Charles E. Wilson, who was known to hold forward views on the subject of race relations, to be its chairman. Additionally, he appointed the late president's son, Franklin Roosevelt Jr., whose mother was in the vanguard of civil-rights activism; Charles Luckman, president of Lever Brothers; three respected clerics, Rabbi Roland Gittelsohn, Catholic bishop Francis Haas, and Episcopal bishop Henry Sherrill; two labor leaders, James Carey of the CIO and Boris Shishkin of the AFL; past president of the Knights of Columbus Francis Matthews; John Dickey, president of Dartmouth College; former senator Frank Graham, president of the University of North Carolina; Channing Tobias, director of the Phelps-Stokes Fund, which promoted educational opportunities for people of color; Morris Ernst, cofounder of the American Civil Liberties Union; Mrs. M. E. Tilly, of the Methodist Church; and Sadie Tanner Alexander, an African-American lawyer from Philadelphia with a Ph.D. in economics and a reputation as an uncompromising advocate for racial equality.

All of these people, balanced by profession, color, religion, and region, held views on civil rights that were ahead of the prevailing sentiments in Washington and much of the country. Truman knew they would produce an honest and far-reaching report, and he told them he wanted "our Bill of Rights implemented in fact. We have been trying to do this for 150 years. We are making progress, but we are not making progress fast enough." He referred to the rise of the Ku Klux Klan and the race troubles of the early twenties and told them, "I don't want to see any race discrimination. I don't want to see any religious bigotry break out in the country as it did then." He gave them a broad mandate, including subpoena power, and instructed the federal government to cooperate fully with them. He asked them to complete their report by the autumn of the following year.

Six months later, he addressed a conference of the NAACP, the first American president to do so, from the steps of the Lincoln Memorial. A few days before, he had written to his sister, Mary Jane, worried that their mother wouldn't care for his remarks. Their colorful mother, who as an eleven-year-old had been forcibly evacuated from the family farm by Union troops, had remained ever after quite firm in her disdain for northerners and in her racial prejudices. In a story recounted in the memoirs of White House butler Alonzo Fields, Martha Ellen Young Truman, during a visit to the White House, listened at the dinner table as the president mentioned the name of someone to his dinner guest. "Isn't he a Yankee?" she asked Truman.

"Yes, Mother, but you know there are good Yankees as well as bad and good Rebels," Truman remarked.

"Well," his mother responded, "if there are any good Yankees, I haven't seen one yet."[7]

In the letter to his sister, Truman wrote, "I have to make a speech tomorrow . . . and I wish I didn't have to make it. . . . Mamma won't like what I have to say because I wind up quoting old Abe. But I believe what I say and I am hopeful we may implement it."[8]

As Truman stood before ten thousand people assembled on the Washington Mall at four o'clock in the afternoon, and delivered his nationally broadcast address, Walter White, who stood beside him, thought it the equal of the Gettysburg Address, if not in its eloquence, then in the political courage it represented, with its direct appeal for federal antilynching laws and an end to poll taxes, discrimination in the workplace, and inequities in public education. "We must make the Federal Government a friendly, vigilant defender of the rights and equalities of all Americans," Truman promised. "And again I mean all Americans." And he based his appeal not in political necessity alone but in its deeply moral importance.

> Many of our people still suffer the indignity of insult, the narrowing fear of intimidation, and, I regret to say, the threat of physical injury and mob violence. Prejudice and intolerance in which these evils are rooted still exist. The conscience of our Nation, and the legal machinery which enforces it, have not yet secured to each citizen full freedom from fear.
>
> We cannot wait another decade or another generation to remedy these evils. We must work, as never before, to cure them now.

When the president sat down, he turned to White and said, "I mean every word of it—and I'm going to prove that I do mean it."[9] And he did.

The president's Committee on Civil Rights presented its 178-page report to Truman on October 29, 1947. The report, entitled *To Secure These Rights,* detailed the many ways in which African Americans did not possess the right Truman insisted they must possess: freedom from fear. It documented recent lynchings and other gross civil-rights abuses and the myriad forms of discrimination that afflicted every facet of life for blacks in the south and elsewhere. It made thirty-five specific recommendations for executive and legislative remedies, including federal antilynching laws, a federal law to abolish the poll tax, protections of voter rights, desegregation of interstate commercial travel, and the integration of the armed services and civil service, the latter having been segregated by Woodrow Wilson in 1913. Truman embraced them all. *The Washington Post* described the report as "social dynamite" in its call "for immediate and bold action to wipe out segregation and discrimination from the American way of life."[10]

As Truman prepared to deliver his 1948 State of the Union Address, first among his administration's legislative priorities were the recommendations of his civil-rights committee. He knew what he was up against. A Republican Congress and a Democratic caucus dominated by southern segregationists would not accept such drastic actions to remedy something many of them did not view as a problem. Of greater concern were the forthcoming national elections, in which Democrats hoped to recover their congressional majorities, and a radical new approach to race relations wasn't going to do anything more than alienate southern Democrats. Truman, too, was facing reelection, but that wasn't as great a concern to Democrats in Congress. They, like a lot of Americans, knew the accidental president who was now pestering them about civil rights would lose, probably by a lot.

Harry Truman, of course, knew nothing of the sort, although he did recognize the virtual impossibility of getting his civil-rights program through Congress. But he thought it important to try. His advisors were divided about whether the initiative would, on balance, help or hurt his reelection chances. Many believed that the growing importance of the black vote in urban centers of the north would offset any defections in the south. But others thought it was an incredibly risky, if courageous, gamble. Henry Wallace, a former FDR vice president, was going to run for president as a progressive and could, they worried, siphon off some of the very votes Truman hoped to pick up on this issue.

In the country, there was very little division concerning the president's policy. Americans were against it. According to a Gallup poll, only 6 percent of Americans approved. In the south, where Truman was most vilified, he had a 57 percent disapproval rating.[11] Talk was already growing that a popular segregationist like Strom Thurmond, governor of South Carolina, might bolt the Democrats and run for president as a states' rights candidate. Although it would have been unnatural for Truman not to have been discouraged by the imposing political hostility he encountered, he gave little indication that he could be deterred.

In his January address, Truman promised that he would soon call for the legislation necessary to implement his committee's recommendations, which was his highest priority for the year. "Our first goal," he declared, "is to secure fully the essential human rights of our citizens." On February 2, 1948, he sent the formal message to Congress, which contained ten points from the committee's recommendations, including an antilynching law, desegregation of interstate commerce, and a measure to protect voters' rights. One would like to think that, even in those unenlightened days, members of Congress, no matter what region they hailed from, would have been more favorably disposed to support an antilynching law. Who could sanction murder? In truth, many of the southern Democrats who opposed the law were not advocates of lynching. Even Strom Thurmond had pressed for tough antilynching laws and prosecution in South Carolina. But neither would they let the federal government intrude on their states' rights to write and enforce their own criminal statutes.

Friends from home, as well as Truman's many friends in Congress, who included southern Democrats, counseled him to abandon his determination to force the civil-rights issue. Congress wasn't going to pass his legislation, and he was only hurting himself with voters he needed. The Republicans were going to nominate popular governor Tom Dewey of New York, a formidable opponent, and his friends couldn't help Truman if he kept after them about the Negro's rights. Truman was unconvinced.

To one delegation of southern friends, he responded that he understood their point of view, for his "own forebears were Confederates." His grandparents had been slaveholders, and as children his parents had been imbued with affection for the Confederacy. But, he said, "my stomach turned over when I learned that the Negro soldiers, just back from overseas, were being dumped out of army trucks in Mississippi and beaten." And to a friend from Missouri who had cautioned him, he responded at length and strongly:

> I am not asking for social equality. . . . I am asking for equality of opportunity for all human beings, and as long as I stay here, I am going to continue that fight. When the mob gangs can take four people out and shoot them in the back, and every-

body in the country is acquainted with who did the shooting and nothing is done about it, that country is in a pretty bad fix . . .

When a mayor and a City Marshall can take a negro Sergeant off a bus in South Carolina, beat him up and put out one of his eyes, and nothing is done about it by the State Authorities, something is radically wrong with the system.

On the Louisiana and Arkansas Railway when coal burning locomotives were used, the Negro firemen were the thing because it was a back-breaking job and a dirty one. As soon as they turned to oil as a fuel it became customary for people to take shots at Negro firemen and a number were murdered because it was thought that this was now a white-collar job and should go to white men. I can't approve of such goings on and I shall never approve of it, as long as I'm here. . . . I am going to try to remedy it and if that ends up in my failure to be reelected, that failure will be in a good cause.[12]

At the 1948 Democratic convention in Philadelphia, a young senator, Hubert H. Humphrey of Minnesota, led a floor fight to place the president's civil-rights program in the party platform and gave one of the most memorable speeches of his career. Truman had been agreeable to keeping the civil-rights plank from the last party convention, even though that plank had offended southern delegates. But he quickly got behind Humphrey's efforts, which prevailed, and which provided the excuse for a walkout by some of the southern Democrats. Truman's speech accepting the nomination was a rousing one and well received, although delivered at nearly one in the morning after the long roll call giving the nomination to him was finally concluded. (Senator Richard Russell of Georgia, a hurriedly chosen southern protest candidate, received 263 votes to Truman's 948.) In his speech he introduced the theme that he would hit over and over again in the campaign, from whistle-stop to whistle-stop: the do-nothing Republican Congress. And to prove it was a do-nothing Congress, he was going to call it into special session on July 26, "Turnip Day" in Missouri, and insist that it pass his legislative program, including his civil-rights bills. The crowd loved it. The Republican Congress didn't, including the southern Democrats who were outraged by the new provision in the platform.

On July 17, in Birmingham, Alabama, southern Democrats, "Dixie-crats," held a convention to nominate Governor Thurmond as the presidential nominee of the hastily formed States' Rights Party. Ten days later, the progressives nominated Henry Wallace as their standard-bearer. Truman's goose was cooked. Tom Dewey was as good as president already. But Truman didn't seem to share in the gloom. He was enjoying himself. On the same day that he called an angry Congress into session, he stunned Washington by ordering the integration of the armed services and the federal workforce, undoing years of military tradition and Woodrow Wilson's segregationist policy in one stroke of the pen.

Of course, Congress declined to pass a single one of the president's initiatives and promptly adjourned two weeks later. It didn't matter. Truman had made his point about the "do-nothing Republicans." He barnstormed the country and put up a spirited fight. His crowds grew larger and more enthusiastic, and the press, which liked him and was sympathetic, enjoyed it. But most reporters knew, as did almost all professional politicians, that Truman would soon be out of job. Truman didn't know it, however. And, as it turns out, a lot of voters weren't so sure he should lose either.

One of his closest aides, Clark Clifford, accompanied Truman on his whistle-stop tour. At a station stop one morning, he got off the train to buy a copy of *Newsweek,* which had surveyed fifty well-known political experts, all of whom said Dewey would beat Truman. When Clifford boarded the train, he tried to hide the magazine from Truman. But Truman insisted that he show it to him. He read the article, turned to Clifford, and said, "I know *every one* of these fifty fellows. There isn't one of them has enough sense to pound sand in a rat hole."[13]

In the late evening of Election Day, November 2, 1948, things were looking a little better for the president. When he went to bed that night he was ahead in the popular vote, though New York and Pennsylvania had gone for Dewey. By the time he awoke, it was over; a little after ten the certain winner, Governor Dewey, conceded the election. Thurmond had carried four southern states, Wallace none.

In the freezing cold of a clear January morning, the favorite son of a segregated state, who had been raised to revere Robert E. Lee and the lost cause of the Confederacy, was inaugurated president of the United

States. His second term was to be as consequential as his first. The Soviets would test their first atomic bomb. The United States would go to war in Korea. Truman would fire the iconic General Douglas MacArthur for insubordination. He would never be overwhelmingly popular. His reelection had been a narrow one, without much of a mandate from the American people. But he pressed his initiatives, including his civil-rights program, no matter the obstacle.

His unilateral decision to integrate the armed services and the civil service were groundbreaking enough. But he pushed many of his other proposals forward as well. He also nominated to the Supreme Court justices who began to move the court away from its sanction of segregation, articulated in the landmark *Plessy v. Ferguson* decision. The Court's decisions in segregation cases heard during Harry Truman's years in office paved the way for the Court to reverse itself entirely in *Brown v. Board of Education,* two years after he left office, and signal the start of a full-scale national struggle to ensure to every American the rights promised in the Constitution. And although historians have been kind to Harry Truman, as well they should be, later administrations received the greatest share of credit for moving America past the ugly chapter in our history that prevailed when Truman entered office. But when the great struggle for civil rights progressed to its greatest triumphs in the administration of Lyndon Johnson, most of the country had abandoned its support for segregation. When Harry Truman decided that his office imposed on him the obligation to protect the constitutional rights of all Americans, most Americans were no more ready for the direction he intended to lead the country than was his own mother. In his belief that it was a moral imperative to secure these rights to all Americans, he was virtually alone among many of his race, his political peers, those who had raised him, and the people with whom he had his longest and closest attachments.

There is so much to admire about Harry Truman: his improbable rise from such modest beginnings; his decisive and wise leadership at a crucial turning point in the history of his country and the world; the soundness of his character; and the pure enjoyment one derives from watching the man whom many liked but few believed in confound all the experts, who didn't have enough sense to pound sand in a rat hole.

He was, as one historian aptly put it, "a man whom history will delight to remember."

One could spend many months searching his words and actions for a greater understanding of why this son of Confederates found the resolve to place before his party, before his political future, before his affection for the plain folks who were his kin and neighbors, the rights of Americans who he himself could casually call "niggers." In his retirement, during which his popularity climbed to heights it had never reached during his presidency, he rebuffed a reporter's request that he reflect on his improbable life. "I never like to go back and retrace my steps," he said. "I did what I had to do, and that is that."[14]

He was the president of all Americans, the highest constitutional officer in the land. He did what he had to do, and that was that.

THE PARADOX OF WAR

When war comes, a million tragedies ensue. The lives of a nation's finest patriots are sacrificed. Innocent people suffer. Commerce is disrupted, economies damaged. Strategic interests shielded by years of patient statecraft are endangered as the demands of war and diplomacy conflict. However just the cause, we should shed a tear for all that is lost when war claims its wages from us. And while war occasions much heroism and nobility, it surely has its corruptions as well. That is what makes it so terrible a thing even when unavoidable, even when fought for purposes our conscience affirms as just.

My grandfather commanded a task force of aircraft carriers in the Pacific during World War II. He believed war was the most ruthless endeavor, the purpose of which was to annihilate your enemy. Like all good commanders, he had a wary respect for his enemy's abilities, but he did not let his prudence temper his contempt for them. His frequent insulting references to the character of the Japanese were in accord with the conventions of his time, although when I read them today I wince at their racist overtones. I don't believe they were intended as racist screeds. As combatants often do, he needed to work up a powerful hatred for his enemy. He once recommended "killing them all—painfully." Although it is a sin, hate is an understandable reaction to the losses and atrocities suffered at the hands of your foe, who has killed your friends and is trying to kill you. And this is no small thing: it sustains the soldier in his devotion to the complete destruction of the enemy and helps him overcome the virtuous human impulse to recoil in disgust from what must be done by his hand.

The Christian is commanded to love "thy God with all thy heart . . . and love thy neighbor as thyself." How can the wages of war—its destruction, its cruelties, its corruptions—ever square with that commandment? And knowing of these corruptions, how could one expect that a soldier at war, or the nation that enjoined him to kill its enemies, could do so while holding fast within his heart a piety that resists the most awful depredations, the most intense and terrible furor, a love that seems divine and beyond the capacity of mortal man, the love for an enemy? It is hard to conceive of the experience of war—just or not, even with its selfless sacrifices, its claims of righteousness, its sanction of suffering and making others to suffer for an end that is necessary and worthy—in practice, from day to wearying day, inured though we may become to its many tragedies, as something on the whole more elevated than the hateful business it appears to be.

Reinhold Niebuhr, the eminent American theologian of the last century, recognized these contradictions about the nature of war and man at war. The former pacifist who offered the most astute, eloquent, and persuasive denunciation of pacifism argued that, in essence, there are worse things than war, and human beings have a moral responsibility to oppose those worse things, even by violence if necessary. A man who understood the paradoxes of war, he urged us to fight with all our strength but without hatred. That is easier said than done, of course, but Niebuhr knew that, too.

"To love our enemies cannot mean that we must connive with their injustice," he wrote.

> It does mean that beyond all moral distinctions of history we must know ourselves one with our enemies not only in the bonds of common humanity but also in the bonds of common guilt by which that humanity has become corrupted. The Christian faith must persuade us to be humble rather than self-righteous in carrying out our historic tasks. It is this humility that is the source of pity and forgiveness.[1]

When he spoke of pity and forgiveness, it was God's mercy he referred to, not man's.

Niebuhr was invited to Edinburgh, Scotland, in the late 1930s to deliver the Gifford Lectures, a prestigious forum established, in the words of its founder, Adam Lord Gifford, "to promote and diffuse the study of Natural Theology in the widest sense of the term—in other words, the knowledge of God." Niebuhr used the lectures to elaborate on the theology that gave rise to his model of Christian ethics, "Christian realism," which broke with the predominant theological liberalism and Social Gospel ethics of mainstream Protestantism in that day and its Renaissance-like belief in the perfectibility of man. The lectures were published in what is considered Niebuhr's magnum opus, *The Nature and Destiny of Man.*

When Niebuhr and his wife, Ursula, traveled through Great Britain en route to the lectures, they stayed briefly in a cottage in Sussex. There they were reunited with Dietrich Bonhoeffer, a young German Lutheran theologian and pastor of deep conviction, uncommon moral clarity, and extraordinary courage. Several years before, Bonhoeffer had been a student at the Union Theological Seminary in New York, where Niebuhr was a professor. Though each respected the other, they had disagreed then. Bonhoeffer had rejected Niebuhr's conception of Christian ethics, with its insistence on social responsibilities, as too worldly. He returned to Germany as Adolf Hitler rose to power and for the previous several years had taught in a seminary of the Confessing Church, the underground resistance movement of Christians who remained faithful to the Reformation and resisted the claims the Nazi government and ideology made on church doctrine and authority. When Bonhoeffer met with the Niebuhrs in 1939, the tragic events that led to World War II were already in train. Bonhoeffer, who had by then embraced Niebuhr's conviction that faith must be served in action, knew he could not support the German side in the coming conflict, and returning to his country now would put him in a dangerous situation. He appealed to Niebuhr for help in finding refuge in the United States, and Niebuhr quickly secured a teaching position at Union for him.

Bonhoeffer stayed only a few months in New York before he decided to book passage on the last ship to sail for Germany before the outbreak of the war. He explained his reasons in a letter to Niebuhr that has not survived but that Niebuhr has paraphrased: "I have come to the conclusion that I had made a mistake in coming to America. I must live through this difficult period of our national history with the Christian people of Germany."[2] His decision was to cost him his life.

Bonhoeffer and a twin sister were born in 1906 to a prosperous and respected family in Breslau, Germany. His father, Karl, was an eminent professor of psychiatry. At the age of thirteen, Dietrich informed his father he intended to enter the church, a declaration that astonished members of his family who were not particularly religious. He received his doctorate in theology in 1927 from the University of Berlin and was ordained a pastor in the Lutheran church in 1931. While he was still a very young man, his writings were admired for their brilliance and genuine insights. He had a questing intellect, searching widely and deeply in other churches and other cultures to comprehend man's relationship to God and God's will. He was influenced by the Swiss theologian Karl Barth, who had been revolted by the respective claims each belligerent nation in World War I had made on God's support, rendering Him a tribal God, a blasphemy Barth believed had nearly ruined Christianity.

Bonhoeffer strove to understand man's true responsibilities in this world and to the will of his Creator and Savior. He studied nonviolence with Mohandas Gandhi. As a curate for a German congregation in

Barcelona—and during travels to Rome, Mexico, and Cuba—he scrutinized the traditions and doctrine of Roman Catholicism. During the war years, he sought refuge and rest in a Catholic monastery. When assigned the pastorate of a Lutheran church in London, he became a confidant of an Anglican bishop. As a graduate student at Union Seminary, he was distressed by the intellectual conceits of its mostly liberal elites, who derided their fundamentalist brethren. "At this liberal seminary the students sneer at the fundamentalists in America," he protested, "when all the while the fundamentalists know far more of the truth and grace, mercy and judgment of God."[3]

He found greater spiritual solace in the services he attended at Harlem's African-American churches and was deeply affected by their joy and passion, their rich and animating music, and their deep-seated commitment, born of the injustice to which they were subjected, to working actively to improve society. He was ardently ecumenical, but always his theology and his ethical philosophy as they evolved remained centered on the redemptive suffering of Christ.

He came to believe that ethics could not be reduced to general principles. We cannot claim self-justification for our actions, nor can we know with certainty that we are right. We must accept the guilt and the necessity of our actions, which we are called to not by duty or ideology or moral certitude—those are God's to judge—but by Christ's example, which reconciled God to this sinful world. His example summons us to take responsibility for the needs of our neighbors, accept the guilt for any sin committed in the exercise of that responsibility, and submit ourselves to God's mercy. That is how we act in accordance with God's will: by taking responsible action against injustice, against evil. To not act condones evil. And it is better to sin to oppose evil directly than to accept evil in the steadfast devotion to one's private virtue.

We must use our free will, Bonhoeffer believed, to make exceptions to our ethical principles for the sake of coming to the aid of a neighbor in need. Those who believed that Christ's command to love thy neighbor enjoined them from taking necessarily coercive action to oppose an evil or who believed that evil in the world required them to withdraw from it as much as is possible were manipulated by that very evil. To be passive amid the suffering of others was a greater sin than using violence to oppose it. He believed Christ's selfless sacrifice taught us that "what is nearest to God is precisely the need of one's neighbor."[4] And we must not refuse, out of the fear of sin or worldly consequences, to answer that need: "No one who lives in this world can remain disentangled and morally pure and free of guilt."[5] The reality of Christ reconciled the reality of the world, all its corruptions and evil, to the reality of God's infinite love and mercy.

Christ's reality, His will, made us responsible for confronting the monstrous evil of Nazi fascism, with its violent claim to racial dominance, its persecution of Jews and other non-Aryans. Thus, Dietrich Bonhoeffer abandoned the pacifism of his earlier life and took up arms against a greater wrong than the sins he committed. It takes someone of truly astonishing character to seek God's will so perilously. For Bonhoeffer's faith is too easily, if falsely, claimed by those who would commit an evil as great as the one they seek to oppose. The defender of unborn life who would murder an abortion provider is an obvious example but not the only one. Bonhoeffer never misread Christ's reality to venture beyond His will. He did conspire to murder, a sin which he did not self-justify but consigned to God's mercy to forgive. It was, in the reality he confronted and to history, necessary and defensible.

"The church has three possible ways it can act against the state," Bonhoeffer wrote.

> First, it can ask the state if its actions are legitimate. Second, it can aid the victims of the state action. The church has the unconditional obligation to the victims of any order in society even if they do not belong to the Christian society. The third possibility is not just bandage the victims under the wheel, but to jam a spoke in the wheel itself.[6]

He jammed a spoke into the wheel.

In opposition to the Protestant Reich Church founded by Christians who submitted to the Nazi decree to rid the church of all non-Aryan influences, even the Old Testament, two thousand Lutheran pastors formed the Pastor's Emergency League, which became the Confessing Church. Bonhoeffer served as the head of its seminaries, training new pastors and theologians to oppose Nazism. He denounced Kristallnacht as an example of the "godless face" of the Nazis. By the time the Reich had caused Europe to convulse once again in war, the Confessing Church had been largely suppressed by the regime, with several of its leaders arrested, its seminaries closed, and Bonhoeffer forbidden to preach. Many pastors had been forced to sign loyalty oaths to the Reich. Bonhoeffer became more involved in the armed underground resistance in Germany. He sheltered Jews and helped them escape. He traveled abroad secretly to aid the resistance, once meeting with an Anglican bishop in Sweden to discuss the overthrow of the Reich and the peace terms Germany could offer to end the war. He joined a secret group of officers in the Abwehr, German military intelligence, who were plotting to kill Hitler. All this time, throughout the perilous years from 1940 to 1943, he worked on his book *Ethics,* which would offer the ethical basis for the violent actions against Nazism he believed were required of a morally responsible person.

He became engaged in January 1943 to Maria von Wedemeyer. Two months later, he was arrested for arranging financing to help Jews escape to Switzerland. From Tegel Prison in December of that year, he penned his famous letter, "After Ten Years," to his comrades in the resistance, who were demoralized by the realization that years of struggle and terrifying danger had achieved so little success. He offered a poignantly realistic acknowledgment of their weariness, disappointment, and uncertainty that their choice to follow God's will, their selfless sacrifice and acceptance of guilt for their own actions, had made any measurable difference:

> We have been silent witnesses of evil deeds: we have been drenched by many storms; we have learnt the arts of equivocation and pretense; experience has made us suspicious of others and kept us from being truthful and open; intolerable conflicts have worn us down and even made us cynical. Are we still of any use?

His comrades—burdened by guilt, tired of a hard, uncompromising, and dangerous life, and uncertain they would, in the end, strike an effective blow against an evil that remained at large—were asked by him, "Who stands firm?"

> Only the one for whom the final standard is not his reason, his principles, his conscience, his freedom, his virtue, but who is ready to sacrifice all these, when in faith and sole allegiance to God he is called to obedient and responsible action: the responsible person, whose life will be nothing but an answer to God's question and call.[7]

The Nazis believed he had conspired to help Jews escape the camps, but they did not initially know the extent of his resistance activities. He spent his time at Tegel writing poems and letters and worrying about his family and his fiancée, Maria, who devotedly corresponded with him. In her bedroom, where she wrote to him, she marked with chalk the dimensions of his cell, which he had described to her, so she could conjure the experience of communicating directly to him.

After the failed attempt on Hitler's life in 1944, the Abwehr plot and Bonhoeffer's role in it were uncovered. His brother, Karl, and two of his brothers-in-law were arrested. Bonhoeffer was moved to a Gestapo prison in Berlin, where he wrote his last letter to Maria, and from there to Buchenwald. On April 8, 1945, he was taken to Flossenburg concentration camp in the middle of the night. "When Christ calls a man," he wrote, "he bids him come and die."[8] In the early morning of April 9, with the Red Army advancing on Berlin and American artillery firing in the distance, three weeks before Hitler took his own life, Dietrich Bonhoeffer was marched naked to the gallows. A prison doctor recalled that when the guards came for him, he was "kneeling on the floor praying fervently to his God. At the place of his execution he again said a short prayer. . . . In almost fifty years that I worked as a doctor, I have hardly ever seen a man die so entirely submissive to the will of God."[9]

In a final letter to his father, Bonhoeffer offered his last testimony: "This is the end, and, for me, the beginning of life."[10]

Like Bonhoeffer, whom he believed had "grasped the real imperatives of the Christian life," Reinhold Niebuhr had once embraced pacifism, albeit with doubts, as the proper response to Christ's law of love.[11]
He believed it was the responsibility of the church to offer a moral substitute for war. Once an ardent socialist, he was sympathetic to the critique of war as the violent struggle of capitalist imperialism for control
of the resources and means of production. He was a man more at home
with paradox than perhaps any other American intellectual in modern times. During his years studying theology at the divinity school
of Yale University, he gave an early indication of his preferred means
of reasoning. He wrote a paper, "The Paradox of Patriotism," which
recognized that heroism occasioned in the destructive enterprise of
war often evinced some of the noblest virtues: courage, self-sacrifice,
loyalty, and love. He posited the question, Could these virtues aroused
by patriotism be redirected toward pacific enterprises? Arguing in the
affirmative, his paper was persuasive and well reasoned enough to
win third prize in a national competition sponsored by the Carnegie
Endowment for International Peace.

Although he had initially supported America's entry into World
War I, after he toured the Ruhr Valley and witnessed the destruction
and moral outrages wrought by all sides in the war, he wrote in his
diary, "I am done with this war business."

His parents, Gustav and Lydia, had emigrated from Germany and
settled in the eastern part of Missouri and later in western Illinois. Gustav entered the ministry of the Evangelical Synod of North America,
which had its roots in the Lutheran and Reformed German traditions
and is today part of the United Church of Christ. Like other German
Evangelical churches, services at Gustav Niebuhr's church were conducted in German, the language the Niebuhrs spoke at home. As late as
his years at Yale Divinity School, Reinhold struggled to speak English
that wasn't heavily accented. Gustav Niebuhr is remembered as a man
of devout faith, who searched honestly to perceive and follow God's
will. He despised tyranny and felt a personal responsibility to oppose
injustice. Reinhold revered him and remembered that his father "was
probably more responsible than anybody else for the choice of my vocation." When he declared at the age of ten that he intended to enter the

ministry, he explained his reason as a desire to emulate his father, who was, he said, the "most interesting man in town." And when asked years later if he was satisfied with his vocation, he responded, "insofar as I have adequately exploited the vision of my father."[12] Three of the four Niebuhr children became ministers, and one, Richard, was to become as nearly as well respected a theologian as Reinhold.

Reinhold enrolled in two Lutheran colleges, Elmhurst College and Eden Theological Seminary. While he was at Eden, his beloved father lapsed into a diabetic coma and died. The loss, which he painfully felt, also liberated the young man from the narrow confines of his small midwestern German Evangelical world. With his mother's encouragement, he enrolled at Yale, rather than immediately follow his father into the ministry.

At Yale, he embraced the social and theological liberalism of his contemporaries, with its emphasis on the humanity of Jesus and its optimistic faith in the perfectibility of man. He left Yale with a master's degree but before completing work on his doctorate. His studies had bored him, he said, "and the other side of me came out: I desired relevance rather than scholarship."[13]

In 1915, he was ordained a minister and assigned a small church in Detroit for a salary of fifty dollars per month. His widowed mother came to Detroit, too, to keep house and cook for him. The congregation of Bethel Evangelical Church totaled eighteen families when Niebuhr became their pastor. By the time he left thirteen years later, its membership had grown to eight hundred. Part of Bethel's prosperity was attributable to the explosive population growth of Detroit as the burgeoning automobile industry drew thousands of workers to the city. Niebuhr's insistence on the Americanization of his church, ridding it of its predominately German character, also attracted new parishioners. But Niebuhr himself was the main attraction. He was a riveting preacher, erudite but with a common touch and a physically expressive speaking style that was mesmerizing. A tall, slightly stooped, and balding man, he spoke hurriedly and without notes, pausing suddenly before issuing another torrent of words, pacing, shaking, twisting his body, stabbing the air with hands that were always in motion. He seemed consumed by the sermon he delivered and oblivious to all around him and to the performance that was holding his congregation spellbound. The force and intensity of Niebuhr's sermons and his growing stature as a public figure in Detroit attracted notice far afield from his small church.

Bethel was to be his only pastorate, but his experiences there shaped his political and religious thought. Bethel, he said, "determined my development more than any books I read."[14] The hardships of his working-class parishioners encouraged his embrace of an initially mild and eventually more radical socialism, which he espoused from the pulpit, in his writings in religious and secular publications, and from the lectern at various assemblies, as he began to attract national notice as a captivating social activist and intellectual.

Henry Ford was the foil that stimulated and became the primary target of Niebuhr's scathing denunciation of the dehumanizing effects of industrialization. The conditions at Ford's assembly plants were no worse than the conditions in other factories of the day. But the visionary industrialist, who paid his workers the unheard-of wage of five dollars per day, was in Niebuhr's eyes the archetype of the self-serving capitalist who exploited his workers for his own profit in the name of a laudable social purpose. Ford might have, for a time, paid his employees a more generous salary than his competitors, but the vast disparity in wealth between employer and employees; the frequent uncompensated layoffs; the hours of repetitious toil in dismal circumstances; the lack of recourse available to an injured, sick, or dismissed worker; and the indifference of an autocratic management to their fate incited Niebuhr's protest of the injustices he believed self-interested men caused in the name of progress. Ford's moral claim for his labor policies was to Niebuhr an example of the failing that shaped his theological and social convictions: pride, the original sin of Adam's fall from grace, when man invested the pursuit of his self-interest with the divinity of God. When he thundered against capitalism's exploitation of labor, he was really inveighing against the inherent corruption of man and society. Man, Niebuhr believed, when confronted with his own "finiteness," grasped for the attributes of God to allay his anxieties, to sanction his acquisitiveness, his will to power.

Niebuhr rose in national prominence as a crusader for social justice. In the beginning, he preached the optimistic liberalism of the Social Gospel: that man is inherently good, and with careful attention to his needs, his education, and economic welfare, human progress was inevitable. The Kingdom of God, where injustice, greed, poverty, and war will have no place, can be replicated on earth. But even in his early profession of this hopeful creed, Niebuhr's doubts were evident. He soon became convinced that the socialism advocated by the Social Gospel's proponents was a self-deluding conceit, a heresy that put God in history. God, Niebuhr argued, was in history only once, when Christ incarnate reconciled Him to man. The profound change in Niebuhr's theology and social liberalism began taking shape even before he left Bethel in 1928 for Union Theological Seminary, where he would teach a subject of his own devising, "applied Christianity," and become the most eminent and influential theologian of his time.

Once, while Niebuhr was in Detroit, a young newsboy who had heard him preach nonviolence stopped him on the street and asked his counsel on an ethical dilemma the boy was grappling with. Other newsboys were trying to run him off the corner on which he plied his trade. If he did not fight to hold on to his little territory, he could not sell his papers, and his family's poverty would become extreme. What did Niebuhr believe was the right thing to do? He spent a moment reflecting on the boy's predicament before offering a three-word response: "Defend your corner."

By the time Niebuhr arrived in New York, a biographer-described "uncouth country bumpkin with decidedly dubious scholarly credentials," he had shed many of what he had come to see as liberalism's self-righteous delusions.[15] The Christian idealism of the youthful, sensitive pastor began to yield to the pragmatism of a sturdy and clear-eyed Christian realist who saw in human beings and in society the primacy of self-interest that will always undermine social justice. He was a member of the Socialist Party and one of the party's candidates for public office, a founder of the Fellowship of Christian Socialists, and the chair of the Fellowship for Reconciliation, an organization of pacifists who viewed war as the greatest evil of all. But the changes in his thinking soon led him to abandon not only pacifism but the moral conceits of socialism. These changes in his political views originated in his rejection of the liberal theology prevalent in American Protestantism of the time and his return to the orthodoxy of the Reformation, with its tragic view of human nature that exposed the pretensions of contemporary idealists. "About midway in my ministry," he wrote, "I underwent a fairly complete conversion of thought which involved rejection of almost all the liberal theological ideals with which I ventured forth in 1915."[16]

In his seminal *Moral Man and Immoral Society,* Niebuhr explains the sea change in his religious and political views by arguing for an interpretation of human nature that traces its origins to the fifth century and the theology of St. Augustine. The Gospel of Jesus Christ commands man to exercise perfect Christian love, but as Christ's suffering revealed, man is by nature incapable of such perfect love. Human consciousness recognizes "the ego as an insignificant point amidst the immensities of the world."[17] Man, in his distress, tries to aggrandize himself with a larger purpose, invest himself with absolute moral authority, particularly in the society he seeks to structure, "to universalize himself and give his life a significance beyond himself."[18] Selfish desire corrupts man in all his social pursuits no matter how well intended. Utopian schemes, no less than the basest impulses of human beings, manifest that moral conceit, the original sin of pride, which makes an idol of our individual and collective goodness. Those who believe that Christ's perfect love is more than an ideal for which man should strive but, in fact, is attainable by human beings practice a heresy. They credit their own efforts with making a place for "Christ in history, whereas the only true Christ is he who was crucified in history."[19] "The quintessence of sin," he later wrote, "is, in short, that man 'changes the glory of the incorruptible God into the image of corruptible man.' He always usurps God's place and claims to be the final judge of human actions."[20]

His tragic view of human nature begs the question: how, then, can human beings follow Christ's commandments if we are so inherently corrupted by self-interest? What can we do to compensate for our sins and still seek and serve God's will? We must stop deceiving ourselves, Niebuhr answers. We must humble ourselves and recognize our sinful nature. We must work in history to establish the human derivative of Christ's perfect love, justice. The former was witnessed only in Christ incarnate and will not be known again until the end of history. But justice can be done by man in history, if we realize that even this pursuit will be corrupted by claims of absolute moral authority.

His was not as pessimistic a view of human nature as it might sound to the reader who, like the authors, lacks Niebuhr's insights and brilliance. He believed in the "indeterminate possibilities" of mankind, if we guard against the comforting delusions conceived in our self-interest. In the pursuit of justice, as in all attempts to follow God's will, we must accept that self-interest disguised as moral absolutism will destroy the justice we seek; the end of our will to do good becomes the will to our own power if unconstrained by moral, legal, and physical means. "Pride," he wrote, "is the religious dimension of the sin that flows from absolute power; and injustice is its social dimension."[21] Thus, Marxism in Stalin's Soviet Union became the primacy of the Communist Party and the tyrant who dominated it; the very justice for the worker that Marxism was conceived to promote was destroyed by the pride and selfishness inherent in the means employed to achieve it, unconstrained as they were by any legal, moral, or physical impediments. We must understand this paradox. We must establish and defend strictures on our own conduct that will protect justice from the demands of our egos. And we must have the humility to accept the guilt we share in by the actions we might be required to take to do justice. The ends do not justify the means. All attempts at self-justification are vain and will invariably lead to evils like Nazi fascism and Stalin's communism. To fight injustice we may very well sin. Here is the pragmatism, the realism expressed in the acknowledgment of lesser and greater evils, that is saved by the recognition that even the lesser is still evil, and mankind must submit to God's final judgment and love, not to himself, for forgiveness.

Niebuhr first came to reject nonviolence by recognizing that the justice in history that socialism sought could be achieved only by coercive, possibly even violent, means. Surely to do violence against another is a sin. But Niebuhr accepted it as potentially necessary to oppose a worse evil. Then, as he observed how socialism in the Soviet Union sacrificed justice to the instrument of power that was awarded sole authority to define and defend it, he came to believe all utopian movements were susceptible to the same corruption. He came to appreciate the forms of democratic government, imperfect and slow as they are, as the best means of protecting justice from the self-interest of both reformers and reactionaries. The individual is better able to constrain his ego through the exercise of the highest virtues, selflessness, courage, compassion, and love. Far harder is it for the state or any political organization to resist the demands of self-interest. It must be coerced by the legal protections of justice.

The American Constitution seems an almost perfect reflection of Niebuhr's political philosophy. Our founders wrote into the basic law of our country—with its elaborate checks and balances, its equality under the law—protections again the corruption of power they knew even they were susceptible to. Democracy, Niebuhr believed, admits man's flaws and labors to protect justice from them. He quit the Socialist Party and helped found the Union for Democratic Action, which in the Cold War became Americans for Democratic Action, the anti-Stalinist organization of American liberals. He became an admirer of Franklin Roosevelt, who he believed was trying to save capitalism from the destructive competition that was the unavoidable result of its laissez-faire principles, though within the constraints of constitutional law that guarded against his own self-interested aggrandizement of power. Niebuhr expressed his preference for democratic governance and his understanding of its nature in one of his most famous paradoxes: "Man's capacity for justice makes democracy possible; but man's inclination to injustice makes democracy necessary."[22]

Very early on, Niebuhr perceived in the fascist challenge to liberal democracy, and the Nazis' persecutions, a great evil that must be opposed with force. And he became the sharpest and most vociferous critic of pacifists who denounced resorting to the evil of violence to combat another evil. Pacifists, who believed by their example that they were promoting Christian love, were in reality assisting injustice and making war inevitable. Their morally arrogant piety, he argued, substituted an antihistorical and anti-Christian faith in the perfectibility of man for the justice that can be done on this earth and our submission to the mystery of God's mercy. To a prominent pacifist of the time, who claimed to "detest Hitlerism" but detested war even more as a sin "against the revealed righteousness of God," Niebuhr replied:

> You are willing to slightly favor the Allies against Hitler, but you are unwilling to allow such discrimination to result in an action in favor of one side against the other. To allow such an action is to involve yourself in sin. Your difficulty is that you want to live in history without sinning. There is no such possibility in history."[23]

Americans who claimed a religious foundation for their pacifism and isolationists who expressed only a fear and contempt for the political turmoil of the old world demanded Roosevelt adhere to the Neutrality Act and avoid any action or statement that might appear to take sides in the coming war. Niebuhr denounced the act as a pernicious abdication of moral responsibility. "The protagonists of a political, rather than a religious pacifism end with the acceptance and justification of, and connivance in tyranny," he wrote. "They proclaim that slavery is better than war. I beg leave to doubt it and to challenge the whole system of sentimentalized Christianity which prompts good men to arrive at this perverse conclusion."[24] He greatly admired Winston Churchill, who he believed shared his realism and who accepted his responsibility to deal with the world as he found it, not as he wished it to be. He urged his country's political leaders to emulate the man who led Britain in its finest hour. "Rarely has a man so gifted," Niebuhr wrote about Churchill's elevation to prime minister, "with every art and wisdom of statesmanship found his hour so providentially as when Churchill was called to the helm in Britain's and the world's darkest hour."[25]

One evening as Niebuhr delivered his Gifford Lectures in Edinburgh, anti-aircraft guns fired at Luftwaffe bombers within earshot, and his audience began to squirm. Niebuhr, utterly absorbed in his address, pacing the stage and flailing his arms, had heard nothing and assumed his audience's evident distress was in reaction to something he had said. His Gifford Lectures were the greatest success of his career, perhaps, the most complete and compelling exposition of Christian faith ever offered by an American theologian. They were widely discussed and debated, and his critique of power's corruptive influence helped persuade his country that reason and love alone were insufficient to triumph over the evil men will do. He began his first lecture with the question, "How shall man think of himself?" He later wrote that it was "the only subject I could have chosen because the other fields of Christian thought were beyond my competence. I lectured on 'The Nature and Destiny of Man.'"[26]

He could be quite acerbic in his criticism, describing pacifists on more than one occasion as "parasites." He was a vigorous and unrelenting polemicist who was better, some wrongly criticized, in destroying an opponent's argument than in propounding his own. He asked and gave no quarter in public or theological disputes. But he tried diligently to attack the position and not the person. He was warm and generous in his personal relations. He held kind personal regard for even those to whom he was a fierce antagonist. He loved teaching and lavished attention on his students, who revered him. He was as mindful of the sin of pride in his own life as he was in the affairs of humanity. Those who knew him well spoke of his humility with reverence. One of his students observed that "the man who so tellingly reacquainted a whole theological generation with the sin of pride was himself so singularly free of that shortcoming."[27] He took pains to subject his own views to scrutiny for the arrogance he deplored in the idealism of others, and which he warned his country to avoid.

During the Cold War, he was as ardent an opponent of communism and the Soviet Union as he had been of fascism and the Third Reich. But he cautioned against investing the policy of containment with the authority of a moral crusade. He was an intimate of many of the generation of "wise men" who led American foreign policy in the early postwar years, and his influence shaped their worldview. He battled idealism in American foreign policy even as it rightly opposed tyranny, perceiving in America's missionary zeal to promote democracy abroad the pride he viewed as heresy. In 1952, he published *The Irony of American History,* in which he warned us against arrogantly ascribing to ourselves an innocence that no human agency could possibly possess, even while subjecting the enemy we confronted to his stark and unsparing judgment. "We are defending freedom against tyranny and are trying to preserve justice," he wrote, "against a system which has, demonically, distilled injustice and cruelty out of its original promise of a higher justice." To succeed in this great contest, he warned, we would have to take "morally hazardous actions to preserve our civilization. We must exercise our power. But we ought neither to believe that a nation is capable of perfect disinterestedness in its exercise, nor become complacent about particular degrees of interest and passion which corrupt the justice by which the exercise of power is legitimized."[28]

He believed that in Vietnam we had fallen into the trap of deluding ourselves that we were invariably a force for goodness in the world, and he was a vocal opponent of the war. Power exercised by the best of nations still involved corruption and required in its exercise those "morally hazardous actions," which he felt demanded our humility. I must confess I find it surprising that a man who had never been in combat himself could arrive at so exact an understanding of the enterprise and express the moral ambiguity that is inescapable for the soldier who must kill to defend his country. Many of those who have had that experience feel that ambiguity keenly. For many, it is the stuff of nightmares that last years beyond the experience. Yet few could claim to understand or express the dilemma as precisely and comprehensively as Niebuhr did. Ours is seldom more than an instinctual dread that gives us hints of self-knowledge. We feel what we have done to be right and necessary, but what it entailed, what was done to us and by us, will always disturb our memory of it. We may attempt to alleviate the tragedy with hate for our enemy or pride in our loyalty. Niebuhr, rightly, urges us to seek happiness in our humility, in moments of triumph and despair.

I do not agree with all of Niebuhr's distrust of impassioned idealism in foreign or domestic affairs. Obviously, if unchecked by colder calculations of our interests, it can lead us astray. But few of us can be animated to take risks for justice, as Niebuhr was, by appeals to realism. Perhaps some statesmen can remain so dispassionate, but it is hard for the soldier to risk his life for an irony or for the public to support him in that endeavor without the inspiration that we are doing a necessary good for the world because we are, as a nation, concerned with doing good. To do justice in our country or in the world may not be as difficult a thing as exercising the perfect love of Christ, but it is a hard thing nonetheless, as Niebuhr recognized, and it requires greater inspiration than realism offers us. It comes at great sacrifice, whether on the streets of Selma, Alabama, or in the bloodstained snows of the Ardennes forest. America was conceived as an example to the world, and while our pride in that purpose may indeed be sinful, it has made this world a better, more just place.

That is not to argue that we should march into the world to do good unchastened by the knowledge that we are, in the end, finite and weak and sinful creatures. Nor is it to suggest that even in a just cause our actions are unstained by some evil. We can only hope to serve justice better than we have served our self-interest—no easy task. On that subject, Niebuhr, like the man he considered the "greatest American theologian," Abraham Lincoln, was exceptionally insightful.

It is natural to wonder whether Niebuhr, were he alive, would have supported or opposed the war in Iraq. Would he have defended or been uncomfortable with appeals to instill democracy in that country? He had in years past doubted the efficacy of such a project in that particular region of the world. Perhaps he would condemn it as an arrogant presumption that led us to do more harm than good. But then Niebuhr, while thoroughly realistic, was never a pessimist or cynic. He believed we have a responsibility to oppose injustice but that we must do so mindful of our own pretenses. America's intervention in Iraq did vanquish a particularly malicious tyranny, even as we struggle to prevent another from taking its place. Would he have perceived in the Iraq war a realistic response to injustice and a threat to our security, or just pretentious idealism? And if the latter, would he argue we should withdraw from that country, after our many mistakes in the prosecution of the war, if doing so would lead to a humanitarian catastrophe and even greater threat to our own security interests?

One could ask the same question about the appeals to our moral superiority that summoned Americans to battle after the attacks of September 11. Would he deplore them as a milder form of the arrogance and absolutism claimed by the terrorists who hate us? I doubt it. As Niebuhr argued in his criticism of pacifism, there are moral distinctions in history, and we have a responsibility to defend the right against the wrong. It is obvious that our cause is morally superior to that of our enemies, for whom the taking of innocent life is the object of war and not a tragic consequence of it. To argue that distinction is not to claim we are morally perfect but to recognize that we and not our enemies prosecute a morally legitimate claim. That a desire for vengeance, which God has admonished us to leave to His judgment, has surely animated our response as well does not forfeit our claim to justice or relieve us of our responsibility to serve it. In this contest, sinners though we are, we are better than our enemies.

The divisions in our country over these questions are pronounced and increasingly bitter. Both sides claim Niebuhr for their own. Which is right? One or the other? Both? Neither? The best we can hope for in this life, he would tell us, is a proximate justice. Have we served that end? I think we have tried to. Others disagree. Perhaps we can all agree with this:

> Nothing that is worth doing can be achieved in our lifetime; therefore we must be saved by hope. Nothing which is true or beautiful or good makes complete sense in any immediate context of history; therefore we must be saved by faith. Nothing we do, however virtuous, can be accomplished alone; therefore we are saved by love. No virtuous act is quite as virtuous from the standpoint of our friend or foe as it is from our standpoint. Therefore we must be saved by the final form of love which is forgiveness.[29]

"What would Jesus do?" was for a time a question posed frequently by opponents of the war in Iraq and the broader struggle against Islamic terrorists. I have more confidence that I know how the man who wrote the passage above, who knew the human condition was both tragic and redeemable, would answer that question than how he would judge both sides of our current debate. I think Reinhold Niebuhr and Dietrich Bonhoeffer would answer it by reminding us that as long as we breathe, we do not live in the Kingdom of God. What Jesus would do is not something mankind can do. We make an idol of ourselves to think otherwise. Jesus sees the acts of terrorists and the government that calls a nation to battle against them; He sees the protestor who condemns a war and the soldier who kills in it; and He weeps for the creatures He died to redeem. And then, if we are contrite, He forgives us our sins.

THE QUALITY OF MERCY

T he witness arrived promptly on Thursday morning, October
17, 1974, and took his seat before the members of the subcommittee. He was composed and confident while waiting for the
chairman to finish his opening remarks, after which the witness would
give his formal testimony and answer the members' questions. The
hearing room was filled to capacity with television cameras, reporters,
congressional staff, and spectators. Subcommittee hearings do not typically attract such a crowd. Most often, they are attended by a handful of
lobbyists and a few other parties with interests in the subject under consideration. On the occasions when they do attract great attention, matters are usually so controversial that the scheduled witnesses are either
quite intimidated by the spectacle or, if they unwisely crave attention,
thrilled by their opportunity to shine in the public spotlight. This witness was neither. He was accustomed to it. He had attended many committee hearings, and he knew the members quite well. He counted some
of them as his friends. Others were his adversaries, but he was the kind
of fellow who rarely considered a political adversary a personal enemy.

He was, after all, a man of the House, a well-liked twenty-five-year veteran of Congress who had risen to the top of his party's leadership, revered its traditions, cherished the cross-party friendships he had formed there, and understood the personalities and political dynamics that would make today's proceedings, as unusual as they were, predictable. Congress had been his life, a life he had enjoyed.

Barely a year before, he and his wife had made the difficult decision to leave Congress after his next term, so he could devote his remaining professional years to practicing law and earning enough money to provide for their comfortable retirement. Events had interceded. He had, in fact, left the House but earlier than he had intended. On this day, he appeared before the committee not as a member of Congress or as a former member but in his new capacity, as chief executive. The witness, Gerald R. Ford, was president of the United States.

The matter he had come to discuss was a serious one: whether he had promised his predecessor, Richard Nixon, a pardon before Nixon had resigned the presidency. Some of the more aggressive and liberal members, including a few who were to question him today, strongly suspected that he had. But most members, Democratic and Republican, knew him better than that. After all, Congress, to which he was showing the unprecedented courtesy of testifying before one of its committees, felt it had as much at stake in the success of his unique presidency as he did.* The country had not elected him president. Congress had.

He was a decorated navy veteran of the Pacific theater in World War II, first elected to Congress in 1948. He was a hardworking legislator, politically astute, and popular with members of both parties. He had always been well liked. A star athlete in high school; an MVP center on the University of Michigan football team; a football coach and law student at Yale University; a promising young lawyer in Grand Rapids, Michigan; handsome, pleasant, and popular with the opposite sex: Gerald Ford made friends easily and kept them. Less than a month before his first election, he had married the former Elizabeth Anne

---

*No other president is known for certain to have volunteered to testify before a congressional committee.

Bloomer Warren, Betty, who became his most trusted confidante. They were an active and attractive couple who thrived on the capital's hectic social life.

I'm always skeptical about nostalgia for a past when Washington seemed less divided by partisanship and personal acrimony. It is unlikely there ever existed quite the golden age of bipartisan harmony and generous civility that frustrated citizens imagine has been lost. Politics has always been a rough business and attracted its share of schemers, scoundrels, and the self-interested. But it is fair to say that for most of the years Jerry Ford served Michigan's Fifth District, members of Congress socialized together more often, seldom considered party membership an impediment to friendship, and seemed to rank the national interest considerably above partisan or personal ambition. Perhaps this betrays my own naïveté.

Common to every generation of Congress is a corps of backbenchers, Young Turks who chafe at the status quo and militate for stronger, more active leadership. They are more commonly found in the ranks of the minority party, particularly in the House of Representatives, where the rules are quite restrictive compared to those in the more freewheeling Senate. The influence and legislative opportunities for members of the minority are less often seized than granted as a courtesy and occasional necessity by the majority leadership. This always becomes frustrating to even the most mild-mannered and gregarious members. I was once a Young Turk during my two terms in the House, which given my personality is not particularly surprising. But that role strikes me as incongruous with Gerald Ford's personality, or at least the personality of the mature elder statesman he was when he became a national figure. He was most often described as nice, solid, dependable, likable, and thoughtful. I never imagined him as a hard charger but more as the kind of Republican leader who grew accustomed to life in the minority and didn't show an aggressive interest in breaking any china to seize control of the institution. That is, however, an inaccurate portrait.

With the support of similarly inclined House Republicans, he ran against the old guard in 1961 to claim the third-ranking position in the Republican leadership. Two years later, he was elected Republican leader in the House, a position he kept for his remaining ten years in Congress. He worked diligently every election season to try to win a Republican majority and satisfy his highest professional ambition: to become Speaker of the House. He never succeeded in that endeavor but was well regarded by political confederates and opponents alike as a skillful and responsible leader of the opposition.

He was well known and respected in Washington and among Republican Party activists, but he was far from a national figure. Although Richard Nixon is reported to have included him in his list of potential vice presidents in 1968, it is unlikely that he received serious or lengthy consideration. He was a man of the House, and to most Americans who knew him, as much as they liked and respected him, he was not presidential material. Perhaps he lacked the self-conscious striving, boldness, and instinct for distinguishing himself from his contemporaries that are thought to be typical traits of presidential aspirants. Nixon had them, to be sure. Ford, it seems, had something else. And that something else made him president just as surely as Nixon's qualities had made him.

"Tell the truth, work hard, and come to dinner on time" was the ethic impressed on young Jerry Ford by his strict and devoted parents. His mother had married poorly. Her husband drank and beat her. She waited for their son to be born, and then she divorced her husband. Two years later, she met and married a good man and gave her son his name, Gerald Ford. They raised him to be an upright man. His mother was alert to signs in her son's personality of his natural father's temper, and whenever anger got the better of him, she made him recite Kipling's poem "If." "If you can keep your head when all about you / Are losing theirs and blaming it on you."[1] The self-control she taught him helped him earn his adult reputation as a deliberate, thoughtful, and imperturbable man who kept his head in tense situations. On all the great occasions of his life, good and bad, he recited the prayer he had learned from his mother, Proverbs 3:5–6.

Trust in the Lord with all thine heart; and lean not unto thine own understanding.
In all thy ways acknowledge Him, and He shall direct thy paths.

When a wealthy man whom he had never seen or heard from appeared unexpectedly in Grand Rapids one day, announced he was Ford's father, and asked his sixteen-year-old son if he would like to come live with him, Jerry calmly replied, "No, thanks, I like it here."[2]

One of the first Republican members to welcome him to Congress was an ambitious young politician, lawyer, and fellow navy veteran from southern California, Dick Nixon. The two future presidents were friends in the early years of their careers. Though they were never the closest confidants, Ford and Nixon shared a bond deeper than political affinity. They felt a kinship as self-made men who had risen to prominence from humble beginnings and the hardships of the Great Depression.

How much a role that kinship played in Nixon's decision to eventually nominate Ford as his vice president will never be known. Surely, Ford's years of faithful support of Nixon's ambitions and his defense of Nixon as the Watergate scandal threatened his presidency were marks in his favor as Nixon contemplated a successor for the disgraced Spiro Agnew. But Nixon is believed to have had few genuinely close friends. Nor is he considered a man who ranked friendship or much else above political necessity. While he liked Ford, he reportedly didn't think he possessed the skills of a master politician or the experience to be a great statesman on the world stage, qualities that Nixon proudly believed he possessed.

Ford lacked other Nixon qualities as well. He was not a man who nursed grudges or who felt so keenly the relentless approach of threats from determined political enemies. Politics was intensely personal for Richard Nixon, and in the end that failing overwhelmed his brilliance. Even paranoids have enemies, and Nixon certainly had his share. He could argue with some cause that his opponents had cheated him out of the presidency in 1960, and he had suffered the injustice stoically, with little appreciation for his self-denying statesmanship from his antagonists in the media and Democratic Party. But his constant dwelling on the threats they posed to him had the perverse effect of always recruiting new names to his lengthening list of enemies.

He was a man of contradictions, whose weaknesses and strengths were unusually closely related. He suffered every slight—from the deprivations of his childhood to the mocking insults of the elite political world he had bulled his way into through hard work, intelligence, and risk taking. Yet he prided himself on being tougher and smarter than his detractors. He admired strength and possessed it, yet felt vulnerable to attack by the weakest adversary. He appeared to crave acceptance by the very people he most despised. It's hard to miss in his poignant and futile quest for elite and popular acceptance a nagging sense of inferiority. But it is hard also to ignore his confidence that he was superior to whatever human or historical obstacles sought to deny his rise to greatness.

He was mocked and despised for his pursuit of Alger Hiss, whose now quite evident treason occasioned little retrospective reevaluation of Nixon's judgment. He was nearly bounced from the ticket with Eisenhower, yet survived. He was defeated for the presidency in 1960 by his social opposite, Jack Kennedy. Two years later, he lost a race for governor of California and was consigned by the cognoscenti to political oblivion. Within six years, he was elected president. In 1972, he was reelected by one of the largest majorities in American political history, without, it seems, the widespread public affection such a triumph usually entails. After he resigned the presidency, reviled even by those who had once been his most ardent supporters, he managed by force of his prodigious will to rehabilitate himself and stake a fair claim to the role he had always craved: elder statesman, whose counsel was valued by world leaders and ambitious American politicians. He was a complex, unique, and fascinating American. It is hard to imagine the American political stage will ever see another quite like him.

Honesty obliges me to concede that while I share much of the conventional view of his faults, my criticism is tempered by my respect for his proven skills as a foreign-policy leader and his ability to guide our country through a dire moment in world affairs. And I admired his strength of will, which for me and my fellow prisoners of war meant the difference between liberty and continued captivity. Most of us believe that had he not ordered the Christmas 1972 bombing of

Hanoi, against political, media, and popular opposition, the North Vietnamese would have insisted on even better terms in the Paris negotiations, and we would have remained for some indefinite period their captives. I owe Richard Nixon a sizable debt, which gives me pause when assessing his faults. And it is hard for me to understand the exuberance that some of his critics bring to charting his epic fall from power.

Gerald Ford respected Richard Nixon. In the years that had passed since their early friendship, they spent little time in each other's company. After Nixon was elected president, Ford probably resented, as did other congressional Republicans, the imperious way in which the Nixon White House treated them. But he admired his talents and strength and loyally supported the remarkable man who had beaten all the odds to become leader of his party and country.

He might have lacked Nixon's political gifts, but Gerald Ford possessed other qualities that would have well served the man he succeeded as president: equanimity, unashamed humility, steady confidence, and a greater faith that virtue was its own reward. Ford was at the end of his career when history called him. He was justly proud of his accomplishments. He was not a wealthy man, but he had provided his wife and four well-raised children opportunities he had never had as a boy. He could leave politics trusting he had made the most of his opportunities and had rendered his country good service.

By the time the Justice Department informed Spiro Agnew and the White House that it had sufficient evidence to indict and convict the vice president for accepting bribes, the cancer that was Watergate, to use John Dean's memorable phrase, had metastasized in the White House. The Senate Watergate Committee had been impaneled, and its televised hearings had shocked Americans for months. Dean had delivered his damning testimony. White House aide Alexander Butterfield had disclosed the existence of the White House taping system, which had captured Nixon and his senior aides attempting to cover up administration connections to the Watergate burglars. Nixon's closest aides, H. R. Haldeman and John Ehrlichman, had resigned, as had Chuck Colson, Dean, and various other White House staff members. Elliot Richardson had been appointed attorney general, and he had appointed Archibald Cox as special prosecutor to investigate the scandal. Cox had subpoenaed nine of the tapes. The White House had refused to relinquish them, and the whole sorry mess was in the federal courts.

Agnew's resignation on October 10, 1973, triggered for the first time the vice-presidential vacancy provision of the Twenty-fifth Amendment, which provided for the selection of a new vice president by presidential nomination, followed by House and Senate confirmation. The search for his replacement was well under way by the time Agnew agreed to plead nolo contendere to one felony count of failure to pay his taxes. Nixon would have to choose carefully, consult with Democratic leaders on Capitol Hill, and ultimately defer to their wishes. The president was playing a weak hand. Democrats would not be inclined to replace Agnew with someone they neither trusted nor liked, confident, as they were, that Nixon's presidency would not last its full term and that whomever they confirmed would soon become the thirty-eighth president of the United States.

Nixon preferred the former Democratic governor of Texas, John Connally, whose own election as president in 1976 Nixon hoped to engineer. But Mike Mansfield, the majority leader in the Senate, and Carl Albert, the Speaker of the House, made it clear to the White House that they would reject his nomination. Connally's support for Nixon's reelection and his recent party switch had made enemies of many Democrats, while many Republicans still distrusted him. There were other names Nixon considered, or at least went through the motions of considering, while his aides polled Republican leaders and activists for their preferences. Nelson Rockefeller and Ronald Reagan were among the most popular with party regulars, and they, along with Connally and one other candidate, were on the president's short list. Republican senators had no clear preference, reflecting the typical independence of members of that body. House Republicans overwhelmingly preferred one man: their leader, Gerald Ford. Even more important, the Democratic leaders who ran Congress favored him, too.

Nixon had quietly met with Ford hours before Agnew resigned. He did not offer him the job, or ask if he was interested in it, or inform him

that Agnew was to resign that same day. He discussed the Agnew problem with him and the other troubles that were assailing his presidency.
Ford left the White House puzzled as to the reasons the president had
taken him into his confidence.[3]

As soon as Agnew resigned, Ford was called back to the White
House with Senator Hugh Scott, the Senate minority leader. Nixon
asked them to solicit their colleagues' preferences for a new vice
president. When their meeting concluded, Speaker Albert and Majority Leader Mansfield were shown into the Oval Office. Nixon was a
canny politician, and he knew these two men were to determine his
eventual choice. With barely more than a word, they could veto any
candidate Nixon suggested. While Nixon still had support from conservative Democrats in Congress, Albert and Mansfield could easily
corral enough votes to reject any nominee they opposed. Nixon would
need these two elder statesmen to beat back any left-wing challenges to
his nominee. Nixon also knew that his odds for completing his term
were no better than fifty-fifty. Albert and Mansfield would have rated
them much worse. Any recommendation they made would not be
entirely free from considerations of their party's interest, but they were
also patriots. They would not recommend someone who they believed
would not bring solid civic virtue to the office and, in the event of
Nixon's resignation, restore the public's trust in the institution of the
presidency.

At first Albert declined to offer a preference to the president. But
after Mansfield took the opportunity to mention a couple of names,
Albert identified only one man Democrats could support. Mansfield
quickly agreed. Although Nixon soon left for Camp David to make
his final decision from a Maryland mountaintop, the choice had been
determined, for all practical purposes, at that meeting. As a Democratic leader remarked the following year, "Congress made Jerry Ford
President."[4]

After the two men left the White House, Nixon authorized two
aides, Melvin Laird and Bryce Harlow, two distinguished men in
their own rights and friends of Gerald Ford, to sound Ford out on his
interest in being vice president. Laird placed the call to Ford's home.
Ford was interested but asked for a few hours to discuss the offer with

the person whose advice he valued most, his wife, Betty. Several hours later, he called Laird and told him they had both agreed: he would accept the nomination if it was offered him. Laird so informed the president.

Nixon left for Camp David. When he returned, he had, as expected, decided on Gerald Ford. Gerald Ford might not have been a political celebrity or possess Nixon's shrewdness or the historical sweep of his intellect, but he was a solid citizen, an accomplished legislator, and, to the extent Nixon considered any other human being outside his most intimate circle deserving of the adjective, Jerry Ford was trustworthy. Most important, a Democratic Congress would confirm him.

Reportedly, Nixon also believed that choosing Ford would help protect him from being driven from the presidency. It is a less charitable conclusion about Nixon's motives than I would care to offer, though I cannot speak with any authority to all the thoughts that occurred to him. Some who were in a better position to judge his motives claim that Nixon believed Congress would be reluctant to decide on a course of action that could lead to Ford's elevation to the presidency, an office Nixon believed—and assumed Congress believed—was too important to trust to Ford, who lacked the abilities to execute the tremendous responsibilities of an American president. The Cold War, the yet-unfinished war in Vietnam, trouble in the Middle East, Nixon's détente diplomacy with the Soviet Union, and his opening to China made the presidency of the United States the center of events that would determine the history of the world for generations after. If Nixon's critics are right, and he did indeed have this cynical political reason for the selection, as he was often known to have had, it was among the most serious of his many miscalculations.

Carl Albert and Mike Mansfield didn't recommend Ford because they believed him seriously unsuited for the office. Had Spiro Agnew remained in office, they might very well have worried that impeachment proceedings against Nixon could saddle the country with an utterly unacceptable successor. But they knew Gerald Ford to be a man of unchallenged integrity, honest, hardworking, fair-minded, and patriotic. As far as they were concerned, he was just the right man to replace the man who had badly damaged the presidency and the country.

Ford met with the president one last time before his nomination was officially announced and sent to Congress. In that meeting, Nixon, who still harbored hopes to have John Connally elected president, extracted a commitment from Ford that he wouldn't run for the office in 1976. Ford was happy to give it. He had no intention of running for president. He considered the office he was about to enter to be an unexpected honor. Even were he to become an accidental president, and he was aware of the possibility, he would use the opportunity to render one last good service to his country before retiring from public life. It is unusual in American political life that humility captures the highest office in the land, but it was Ford's humility and decency that made him president and offered the country the kind of leadership we most needed at the time, the selfless kind. And it immediately became clear to most of Congress and the country they were going to need it.

On the same day the White House sent Ford's nomination to Congress, the U.S. Circuit Court of Appeals had ruled 5–2 to affirm District Court Judge John Sirica's demand that he be provided the nine Watergate tapes subpoenaed by Special Prosecutor Cox and the Senate Watergate Committee so he could rule on the administration's claim of executive privilege. Alexander Haig, Nixon's chief of staff, a formidable man whom many considered regent of the crippled Nixon White House, summoned Attorney General Elliot Richardson to the White House.

At Nixon's instruction, Haig informed Richardson that the White House intended to provide summaries of the tapes to a senior Senate Democrat friendly to the president, John Stennis, who would review them. The reason was obvious. Nixon had been the only person in the White House to review the tapes. He knew what they contained: clear evidence that he had obstructed justice by directing the cover-up. He had no intention of releasing them from his sole custody.

A constitutional crisis was fast approaching. The short clock on Richard Nixon's presidency had started to tick.

Liberal backbenchers in the House wanted their leadership to drag out Ford's confirmation hearings in the hope that it would give them time to find something in his background that would disqualify him. Their real purpose was to keep the office vacant while they impeached President Nixon. Speaker Albert was third in the constitutional line of succession to the presidency. They wanted him to replace Nixon, not a Republican, any Republican. It was an appalling idea for several reasons and reflects little credit on its proponents.

The nation reelected a Republican president and vice president by an immense mandate less than a year previously. Democrats who wanted to stage a coup to place one of their own in the office the people had denied them risked compounding partisan divisions and making it virtually impossible for anyone to govern the country. When Watergate had run its course, the nation would ache for stability. It might take years to restore the public's trust in our governing institutions. Had Speaker Albert ascended to the presidency, a job he expressly did not want, even the beginning of national reconciliation would be delayed for at least the balance of Nixon's term. And Democrats would have proved to the country that they were as self-interested and underhanded as the man they had forced from office.

Their choice of targets proved their colossal misjudgment as well. They weren't going to find anything unethical in Jerry Ford's background. Indeed, in his lengthy and extensive background check, all investigators discovered was a single disallowed tax exemption for two suits Ford had purchased for the Republican convention and had claimed as a business expense.

The Democrats who advocated obstruction were few in number. Most were relative newcomers to Congress, and it showed in their unseasoned judgment. Fortunately, Carl Albert, Tip O'Neill, Peter Rodino—chairman of the Judiciary Committee, who would oversee impeachment proceedings should it come to that—and other senior Democrats could be counted upon not to use a divisive national tragedy to seize power for themselves. Counting on Ford's patience and maturity, Rodino allowed restive Democrats on his committee to ask Ford tough questions during his confirmation hearing. But he didn't let things get out of hand. Nor did the leadership acquiesce in any attempts to delay Ford's confirmation. Working with Ford as minority leader, they stalled congressional demands to begin impeachment proceedings in the House Judiciary Committee. They knew if the president was impeached or about to be impeached before Ford's confirmation, it might become impossible to get Jerry Ford into office before Nixon resigned or was convicted in a Senate trial.

Ford took it all in stride, unruffled by the indignities occasioned in most confirmation hearings or, apparently, by the magnitude of the changes in life and responsibilities he was about to experience. As controversy raged throughout the capital, he sat erect in his hearings before the House Judiciary Committee and the Senate Rules Committee, broad shouldered, square jawed, his natural humility and decency plainly evident, handling antagonistic questions on all manner of Watergate-related questions good-naturedly and, if not with eloquence, with an easy grace. One of the more difficult questions put to him was offered by Nevada senator Howard Cannon, chairman of the Rules Committee: "If a President resigned his office before his term expired, would his successor have the power to prevent or terminate any investigation or criminal prosecution charges against the former President?"

"I do not think the public would stand for it," Ford answered.

Both House and Senate committees reported his nomination favorably. On November 27, the Senate voted 92–3 to confirm him. Nine days later, the House did likewise, 387–35. Ford took the oath of office that night on the House floor, with the president in attendance.

Ford spent as much as he could of his brief vice presidency on the road, speaking to various Republican and civic organizations. Nixon wanted him closer at hand to help convince House Republicans to oppose an impeachment resolution. Ford wisely stayed away, intentionally distancing himself from the firestorm that was consuming the Nixon presidency. On July 24, 1974, the Supreme Court ruled against the president's claim of executive privilege and ordered the tapes turned over to Special Prosecutor Leon Jaworski. A desperate Nixon explored various options, most of them wildly implausible, to avoid compliance with the court's order and the inevitable consequences that would follow. But everyone else in the White House knew the Nixon presidency was over. It would take another couple of weeks for the president to accept that verdict, but no one had any doubt that, by his own hand, Nixon had inflicted a mortal wound on his presidency. On July 27, the House Judiciary Committee voted 27–11 to recommend the first article of impeachment, obstruction of justice. On July 29 and 30, respectively, the committee recommended the second article, abuse of power, and third, contempt of Congress.

On August 1, Al Haig asked to see Vice President Ford. Shortly after the Court's ruling, Nixon had for the first time allowed his lawyers and Haig to listen to the tape he knew would convict him. It was a recording of a June 23, 1972, conversation between the president and Haldeman, in which Nixon ordered his chief of staff to have the CIA pressure the FBI to terminate its Watergate investigation, a clear obstruction of justice. Haig intended to inform Ford that Jaworski and Congress would soon possess the damning evidence and tell him the president would like Ford's views about whether he should resign. He also intended to raise the possibility that Ford would pardon the president once he left office. When he arrived in Ford's office, he was annoyed to find Bob Hartmann, Ford's chief aide, with whom he was mutually antipathetic. He limited his discussion to informing Ford that the tape, the contents of which he did not describe in detail, was soon to be public and probably fatal to Nixon. A few hours later, he seized an opportunity to meet with Ford again, privately, and in that meeting he asked the vice president for his advice about whether Nixon should resign and discussed with him the idea of a pardon.

One of the president's lawyers had prepared a carefully researched memorandum, asserting the constitutionality of a presidential pardon in advance of the ex-president's actual indictment. Ford listened but made no commitment and asked for time to consider the matter. He believed he was acting as he always did before forming an important opinion, thoughtfully and carefully. Hartmann and Jack Marsh, a former congressman and the other most senior Ford aide, were appalled. They informed Ford that Haig had clearly offered Ford a deal, the presidency for a pardon, and Nixon had surely authorized the overture. At a minimum, they argued, Haig was trying to use Ford's consideration of a pardon as the means to induce Nixon to resign.

Congress and the public would quite likely consider such an arrangement an obstruction of justice itself. Were Haig to believe that a deal
had been offered and considered, Ford's presidency would be crippled
before it began. Ford rejected their interpretation of the meeting, saying he had made no such promise, nor had Haig asked for one. They
responded that Haig had carefully laid the question on the table, and
the very fact that Haig believed he was considering it was so potentially dangerous that Ford must immediately correct the impression by
telling Haig, "No deal." They persuaded Ford to seek the counsel of
Bryce Harlow, a man whose judgment Ford greatly respected. Harlow
agreed with Hartmann and Marsh. So did Betty Ford. Their concern
convinced Ford to call Haig and read a written statement, witnessed
by Hartmann and Harlow, informing Haig that he had "no intention
of recommending what the President should do about resigning or
not resigning, and that nothing we talked about yesterday afternoon
should be given any consideration in whatever decision the President
may wish to make."⁵

Haig replied, "You're absolutely right." The president's chief of
staff returned to his most urgent task: persuading Richard Nixon to
resign.

Nixon knew he was finished, but the enormity of the consequence of his mistakes—resignation in disgrace from the office he
had labored and schemed for most of his adult life—further unsettled his judgment. He wavered between surrendering abjectly and
mounting one last, impossible fight against the vast powers arrayed
against him. Haig made sure, to the extent he could, that anyone the
president consulted would insist that his impeachment and conviction
were beyond doubt, and that he would serve the country and himself
better if he would resign immediately. A week later, the broken man
agreed.

On August 8, the president asked his vice president to come to the
Oval Office. There, he informed Gerald Ford that he would become
president of the United States the following morning. Jerry and Betty
Ford watched the president announce he would resign his office on
television in their Alexandria, Virginia, home. When the broadcast was
finished, they retired for the night. Before falling asleep, they recited

together Proverbs 3:5–6. *Trust in the Lord with all thine heart . . . and He shall direct thy paths.*

It might strike many as surprising that after narrowly averting a nearly catastrophic misunderstanding with Al Haig, the new president who took office on August 9, 1974, with a heartfelt assurance to his country that "our long national nightmare is over" would so soon after begin to seriously consider pardoning his predecessor. But those who believed President Ford had indeed conspired in a quid pro quo or were shocked by his decision understand him little better than had Al Haig and Richard Nixon. His friend and domestic policy advisor, James Cannon, offered a brief and exact summary of the greatest quality Gerald Ford brought to the presidency: "Ford had a quality rare in politicians: He could come close to separating his own political gain from what he believed to be the national interest."[6]

On Ford's first day as president, reporters grilled his new press secretary, former reporter Jerry terHorst, with questions about the disposition of Richard Nixon's records and tapes and whether the new president had given any thought to pardoning the former president. TerHorst replied by asserting that Ford had opposed a grant of immunity during his confirmation hearings. That was not accurate. Ford had observed that he didn't think the American people would support a pardon and arguably left the impression that he could be expected to defer to public sentiment. But he hadn't said he would not consider granting one, and he had never been asked directly if he would. That was to change in the days ahead.

By prearrangement with the former president, Al Haig, who remained temporarily as chief of staff, ordered the shipment of the White House tapes to Nixon in San Clemente, California. A young lawyer, Benton Becker, whom Ford had brought from his congressional staff to work as a White House legal counsel, had noticed Air Force personnel loading file boxes into a caravan of trucks. When he learned they were the tapes and other records, he ordered a halt to the transfer until he could ascertain that the new president had authorized it. The press got wind of it and badgered terHorst for an explanation. Democrats in Congress introduced legislation to keep government control of all Nixon tapes and presidential records. Haig, who had promised to get Nixon the tapes, insisted that Nixon, like presidents before him, retained ownership of his records. Hartmann, Marsh, and Ford's chief legal counsel and former law partner, Phil Buchen, were adamant that they remain where they were.

Leon Jaworski and his team of determined lawyers were methodically building a case to prosecute the former president, and all of Washington buzzed with speculation about when the first indictment would be handed down. Seven senior aides, including John Mitchell, the former attorney general, Haldeman, Ehrlichman, and Colson had already been indicted and were awaiting trial. Although he had sincerely hoped Nixon's resignation would begin to close the chapter on the nation's obsession with Watergate, Ford could see that the scandal had the potential to dominate his presidency, as events moved slowly but surely toward the conviction and possible imprisonment of a disgraced former chief executive.

Ford served in difficult times. The North Vietnamese Army violated the Paris Peace Treaty and marched south, while six thousand U.S. military personnel remained in country. Relations with the Soviet Union were at a critical point. Ford was responsible for directing the development of a new relationship with China. The effects of the Yom Kippur War were still being felt, not the least of which were skyrocketing energy costs. Inflation had spiked to 7 percent. All these problems, and many others, required his urgent attention, and he intended to address them as forthrightly as he could. But he now plainly recognized that Watergate would potentially cripple his ability to get on with the important business of the country. Worse, the national morale and the public's faith in its governing institution had not risen much beyond its low ebb.

The country had been little placated by Nixon's resignation but had plainly been cheered by the down-to-earth fellow they barely knew who had succeeded to the office. Ford was reported to have made his own breakfast on the morning he took office, and that simple act was regarded as evidence that the country now had a man closer in values and style to the people he served. His inaugural address was well received by Congress, the media, and the public. Ford had been greatly moved by the warm welcome he received from his former colleagues during his first address to Congress four days after he took office, when he had told them he was not his own man, but theirs, and the people they represented. Within days, the new president could claim a 71 percent approval rating. A glimmer of optimism could now be faintly perceived through the gloom of Watergate. But Ford knew, as did many others, that if Watergate continued to consume the full attention of the country, his greatest hope, to reconcile the nation to its government, would be suffocated in the endless aftermath of the scandal.

So, privately at first, he began to consider pardoning Nixon. He knew it would be unpopular with the press, with Democratic and many Republican politicians, and with much of the public. But he thought whatever initial outrage a pardon provoked would soon give way to the relief everyone would feel to finally be rid of the entire distressing episode.

He never seemed to factor his own political future into his deliberations. He took office intent on serving out Richard Nixon's term and then retiring. Henry Kissinger had persuaded him that his credibility as a world leader would be undermined if he was viewed from the outset as a lame duck. So, from then on, he kept his intentions quiet. But he had not yet changed his mind. He had a job to do, and his injured country required his best service free from personal considerations, and he intended to expend every effort to provide it.

As he started to replace Nixon's staff with his own and put his own imprint on the office, he began his initial discussions with his aides about the pardon. He took his three closest aides, Hartmann, Marsh, and Buchen, into his confidence on August 30. They responded with complete opposition to the idea of a pardon, at least before Nixon had been charged with a crime. He heard them out patiently and then told them he couldn't govern under these conditions. He tasked Buchen with researching his authority to pardon someone before they had been indicted. He asked Kissinger for his views. Kissinger supported the idea but warned Ford that there would be great public opposition to the move. Jack Marsh met with

Ford privately to warn him that if the August 1 deal that Haig had presented became known, it could taint the pardon with suspicions. Ford acknowledged the risk. He authorized Buchen and Benton Becker to inform Nixon's attorney, Jack Miller, that the president was considering a pardon and that a statement of contrition from Nixon would be appreciated. Buchen also met with Leon Jaworski to see if he indeed intended to indict Nixon and, if so, how long the nation would endure a public trial. Jaworski informed him that it was quite likely the former president would be indicted on several felony counts, and that it could take one to two years before the case were brought to court, an objective jury could be found, and the defendant tried, confirming Ford's worst suspicions. Buchen was also charged with ascertaining whether Jaworski would accept the president's power to pardon Nixon in advance of his indictment or raise any other public objection to the pardon. Jaworski seemed to imply carefully that he would not.

His mind made up, Ford sent Benton Becker to San Clemente to try to negotiate with Nixon over the tapes and, if he could, get a statement of contrition that could be released coincident with the pardon. Benton was met by Nixon's press secretary, Ron Ziegler, who began their discussion with a hostile rejection of the idea that Nixon would apologize for anything. Cooler heads prevailed, and the discussion continued. Benton had been charged by Ford with getting the best deal he could but not driving so hard a bargain that Nixon or his aides would conclude that they couldn't accept a pardon under those conditions. Ford told Benton he had resolved to grant the pardon irrespective of the recipient's cooperation on other matters. Nixon's aides, who excused themselves occasionally to confer with their boss, agreed in the end to a lopsided agreement on the tapes that favored Nixon's possession of them and to a statement that acknowledged and regretted Nixon's mistakes in judgment but that was far from the full-throated confession and apology the country and Ford's aides would have preferred. Before he returned to Washington, Benton asked for and received a brief audience with Nixon. What he saw and reported to Ford was a man utterly broken, physically and emotionally, confirming reports that Ford and his aides had received that the former president might not live long enough to go to trial. This circumstance, too, weighed on Gerald Ford's mind. He regretted the suffering of the man whom he had once highly respected but who had betrayed him as he had betrayed so many others. Benton's very limited success did not seem to overly trouble the president. Ford had resolved to move on, no matter what.

On the morning of September 8, Gerald Ford walked across Lafayette Square to St. John's Episcopal Church to attend Sunday services and take communion. The day before, he had informed a few members of Congress of his plans, and their reactions ranged from respectful to downright hostile. Barry Goldwater was appalled. Ford's pal Tip O'Neill warned him that the pardon would end any hope Ford might have of remaining in office after 1976. Jerry terHorst, who had been informed of the pardon the day before, arrived to work on Sunday with a letter of resignation in his pocket and couldn't be persuaded to reconsider.

At 11:05 a.m., Gerald Ford told the country he had pardoned Richard Nixon, assuring his fellow citizens he "was certain in my own mind and in my conscience that it is the right thing to do." The reaction was swift and universally negative, far worse than Ford had anticipated. Editorial writers from one end of the country to the other denounced him. Liberal and conservative columnists questioned his judgment, his motives, and his sense of justice. The public's anger was just as sharply negative and overwhelming. Virtually overnight, Ford's approval ratings dropped thirty points. Congress promised an investigation and in short order filed resolutions of inquiry demanding answers from the president about collusion with Nixon. Rather than lie to the press, public, or Congress and say that no discussions about a pardon had occurred prior to Ford's succession, the president determined to break with precedent and volunteered to testify personally on Capitol Hill and answer any question related to the pardon. He consulted with Carl Albert and Mike Mansfield before he made the offer. Albert welcomed it as the right course of action. Mansfield assented to his appearance as well, but, out of respect for the presidency and the president, told Jack Marsh to tell the president he shouldn't make a habit of it.

During the hearing, Ford volunteered the details of his meeting with Haig, his rejection of the implied deal, and the factors he weighed to arrive at his decision. Many of the questions directed to him were dripping with skepticism. The younger, more militant members were predictably aggressive, but within bounds. Senior Democrats were, as usual, rooting for him and confident that his bold gesture would in time end suspicions and heal the wounds the pardon had seemed at first to reopen. Ford kept his cool, and when his frustration mounted, he stated forcefully and convincingly, "There was no deal, period, under no circumstances."

His performance did, for the most part, remove any serious suspicion that Ford had done something underhanded and possibly illegal. But he still paid a heavy political price. His party was trounced in congressional elections a few weeks later, and a whole new crop of Watergate babies arrived in Washington to press aggressively their agenda for change and to make life as miserable as possible for the man who had pardoned their great nemesis. Ford managed the affairs of state quite well for the balance of his term and, despite all the turmoil occasioned by the pardon, came to enjoy his job. When he decided to reverse himself and seek election in his own right in 1976, he was challenged in the primaries and nearly beaten by the popular former governor of California, Ronald Reagan, who clearly claimed the hearts of Republican activists. And in the general election, he was defeated by a little-known former governor of Georgia. It was, of course, a terrible disappointment to the president and his family and friends. But he handled it with his usual equanimity and self-effacing modesty. He never considered himself indispensable to his country, and he knew it would get along well enough without him. He left office with no bitterness, a little regret, but mostly gratitude for the great privilege that had come so unexpectedly to him.

Near the end of his presidency, Richard Nixon told his sons-in-law, Ed Cox and David Eisenhower, "the tragedy must be seen through until the end as fate would have it."[7] As fate had it, the tragedy reached its end in the capable hands of Gerald Ford. Though it was hard to see at the time, he had helped his country move beyond the crippling effects of Watergate and spared a disgraced president from further unnecessary torment. He had risen to the challenges of his office and the times with courage and confidence and had acquitted himself admirably. The surprise of the wisdom of the accidental president was that it was no surprise. As expected by those who knew him best, Jerry Ford had simply remained himself.

INSPIRATION

Only a brief explanation is required here for our identification of this last and honorable kind of decision. The quality of inspiration we refer to is found in those decisions whose authors have felt beckoned by a sense of duty or the demands of justice simply to do what is right; who use just means to secure just ends; and who are prepared to suffer whatever price they incur for their faithfulness. They are decisions made by those who feel and act upon a perceived moral obligation to a cause, to their conscience, or to God. They are rare in history and sublime in the eyes of humanity. They summon their witnesses to greatness as they reaffirm the potential within us all to rise above our nature and serve a cause greater than our self-interest.

NO HOLIER PLACE

In the end, all soldiers fight for the same cause. Some defend the right and some the wrong. Some embrace the cause their nation summoned them to fight. Some perceive other interests of the state in their summons, less noble or selfless perhaps, but serve out of sense of patriotic duty. Some fight because they are professional soldiers and proud to do the job they have been trained to do. Some fight to prove themselves or to avenge an injury to their country's honor or their own. Some fight because they would be ashamed not to or to make something of themselves in the exhilarating challenge and spectacle of combat. Some fight to make the world better and some to keep the world from threatening their little piece of it. Some fight eagerly and some reluctantly.

But in the upheaval of war, that great leveler of ego and distinction, things change. War is a remorseless scavenger, hacking through the jungle of deceit, pretense, and self-delusion to find truth, some of it ugly, some of it starkly beautiful; to find virtue and expose iniquity where we never expected them to reside. No other human experience exists on the same plane. It is a surpassing irony that war, for all the horrors and heroism it occasions, provides the soldier with every conceivable human experience. Experiences that usually take a lifetime to know are all felt, and felt intensely, in one brief passage of life. Anyone who loses a loved one knows what great sorrow feels like. And anyone who gives life to a child knows what great joy feels like. The combat veteran knows what great loss and great joy feel like when they occur in the same moment, the same experience. It can be transforming.

However glorious the cause—liberty, union, conquering tyranny—it does not define the experience of war. War mocks our idealized conceptions of glory, whether they are genuine and worthy or something less. War has its own truths. And if glory can be found in war, it is a different concept altogether. It is a hard-pressed, bloody, and soiled glory, steely and forbearing. It is the decency and love persisting amid awful degradation, in unsurpassed suffering, misery, and cruelty. It is the discovery that we belong to something bigger than ourselves, that our individual identity—tested, injured, and changed by war—is not our only cherished possession. That something is not an ideal but a community, a fraternity of arms. Soldiers are responsible for defending the cause for which their war is fought and for which they will lay down their lives. But it is their war, and they have their own causes.

In the immediacy, chaos, destruction, and shock of war, soldiers are bound by duty and military discipline to endure and overcome. Their strongest loyalty, the bond that cannot break, is to the cause that is theirs alone, the cause for which they all fight: one another. It is through their loyalty to comrades in arms, their exclusive privilege, that they serve the national ideal that begat their personal transformation. When war is over, they might have the largest but not exclusive claim on the success of their nation's cause. But their claim is shorn of all romance, all nostalgia for the crucible in which it was won. From that crucible they have but one prize, one honor, one glory: that they had withstood the savagery and losses of war and were found worthy by the men who stood with them.

———

W<small>HEN</small> "the blue-eyed child of fortune," Robert Gould Shaw, rushed to war, he shared in the common excitement that the long-delayed reckoning was finally at hand.* The question of slavery that had tested the nation since its inception had finally pushed things to the inevitable and decisive confrontation. Abraham Lincoln had been elected president, and the south, claiming its liberty imperiled, resolved to sever its bonds to our Union. Now the thing would be decided once and for all.

When southern batteries fired on Fort Sumter, Shaw was among the first to answer the Union's call. The new president had beseeched the states loyal to the Union to send their militia to the immediate defense of the nation's capital. The Seventh New York National Guard was the first to arrive. Marching in its ranks were many sons of the New York elite, intent on proving their manhood and patriotism in a war they believed would be over as quickly as it had begun. They had enlisted for thirty days—long enough, many believed, to settle the matter. Shaw, who marched with them, had a somewhat different expectation. He wasn't sure the Union could be reconstituted by force of arms. But whether it could or not, the north could at least strike a blow to avenge the injury the south and its peculiar institution had inflicted on America's honor. If the Union could not be saved, Union armies could still give a good accounting of themselves in battle. Private Shaw could say he had done his part to ensure that he and his country had left the field with their honor intact and had left their errant southern brethren to suffer alone the shame of their disreputable cause.

He had always been sensitive to slights against his honor, even when they weren't intended. As he grew older, he felt insults to his country just as keenly. Now he marched to punish the offender. He would be glad if the more glorious cause of Union—and his parents' cherished object, abolition—prevailed in the bargain. But he was an instrument of retribution and intent on its execution. As he paraded cheerfully with his friends and fellow sons of privilege, past the cheer-

———

*From William James's oration at the dedication of the Augustus Saint-Gaudens memorial to the Fifty-fourth Massachusetts Infantry.

ing multitudes down Broadway to Battery Park and a waiting transport ship, Shaw looked forward to an early opportunity to teach the south a lesson, followed by quick return home. War was to change all that.

He belonged to a prominent family of wealthy merchants. His parents, Francis and Sarah Sturgis Shaw, were well-connected progressive reformers and ardent abolitionists. His father had retired from business at thirty-two, intent on devoting his time exclusively to his family and the social causes he generously supported. He moved the family to West Roxbury, Massachusetts, to be near Brook Farm, the utopian community founded by eminent intellectuals and progressives, such as Ralph Waldo Emerson and Nathaniel Hawthorne, and remained their until Sarah Shaw's failing eyesight necessitated a move to New York. Their friends included most of the leading abolitionists and social reformers of the day, whose intense and animating passions they shared in full. Sarah Shaw was particularly devoted to her causes, and none more so than ending the deep shame of slavery.

Shaw was her only son, born on October 10, 1837, and she cherished him as he cherished her. But her motherly care to instruct him in the duty of wealth and privilege to alleviate human suffering did not always inspire strict filial piety to her causes. He was raised to be an abolitionist. His family's entire social world revolved around the cause. His playmates were the children of abolitionists. The churches where his family worshipped were led by abolitionists. His parents spoke, as he one day remonstrated with his mother, of little else besides the abolition of slavery. He queried his parents and their friends about the conditions of slaves, the economic system that depended upon their bondage, and the latest social or political development that could help advance the cause of their emancipation. He knew the cause well and understood its arguments. He never doubted its convictions. But he was not a devoted abolitionist. Nor, perhaps, did he share his parents' faith in every person's ability to rise above the circumstances of their birth if they were free from oppression. He might have been an abolitionist of the head, but not of the heart. He did not suffer emotionally from the terrible injustice. He knew it to be wicked, but it was not his responsibility to vanquish it. He was not a fanatic, as abolitionists were often considered by southerners and even stalwart unionists, who worried that hastening slavery's end before southern society had learned to live without it would precipitate the conflict they dreaded.

He was a rebellious boy, but no more so than other boys searching for some identity distinct from that of their parents. He was selfish and possessed an arrogant sense of entitlement, but no more so than was typical among the children of the wealthy. He hated his school and petulantly denounced it in letters to his family. When his mother chastised him for not regularly writing her, he responded, "I don't want to write every week; it's too much trouble. I shall only write when I want something."[1]

In 1851, the family left for a five-year tour of Europe. Robert completed his secondary education first, at a boarding school in Switzerland, and then studied for two years with tutors in Hanover, Germany. In Hanover, he enjoyed his first taste of liberty and indulged himself. He took rooms in a private home, and though he was only fifteen when he arrived, no authority determined his schedule or behavior. He spent his evenings at the theater and opera or at parties, where he developed a taste for spirits. He traveled around Europe independently. He made friends, flirted with girls, stayed out late, generally enjoyed himself, and, for the first time in his life, did not suffer the homesickness that often plagued him when he was separated from his family. As he considered his future and speculated about what career he might best be suited for, he wrote his mother, "I have no taste for anything excepting amusing myself."[2] He wrote frequently and often pleaded for money after exhausting the last sum he had received. He also warned his mother that now that he had become accustomed to his independence, she should not expect him to live under stricter authority when he came home. "It's very unwillingly that I ask you to let me do anything," he complained, "because that's submission."[3]

While on holiday with his family in Sorrento, Italy, he was introduced to the celebrated actress Fanny Kimble. She was an abolitionist who curiously had married a slaveholding plantation owner in Georgia. She fascinated the Shaws with her accounts of life in the south and the personal lives of the slaves who had worked her husband's rice fields and whose emancipation she championed.

In 1855, Robert wrote his mother about a party he had attended where a man had "railed against America."[4] Shaw took the insult personally and expressed a desire to exact retribution, preferably through violence.

In 1856, the Shaws went home to their new mansion on Staten Island. Robert left that fall for Harvard, where he was an indifferent student but socially active and popular. He had grown to be a handsome young man, with blond hair, expressive blue eyes, and fine features. He was five-foot-five and insecure about his stature. But he had charm and grace, was well spoken, and attracted sufficient favorable attention from young ladies. He formed many friendships at Harvard that he would soon renew and strengthen under much less pleasant conditions.

He left Harvard at the conclusion of his third year and accepted employment as a clerk in the New York mercantile office of his uncle, George Russell. He quickly wearied of that, too, and complained at having been persuaded to spend long hours on work that didn't interest him. He had little idea what he wanted to do with his life, but, whatever it would be, he wanted it to be exciting. In 1861, history gave him the chance, and he wasted no time in seizing it.

At Harvard and in New York, he had stayed apprised of the progress of the abolitionist movement and was as gladdened as his parents by exciting political developments, including the formation of the new Republican Party. He followed with fascination, as did most of the country, north and south, the trial and hanging of John Brown, whose raid on the federal armory at Harpers Ferry served as a call to arms. In 1860, Shaw cast his first vote for Abraham Lincoln. It is unclear whether these developments inspired a more active devotion to his parents' cause or kindled his desire to fight. He joined the Seventh for the excitement he craved and the opportunity to "bully southerners" for a change, after slave power had bullied the country for its first eight decades and sullied her honor.

Shaw's thirty-day enlistment with the Seventh occasioned nothing more memorable than the regiment's bivouacking in the House of Representatives and a brief private meeting with the new president, arranged by Secretary of State William Seward. He had voted for Lincoln, but until he met him Shaw shared an impression of him common among eastern sophisticates: that of a tall, ungainly, backcountry rube. After their meeting, however, Shaw felt differently.

After waiting a few minutes in an antechamber, we were shown into a room where Mr. Lincoln was sitting at a desk perfectly covered with papers of every description. He got up and shook hands with us both, in the most cordial way, asked us to be seated, and seemed quite glad to have us come. It is really too bad to call him one of the ugliest men in the country, for I have seldom seen a pleasanter or more kind-hearted looking one.[5]

The Seventh spent most of its time in ceaseless drilling. But irrespective of his unremarkable month of active duty, Private Shaw, for the first time in his young life, believed he might have found an occupation that engaged his head and heart. As the regiment prepared to return to New York, he used his family's connections to secure an officer's commission in the Second Massachusetts Regiment. The Second's officer corps boasted a good many privileged Bostonians, many of whom Shaw knew quite well from childhood and Harvard. The regiment trained at a quickly organized camp in West Roxbury, where Shaw had spent his early childhood. He felt entirely at home there and thrived in the convivial society of his fellow Brahmins. The friendships he renewed there were, in the trials they were soon to face, to be transformed into his most treasured relationships outside his family.

The Second was assigned garrison duty at Harpers Ferry. In the early days of the war, Lincoln was intent on avoiding any provocation that might encourage the border states to leave the Union, and one of the regiment's early responsibilities was the apprehension of runaway slaves and their return to their owners. Shaw found the duty distasteful, but he did not shirk it.

For Shaw and his fellow officers of the Second, life in camp was not all that arduous in the early days of the war. To the extent practical, they continued to live the lives of privilege they had always known—but the privileges were now of rank rather than wealth, and this reinforced class distinctions they considered the natural order of things. Their present duty was far from taxing or particularly dangerous and afforded them time and opportunity to indulge creature comforts familiar to them. They took quarters in private homes near their camp, attended balls, and dined and drank well. Shaw maintained regular correspondence with his family and with a young lady, Annie Haggerty, whom he had accompanied to the opera shortly before the war began and whom he could scarcely stop thinking about ever since. When Shaw suffered dysentery, he employed the services of a private nurse, who attended him in his comfortable, well-appointed lodgings. He recovered quickly. Unfortunately, many of the enlisted men who suffered the affliction, in less hospitable circumstances, did not fare so well.[6]

Throughout the summer, autumn, and winter of 1861, the regiment saw little action beyond a brief skirmish with Confederate cavalry. They spent the months learning to become soldiers. In the first major battle of the war, at Bull Run in July, Union forces were chased from the field in an ignominious rout. Command of the Army of the Potomac passed from General Irvin McDowell to General George McClellan, who, despite his shortcomings as a fighting general, proved to be a genius at training and organizing an untested army into a disciplined fighting force. The officers of the Second Massachusetts, and Shaw in particular, embraced the stern discipline McClellan imposed on them and took pride in the transformation it wrought. Henceforth, the Second would be known for the exacting discipline its officers insisted upon, which could seem more than a little overbearing to the men under their command. Young Lieutenant Shaw was hardly a martinet, but he was an uncompromising enforcer of good order and discipline, and he rarely had second thoughts about harshly punishing even lesser infractions of the rules.

In October 1861, the regiment was ordered to Balls Bluff near Leesburg, Virginia, where the Fifteenth and Twentieth Massachusetts regiments were being mauled by the Seventeenth Mississippi. When they arrived, the battle had ended in another complete defeat. Shaw got his first hard look at war, finding several friends among the dead and wounded, including Oliver Wendell Holmes Jr., who had been gravely wounded, shot in the leg and through his lungs. But it wasn't until the late spring of 1862 that Shaw's faith in his regiment's professionalism was to be tested under fire and he began to experience the real transformative power of war. In late March, the regiment marched with General Nathaniel Banks's corps chasing the elusive Stonewall Jackson through the Shenandoah Valley. On the twenty-third, the Second fought its first battle at Front Royal, Virginia. It fought there again two days later. Shaw remained composed throughout, even though Jackson's corps won both battles handily and Shaw suffered a slight wound when a minié ball struck him precisely where his gold watch was lodged in his vest pocket. Shaw was disappointed to watch his regiment succumb to the Confederate assault, but it managed to retreat in reasonably good order, and Shaw earned the respect of his men for his gallantry and coolheadedness under fire.

On August 9, the regiment faced a sterner test. Banks's corps again squared off unsuccessfully with Jackson in the Battle of Cedar Mountain, in Culpepper County. The Second Massachusetts was caught in a withering cross fire, and 16 of its officers and 162 men were killed, wounded, or captured. Shaw was not among them. At the time of the battle, he was serving as an aide to his brigade's commanding officer, General George Gordon. He was nevertheless exposed to fire and again acquitted himself bravely. He wrote friends and family afterward that he was much distressed by the loss of so many friends and terribly moved by their gallantry. He was promoted to captain the next day.

A little more than a month later, Shaw and the Second fought in the greatest bloodletting of the war, a ferocious battle between Lee's Army of Northern Virginia and McClellan's Army of the Potomac near a little Maryland creek called Antietam. Confederate armies had successfully driven Union forces from Virginia, and the daring Lee had now crossed the Potomac to fight the enemy on its territory. McClellan's army arrived at Antietam on September 15, with three times the number of Lee's forces. Had McClellan attacked as soon as possible, even the resourceful Lee could not have escaped an encounter with such a massively superior force. But the ever-cautious McClellan waited until the seventeenth to order the attack. By then, Lee had been reinforced by General James Longstreet's First Corps and Jackson's Second Corps. Though McClellan still possessed a two-to-one advantage in men over Lee, his battle plans were ill conceived and ill executed. He never massed his forces in sufficient concentration to press his advantage, and Lee skillfully moved his forces to counter each assault. Nevertheless, the soldiers McClellan had expertly trained fought bravely, and the battle, which lasted twelve hours, was fought to a draw.

The Second Massachusetts, still part of General Gordon's brigade, fought in the army's Twelfth Corps, under a newly arrived commander, Major General Joseph Mansfield. They fought exceptionally well and drove the rebels from the infamous cornfield, which changed hands several times during the battle. Shaw and his comrades marched over "such a mass of dead and wounded men, mostly Rebels. . . . I never saw before; it was a terrible sight, and our men had to be very careful to avoid treading on them; many were mangled and torn to pieces by artillery, but most of them had been wounded by musketry fire. We halted right among them and the men did everything they could for their comfort, giving them water from their canteens and trying to place them in easy positions."⁷ Shaw was, again, slightly wounded. General Mansfield suffered a mortal wound early in the fighting and died the next day.

At the battle's end, McClellan's army had suffered 12,401 casualties, 2,108 killed. Lee lost 10,318 men, 1,546 dead. These numbers, representing one quarter of McClellan's forces and almost one third of Lee's, were the highest casualties suffered on a single day in all the wars in American history. Captain Shaw no longer thrilled at the prospect of fighting to avenge American honor. He had matured and was a much graver man than the boy who had paraded off to war as if it were a lark. He began to write in letters to his family and Annie Haggerty of his desire that the scourge soon pass. But no one thought that was likely anymore.

Although he had again out-generaled his adversary, Lee had left the field first and drove his army back to Virginia. That was enough for northern papers to declare Antietam a Union victory. And it was enough for Abraham Lincoln to execute the boldest political decision of his presidency. One week later, he issued a preliminary Emancipation Proclamation, declaring that unless the Confederate states agreed to rejoin the Union by January 1, 1863, he would decree their slave populations to be free. On January 1, the Confederacy having spurned the offer, he did as he warned.

To the south's disgust and horror, talk immediately began in the north of raising new armies of freed slaves to crush the armies of their former masters. Captain Shaw didn't share his family's exuberant reaction to the proclamation. He had long supported the idea of using African-American regiments to help quell the rebellion. But he doubted the proclamation would offer a significant practical advantage to northern armies and worried that it would only aggravate the terrible cruelties already occasioned by the war. He wrote his family, "I suppose you are all very much excited about it. For my part, I can't see what practical good it can do now. Wherever our army has been there remain no slaves, and the Proclamation will not free them where we don't go . . . Jeff Davis will soon issue a proclamation threatening to hang every prisoner they take, and will make this a war of extermination."[8]

Shaw and the regiment spent a quiet winter in quarters near Antietam in Sharpsburg, Maryland, and at Fairfax Station, Virginia. He was granted a furlough home and spent Christmas with his family before traveling to Lenox, Massachusetts, to visit Annie Haggerty and her family to discuss the couple's future plans. Sometime after Antietam, the weary and seasoned veteran had written Haggerty a letter in which he proposed marriage, and she had accepted.

Tired of war though he may have been and happy as he was in the company of the woman he loved, Shaw was pleased to return to his regiment after the holidays. It was where he belonged. Indeed, he had never felt so connected to anything else in his life, with the exception of his family. In his eagerness for recognition and rank, he might have once considered opportunities elsewhere, but no more. He had buried friends, attended them in moments of extreme duress, and discovered with them how great a catastrophe is war. He had seen the men of his regiment face the worst, bend their backs, and march into the withering fire. It was his home, and he intended to remain with it to the end, even if he never left it alive. He would no longer be satisfied with one good retaliatory blow to restore national honor. The south must be compelled to accept reunion. Too much had been sacrificed to settle for anything less. "I would rather stay here all my life," he wrote, "than give up to the South."[9] Unless he was killed, he planned to stand with his brother officers and men of the Second Massachusetts to the last battle of the war. But the war, and the cause he had been raised to revere, had other plans for him.

Union ranks had been seriously depleted by elapsed enlistments, desertions, and casualties in the field. Congress authorized a draft of all men between the ages of twenty and forty-five. The act was very unpopular and sparked an enormous riot in New York City and smaller ones elsewhere. Nearly as unpopular, except in the areas where abolitionist sentiment prevailed, were efforts to raise African-American regiments. But necessities of war require politicians to make unpopular decisions. When Massachusetts governor John Andrew wrote to him for permission, Secretary of War Edward Stanton quickly authorized him to raise new regiments, which "may include persons of African descent, organized into special corps."[10]

When Francis Shaw arrived unexpectedly at his son's winter camp, he carried a letter for Robert from Governor Andrew offering him a colonelcy and command of the Fifty-fourth Massachusetts Infantry, a "Colored Regiment" the governor intended to organize "as part of the volunteer quota of this state—the commissioned officers to be white men." Shaw turned the offer down. He could not leave the regiment he loved, and his matured ego permitted him to question his own inadequacies. War will do that. Even as a soldier finds he possesses greater courage and strength than he once imagined he had, he learns also that he is far less significant as an individual than he once believed. In the vast and relentless enterprise of war, one soldier's fate matters only to his family and to the soldiers who fight to his right and his left. War might not strip your identity from you, but it makes short work of any exalted notions of self-importance. You are only as important in this world as you are to your military unit. Whatever pretense you once indulged, whatever sense of entitlement you claimed in youth, is all shorn away. All you have left is your responsibilities and your determination not to disgrace yourself in their execution. You must earn your way in war with courage and skill. It is not that you learn to doubt yourself. On the contrary, soldiers who discover that they are equal to the trials of war generally have a more genuine confidence in themselves than they had previously. But they no longer assume that by virtue of the happy accidents of their birth they are equal to any responsibility, any honor. They have learned not to make presumptions like that.

Robert Gould Shaw did not think he was the right man to shoulder the responsibility offered him. Raising such a regiment would be popular in his parents' circle and accepted as a necessity elsewhere. But many Americans, north and south, would despise the idea. The regiment would have to prove itself so exemplary that it would confound skeptics and silence critics. Men without a lick of military experience from a race that contemporary prejudices—which Shaw was far from free of—held lacked the discipline, courage, and intelligence to be good soldiers would have to become as effective a fighting force as any other in the field. If the regiment failed in any way, in training or fighting, it would do more harm to the cause of abolition and equality between the races than its success would do to advance it.

The men of the Fifty-fourth Massachusetts would have to find not only the courage every soldier needs in battle but the courage to endure injuries from the countrymen they fought for; the courage to carry on their own shoulders the aspirations of an entire race; the courage to know when they took the field that, were they to be wounded or captured, they could expect no mercy from their foe. The south issued its own proclamation, as Shaw had foreseen they would: any Union soldier of African descent or any of his commanders, whatever their race, could be tried and executed. He was right to doubt whether he was suited to such a burdensome command, where "loneliness was certain, ridicule inevitable, failure possible."[11]

He wrote the governor a letter declining the offer, and his disappointed father carried it to Boston. Both his parents had exulted that their beloved son had been offered the command, in the vanguard of the cause they had devoted their lives to. He had respected their beliefs and shared them intellectually, if not with the ardor they possessed or with their sense of personal responsibility. His mother was crushed when she received a telegram from her husband informing her of Robert's decision. Surely, her son knew she would be. And their disappointment and the values they had labored to impart to him weighed on him.

He sought advice from his brother officers. Encouraged by their support, he reconsidered. Perhaps he had made a purely personal decision when personal considerations were not supposed to take precedence over military ones. Perhaps black regiments could be formed into effective fighting forces that would hasten a successful end to the war. Perhaps he was experienced enough in imposing discipline and commanding men in the field that he would prove equal to task. Perhaps, for reasons he did not fully understand, providence had given him a unique responsibility to right a grave injustice. It would be a hard thing to leave his regiment, but it might be dishonorable not to.

When his father returned home, he was delighted to find a telegram waiting for him from his son, asking him to destroy his letter of refusal and to wire the governor that he accepted the command. His mother, who had "shed bitter tears over his refusal," now wrote her son to express her "deep joy" over his decision: "Now I feel ready to die, for I see you willing to give support to the cause of truth that is lying crushed and bleeding."[12]

Shaw arrived in Boston on February 15, 1863. Recruitment for the new regiment was already under way. The governor had pressed many leading African Americans into the cause of raising the regiment. They were notably aided by the country's most eloquent advocate of emancipation, Frederick Douglass, who exhorted men of his race to follow the example of his two sons, Lewis and Charles, and enlist in the Fifty-fourth. Free African Americans from cities throughout the northeast signed enlistment papers for the promise of fighting for freedom, thirteen dollars per month in pay, and a three-dollar clothing allowance. The regiment's full complement of one thousand soldiers was quickly filled.

Shaw selected most of the regiment's twenty-nine officers, although Governor Andrew had selected his second in command, Norwood Penrose Hallowell, a Pennsylvania Quaker from the Twentieth Massachusetts and veteran of Antietam, as well as his brother, Ned Hallowell, as third in command. They trained their regiment at Camp Meigs, south of Boston. Shaw proved an austere and uncompromising disciplinarian. Every infraction, every incident of disobedience or failure to understand orders, was punished. Gone was the carefree soldier who marched to war in 1861 and the convivial young man who warmed to the society of fellow officers. In his place was a grave man intent on a grave duty. He had a higher obligation than merely preparing men adequately for combat. He had accepted a cause as well as a command,

and his execution of the latter would determine the progress of the former.

How ironic, then, that he initially held the men under his command in lower esteem than they deserved. Shaw's racism was of a lesser order than the crueler forms common then. He was not a cruel man but a man of wealth and privilege, whose keen sensitivity to class distinctions had only lately been altered by war. He would have been a man of uncommon wisdom not to accept his race's superiority over a race of slaves and the children of slaves. He was not that wise. But his racism manifested itself mostly in a smug paternalism. "Whatever their habits of life may be," he wrote, "they certainly are not bad or vicious; they are perfectly childlike. No more responsible for their actions than so many puppies."[13] Yet most of the men could read, and many were decently educated, having lived at length in the north. Later, Shaw professed himself "perfectly astonished at the general intelligence these darkeys display."[14] His private references to them as "darkeys" and "niggers" were to stop in time. He was a better man than his prejudices. Shaw initially had a hard time seeing the men under his command as individuals. That was to change in time, too.

Reveille woke the men at 5:30. This was followed by hours of drill, inspection, marches, and weapons training. "Particular attention should be paid," Shaw instructed his officers, "to the soldierly bearing of the men, and their steadiness in the ranks."[15] He recruited a regimental surgeon to inspect the men and to refuse the services of any who gave the slightest appearance of not being able to endure the rigors of military life. He was tough and kept his distance from the ranks, maintaining as serious a bearing as he could. These men, he knew, must be more than good fighters. They had to be, and give the appearance of being, the most disciplined, squared-away regiment in the army. No man was to leave the camp for any reason without first being inspected by an officer. He saw to it that they were well fed and clothed and not denied anything a white regiment would receive, although they had to wait until May before the wooden rifles and old muskets they had been issued to train with were replaced by one thousand new Enfield rifles.

Within two months, Shaw and his officers marveled at the exceptional performance of their men. Visitors to the camp shared their pleased astonishment. A Boston reporter who had observed the regiment parade wrote: "They marched well, they wheeled well, they stood well, they handled their guns well, and there was about their whole array an air of completeness, and order, and morale, such as I have not seen surpassed in any white regiment."[16]

In their quick and determined transformation from raw recruits to proud soldiers, the men of the Fifty-fourth earned many admirers, even among those who had doubted the success of the enterprise. They had no greater admirer than the colonel who commanded them. As Shaw watched their progress, his regard for them began to change. He was starting to see them as individuals and capable soldiers. He spent more of his leisure in their company, welcomed opportunities for personal contact with them, offered words of praise when merited, and took a personal interest in their lives. He had come to respect them, and they him. And as their personal bond strengthened, so, too, did Shaw's devotion to the cause they shared. When his men were mustered into service at the end of May, Shaw remarked, "Truly I ought to be thankful for all my happiness and success in life so far; and if the raising of colored troops proves such a benefit to the country and to the blacks . . . I shall thank God a thousand times that I was led to take my share in it."[17]

Robert Shaw and Annie Haggerty were married in New York City on May 2, 1863. Both families initially objected to the wedding. The groom was soon to return to war, and both sets of parents thought it sensible to postpone the marriage until the country had returned to more ordinary and certain times. Shaw's mother worried that his marriage would distract him from the sacred cause that had been entrusted to him. But Shaw would not be dissuaded. He wanted to enjoy this last happiness in the event that life would afford him no other. The bride and groom enjoyed a short honeymoon at the Haggertys' summer home in the Berkshires, before the governor summoned Shaw to camp. The regiment had received orders to report to Major General David Hunter, commander of the Department of the South, at Hilton Head, South Carolina.

Shaw and Annie spent their last days together at a boardinghouse near Camp Meigs as Shaw and his officers readied the regiment for

departure and war. The regiment received its colors from Governor Andrew in a well-attended public ceremony on May 18. Andrew
reminded the Fifty-fourth that the hopes of an entire race marched
with them. "I know not," he told them, when "to any given thousand
men there has been committed a work at once so proud, so precious,
so full of hope and glory as the work committed to you." Shaw assured
the governor that the regiment understood "the importance of the
undertaking."[18]

Ten days later, the Fifty-fourth Massachusetts Regiment paraded
through the streets of Boston to Battery Wharf, where they boarded
the steamer *DeMolay,* which was to carry them to war. Boston had never
seen such a spectacle, and most of the city turned out for the occasion.
A thousand well-trained soldiers of African descent, shouldering rifles,
their military deportment impeccable, marched proudly past thousands
of cheering Bostonians (and a smaller number of heckling detractors),
a drum-and-bugle corps in the van, their mounted officers splendid in
dress uniform and bearing. Riding at the head of the column on a spirited black horse was their commanding officer, Colonel Robert Gould
Shaw, his handsome, unlined face a study of dignity and concentration. As he passed his family and young wife gathered in front of his
mother's childhood home, he raised his sword and pressed it to his lips.
Then he snapped his head forward, lowered his sword, and marched
his men to their destiny.

The regiment came to a halt on Boston Common and stood at parade
rest as various dignitaries offered them their praise and best wishes. At
the conclusion of the ceremony, the officers and men were given a few
minutes of liberty to bid their loved ones farewell. Before ordering the
regiment to re-form and proceed to Battery Wharf, Shaw embraced his
parents, sisters, and wife. He was never to see them again.

They arrived at Hilton Head a week later. General Hunter inspected
the regiment, complimented its commander on its appearance, and
ordered it to camp near Beaufort, South Carolina. As they steamed
upriver, the men of the Fifty-fourth turned their fascinated attention
to the passing grand plantations of the rice coast, most of them vacant
save for the former slaves who remained after the owners had fled the
approach of the Union army.

Two days after the regiment made camp, Hunter ordered it to St. Simon's Island, Georgia, where it was to join with Colonel James Montgomery's Second South Carolina regiment. Montgomery was a dedicated abolitionist, who had fought in Kansas with John Brown. He had formed a "contraband regiment" of liberated slaves, which he used as an instrument of vengeance against the wicked southern culture that had kept them in bondage. Despite the common race of their ranks, the differences between the two regiments were readily apparent. Shaw led a disciplined, well-trained regiment of African Americans who had either escaped bondage long ago or had been born in freedom in the north. Most were educated. The men of Montgomery's Second had little training in military discipline or tactics, and few had any formal education. Until recently, they had toiled on some of the very plantations that their colonel ordered them to pillage and destroy.

Shaw had hoped for better duty than "bushwacking" with a contraband regiment. But when Montgomery ordered him to accompany the Second on a raid up the Altamaha River to Darien, Georgia, he raised no objection and ordered his regiment to muster out and board the transport ships that took them upriver. When they arrived, Montgomery ordered the town shelled. When the guns ceased their bombardment, the regiments marched into the center of the town, meeting no resistance along the way. All of Darien's white citizens had fled the town.

Montgomery ordered both regiments to loot the well-appointed mansions arrayed along the town's streets. Shaw told his officers to assemble a detail to enter the empty houses and "take out anything that can be made useful in camp."[19] But when Montgomery ordered his regiment to burn the town, Shaw was revolted. The residents of Darien had offered no resistance. Had they done so, it would have justified such extreme measures. As they had not, he considered razing dishonorable. Had not Montgomery issued a direct order for a company of the Fifty-fourth to help fire the surrounding buildings, Shaw would have kept all his men assembled in the town square. As it was, he could only watch with disgust as some of his men dutifully set torches to warehouses, shops, and houses.

After the Fifty-fourth returned from the expedition, Shaw wrote Annie about having been a part of "this dirty piece of business."

Besides my own distaste for this barbarous sort of warfare,
I am not sure that it will not harm very much the reputation
of black troops and of those connected with them. . . . I have
gone through the war so far without dishonour, and I do not
like to degenerate into a plunderer and robber,—and the same
applies to every officer in my regiment. There was not a deed
performed, from beginning to end, which required any pluck
or courage.[20]

There was no justification that he could see for the town's indis-
criminate destruction, and he worried until the end of his life that his
association with the action had disgraced himself and the men whom he
had the honor to command. "After going through the hard campaign-
ing and hard fighting in Virginia, this makes me very much ashamed
of myself," he told his wife.[21] His concerns were well founded. Both
northern and southern newspapers reported the atrocity, and while
condemnation in the south was angrier and more vituperative, northern protests were heard as well. Shaw knew the incident had stained the
honor of his regiment, strengthened northern objections to a "Colored
Regiment," and bolstered claims that African Americans would revert
to "savagery" if given arms and license to kill. He wrote General Hunter's adjutant asking if Hunter had, as Montgomery claimed, ordered
Darien burned or if Montgomery had acted on his own initiative. He
was little placated when he received the answer that Montgomery had,
indeed, been following Hunter's orders. He must have welcomed, then,
President Lincoln's decision to relieve Hunter of his command and
replace him General Quincy Gilmore.

Determined to repair the damage to his regiment's reputation, Shaw
again imposed stringent discipline on his ranks, punishing severely any
man whose conduct could subject the regiment to additional criticism.
He drilled the men excessively and every evening ordered them to
assemble for dress parade and his inspection. But Shaw knew that only
the regiment's performance under fire would silence its critics.

On June 30, the enlisted men of the Fifty-fourth mustered to receive
their pay and were aggrieved to discover that the standard monthly pay
and allowance they had been promised had been reduced for colored

regiments to ten dollars, with an additional three dollars deducted to compensate the government for their uniforms. As angry as the men were, none was more incensed by the insult than their commander. His men had been trained as arduously as any white regiment. They were prepared to suffer and sacrifice as much as any white regiment. They had been promised a meager wage in accord with the payment of every other regiment. To deny them their due was not just bad faith but an official offense that deliberately accorded his regiment a lower station in the regard and gratitude of the nation they served. He would not stand for it. He advised his men to refuse all pay until the insult was withdrawn and they were given their full pay. He and his officers would do the same. Eventually, the Army relented.

Sick of the contempt and indifference the Fifty-fourth was made to suffer, Shaw badgered his superiors for the chance to put an end to northern doubts, and possibly even his own, that a colored regiment could fight as well as any white one, and that he was capable of leading them. Their first chance came rather unexpectedly. Gilmore had decided the time had arrived to take the citadel that had started the war, Charleston, but initially intended to keep the Fifty-fourth separate from white regiments in the main theater of operations. Shaw complained to his brigade commander, Major General George Strong, who knew and liked him. Strong promised Shaw he would see what he could do for the Fifty-fourth at some point in the campaign. On July 8, Gilmore ordered the regiment to James Island, where they were to provide a diversion from the main objective. Gilmore planned to take the island fortresses that protected Charleston harbor, the last of which would be Fort Sumter, before launching an assault on the city itself. His first objective was Morris Island and the reduction of its earthwork stronghold, Fort Wagner. Seven companies of the Fifty-fourth arrived on James Island and were assigned picket duty alongside companies from white regiments, not long after the first assault on Wagner was tried and repulsed, with heavy losses.

At dawn on July 16, a regiment-size force of Confederate infantry attacked the advanced picket guard on James, including 250 soldiers from the Fifty-fourth, who stoutly resisted the assault until reinforcements arrived. Retreating in good order in the hail of gunfire from the numerically superior rebel force, Shaw's men held their final position until the enemy broke off the attack. Shaw and his officers were moved by the courage and professionalism of their men, who in this battle earned the commendation of the division commander and the respect of the white Union soldiers who had fought alongside them. A soldier in the Tenth Connecticut Infantry Regiment wrote home, "But for the bravery of the Massachusetts Fifty-Fourth (colored), our whole regiment would have been captured. . . . [T]hey fought like heroes."[22]

At last, the Fifty-fourth had joined the war, and in their first opportunity to prove their mettle had shown they were the equal of any regiment in the Union army.

Gilmore ordered the Fifty-fourth, along with the Tenth Connecticut, to come to the assistance of the main federal force on Morris Island. The men made an arduous seven-hour night march through drenching rain to their embarkation point, boarded a steamer for Folly's Island, where they marched another six hours to reach another steamer that ferried them to Morris. After landing on Morris at 5:00 on the afternoon of July 18, they marched two hours more to their assembly point on the south end of the island, where Shaw reported to General Strong. Since their action on James Island, the men had had nothing with which to nourish themselves save coffee and hardtack. The officers had eaten no better than the men.

Strong informed Shaw that Gilmore had ordered another attack on Wagner that night. He offered the Fifty-fourth the privilege of leading the attack. It was not an order. Shaw could have declined. His men had had little rest since the fight on James and were exhausted, so Strong would have understood had Shaw refused the offer. But he did not. Nor would his officers and men have wanted him to. They had come to fight and to prove again their worth and honor. They welcomed the privilege offered them. In the words of Shaw's biographer, Russell Duncan, "Shaw knew that the key to Charleston lay at the end of the beach. If black men could storm the fort and open the door to the birthplace of the rebellion, the symbolism would be enormous. His duty was never clearer."[23]

But Shaw had another reason to decline the duty. After the Confederate attack on James had been repulsed, Shaw had confided in Ned

Hallowell that he had a premonition he would be killed in the next battle. He wrote a letter to Annie, informing her of the regiment's success on James and assuring her that "what we have done today wipes out the memory of the Darien affair, which you could not but grieve over." But he intended the letter as a farewell rather than a war bulletin, signing off with "Good bye, darling, for the night."[24]

Gilmore felt confident that the previous assault on Wagner had so tired and depleted the ranks of its defenders that it could be taken by a frontal assault. Union gunboats had been battering Wagner with a continuous barrage for twenty-four hours. The Fifty-fourth would have to charge with bayonets fixed for six hundred yards over a narrow spit of sand, with the ocean on their right and a creek to their left. Their ranks would be compressed and terribly vulnerable to artillery fire. Still, Gilmore felt certain that once the men reached the fort's sand walls, the exhausted defenders would be quickly overcome in hand-to-hand combat. Before his men assembled, Shaw asked a friend, New York *Tribune* correspondent Edward Pierce, to take some of his personal papers and letters to his wife and family and see that they were safely delivered in the event of his death.

As the men of the Fifty-fourth moved into position on the evening of July 18, they marched through thirteen supporting regiments of white troops, who cheered them. The slight, boyish colonel who commanded them spurred his horse to the front of the column and dismounted. He ordered his men to form two battle lines, fix their bayonets, and wait for the signal to begin the attack. While they waited, he walked among them, sat with them, and talked with them informally and warmly.[25]

The gunboats ceased their barrage at seven o'clock. At 7:45, Shaw stood in the front of the columns, drew his sword, exhorted his men to "prove yourselves," and ordered them forward. Two hundred yards from the fort, artillery from Wagner and Sumter fired into their ranks, and Shaw gave the order to march at the double-quick. Wagner's defenders had survived the daylong barrage in surprisingly good order. Seventeen hundred Confederate soldiers now opened up on the Fifty-fourth with artillery and rifle fire, as the attackers came within one hundred yards of the fort. The narrowness of the beach they streamed across forced the men to run shoulder to shoulder.

Shaw waved his sword as his men briefly faltered, and he yelled, "Forward, Fifty-fourth." The defenders had dug a moat around the fort, and it was now filled with four feet of standing water. Men jumped into the ditch, lost their footings, fell into the water, picked themselves up, and climbed out of it. In front of them was their colonel. He was among the first to scale the wall and reach the parapet. He shouted encouragement to his men, holding his sword aloft. A bullet pierced his heart, and he fell dead into the fort.

The regiment managed to fight on Wagner's walls for an hour before their retreat was finally ordered. Nearly half their number had been killed, wounded, or captured. To military historians, it is just another futile charge in a war that saw so many futile charges. But the courage and fierce determination of the fighting regiment that had led it transformed the regiment's losses into a sacred sacrifice in the glorious cause of freedom.

William James, whose brother Wilkie served in the regiment and had been wounded in the assault on Wagner, years later wrote his brother, the novelist Henry James, "Poor little Robert Shaw erected into a great symbol of deeper things than he ever realized himself." I think James was wrong. Shaw knew what he was about when he led the charge on Wagner—proving black men equal to white men—and to do so he marched to the death he was certain awaited him. He had taken as his own his family's crusade, led men into battle whom he had once judged to be his inferiors, had formed with them the unique and insuperable bond of men at war, and been transformed by it in life and in death.

Although witnesses later disputed the account, northern newspapers were filled with angry denunciations of the subsequent behavior of the rebel defenders of Wagner. They had buried Shaw with his fallen men in a common grave. When a Union officer approached under a flag of truce and asked for the body of the fallen colonel, the Confederate commander turned him back. "We have buried him with his niggers," he is reported to have said. When word of the offense reached Francis Shaw, he responded that there could be found "no holier place" for his son's burial. When Wagner finally fell to Union forces, Shaw's father wrote the War Department to insist that his son's grave not be disturbed.

The Atlantic tides have long since washed away the sands where Fort Wagner once stood. Somewhere beneath its waves rests the body of Robert Gould Shaw and the bodies of the other men of the Fifty-fourth who stood, fought, and fell with him. A nurse who treated some of the wounded after the failed attack noted how anxious they were about the fate of Colonel Shaw and how deeply they grieved when they learned he had perished.

"They loved him," she wrote.[26]

DUTY TO THE DEAD

T he work begins with the story of a frozen salamander. The writer recounts an article he and friends had read in a scientific journal about the discovery in the Russian Far East of a stream frozen for tens of thousands of years that contained perfectly preserved specimens of prehistoric fauna, which those present at the discovery broke from the ice and immediately consumed. He remarked how the average reader must have been astonished to learn that a frozen salamander could still be edible after epochs. But he and his friends were astonished for another reason: the sly subversion introduced by the article.

These creatures were then living in "that amazing country of Gulag," where a starving man, "from that powerful tribe of zeks" (a colloquialism derived from an abbreviation of the Russian word for inmate), would see a frozen salamander, hack it from the ice, roast it, and eat it before he asked whether their meal might have been of greater interest and service to natural historians.[1] Aleksandr Solzhenitsyn was a *zek*.

How had he come to recount this darkly humorous anecdote? He had chosen it for the preface to the book he began in 1958, which took him ten years to write and another six years to get published. But for Solzhenitsyn the story began in 1945, in East Prussia, as the Red Army pushed toward Berlin in the last weeks of World War II.

A decorated captain of artillery, in command of a forward battery that had served with distinction on the front lines since 1942, Solzhenitsyn was a model of Soviet manhood. He was raised in the northern Caucusus, in Rostov-on-Don, by his widowed mother. His father, who had served as an artillery officer in World War I, had been killed in a hunting accident six months before Solzhenitsyn was born. Though poor (their home had been a room in a converted stable), he was a prizewinning schoolboy; a dedicated communist youth leader; and a gifted university student with degrees in mathematics and physics, who had brought a copy of *Das Kapital* with him on his honeymoon. He was a tough, exacting, and disciplined officer, with an unblemished record, two medals, and, until then, unquestioned loyalty to his homeland and the purposes and glory of the Soviet state. He was also an intelligent and sarcastic man, who, though a loyal communist and admirer of Lenin, had a more jaundiced view than was wise of the current father of the Soviet peoples, Joseph Stalin.

In a letter to a school friend serving in another sector of the front, Solzhenitsyn had included not very well disguised references to Stalin, criticizing what he perceived as the political shortcomings of the man with the mustache. To western eyes, such vague and minor breaches of discipline would be considered no more than the typical grumbling of a war-weary soldier. But to Soviet counterintelligence, which received Solzhenitsyn's opened letter from Red Army censors, to criticize Stalin was to betray the motherland. His indiscretion constituted anti-Soviet propaganda in wartime and, as such, was treasonous. He was arrested.

"One pallid European February," he wrote, he was taken "from our narrow salient on the Baltic Sea, where, depending on one's point of view, either we had surrounded the Germans or they had surrounded us."[2] He was brought to brigade headquarters and instructed by the colonel who was his commanding officer to surrender his pistol. Two counterintelligence officers then grabbed his arms, stripped his officer's insignia from his cap and shoulders, and placed him under arrest. When he demanded to know why, the brigade commander answered him, over the objections of the counterintelligence officers, "You have a friend on the First Ukrainian Front."[3] In a further breach of protocol, the colonel, who had never before shown much affection or even courtesy to Solzhenitsyn, shook the hand of his fellow veteran of the war's cruelest fighting, and wished him happiness.

Happiness, at least as it is normally appreciated, would find him only many years from that unhappy day. For the next eleven years, Aleksandr Solzhenitsyn was a zek, an inhabitant of the chain of islands that crossed the breadth of the Soviet Union, the gulag archipelago.

He was interrogated at Moscow's infamous Lubyanka Prison, where interrogators beat the truth—or what, for their purposes, adequately served as the truth—from hapless prisoners. He was charged with proposing the formation of a new communist party and convicted and sentenced in absentia to eight years in the labor camps. He served the first few months of his sentence in camps in and around Moscow. The next year, he was sent to a research institute at Marfino Prison in Moscow, where his background in mathematics could better serve the interests of the state.

The young artillery captain, a witness to human sacrifice on a colossal scale in the largest theater of war in history, the eastern front, might have fleetingly entertained doubts about the party and its ideology. Perhaps they were driven by his growing dislike for Stalin and the mindlessly destructive policies he inflicted on the Red Army, where the best officers were often not singled out for commendation but removed and, often enough, shot. But however slightly evolved his views had become on the front lines of that hard and desperate war, they were transformed during his imprisonment. At Marfino, the ideological blinders imposed by the state on its citizens from birth to death began to slip from his eyes as he glimpsed the monstrosity that Marxism-Leninism had become under Stalin. He became increasingly truculent and uncooperative with his superiors at the research institute. And, when his intelligence and expertise became less valuable to the state as his insubordination became more of a provocation, the state dispensed with his intellect and consigned his body to other, less tolerable work in its slave-labor economy. In 1950, he was dispatched to a new labor camp in Ekibastuz, Kazakhstan, which had been built to hold exclusively zeks whose crimes were political. There he would serve out, if he survived, the balance of his sentence.

At Ekibastuz, he worked as a bricklayer, miner, and iron smelter. And he wrote poetry, on scraps of paper he purloined, committed to memory, and destroyed. He had always been a writer. His mother was an educated woman, though she worked as a typist and stenographer to earn the family income, and with his aunt Irina had instilled in Aleksandr an abiding love for books. From an early age he wished to follow in the footsteps of his heroes: Dostoyevsky, Tolstoy, Turgenev, and Pushkin. He excelled as a writer at his high school and even began to submit stories to magazines, albeit without success. But his family's dire financial straits and his mother's poor health prevented him from attending a university with a distinguished literature department. So he studied mathematics and physics at the University of Rostov, where he won a scholarship in his last year, while satisfying his greater intellectual hunger by taking correspondence courses in literature from the Moscow State University. He graduated in 1941, having married his college girlfriend, Natalia Reshetovskaia, the year before and settled into the life of a provincial high school mathematics instructor before the Wehrmacht invaded Russia in June 1941, and the Red Army claimed his services.

Of course, as he later recognized, the disappointment he experienced when circumstances denied him a literary career was but a minor inconvenience. Had he been a writer or a Russian-literature teacher, he wouldn't have spent half of his sentence in the comparatively comfortable accommodations of a scientific-research institute. He would have spent it all at hard labor and, by his own admission, would probably not have survived it. He had known human suffering in the war, but even that hadn't prepared him for the criminal degradation of human dignity that was, as a matter of course, life in a hard labor camp, where a bowl of gruel, a small, unexpected kindness, and the blackest humor was all the comfort allowed a zek. Long hours of backbreaking and dangerous work, extreme weather conditions, near starvation, injury, and disease were the routine. Beatings, torture, and intentional as well as indifferent cruelty were its methods. Many millions passed through the camps, and millions of them never emerged again from the country of gulag. He was one of the lucky ones, barely.

He developed stomach cancer at Ekibastuz. The tumor was operated on with only a local anesthetic, but surprisingly was successfully removed. In 1953, after he was released from Ekibastuz and ordered into permanent exile in Kokterek in southern Kazakhstan, the cancer recurred and nearly killed him. He wrote in a short autobiography, "At the end of 1953, I was very near death. I was unable to eat, I could not sleep, and was severely affected by the poisons from the tumor."[4] He was given permission to seek treatment at a hospital in Tashkent, the Kazakh capital. One assumes the presence of the miraculous that a person feels after a narrow escape from death pushed Solzhenitsyn to make something more of his life than had been in prospect in his early life in Rostov and that he would have dismissed as pointless fantasy during his years in the gulag. He returned to teaching mathematics and physics, but he returned to writing as well. He remembered his years of exile in Kazakhstan as some of the happiest and productive of his life. When he was released from exile in 1956, three years after Stalin's death, he continued the work begun in Kokterek.

From his memories of Marfino, he constructed *The First Circle;* from the hospital at Tashkent, *The Cancer Ward;* and from the camp at Ekibastuz, the masterpiece *One Day in the Life of Ivan Denisovich.* He wrote because he was meant to write, meant from his earliest youth, immersed in the beauty of the greatest Russian literature, and meant to carry that special responsibility from the land of zeks, the inescapable moral obligation to use the instrument of his memory to render comprehensible the incomprehensible.

He wrote diligently, comprehensively, profoundly, and in secret. Why? What good is a silent memory when the forgotten deserve justice? This way, he might avoid the despair of having his work confiscated and destroyed or the frustration of having his work rejected by publishers as inadequate or politically unacceptable. Worse, making public his work, his memories, might cost him the measure of happiness he then enjoyed. It might send him back to the gulag. For whatever reason, he kept his work to himself and to his wife, Natalia. They were divorced when he was sent to Ekibastuz. She had married another man while he suffered there. But they reunited and remarried when he returned from exile and settled in Ryazan, about one hundred miles from Moscow. "During all the years until 1961," he wrote, "not only was I convinced that I should never see a single line of mine in print in my lifetime, but also, I scarcely dared allow any of my close acquaintances to read anything I had written because I feared that this would become known."⁵

He was a writer with unusual gifts, utterly devoted to his art, brilliant and exacting, producing work that would stun not just literary worlds but the entire Cold War political world, and he was resigned to being unread, until "this secret authorship began to wear me down."⁶ Following Khrushchev's 1956 denunciation of Stalin at the Twentieth Communist Party Congress and the cultural thaw Khrushchev encouraged at the Twenty-second Congress in 1961, Solzhenitsyn mustered the courage to send *One Day in the Life of Ivan Denisovich,* a fictitious account of one day's suffering in a poor peasant's life in a labor camp, to the literary journal *Novy Mir* (New World). The magazine's gifted editor, Aleksandr Tvardovsky, recognized it as a work of genius, compared it to Tolstoy, sent it to Khrushchev for the premier's permission, and published it. Tvardovsky said that while reading the manuscript late at night "he was so moved by its power that he got out of bed, put on a suit and tie and sat up the rest of the night reading . . . because it would have been an insult to read such an epic in his pajamas."⁷

Instantly, critics lavished praise on his book. Party organs welcomed it as a work of great political significance in the cause of correcting Stalin's many abuses. By the following year, after it had been translated and published abroad to widespread and nearly universal acclaim, Solzhenitsyn had become the most famous living Russian writer, arguably the most famous living writer in the world.

Success was good to him. He was embraced by the party and pressed into the bosom of official Soviet life. Khrushchev lauded him. The Union of Soviet Writers welcomed him into its ranks. He bought a car; attended cultural events; ate better; slept comfortably; lived well. And he wrote. In 1958, before his star ascended, he had begun work on the book that was to change the world. And he kept at it after 1961, despite his apprehension that the enterprise was too big and difficult to complete—despite the allure of celebrity and the risk of losing everything for the sake of his memories. For what good are silent memories to the forgotten, to the dead?

Solzhenitsyn had decided to write, in seven parts, a history of the gulags, which were not first conceived, as popular opinion held, in Stalin's malevolent paranoia, but by Lenin himself, who in the earliest days of Bolshevik rule provided the legal justification for strengthening the party's hold on power by establishing slave-labor camps. Stalin, of course, had expanded the system beyond Lenin's vision.

The writing began in fits and starts. Another round of cancer treatment interrupted him. And he had doubts that, lacking any access to official records, his own experiences—what he "was able to take away from the Archipelago on the skin of my back, and with my eyes and ears"—provided sufficient material on which to base such an immense undertaking.[8] He set it aside. But after the publication of *One Day in the Life of Ivan Denisovich,* Solzhenitsyn began to receive hundreds of letters from gulag survivors, and the letters and accounts obtained in conversations and memoirs from a total of 227 witnesses gave him the material necessary to complete the work.

His experience of official favor was a brief one. Between 1962 and 1964, he managed to have a few short stories published. But after Khrushchev was deposed in 1964, the party, which had had enough of official tolerance for the intellectual and artistic avant-garde, once again regarded the now-famous author with suspicion. In 1965, the KGB seized the manuscript of his novel *The First Circle,* along with many of his notes for that and other projects. He was refused permission to publish other works, so he had them published in the Soviet Union as samizdat and managed to smuggle *The First Circle* and *The Cancer Ward* to the west for publication. In 1969, for these and other offenses, he was officially expelled from the Union of Soviet Writers.

But in 1964 he had began to work diligently on *The Gulag Archipelago,* writing sixteen hours a day, in two eight-hour shifts. He completed the second draft in two and half months, from late 1966 to early 1967. In the spring of 1968, he worked feverishly to finish and microfilm the work in anticipation of sending it abroad for publication. On June 2, 1968, it was done. One week later, a friend carried the microfilm rolled in a capsule to Paris. Five years were to pass before it was published.

Solzhenitsyn had to make three decisions before *The Gulag Archipelago* and its truths, which were to wreak enormous damage on the Soviet system of oppression and hasten the demise of the entire post-war balance of power, would be available to the world. The first, of course, was the decision to write it. Even had the period of cultural liberalization in the Soviet Union lasted indefinitely, Solzhenitsyn's truths would still have greatly offended Stalin's successors. Among them were the accusation that Lenin shared culpability for the gulags; and the recognition that the Soviet people themselves, not only Stalin and other Soviet leaders, must accept part of the responsibility for these crimes. His second decision was to send the manuscript abroad for publication, knowing that he would never receive permission to publish it in the Soviet Union. The third decision was to order its publication.

Each decision carried enormous risks for Solzhenitsyn. They could result in the confiscation of all his other ambitious writing projects. They would certainly end any hope he might have had for a return to a normal writing life, living and publishing in the country he loved so deeply. They would place at grave risk those brave souls who had given their memories to *The Gulag Archipelago*. They might even return him to the place were he had discovered his great truths, the land of gulag. Each decision was fateful. That he made them is the only evidence necessary to prove George Kennan's praise of Solzhenitsyn's "immense courage and stoutness of heart."[9]

Each decision was influenced by various factors, but all shared one principal imperative. "I could have enjoyed myself so much," he wrote of the anxious days after his messenger left with the manuscript but before he learned of its successful delivery, "breathing in the fresh air, resting, stretching my cramped limbs, but my duty to the dead permitted no such indulgence. They are dead. You are alive: Do your duty."[10]

He had just learned that both *The First Circle* and *The Cancer*

Ward had been published almost simultaneously in the west. His fame was sure to be even greater than before, though the Kremlin's displeasure with the noisy, recalcitrant, provocative celebrity writer was sure to grow more intense and dangerous. "Sending the Gulag would be a rash, very risky, business, but opportunities were few, and there was no other in prospect. Right, I would send it. The heart had surfaced from uncertainty only to plunge into another. There was no rest."[11]

He had the opportunity. There might not be another. Despite his fears and his many sound reasons to withhold his memories until a safer time, he seized it. After an anxious week worrying that the manuscript might be seized by customs and the weight of the Kremlin's wrath might soon come crashing down upon him, he learned that it had reached Paris safely. He rejoiced and began work on his newest project, a history of the events that produced the Russian Revolution, beginning with a seminal early battle between the Imperial Russian Army and Germany in World War I.

The decision to authorize publication, however, was to wait. He initially intended the book to be published in late 1970. He correctly anticipated that he might receive the Nobel Prize for Literature that year, which would, of course, greatly increase his international stature and complicate the Kremlin's reaction to the offense. But when that moment arrived, the new Nobel laureate hesitated. Why? He had his reasons. He had planned to travel to Stockholm to accept the prize but, worried that he would not be readmitted to the Soviet Union, canceled the appearance. He had fallen in love with another woman, Natalia Svetlova, and married her, and the comfort of his new love restrained him from risking separation. He was already pressing his luck. His protests against the Kremlin's repression of human rights were becoming more frequent and bolder, and he was becoming as celebrated a dissenter as he was a writer. A propaganda campaign criticizing him was well under way in the many organs the Kremlin used to indicate its official displeasure and warn miscreants that a more troublesome fate might be in store for them. He was not entirely satisfied with the manuscript and felt it could be improved with further additions. Those whose memories and names were etched into the work would be at risk of persecution, and he had a duty to the living as well as the dead. And he wished to continue working uninterrupted.

Solzhenitsyn's biographer Michael Scammell summarized his subject's state of mind:

> He could not say when he would be ready to publish. Apparently, he was thinking of publication in about two years time, but the main thing was that the manuscript was safe. He had done the first part of his duty to the living and the dead. The testimony was complete. But to publish it would be to let off a bomb, in whose explosion he himself might perish. For this sacrifice he was not yet prepared.[12]

Years passed, and with every new deadline missed, he anguished over his delay, alternately defended and questioned his reasons, and chastised himself for his weakened resolve: "Whatever comfortable excuses I reclined on, to those who had been taken four to a sled and tipped like frozen logs into camp burial pits, my reasons would look most unreasonable."[13]

But still he waited. "He was anxious," Scammell wrote, "to postpone the moment of decision for as long as possible—and to be in command of the decision himself when the moment came."[14] The moment came in September 1973. Though they did not make it for him, the KGB, as it often did, forced him to face the moment, summon his ample courage, risk everything, and order the publication of *The Gulag Archipelago*.

On September 1, 1973, Solzhenitsyn received word from Leningrad that his typist had been interrogated by the KGB for five days in August and under duress had confessed the existence and whereabouts of a copy of the manuscript, buried in a garden in the country, which they promptly dug up and seized. His typist, distraught over her action, had committed suicide two weeks after her release. Solzhenitsyn glimpsed divine intervention in the precipitous turn of events: "I felt the finger of God: Sleepest thou, idle servant? The time has long since come and gone. Reveal it to the world!"[15]

And so he did. He sent word to Paris to publish the first volume of the book. On December 28, he listened on the radio as the BBC

Russian-language broadcast announced the publication in Paris of *The Gulag Archipelago*. "And now" he later wrote, "it was no longer on my back, but set where all could see it—that unwieldy stone, that great petrified tear."[16]

The international reaction was swift, enormous, and awestruck. I cannot think of a book published in my lifetime that made such a profound impact not only on its readers and the history of literature but on the political history of the world. It was, George Kennan wrote, "the greatest and most powerful political indictment of a political regime ever to be leveled in modern times."[17] Saul Bellow in a letter to *The New York Times* declared that "the word 'hero,' long in dispute, has been redeemed by Solzhenitsyn . . . what [he] has done in revealing the brutality of Stalinism, he has done also for us. He has reminded every one of us what we owe to the truth."[18]

The ultimate political impact of *The Gulag Archipelago* cannot be overstated. In the west, it disabused minds sympathetic to the Soviet Union and to the memory of Lenin of their conviction that the regime's crimes had been the result of one diseased, power-mad dictator, Stalin. Now they could see that Lenin and all his successors, who had championed the state's absolute superiority to the individual, were as responsible for those crimes as were the torturers and executioners they employed. Totalitarianism itself was the crime, even that form that purported to serve Marx's utopian goals, and the guilt should be shared by all in the Soviet Union and in the west who thought otherwise or averted their eyes or waited for things to get better. Solzhenitsyn had struck the blinders from their eyes. He made them see.

The book's publication spelled the beginning of the end for western European communist parties, which had grown stronger in recent years and had competed seriously for power within democracies. More than any other event, publication of *The Gulag Archipelago* forced their decay and ultimate collapse.

In the Soviet Union, too, the doomsday clock started ticking again, having been frozen when Leonid Brezhnev replaced Khrushchev. Solzhenitsyn's bravery, as much as his powerful and emotive prose and the stark truths it revealed, robbed the regime of its last claims of legitimacy in the eyes of its people. Only brute force could be used now to hold on to power. And force is expensive and exhausting when challenged. Propaganda, the official dissemination of a library of lies, an entirely fabricated history, lost its hold on the imagination and loyalty of its audience, although it still tried to work its old magic. *Pravda* denounced Solzhenitsyn in an article entitled "The Path of a Traitor." Tass dismissed the book as a novel. But no one believed them anymore. Neither the regime, he wrote, "nor those who came after would free themselves from the trouble I had brought crashing down on them—not in fifty years."[19]

On February 12, 1974, Solzhenitsyn was arrested and charged with treason. The next day, he was expelled with his family from the Soviet Union. He lived briefly in West Germany and Switzerland before immigrating finally to the United States, where he lived and worked in relative solitude. Twenty years later, when the Soviet Union's long death rattle, which he had done so much to cause, finally ended, the man who had the privilege of presiding over its demise, Mikhail Gorbachev, welcomed Solzhenitsyn back to his country as a hero. Solzhenitsyn went home and brought his memories with him.

Memory can be more powerful than other forces of nature—the midsummer drought, the early-autumn hurricane, the spring flood, the winter blizzard—that find the structural flaws of human endeavor, give them a shove, and turn the work to rubble. Memory, too, can expose and push and destroy. But it can also provide the mortar to build from the rubble something better, something more lasting.

We know what they helped destroy. But what did Solzhenitsyn's memories help to build? We may not know the full answer for some time. To history, in its poor imitation of God's timeless judgment, one man's life lasts no longer than the spark of a struck flint. But the flame it kindles lasts a bit longer, and thus the full achievement awaits a later, posthumous judgment. Perhaps his memories will not help build what he hoped they would: the great nation of small communities, rigorously spiritual, where the motherland's sacred soil is revered, where a solemn, obsessive regard for seeking truth resists the cruel oppression of soulless tyranny. Whatever their final achievement; whatever the virtue or plausibility of their author's vision; whatever the progress of his nation; his memories, the truths they declared, and the changes they wrought will be potent still, beyond his grave, in the wide expanse of Russia and in the eyes of the watching world.

Today, some Russians seem to have lost their esteem for Solzhenitsyn and his greatest work and dismiss the author as an eccentric, antimodern crank. Yet should their rulers, formed as they were in the bureaucracies at the core of the Soviet police state, in their nostalgia and egotism attempt to submerge Russia again in a sea of despotism, tomorrow's dissidents will find their duty, to the living and the dead, in his example. From the published memories of Aleksandr Isayevich Solzhenitsyn and his fellow zeks, they can summon their own courage to expose, to push, to destroy, and from the rubble to attempt again to build something better.

THE COVENANT

Abraham Lincoln had never been much of a churchgoer. He had steered clear of the excessive emotions aroused by sectarian feuding and doctrinal disputes that unsettled the frontier village of New Salem, where he lived as a young man. He declined membership in any church, preferring, he said, to defer his formal affiliation with a denomination until the establishment of the first church that claimed for the whole of its confession Christ's commandment to love God with all thy heart and to love thy neighbor as thyself.

When he ran for Congress in 1846, his political detractors accused him of being an infidel. His opponent, the Reverend Peter Cartwright, was a circuit-riding Methodist minister known throughout Illinois for the power of his evangelizing and for the rough justice the frontier preacher could dispense to highwaymen who tried to waylay him or to those who resorted to the threat of violence to settle the finer points of theological disputes. As the accusations of religious freethinking leveled by Cartwright's supporters began to pose a serious threat to his candidacy, Lincoln decided to confront the issue directly. He attended one of the Reverend Cartwright's revival meetings. When Cartwright called on the sinners present to stand if they wished to go to heaven, many did. When he called on those who wished not to go to hell to do likewise, all stood except Lincoln. When Cartwright observed that his opponent had declined both invitations, he asked, "May I inquire of you, Mr. Lincoln, where are you going?"

To which Lincoln, standing to his full height of six feet and four inches, responded good-naturedly

> I came here as a respectful listener. I did not know that I was to be singled out by Brother Cartwright. I believe in treating religious matters with due solemnity. I admit that the questions propounded by Brother Cartwright are of great importance. I did not feel called upon to answer as the rest did. Brother Cartwright asks me directly where I am going. I desire to reply with equal directness: I am going to Congress.[1]

Although he was suspected of being an unbeliever for much of his adult life, he had always been conscious of some higher intelligence directing the affairs of this world. He often quoted from *Hamlet:*

> *There's a divinity that shapes our ends,*
> *Rough-hew them how we will.*

Lincoln's fatalism is so poignant in regard to his life as president, from his plaintive acceptance that he had not controlled events but "that events have controlled me" to the premonitions of his own death, and so sublime in his resolve to prosecute a war he did not want but that he could not lose. Yet it had always been so. In the hardships and heartbreak of his youth, in the personal and political trials of his early adulthood, in his intuition that he was appointed to some great historical purpose, in the recurring bouts of depression that drove him to despair, Lincoln clung to his sense of predestination. As a young man, he proclaimed his faith in the Doctrine of Necessity, which had encouraged speculation that he was a deist. He explained the doctrine in that campaign of 1846 as the belief "that the human mind is impelled to action, or held in rest by some power, over which the mind itself has no control."

No president before or since had ever been more biblically literate than Lincoln. The grim circumstances of his impoverished childhood in the wilds of Kentucky and Indiana offered little in the way of formal education, and the books he used to furnish his mind in his earliest years were few. This would explain how he came to command such a thorough knowledge of scripture, concentrating his prodigious mind on the one learning resource nearest to hand. No politician, it was said, could recall more of the psalms, the prophets, and the New Testament by heart than Lincoln. For a man whose religious beliefs seemed shrouded in mystery and are still disputed to this day, his speeches and even informal conversations were studded with biblical allusions and invocations of the deity, which grew more frequent and more spiritually perceptive as the years passed. The world-shaping events in which he played the most prominent part urged his mind forward to some greater explanation of the suffering of his war-savaged country, which weighed heavily upon him. The aspiring man intent on using his reason to recover the Union from the passions that had torn it apart perceived in the struggle evidence of divine will, to which he could defer part of the burden for the terribly onerous decisions required of him.

Though he never felt compelled to dispel the belief that his religious views were unorthodox or to elaborate on his agreement or disputes with any Christian confession, he was an exemplar of Christian virtue. His exalted place in history is attributed to the singular achievements of his life, his rise from obscurity and extreme poverty to master by wisdom, political genius, and steadfastness his most eventful presidency. But the privileged place he occupied in the hearts of his closest contemporaries and in those later generations of Americans inspired by his life was fastened by admiration for his honesty, selflessness, empathy, humility, unaffected decency, and that tenderness of the heart that never left him through all the trials and suffering of his own life. In the civic religion of Americans, the belief in our exceptionalism, espoused from the Puritans to the abolitionists to those of modern generations who believe that

naked self-interest is inadequate justification for the great work we have
been assigned to do for humanity, he became Father Abraham.

As he prepared to embark on his trip to Washington and his inauguration as president, he bid a touching farewell to the people of Spring-
field, with whom he had lived for a quarter century.

> I now leave, not knowing when or whether I shall ever
> return, with a task before me greater than that which rested upon
> Washington. Without the assistance of that Divine Being who
> ever attended him, I cannot succeed. With that assistance, I can-
> not fail. Trusting in Him who can go with me, and remain with
> you, and be everywhere for good, let us confidently hope that all
> will yet be well. To His care commending you, as I hope in your
> prayers you will commend me, I bid you an affectionate farewell.

Lincoln made many stops along his circuitous route to Washington,
and he used them as occasions to address the constitutional crisis confronting the country and his purposes in resolving it. He addressed the
State Senate of New Jersey in Trenton on February 21, 1861. He recalled
that New Jersey had been the theater of many Revolutionary War battles and had made enormous sacrifices in that conflict for the cause of
American liberty. Linking those sacrifices to the present crisis, and his
purposes to the ideal for which we fought for our independence, he
averred that he was

> exceedingly anxious that this Union, the Constitution, and the
> liberties of the people shall be perpetuated in accordance with
> the original idea for which that struggle was made, and I shall
> be most happy indeed if I shall be an humble instrument in the
> hands of the Almighty, and of this, His almost chosen people,
> for perpetuating the object of that great struggle.

His *almost chosen people*—what a curious description of Americans.
John Winthrop had called upon the pilgrims who traveled with him to
the new world to establish a "shining city on a hill." The Puritan ideal
that they had come to build—a New Jerusalem—presumed their anoint-

ment as God's chosen, not almost chosen, people. And that sense of our exceptionalism that endures to this day, whether it is secular or religious in its orientation, shares a similar conceit: that we have been chosen or at least self-selected to set an example to all nations and are endowed by God or history or both with a distinction that forever sets us apart from others. What was it that Lincoln intended to suggest by adding the qualifier "almost"? I think it was to imply that as he was a "humble instrument in the hands of the Almighty," so were the people he served. It was not to deny that our nation was conceived as an example to mankind and had been blessed by providence with ideals, laws, institutions, and resources intended to serve that end. On the contrary, as he was to remind us, we are "the last, best hope of earth." Clearly he saw the hand of providence in that distinction.

Rather, I believe it was his purpose to remind us that while we may have been assigned this unique role in history, as a nation half slave and half free we had not proved ourselves still competent and perpetually devoted to the task—or indeed, "whether that nation, or any nation, so conceived and so dedicated, can long endure." The crisis that gripped the nation and the great civil war that could ensue were to test mightily our fidelity to that cause. War might reveal that the divine will we had perceived in our conception imposed on us sacrifices and transformation—indeed, a "new birth of freedom"—that we had not expected to bear. Chauvinism and pride in our exclusivity would not answer the question before us and would not be adequate to the great and terrible task at hand. And in the bloodshed and destruction that would ensue, however right the cause or wrong, no Christian, no morally serious participant, could avoid the anguish of what he must do or order others to do. Further, victory would not absolve us from responsibility for the savage work that had been done at our hand. We could only struggle to do justice, to save the nation that best served the cause of justice, to do all that was necessary to accomplish that end, and trust in God to relieve us from the crushing burden of guilt at having paid such a bloody recompense for awful wrong of slavery. Those are the spiritual and temporal convictions that were to echo four years later, when the carnage had reached its apex and an exhausted nation stood humbled even in imminent victory, in the greatest of Lincoln's public addresses, his Second Inaugural.

In his first inaugural address, he had eloquently expressed his desire to avoid the coming conflagration. "I am loath to close," he declared. "We are not enemies, but friends. We must not be enemies." He appealed to his countrymen's forbearance until they were "again touched, as surely they will be, by the better angels of our nature." But close he did, when the south declared its independence from the Union. And he did so with a relentless but not remorseless determination, furious in its consequences even if generous and just in its purposes. This tenderhearted man, who could not bear the thought of hunting animals, was to exhort his general, "hold on with a bulldog grip, and chew and choke as much as possible" until the enemy was vanquished.

In 1864, he wrote a letter to three prominent unionists from Kentucky who had protested the Emancipation Proclamation and the recruitment of African-American regiments that followed. "I am naturally anti-slavery," he wrote. "If slavery is not wrong, nothing is wrong. I cannot remember when I did not so think, and feel." But he had entered the presidency, he reminded them, intent not on ending slavery but on saving the Union: "I have never understood that the Presidency conferred upon me an unrestricted right to act officially upon this judgment and feeling." The Constitution, he believed, had delegated the authority to end or maintain the institution of slavery, as wrong as it was, to the states and not the federal chief executive.

> I could not take office without taking the oath [to preserve, protect, and defend the Constitution]. Nor was it my view that I might take an oath to get power, and break the oath in using the power. I understood, too, that in ordinary civil administration this oath even forbade me to practically indulge my primary abstract judgment on the moral question of slavery. I had publicly declared this many times, and in many ways. And I aver that, to this day, I have done no official act in mere deference to my abstract judgment and feeling on slavery.

Yet once war came and threatened the Union with extinction, he would, he reasoned, lawfully possess the authority as commander-in-chief to end slavery or order any other act that proved necessary to support the armed cause of restoring the Union.

I did understand however, that my oath to preserve the Constitution to the best of my ability, imposed upon me the duty of preserving, by every indispensable means, that government—that nation—of which the Constitution was the organic law. Was it possible to lose the nation, and yet preserve the Constitution?

The letter encapsulates Lincoln's defense of his decision to issue the Emancipation Proclamation. One can see in his argument the working of "cold, calculating, unimpassioned reason." He was buffeted by urgent demands from Radical Republicans that immediate emancipation was a moral and military necessity; cautioned to avoid such a precipitous step by moderate Republicans and loyal Democrats; fearful of exacerbating tensions in the still unionist border states; and mindful that Roger B. Taney–led Supreme Court that had rendered the *Dred Scott* decision would likely consider emancipation achieved through legislation as unconstitutional. Through the first year and a half of the Civil War, Lincoln navigated the debate over emancipation judiciously, carefully weighing the politics, timing, and necessity of doing so.

He ever insisted that his single purpose was to restore the Union and that any other decision he made was adjunct to that larger purpose. He attempted other, less peremptory means of freeing slaves, offering the border states federal compensation for the voluntary emancipation of their slaves and funds to establish colonies for them outside the United States. He signed legislation, after insisting on modifications to earlier drafts, that authorized the confiscation of all slaves employed in the Confederate war effort; ended slavery in the District of Columbia; forbade the return of fugitive slaves, overriding *Dred Scott;* outlawed slavery in all federal territories; ordered the seizure of property, including slaves, of all those who had joined or supported the rebellion; and authorized the enlistment of African Americans in the military. Yet he countermanded orders by generals that had emancipated all slaves within their military jurisdiction. He refrained temporarily from raising African-American regiments. And he resisted ever more insistent entreaties that he issue a proclamation emancipating all slaves in rebel states, in his capacity as commander-in-chief of the army and navy, to avoid legal challenge to the government on the grounds that it had usurped the authority of the states.

His moral convictions, enormous and contradictory political pressures, and military imperatives tested his reason. But he labored mightily, and in the judgment of history prudentially, to proceed only so far as he could claim honestly to have done nothing that had not been intended to restore the Union. After he had decided finally to issue the proclamation, but before it had been publicly announced, he wrote a response to an open letter from Horace Greeley, editor of the New York *Tribune,* demanding that Lincoln issue such a proclamation. "My paramount object in this struggle is to save the Union, and is not either to save or destroy slavery," he replied. "If I could save the Union without freeing any slave, I would do it; and if I could save it by freeing all the slaves, I would do it."

Underlying his prudence was a deep insight, which partisans of all sides would not admit: that slavery was not simply the peculiar institution of the southern states but the collective responsibility of all Americans. The injustice was rooted firmly in our history and not easily eradicated by appeals to the better angels of our nature. When Reverend Elbert Porter visited Lincoln and questioned his reluctance to act, the president explained his caution by observing,

American slavery is no small affair, and it cannot be done away with at once. It is part of our national life. It is not of yesterday. It began in colonial times. In one way or another it has shaped nearly everything that enters into what we call government. It is as much northern as it is southern. It is not merely a local or geographical institution. It belongs to our politics, to our industries, to our commerce, and to our religion. Every portion of our territory in some form or another has contributed to the growth and the increase of slavery. It has been nearly two hundred years coming up to its present proportions. It is wrong, a great evil indeed, but the South is no more responsible for the wrong done to the African race than is the North.[2]

In that last observation, we can glimpse the course of Lincoln's thinking as he came to the course of action that was to direct all his decisions after the first year of the war: the emancipation of the slaves

in the rebellious states, the urging of the Thirteenth Amendment abol-
ishing slavery throughout the United States, and his resolve to prosecute the war by military means that required ever greater casualties on
both sides and the most terrible devastation ever suffered by our country. In the shared guilt for slavery he presents the object that merited, if
anything ever did, the most fearsome exacting of justice on the whole
country. Human beings were only the instruments of that retribution
and were in the hands of a greater power. The theme echoed again
and again in his statements and writings as the war ground on and the
butcher's bill mounted, culminating in the majestic Second Inaugural
Address. In them, we can see how Lincoln was increasingly appealing
to God for solace and finding in the war's prodigious slaughter and the
lamentations for all that had been lost evidence of divine justice.

Lincoln came to believe that the war he had earnestly sought to
avoid could not be avoided, the Constitution he sought to preserve
could not be preserved, and the union he sought to restore could not
be restored until God deigned that the price for the injustice of slavery
had been paid in full. And through the horrible summer, he would look
for a signal from Him that the moment was at hand for the most consequential act of his presidency, to right the wrong that had incurred
His wrath.

He closed his 1864 letter to the prominent Kentucky unionists thus:

> In telling this tale I attempt no compliment to my own sagac-
> ity. I claim not to have controlled events, but confess plainly
> that events have controlled me. Now, at the end of three years
> struggle the nation's condition is not what either party, or any
> man devised, or expected. God alone can claim it. Whither it is
> tending seems plain. If God now wills the removal of a great
> wrong, and wills also that we of the North as well as you of the
> South, shall pay fairly for our complicity in that wrong, impar-
> tial history will find therein new cause to attest and revere the
> justice and goodness of God.[3]

By the summer of 1862, the war was going badly for the north. The
Battle of Seven Pines had been inconclusive, with heavy casualties on

both sides, and it effectively ended the Peninsular Campaign to capture Richmond. It led to Lee's emergence as commander of the Army of Northern Virginia, the Seven Days' Battles, with its dreadful casualties, and McClellan's retreat from the field. Union efforts to open the southern Mississippi valley had stalled, and the critical city of Vicksburg remained under the control of the Confederacy. On August 29 and 30, fifty-five thousand Confederates defeated seventy-five thousand federals in a second rout for the north at Bull Run. On September 4, Lee's army invaded Maryland. The Confederacy showed no signs that its will to continue the struggle was exhausted, while the north's resolve to prosecute the war was increasingly doubtful. In Robert E. Lee, the south had a general whose tactical daring and enterprise Lincoln looked for vainly in his own generals. Many of Lincoln's generals were incompetent, unsympathetic to his aims, or, as in the case of McClellan, openly contemptuous of his authority. Lincoln knew the north "must change our tactics or lose the game" but despaired of finding a general who shared that concern. Everywhere he looked, the prospects for victory seemed distant at best, if attainable at all.

Adding to his heavy burdens of his office was the awful personal tragedy that had nearly broken him: the death in February of that year of his beloved third son, Willie, from typhoid fever. "My poor boy," the grief-stricken Lincoln lamented, "he was too good for this earth. God has called him home. I know that he is much better off in heaven, but then we loved him so. It is hard, hard to have him die!"

In those dark hours, a careworn Lincoln wrote a personal "Meditation on the Divine Will," which his secretaries, John Nicolay and John Hay, said was "penned in the awful sincerity of a perfectly honest soul trying to bring itself into closer communion with its maker" and "not written to be seen of men."[4]

> The will of God prevails. In great contests each party claims to act in accordance with the will of God. Both may be, and one must be, wrong. God can not be for and against the same thing at the same time. In the present civil war it is quite possible that God's purpose is something different from the purpose of either party—and yet the human instrumentalities, working just

as they do, are of the best adaptation to effect His purpose. I
am almost ready to say this is probably true—that God wills
this contest, and wills that it shall not end yet. By his mere quiet
power, on the minds of the now contestants, He could have
either saved or destroyed the Union without a human contest.
Yet the contest began. And having begun He could give the
final victory to either side any day. Yet the contest proceeds.[5]

Historian and evangelical Mark Noll wrote of this brief meditation that
"like a figure from Israel's ancient history, Lincoln was arguing with
God. But it was no longer a domesticated deity, an American God, but
the ruler of the nations. The truth had begun to dawn to Lincoln that
this God was not at the nation's beck and call, but the nation at his."[6]

This then was the man who decided by midsummer 1862 to issue
the Emancipation Proclamation and begin to right the injustice that
had unleashed the fury that was consuming the country. He informed
two members of his cabinet of his intentions on July 13 and a week
later told the full cabinet. The reasons he gave were politically, mili-
tarily, and legally sound. The north's armies were becoming demoralized. Enlistment was declining. Emancipated slaves would provide a
new and abundant source of manpower for the Union ranks. It would
deprive the south of an indispensable economic resource to sustain
their war effort. Foreign intervention on behalf of the south might be
prevented only were the war to focus on resolving the moral question
of slavery and not preserving the republic that many foreign statesmen
had long dismissed as an historical anomaly and destined to disappear.
He had the lawful authority as commander-in-chief to order it done as
a military necessity.

In the second meeting, some cabinet members expressed concern
that it would be too dangerous a step and too provocative to the border states. Others urged its immediate promulgation. A few suggested
revisions to the preliminary draft they had been shown. Secretary of
State William Seward advised caution and urged Lincoln to at least
wait until an important Union military victory had been gained to dispel the impression that he acted out of desperation. Lincoln adjourned
the meeting resolved to proceed but uncertain of when.

At some point thereafter, he later indicated, he made a covenant with God that if the Union were to attain an important victory against Lee's forces, he would issue the proclamation. September 17 saw the greatest casualties ever suffered in a single battle in American military history, nearly twenty-three thousand dead and wounded at Antietam. But Lee had withdrawn from the field first, and Lincoln had the victory he had waited for. He immediately moved to honor his commitment.

He convened his cabinet on September 22 and informed its members that he intended to issue the proclamation that day. He would give the Confederacy one hundred days to end its rebellion. If the rebellious states persisted, he would declare all slaves in them to be forever free. He would not have the power to enforce the order until Union armies conquered the states that were the subject of the proclamation, but he would have put the south and the world on notice that henceforth the war would be fought to end the cause for which the south had seceded from the Union. He had already explained the reasons for his decision in the earlier cabinet meeting. Now he gave his ministers his final justification for daring to act so decisively. Secretary of the Navy Gideon Welles recorded it in his diary:

> The President remarked that he had made a vow, a covenant, that if God gave us the victory in the approaching battle, he would consider it an indication of Divine will, and that it was his duty to move forward in the cause of emancipation. It might be thought strange, he said, that he had in this way submitted the disposal of matters when the way was not clear to his mind what he should do. God had decided this question in favor of the slaves. He was satisfied it was right, was confirmed and strengthened in his action by the vow and the results.[7]

When his wife, Mary, a daughter of Kentucky slave owners, questioned the decision shortly before he announced it, Lincoln replied, "I am under orders. I cannot do otherwise."[8]

The proclamation itself had, in the words of historian Richard Hofstadter, "all the moral grandeur of a bill of lading."[9] It was drafted in quite prosaic language. Lincoln wisely understood that he must defend it on legal grounds, not moral. The moral question was to be settled by force of arms and in the merciful peace he hoped to establish. He had to defend it as a military necessity, consistent with his powers as commander-in-chief, to avert a challenge in the Supreme Court. He closed the proclamation with an appeal for the higher approval he now sought so earnestly: "And upon this act, sincerely believed to be an act of justice, warranted by the Constitution upon military necessity, I invoke the considerate judgment of mankind and the gracious favor of Almighty God."

When he signed the final proclamation on January 1, 1863, his hand trembled. He attributed the unsteady signature he produced to the effects of shaking hundreds of hands at a New Year's reception that morning. "I never, in all my life," he said, "felt more sure that I was doing right by signing this paper."

The public reaction was not as strongly in favor of his decision as he had hoped. Northern Democrats as well as conservative Republicans and agnostics on the question of slavery opposed it, and the November elections that year saw Democratic majorities elected to Congress. It was a difficult blow, although he avowed that despite the difficulties engendered by the decision he would rather die than take back a word of it. The reaction to his decision, along with further military setbacks, seemed to presage his own defeat in 1864 to his failed general, McClellan, the Democratic candidate, who promised the war-weary nation that he would negotiate a peace with the Confederate states. General Sherman's conquest of Atlanta changed all that, in the nick of time. In the north's euphoria over the victory, the man who more than any other had won the day was returned to office. It is hard not to see the hand of providence in that.

"The truly remarkable thing about Lincoln's religion," Mark Noll wrote,

> was how these circumstances drove him to deeper contemplation of God and the divine will. The external Lincoln, casual about religious observance, hid a man of profound morality, an almost unbearable God-consciousness, and a deep belief in the freedom of God to transcend the limited vision of humanity.[10]

There is no story in American history as inspiring as the story of Abraham Lincoln. I doubt there ever shall be. And no part of Lincoln's story is more moving than his transformation from the ambitious young man who believed reason could summon our better angels to the weary and beleaguered president who believed that only providence could. After the disastrous Union defeat at Fredericksburg, just ten days before he issued the final proclamation, Lincoln asked despairingly, "What has God put me in this place for?" The burdens of his office were too great for such a compassionate man to bear alone. Neither his own resources nor the support of any other person could sustain him in such a trial or ease his stricken conscience, so pained by the terrible costs exacted by the war he steadfastly prosecuted. Only God could bear the weight of it. And to God he turned to share the burden.

Of all the great and difficult decisions of his presidency, none was more consequential or just than that to issue the Emancipation Proclamation. And in no matter had he looked more sincerely to God for guidance. He brought all the force of his political genius, natural strategic foresight, and lawyer's skills to the decision. He defended it as a practical necessity and wrote it like a lawyer's brief as if to mask its great moral force. But he knew what he was about. The awful war, which would claim him as one of its last victims, was punishment for an injustice, in which both sides had been complicit. Justice must be done, and he was its instrument.

It is beyond my talent to explain the moral insights that guided Lincoln's decision to issue the Emancipation Proclamation and informed his view of the war in words as inspiring as those offered by the man himself. Nor has anyone ever revealed the full wisdom and goodness of his character better than he himself did in the last major public address of his life. It is fitting to close the last chapter of this book on decision making with the words—the most eloquent, prophetic, and prayerful ever uttered by an American statesman—of the most important decision maker in our history. We defer to Lincoln, then, for an explanation of the profound reckoning that saw his nation through the great trial and for guidance to understand our responsibilities to the great nation he saved.

Neither party expected for the war the magnitude or the duration which it has already attained. Neither anticipated that the cause of the conflict might cease with, or even before, the conflict itself should cease. Each looked for an easier triumph, and a result less fundamental and astounding. Both read the same Bible, and pray to the same God; and each invokes his aid against the other. It may seem strange that any men should dare to ask a just God's assistance in wringing their bread from the sweat of other men's faces; but let us judge not, that we be not judged. The prayers of both could not be answered—that of neither has been answered fully. The Almighty has his own purposes.

"Woe unto the world because of offenses! for it must needs be that offenses come; but woe to that man by whom the offense cometh." If we shall suppose that American slavery is one of those offenses which, in the providence of God, must needs come, but which, having continued through his appointed time, he now wills to remove, and that he gives to both North and South this terrible war, as the woe due to those by whom the offense came, shall we discern therein any departure from those divine attributes which the believers in a living God always ascribe to him? Fondly do we hope—fervently do we pray—that this mighty scourge of war may speedily pass away. Yet, if God wills that it continue until all the wealth piled by the bondsman's two hundred and fifty years of unrequited toil shall be sunk, and until every drop of blood drawn by the lash shall be paid by another drawn with the sword, as was said three thousand years ago, so still it must be said, "The judgments of the Lord are true and righteous altogether."

With malice toward none; with charity for all; with firmness in the right, as God gives us to see the right, let us strive on to finish the work we are in; to bind up the nation's wounds; to care for him who shall have borne the battle, and for his widow, and his orphan—to do all which may achieve and cherish a just and lasting peace among ourselves, and with all nations.

Amen.

AFTERWORD

On the day after the New Year's holiday in 2007, Wesley Autrey was taking his two young daughters to Times Square, where he was to drop them off with their mother before he continued on to his construction job in Brooklyn. As they passed through the turnstile at the 137th Street and Broadway subway stop in Harlem, Autrey saw Cameron Hollopeter, a twenty-year-old student at the New York Film Academy, suddenly collapse from a seizure. Autrey and two other commuters rushed to the young man's aid. After instructing the station agent to call for assistance, Autrey placed a pen in Hollopeter's mouth to stop him from biting his tongue. A moment later, the woozy Hollopeter opened his eyes, struggled to his feet, and staggered off the platform. He fell between the two rails as a southbound train approached the station.

The first commendable thing Wesley Autrey did was to recognize he had a personal decision to make—and he had only an instant to make it. He was not just an observer but a man with a choice. Should he risk his own life in an attempt to save another's? Or should he remain with his daughters as they witnessed the horrible and psychologically scarring scene of another human being destroyed in a gruesome accident? No doubt there were many decent people on the subway platform that afternoon. But how many of them recognized that they had choices as well? Perhaps others did. Perhaps someone would have acted had Autrey not done so. By raising the question, I intend no disrespect to any of the people present at the moment a young man's life was in peril. On the contrary, I think it is completely understandable that someone would witness such a calamity and simply be too stunned to act, to think, to do anything other than look on in horror or with only the thought to turn away from the imminent tragedy. It is not the most natural reaction to see in that shocking and sudden situation an occasion for making one's own choice. There is, obviously, hardly time to think at all. There is only the moment, and any reaction is unlikely to be more than an instinctive one.

I assume Wesley Autrey's instinct to act was a learned one. He was a navy veteran of the Vietnam War, and his training would have prepared him to recognize and make an instant, fateful decision. I, too, share a similar military background, although many years have passed since I was trained, and the effects have probably atrophied. But even were I still in uniform, I do not know whether I would have done as Wesley Autrey did. Would I have realized in time that I had a responsibility to make a decision? Would I have made the right decision? Or would I have simply stood—eyes wide and mouth open, my frozen mind only receiving and not sending signals, as the train, the screech of its brakes on the rails splitting my eardrums, was impelled by its momentum toward its hapless victim—and watched as young Cameron Hollopeter's life came to an abrupt and grisly end? I cannot honestly say. Vanity inclines me to answer in the affirmative. Hard-learned humility encourages doubt. It is never certain that we will be the kind of person we hope to be in a crisis.

Perhaps Autrey was raised exceptionally well; taught that it is a moral imperative to come to the urgent need of another; raised so well that an act of conscience becomes a physical instinct. Or perhaps the influence of others and the experiences of his life had so well shaped his character that his empathy acquired great courage. I know little about his life, other than that he is a construction worker, a veteran, a resident of the great city of New York, a father, and a brave man. Like the rest of the country, I'm only an admirer who speculates and makes assumptions about a man who did something extraordinary that I cannot be certain I would have done. I don't believe anyone is born a hero or a coward any more than they are born to make sound and courageous decisions in an instant or at length. Something, someone helped him become the man he is; prepared him to act in a crisis; taught him to be alert and think amid surprise and chaos; imparted to him a sense of duty that confusion, shock, and fear could not suppress. He is obviously a man of many commendable virtues. But virtues are our second nature, not our first. They are acquired laboriously over time by our own trials and with the assistance of others. And virtues that become almost instincts that overpower the instincts we are born with, the first among them self-preservation, are the most difficult to acquire of all. Whoever helped Wesley Autrey become the man he became, his parents or teachers or ministers or coaches or the navy, God bless them, too. They helped to save a life that day.

I was born into a military tradition. My father and grandfather were navy admirals who were single-mindedly devoted to their service and their country. They could not have imagined a better life. They and my mother and the Naval Academy labored to impart to me the sense that a truly rewarding life could never be lived in service to oneself alone. Happiness, lasting happiness, is found in the possession of virtues required to serve a cause greater than oneself. It took me years to learn that lesson, and even now I cannot claim to heed it as faithfully as they did. But they helped to embed in my conscience a sense of self-worth that was measured by how close I approached or how far I fell from the standard they set.

When I was in high school, I was blessed to have had an English master and football coach who also sought to teach me by example values that could give my life and my decisions qualities that I might never have possessed had I been left to my own devices. William B. Ravenel had been a star running back at Davidson College and had earned a master's degree from Duke University. He had served in Patton's tank corps in World War II and survived its hard encounters with Hitler's panzer divisions. He was, when I knew him, a lieutenant colonel in the Army Reserve and the only master at school who still served in the military. He loved English literature, especially Shakespeare, and had a very effective way of communicating his enthusiasm to us and encouraging us to share it. He was a hero to his students, and we wanted to like what he liked.

I was something of a discipline problem as a boy—the problem being I didn't like discipline. I had often found myself on the weekend working off demerits I had incurred during the week for various infractions of school rules and other discourtesies. The school authorities wisely charged me with raking the leaves and doing other sundry chores in Ravenel's yard. I have no idea why he took an interest in me. At the time, I had little to recommend myself. But he did, to my great benefit.

He used the occasions to talk at length to me about everything that interested me: history, English literature, sports, girls, his war experiences and those of my father and grandfather. I began to confide in him things I rarely confided to my friends. I told him I was bound for the Naval Academy and a career in the navy, something I wasn't particularly thrilled about at the time. And he counseled me about that, wisely. He did not encourage me to refuse or accept that destiny but to consider it carefully and comprehensively, with equal attention to its sacrifices and its many compensations. To be honest, there was nothing either of us could do about it anyway. The men in my family made their careers in the military. It wasn't even discussed in terms of whether or not a son would go into the military. It was just assumed. To have considered it as a question would have been as peculiar as pondering whether I would need to shave when I grew up. But Ravenel did consider it as a question and subtly encouraged me to do so as well and to come to the conclusion that, indeed, the navy was where I belonged. And while I cannot say that I entered the Naval Academy with any particular enthusiasm, I did not arrive there with the resentment I might have had but for his counsel.

In my senior year, a member of our junior-varsity football team, which Ravenel coached, had broken training. The violation was serious enough to warrant expulsion from the team. Ravenel deferred the decision to us and observed without comment our deliberations. My high school had an honor code, and most of us took care to keep our petty crimes well short of violating it. Matters of honor were taken seriously there, and the general opinion of the team was that the boy should be expelled, even though his offense had not been a violation of the code. I disagreed, however, and said so. Our teammate had broken training but hadn't been discovered doing so by anyone. He had confessed his transgression himself, without coercion or even questioning. He had felt bad and owned up, and I thought this was a mitigating factor. Also arguing for leniency was the fact that he had not signed, as the rest of us had, a pledge to abide faithfully by the training rules, as he feared in advance that he might fall short. I made my case in somewhat heated argument that he had felt remorse and confessed and no further disciplinary action was necessary. He had not acted dishonorably. Ravenel felt the same, I later learned. But he kept his own counsel as he watched us debate the boy's future. I suspect he knew that all of us on the team, who revered him, were trying to acquit ourselves in this decision in some way that would seem admirable in his eyes. Eventually, although he gave few clues to his preference other than one or two brief nods as I spoke, most of the team came around to my argument, suspecting as I did that Ravenel was on the side of leniency. At the end of our discussion, when it became clear we would probably vote to drop the matter, we asked his opinion, and he offered that he felt that was the wisest course. So we voted to let our relieved teammate off, and disbanded our little court-martial. Afterward, Ravenel told me how pleased he was with the decision, even more pleased that his boys had reasoned the thing out for themselves, and that I had led the way.

In the years ahead, I had a pretty eventful life in the navy and confronted decisions with consequences more fateful than one boy's career on a high school football team. To make them, I had the examples of other men, brave men who shared my circumstances, to guide me. The one decision in prison I am most proud of I made primarily because I couldn't bear the shame of their disapproval. I did not always make the right decision, then or since, but I managed many of the important ones without erring too greatly. I can say that in every one of those serious encounters, in addition to heeding the influence of my friends and family, I imagined what Ravenel would have done and tried to do accordingly. I never forgot him and the things he taught me, and I will never forget him, though my excellent teacher has long been dead.

I am a man with public responsibilities, which I have sworn an oath to bear faithfully. My occupation requires me to make decisions that are, by that oath, intended to benefit others. They are not supposed to be made to benefit me personally or, if they do, only inasmuch as I am a citizen of the state I represent and the nation I serve. But in truth, it is asking too much of human nature to expect that exclusively personal considerations will never influence a politician's decisions. Only the rarest of us could make such a claim, and even they would be loath to do it. But I can say that while I have made sound and not-so-sound decisions as a member of Congress—and have made the latter even when I sincerely believed them to be in the public interest—the worst decisions I have made, not just in politics but over the course of my entire life, have been those I made to seek an advantage primarily or solely for myself.

Two of the more famous or infamous occurred while I was in office. I once attended a meeting with federal regulators at the behest of a contributor to my campaign, whose interests they were investigating. I did so for no other reason than I valued his support. While I took no action to pressure the regulators to reconsider their investigation—or any action at all after they informed me of the seriousness of the charges they were preparing against my supporter—had I weighed the question of honor it occasioned and the public interest more than my personal interest to render a small service to an important supporter, I would not have attended the meeting. I soon regretted that decision very much.

When I ran for president in 2000, I took a position I knew to be wrong on a controversial public issue that had a moral component because I thought it might help me win the primary in the state the issue concerned. That, too, I regretted. For in addition to the fact that it did me little political good, it caused me to be ashamed of myself, and it's a little late in life to bear that kind of burden.

In both instances, I lacked humility and an inspiration to some purpose higher than self-interest, which proved the cause of my error. They have not been the only times when I have lacked those qualities. But I have learned by painful experience, and I suspect I will have future occasion to relearn, that those two are the most important qualities of a good decision, and all the more so when it is a hard decision.

They were the two most obvious qualities of Wesley Autrey's decision to save an unfortunate boy's life at the risk of his own. He had an astonishing awareness of the situation, given the shock that naturally would have interfered with his thinking and slowed anyone's reaction time. He saw the train approaching and knew the boy was incapable of saving himself, knew he would be either struck by the train or killed when he touched the high-voltage third rail. But he also recognized that even if he failed to get Hollopeter off the tracks, there was another way he might prevent his death.

He had foresight of sorts. He worried about how grievously his daughters would be affected were they to witness such a horrible thing at such young ages. He grasped all this in an instant, knowing he must act without hesitation. He knew when there wasn't enough time to get Hollopeter to the safety of the platform and when to make another even more daring decision. He had the confidence, the fortitude, to do what he knew was right.

"I had a split-second decision to make," he recounted. "Do I let the train run him over and hear my daughters screaming and see the blood? Or do I jump in?" He looked to see that the two women who had also come to Hollopeter's assistance were holding his daughters by the hand, and then he jumped onto the tracks himself.

Hollopeter was completely disoriented and tried to fend off Autry's attempt to help him. As Autrey tried to wrestle him up to the platform, he saw the white lights of the train. The train engineer noticed there were people on the track and hit his brakes, but it was obvious the train's forward momentum would not be halted before Autrey and Hollopeter had been run over. Autrey noticed a drainage ditch perhaps twelve inches deep between the two tracks and threw Hollopeter in it, covering him with his own body. Two cars passed over them before the train came to a stop. It had cleared Wesley Autrey's head by only a couple of inches, leaving grease stains on his knit cap.

The crowd on the platform could not see the two men and were screaming in horror at what they assumed had happened to them. Autrey yelled from under the train for them to calm down. "We're OK," he called out. "I've got two daughters up there. Let them know their father's OK."

His heroism, spontaneous, alert, and bold, was extraordinary. His humility was uplifting. His first thought was for the boy, not himself, and then his daughters, screaming from the platform. He wasn't a hero, he later protested. "The real heroes are the young men and women fighting in Iraq," he said. Then what was it he had done? "It was being there and helping the next person."

The reader might have noticed that some of the decisions examined in this book, although they might look difficult to us and to informed opinion at the time, weren't perceived as hard calls by the people who made them but rather as the obvious courses of action. It is often that way, particularly with decision makers who possess a sturdy sense of duty—expressed with humility and inspired by some obligation, some cause, some faith—to think and act for the benefit of others first.

Wesley Autrey was going to his job one day when he saw another human being in distress. Without hesitating, he jumped in front of a rushing train to save a stranger's life. And then, his duty done, the cheers from witnesses to his bravery quieted, he took his daughters to their mother and went to work a little late that day.

ACKNOWLEDGMENTS

There are two people without whose help this book could not have been written. Our editor, Jonathan Karp, conceived the idea, suggested many of the subjects, and graciously but insistently pressed us to write it. He was quick and generous with advice when asked, patient with our desperate pleas that we could not finish it, trusting when the writing was going well and encouraging when it wasn't, and always sharp-eyed and wise while editing. Jon has been our editor for nearly a decade now, and what success we have had in this satisfying sideline is as much his accomplishment as ours.

Michael Hill did the research for the book and recommended several of the subjects. As other authors have discovered, he is as reliable and discerning an advisor as he is a diligent, prompt, and thorough researcher. His enthusiasm for the project and his knowledge of and passion for history were indispensable to us as was his encouragement, kindness, and sensibility. We have become friends in the process and are as grateful for that as we are for the exceptional quality of his work.

Our agent, Flip Brophy, was an invaluable source of support, advice, and friendship, and, as always, more confident we were up to the task than were we. John Stauffer, Bruce Sterling, Michael Scammel, Howard Gardner, Robert Dallack, Diane Ravitch, and Richard Fontaine helpfully suggested decisions that warranted inclusion in the book. Although we could not hope to write about them as insightfully or gracefully as they could, we hope we have done well enough to show our gratitude for their kind attention to our request for ideas.

Our excellent copy editor, Timothy Mennel, was perceptive, sensible, witty, and astonishingly quick and thorough. This is the first time we have worked with him, and we hope not the last.

Director of Publicity Cary Goldstein at TWELVE will expertly orchestrate the campaign, and editorial assistant Nate Gray has contributed many good ideas from the beginning of the project. Our thanks to both of them.

Special thanks also to Emi Battaglia, Chris Barba, Maureen Egen, Anthony Goff, Jeff Hookey, Harvey-Jane Kowal, Martha Otis, Bruce Paonessa, Jamie Raab, Jennifer Romanello, Karen Torres, Anne Twomey, Flamur Tonuzi, Thomas Whatley, and David Young at the Hachette Book Group, and to the sales force for your enthusiasm and the production department for grace under deadline pressure.

Lastly, as always, we are indebted to our families for their weary patience with us as we embarked on another extracurricular endeavor that took yet more time from our most important responsibilities.

NOTES

THE MAHATMA AND THE INTRUDER

1. "Rookie of the Year," *Time,* September 22, 1947.
2. David Falkner, *Great Time Coming: The Life of Jackie Robinson.* New York: Simon & Schuster, 1995.
3. "Jackie Robinson and the Integration of Major League Baseball," *History Today* 53 (September 2003): 25–30.
4. Jules Tygiel, *Baseball's Great Experiment.* New York: Oxford University Press, 1983.
5. John R. Austin, "A Method for Facilitating Controversial Social Change in Organizations: Branch Rickey and the Brooklyn Dodgers," *Journal of Applied Behavioral Science* 33 (March 1997): 101–18.
6. Ibid., quoting from *The New Yorker,* June 2, 1950.
7. Ibid.
8. Ibid.
9. Falkner, *Great Time Coming.*
10. Geoffrey C. Ward and Ken Burns, *Baseball: An Illustrated History.* New York: Alfred A. Knopf, 1994.
11. Falkner, *Great Time Coming.*
12. Jackson Lears, "Providence at Bat," *The New Republic,* February 2, 1998.
13. Falkner, *Great Time Coming.*
14. Ibid.
15. "Robinson sparkled in the field and the plate," Larry Schwartz, ESPN.com, July 5, 2005.
16. Falkner, *Great Time Coming.*
17. Carl Rowan with Jackie Robinson, *Wait Till Next Year: The Story of Jackie Robinson.* New York: Random House, 1960.
18. Ibid.
19. Ibid.
20. Falkner, *Great Time Coming.*

21. Tygiel, *Baseball's Great Experiment.*
22. Frank Deford, "Crossing the Bar," *Newsweek,* April 14, 1997.
23. Falkner, *Great Time Coming.*
24. Tygiel, *Baseball's Great Experiment.*
25. Ibid.
26. Ibid.
27. Falkner, *Great Time Coming.*
28. Ibid.
29. Ibid.
30. Ibid.
31. Tygiel, *Baseball's Great Experiment.*
32. Jackie Robinson and Alfred Duckett, *I Never Had It Made.* New York: Putnam, 1972.
33. Falkner, *Great Time Coming.*
34. Robinson and Duckett, *I Never Had It Made.*
35. Tygiel, *Baseball's Great Experiment.*
36. Ward and Burns, *Baseball: An Illustrated History.*
37. Ibid.
38. William Nack, "The Breakthrough," *Sports Illustrated,* May 5, 1997.

SATISFACTION GUARANTEED

1. Lloyd Wendt and Herman Kogan, *Give the Lady What She Wants! The Story of Marshall Field & Company.* Chicago: Rand McNally, 1952.
2. Ibid.
3. Ibid.
4. Ibid.
5. James L. Palmer, president of Marshall Field & Company, "The Origin, Growth and Transformation of Marshall Field & Company," address to the Newcomen Society, Chicago, 1963.
6. Wendt and Kogan, *Give the Lady What She Wants!*
7. Ibid.
8. Ibid.

ROCKET MEN

1. Report of the Presidential Commission on the Space Shuttle Challenger Accident, June 6, 1986.
2. Ibid.
3. Marcia Baron, *The Moral Status of Loyalty.* Dubuque: Kendall/Hunt Publishing, 1984.
4. Jeffrey Kluger, "Time 100: Robert Goddard," *Time,* March 29, 1999.
5. Ernst Stuhlinger and Frederick I. Ordway III, *Wernher von Braun: Crusader for Space.* Malabar, Fla.: Krieger Publishing, 1994.
6. Ibid.

7. Ibid.
8. "Reach for the Stars," *Time,* February 17, 1958.
9. Stuhlinger and Ordway, *Wernher von Braun.*
10. Ibid.
11. Ibid.
12. "Reach for the Stars."

FORESIGHT

1. Richard Tedlow, "The Education of Andy Grove," *Fortune,* December 12, 2005.

"I HEAR THE STEADY DRUMMER"

1. The title of this chapter is taken from A. E. Housman's poem, "A Shropshire Lad," which Churchill is reported to have reflected upon in the anxious days of the Agadir crisis. William Manchester, *The Last Lion.* New York: Random House, 1983.

> *On the idle hill of summer,*
> *Sleepy with the flow of streams,*
> *Far I hear the steady drummer*
> *Drumming like a noise in dreams.*
>
> *Far and near and low and louder*
> *On the roads of earth go by,*
> *Dear to friends and food to powder,*
> *Soldiers marching, all to die.*

2. Manchester, *Last Lion.*
3. Winston S. Churchill, *The World Crisis.* New York: Charles Scribner's Sons, 1923.
4. Ibid.
5. Robert K. Massie, *Dreadnought: Britain, Germany, and the Coming of the Great War.* New York: Random House, 1991.
6. Randolph S. Churchill, *Winston S. Churchill: Young Statesman, 1901–1914.* Boston: Houghton Mifflin Company, 1967.
7. Ibid.
8. Massie, *Dreadnought.*
9. Ibid.
10. Ibid.
11. Churchill, *World Crisis.*
12. Ibid.
13. Peter Gretton, *Winston Churchill and the Royal Navy.* New York: Coward McCann, 1968.

14. Churchill, *World Crisis*.
15. Ibid.
16. Ibid.
17. Ibid.
18. Ibid.
19. Manchester, *Last Lion*.
20. Churchill, *World Crisis*.
21. Ibid.
22. Massie, *Dreadnought*.
23. Churchill, *World Crisis*.
24. Ibid.
25. Ibid.
26. Ibid.
27. Ibid.
28. Sir Martin Gilbert, *Churchill: A Life*. New York: Henry Holt, 1991.
29. Churchill, *World Crisis*.
30. Gilbert, *Churchill: A Life*.

PATENT NUMBER 174,465

1. Maury Klein, "What Hath God Wrought," American Heritage.com.
2. Ibid.
3. Catherine MacKenzie, *Alexander Graham Bell*. Whitefish, MT, 2003.
4. "The Voice Heard Round the World," *American Heritage,* April 1965.
5. Ibid.
6. "Hindsight, Foresight and No Sight," *American Heritage,* June/July 1985.
7. "Voice Heard Round the World."
8. George David Smith, *The Anatomy of a Business Strategy*. Baltimore: Johns Hopkins University Press, 1985.
9. Ron Adner and George David Smith, "The Bell–Western Union Patent Agreement of 1879," Case Study, Copyright INSFAD, 2005, Fontainebleau, France.

TURNING POINT

1. *Time,* June 21, 1982.
2. "Reagan and Russia," *Foreign Affairs,* winter 1982/83.
3. Peter Schweizer, *Victory: The Reagan Administration's Secret Strategy That Hastened the Collapse of the Soviet Union*. New York: Atlantic Monthly Press, 1994.
4. Peter Schweizer, "Who Broke the Evil Empire?" *National Review,* May 30, 1994.
5. "Fencing at the Fireside Summit," *Time,* December 2, 1985.
6. Ronald Reagan, *An American Life*. New York: Simon & Schuster, 1990.
7. Ibid.
8. Ibid.

9. Mikhail Gorbachev, *Memoirs*. New York: Doubleday, 1996.
10. Reagan, *American Life*.
11. Ibid.
12. "Freedom's Team: How Reagan, Thatcher and John Paul II Won the Cold War," *The Wall Street Journal,* June 7, 2004.
13. Reagan, *American Life*.
14. Richard Reeves, *President Reagan: The Triumph of Imagination*. New York: Simon & Schuster, 2005.
15. Ibid.
16. Ibid.
17. Meg Greenfield, "How Does Reagan Decide?" *Newsweek,* February 20, 1984.
18. Reagan, *American Life*.
19. Ibid.
20. Gorbachev, *Memoirs*.
21. Jeffrey Gedmin, *The Hidden Hand: Gorbachev and the Collapse of East Germany*. Washington, D.C.: AEI Press, 1992.
22. Ibid.
23. Ibid.

TIMING

1. Felix Frankfurter, *American National Biography,* John A. Garraty and Mark C. Carnes, eds. Vol. VII. New York: Oxford University Press, 1999.
2. Richard Kluger, *Simple Justice*. New York: Alfred A. Knopf, 2004.

THE MASTER STROKE

1. *Time,* July 19, 1954.
2. Ibid.
3. Harold Mansfield, *Vision: The Story of Boeing*. New York: Popular Library, 1966.
4. "Boeing's 15,000,000 Gamble," *Collier's,* March 19, 1954.
5. Clive Irving, *Wide-Body: The Triumph of the 747*. New York: William Morrow & Co., 1993.
6. "Time 100: Juan Trippe, Richard Branson," *Time,* December 7, 1998.

SELL THE SHAVE, NOT THE RAZOR

1. Russell Adams, *King Gillette: The Man and His Wonderful Shaving Device*. Boston: Little, Brown, 1978.
2. Ibid.
3. "Gillette in His Early Days," *Fortune,* April 1, 2003.
4. Ibid.
5. Adams, *King Gillette*.
6. Ibid.

7. "Gillette in His Early Days."
8. Adams, *King Gillette.*
9. Ibid.
10. "Gillette in His Early Days."
11. Adams, *King Gillette.*
12. http://en.wikipedia.org/wiki/King_C._Gillette.
13. "K.C. Gillette Dead; Made Safety Razor," *The New York Times,* July 10, 1932.

"Shalom, Salaam, Forever"

1. "Two Weeks at Camp David," *Smithsonian,* September 2003.
2. "The Warrior Who Made Peace," *The Jerusalem Report,* March 19, 1992.
3. "Menachem Begin, Guerrilla Leader Who Became Peacemaker," *The New York Times,* March 10, 1992.
4. "The Warrior Who Made Peace."
5. "Zion's Man of Iron," *People,* March 23, 1992.
6. "Anwar Sadat, 1977 Man of the Year," *Time,* January 2, 1978.
7. Anwar el-Sadat, *In Search of Identity.* New York: Harper and Row, 1978.
8. Ibid.
9. Ibid.
10. Ibid.
11. Ibid.
12. Ibid.
13. Ibid.
14. Ibid.
15. "Anwar Sadat, the Daring Arab Pioneer of Peace with Israel," *The New York Times,* October 7, 1981.
16. "Anwar Sadat." *Time.*

Confidence

1. Kenneth P. Williams, *Lincoln Finds a General.* New York: Macmillan, 1949.
2. George B. McClellan, *McClellan's Own Story.* New York: Charles L. Webster, 1887.
3. Williams, *Lincoln Finds a General.*
4. Katharine Graham, *Personal History.* New: York: Knopf, 1997.

Miss What For

1. "Greased Lightning," *The Guardian,* October 16, 2006.
2. "Gertrude Ederle, the First Woman to Swim Across the English Channel, Dies at 98," *The New York Times,* December 1, 2003.
3. *Daily News,* August 6, 1926.
4. "Ederle Crosses the English Channel," *St. Petersburg Times,* October, 5, 1999.

5. "Swim It or Drown, Gertrude of America, 1926," New York *Daily News,* December 12, 2003.
6. "Gertrude Ederle Swims the English Channel," *The New York Times,* August 6, 1926.
7. "Greased Lightning."
8. "Girl Swims Channel," *Chicago Daily Tribune,* August 7, 1926.
9. "Laughing with the First Woman to Swim the Channel," Cynthia L. Cooper, Women's E News, December 5, 2003.

LANDING THE EAGLE

1. *Apollo II* radio transcripts, www.history.NASA.gov.
2. "'The Eagle Has Landed,'" *Houston Chronicle,* July 16, 1989.
3. Ibid.
4. James R. Hansen, *First Man: The Life of Neil A. Armstrong.* New York: Simon & Schuster, 2005.
5. Michael Collins, *Carrying the Fire: An Astronaut's Journey.* New York: Farrar, Straus, and Giroux, 1974.
6. Ibid.
7. Ibid.
8. Hansen, *First Man.*
9. Ibid.
10. Ibid.
11. Charles Murray and Catherine Bly Cox, *Apollo: The Race to the Moon.* New York: Simon & Schuster, 1989.
12. Hansen, *First Man.*
13. "'The Eagle Has Landed.'"
14. Ibid.
15. Hansen, *First Man.*
16. Ibid.

THE SURGEON SCIENTIST

1. Robert Cooke, *Dr. Folkman's War.* New York: Random House, 2001.
2. Ibid.
3. Interview, Academy of Achievement, Washington, D.C., June 18, 1999.
4. Cooke, *Dr. Folkman's War.*
5. Ibid.
6. Interview, June 18, 1999.
7. Interview, *Nova,* PBS, February 27, 2001.
8. Interview, June 18, 1999.
9. Ibid.
10. Cooke, *Dr. Folkman's War.*
11. Ibid.

12. Ibid.

13. Ibid.

14. Interview, February 27, 2001.

15. *The New York Times,* May 3, 1998.

16. *The Economist,* February 10, 2001.

IN COMMAND

1. William Manchester, *American Caesar.* Boston: Little, Brown, 1978.

2. Ibid.

3. T. R. Fehrenbach, *This Kind of War.* New York: Macmillan, 1963.

4. Ibid.

5. Manchester, *American Caesar.*

6. Ibid.

7. Ibid.

8. Interview with General Fred C. Weyand by Colonel Harry Summers, *Vietnam,* 1988.

9. Neil Sheehan, *A Bright Shining Lie.* New York: Random House, 1988.

10. Ibid.

11. John Prados, *The Hidden History of the Vietnam War.* Chicago: Ivan R. Dee, 1998.

12. Sheehan, *Bright Shining Lie.*

13. Marc Jason Gilbert and William Head, eds., *The Tet Offensive.* Westport, Conn.: Praeger, 1996.

14. David T. Zabecki, "Battle for Saigon," *Vietnam,* summer 1989.

15. Interview with General Fred C. Weyand, *Vietnam,* 1988.

16. Stanley Karnow, *Vietnam: A History.* New York: Viking Press, 1983.

17. Ibid.

MA ELLEN

1. "Healing Powers," *Newsweek,* April 3, 2006.

2. "After the Warlords," *The New Yorker,* March 27, 2006.

3. "It's the Little Things—A Reflection on Ellen Johnson Sirleaf's Journey to the Presidency," *Financial Times,* March 24, 2006.

4. Interview, *NewsHour,* PBS, March 23, 2006.

5. Ellen Johnson Sirleaf, address to the U.S. Congress, March 15, 2006.

6. *Meeting the Hard Man of Liberia,* BBC, November 4, 2006.

7. "After the Warlords."

8. "Healing Powers."

9. "It's the Little Things."

10. "After the Warlords."

TO SECURE THESE RIGHTS

1. Laura Wexler, *Fire in the Canebrake.* New York: Charles Scribner's Sons, 2003.

2. Joseph Pierro, "'Everything in My Power': Harry S. Truman and the Fight

Against Racial Discrimination," master's thesis, Virginia Polytechnic Institute and State University.

3. David McCullough, *Truman*. New York: Simon & Schuster, 1992.

4. Pierro, "'Everything in My Power.'"

5. Walter White, *A Man Called White*. North Stratford, NH: Ayer Company Publishers, 1948.

6. Michael R. Gardner, *Harry Truman and Civil Rights: Moral Courage and Political Risks*. Carbondale: Southern Illinois University Press, 2002.

7. Alonzo Fields, *My 21 Years in the White House*. New York: Coward McCann, 1961.

8. Margaret Truman, *Harry S. Truman*. New York: William Morrow, 1973.

9. McCullough, *Truman*.

10. Gardner, *Harry Truman and Civil Rights*.

11. Alonzo L. Hamby, *Man of the People: A Life of Harry S. Truman*. New York: Oxford University Press, 1995.

12. McCullough, *Truman*.

13. Ibid.

14. *The New York Times*, December 27, 1972.

THE PARADOX OF WAR

1. Reinhold Niebuhr, "Our Responsibilities in 1942," *Christian Century*, January 12, 1942.

2. Charles C. Brown, *Niebuhr and His Age*. Philadelphia: Trinity Press International, 1992.

3. "Dietrich Bonhoeffer," www.victorshepard.on.ca.

4. Dietrich Bonhoeffer, *Ethics*. Minneapolis: Augsburg Fortress Publishers, 2004.

5. "Dietrich Bonhoeffer," the Internet Encyclopedia of Philosophy.

6. "The Church and the Jewish Question," public address by Dietrich Bonhoeffer, 1933.

7. Dietrich Bonhoeffer, *After Ten Years: Letters and Papers from Prison*. New York: Macmillan, 1971.

8. Dietrich Bonhoeffer, *The Cost of Discipleship*. New York: Macmillan, 1949.

9. *A Hitler Dilemma*, BBC, April 14, 2006.

10. Ibid.

11. Bonhoeffer, *Cost of Discipleship*, preface.

12. Interview with Reinhold Niebuhr, *McCall's*, February 1966.

13. June Bingham, *Courage to Change: An Introduction to the Life and Thought of Reinhold Niebuhr*. New York: Charles Scribner's Sons, 1961.

14. *Reinhold Niebuhr: His Religious, Social, and Political Thought*, ed. Charles Kegley and Robert W. Bretall. The Library of Living Theology, vol. 2. New York: Macmillan, 1956.

15. Richard Fox, *Reinhold Niebuhr: A Biography*. New York: Pantheon, 2005.

16. Reinhold Niebuhr, "Ten Years That Shook My World," *Christian Century,* April 26, 1939.

17. Reinhold Niebuhr, *Moral Man and Immoral Society.* New York: Scribner's, 1932.

18. Ibid.

19. Reinhold Niebuhr, "Radical Religion" (1939), in *Love and Justice.* Westminster John Knox Press, 1992.

20. Ibid.

21. Reinhold Niebuhr, *Discerning the Signs of the Times.* New York: Scribner, 1946.

22. Reinhold Niebuhr, *Children of Light and Children of Darkness.* New York: Macmillan, 1985.

23. Gordon Harland, *The Thought of Reinhold Niebuhr.* New York: Oxford University Press, 1960.

24. Ibid.

25. Brown, *Niebuhr and His Age.*

26. *Reinhold Niebuhr: His Religious, Social, and Political Thought.*

27. Howard G. Patton, *Reinhold Niebuhr.* Waco: Word Incorporated, 1977.

28. Reinhold Niebuhr, *The Irony of American History.* New York: Scribner, 1952.

29. Ibid.

The Quality of Mercy

1. James Cannon, *Time and Chance: Gerald Ford's Appointment with History.* New York: HarperCollins, 1994.

2. Ibid.

3. Ibid.

4. Ibid.

5. Gerald Ford, *A Time to Heal: The Autobiography of Gerald R. Ford.* New York: Harper and Row, 1979.

6. Cannon, *Time and Chance.*

7. Ibid.

No Holier Place

1. Russell Duncan, *Where Death and Glory Meet: Colonel Robert Gould Shaw and the 54th Massachusetts Infantry.* Athens: University of Georgia Press, 1999.

2. Ibid.

3. Ibid.

4. Ibid.

5. Russell Duncan, ed., *Blue-Eyed Child of Fortune: The Civil War Letters of Colonel Robert Gould Shaw.* Athens: University of Georgia Press, 1992.

6. Duncan, *Where Death and Glory Meet.*

7. Duncan, ed., *Blue-Eyed Child of Fortune.*

8. Ibid.

9. Ibid.

10. Duncan, *Where Death and Glory Meet.*
11. William James's oration at the dedication to the memorial to the Fifty-fourth Massachusetts Regiment, Boston Music Hall, May 31, 1897.
12. Duncan, *Where Death and Glory Meet.*
13. Ibid.
14. Ibid.
15. Ibid.
16. Duncan, ed., *Blue-Eyed Child of Fortune.*
17. Duncan, *Where Death and Glory Meet.*
18. Ibid.
19. Ibid.
20. Duncan, ed., *Blue-Eyed Child of Fortune.*
21. Ibid.
22. Ibid.
23. Ibid.
24. Ibid.
25. Ibid.
26. Ibid.

Duty to the Dead

1. Aleksandr I. Solzhenitsyn, *The Gulag Archipelago: 1918–1956.* New York: Harper and Row, 1973.
2. Ibid.
3. Ibid.
4. Nobel Lectures in Literature, Edited by Sture Allén, Swedish Academy, Stockholm.
5. Ibid.
6. Ibid.
7. D. M. Thomas, *Alexander Solzhenitsyn: A Century in His Life.*
8. *Gulag Archipelago.*
9. George Kennan, "Between Earth and Hell," *The New York Review of Books,* March 21, 1974.
10. Aleksandr Solzhenitsyn, *The Oak and the Calf.* New York: Harper and Row, 1975.
11. Ibid.
12. Michael Scammell, *Solzhenitsyn: A Biography.* New York: W. W. Norton, 1989.
13. Solzhenitsyn, *Oak and the Calf.*
14. Scammell, *Solzhenitsyn.*
15. Solzhenitsyn, *Oak and the Calf.*
16. Ibid.
17. Kennan, "Between Earth and Hell."
18. *The New York Times,* January 15, 1974.
19. Solzhenitsyn, *Oak and the Calf.*

THE COVENANT

1. Carl Sandburg, *Abraham Lincoln: The Prairie Years.* New York: Harcourt, Brace and Company, 1926.
2. Don E. and Virginia E. Fehrenbacher, *Recollected Words of Abraham Lincoln.* Stanford University Press, 2005.
3. Letter to Albert G. Hodges, Abraham Lincoln, April 4, 1864.
4. *Abraham Lincoln: A History,* vol. IV. Century Company, 1914.
5. "Meditations on the Divine Will," Abraham Lincoln and Roy Basler, ed., *Collected Works of Abraham Lincoln.* The Abraham Lincoln Association.
6. Mark A. Knoll, "The Puzzling Faith of Abraham Lincoln," *Christian History,* winter 1992.
7. Allen C. Guelzo, *Lincoln's Emancipation Proclamation: The End of Slavery in America.* New York: Simon & Schuster, 2004.
8. Allen C. Guelzo, *Abraham Lincoln: Redeemer President.* Wm. B. Eerdmans Publishing Co., 2003.
9. Richard Hofstadter, *The American Political Tradition and the Men Who Made It.* New York: Knopf, 2nd revised ed., 1973.
10. Knoll, "The Puzzling Faith of Abraham Lincoln."

INDEX

PHOTO CREDITS

ABOUT TWELVE

MISSION STATEMENT

TWELVE was established in August 2005 with the objective of publishing no more than one book per month. We strive to publish the singular book, by authors who have a unique perspective and compelling authority. Works that explain our culture; that illuminate, inspire, provoke, and entertain. We seek to establish communities of conversation surrounding our books. Talented authors deserve attention not only from publishers but from readers as well. To sell the book is only the beginning of our mission. To build avid audiences of readers who are enriched by these works—that is our ultimate purpose.

For more information about forthcoming TWELVE books, please go to www.twelvebooks.com